Rachel Finnie | Carol Frain | David A. Hill | Karen Thomas

TOP Grammar

TOP Grammar
by Rachel Finnie, Carol Frain, David A. Hill, Karen Thomas

© HELBLING LANGUAGES 2010
www.helblinglanguages.com

11 10 9   8 7   6 5   4
2018 2017 2016 2015

All rights reserved; no part of this publication may be reproduced, stored in a retrieval system, or transmitted in any form or by any means, electronic, mechanical, photocopying, recording, or otherwise, without the prior written permission of the Publishers.

ISBN 978-85-7827-322-4

The publishers would like to thank the following for their kind permission to reproduce the following photographs and other copyright material:
Alamy p144, p151, (CD: Food Icons) p196 (bread), (CD: Food Icons; Ultimate Food) p197 (coffee, chocolate, beer), (CD: Food Icons) p198 (single strawberry, PG Tips), p305; Barbara Bonci p197 (trifle); Corbis p248, p289, p304; Helbling Languages p240, p309; ©iStockphoto.com p28, p30, p34, p63, p78, p104, p194, p196 (eggs), p197 (marmalade, bread, champagne), p198 (cup of tea), p210, p218, p231, p256, p264, p269, p287, p321, p334, p339, p343; Shutterstock p14, p18, p27, p71, p197 (paper, oil, biscuits), p198 (bowl of fruit, three strawberries), p201, p220, p222, p246, p306, p310, p323; book cover of SOMEBODY SOMEWHERE by Donna Williams, reprinted by permission of The Random House Group Ltd p250; Wikimedia Commons p186.

Project managed and edited by Paola Tite
Designed by BNC comunicazione
Cover by Capolinea
Illustrated by Roberto Battestini, Matteo Buffagni, Sergio Cingolani, Valentina Russello, Doriano Strologo
Printed by Orgrafic

Every effort has been made to trace the owners of any copyright material in this book. If notified, the publisher will be pleased to rectify any errors or omissions.

Top Grammar

Top Grammar is a grammar reference book for teenagers and young adults learning English at all levels, from elementary to advanced. It covers all the main grammatical areas of the language.

Top Grammar can be used for individual study, for exam preparation, or in class for specific training on grammar included in the syllabus.

Top Grammar is easy to use, with clear explanations and lots of practice.

The Student's Book contains 25 sections, each focusing on a specific grammar point. In addition, each section has a lexical theme, broadly based on the vocabulary topics covered in the PET and FCE syllabuses.

There is a wide variety of exercises and at the end of each section there is a two-page Review containing revision exercises plus two pages of PET and FCE exam preparation.

The interactive CD-ROM contains extra activities for each of the grammatical areas covered in the book, authentic texts from English and American papers and magazines with exercises and phonetic exercises.

The Teacher's Guide contains tips on how to use Top Grammar in the classroom or for individual study, with practical suggestions on how to develop grammar competence and how to deal with error correction. There are 25 tests, one for each of the sections and the keys to all the exercises and tests.

Online Resources. There is a range of additional exercises for each of the 25 sections available online at www.helblinglanguages.com/onlineresources

Contents

The words of grammar   9

Present *be*
Lexical theme: Friends and family

1	*Be* present simple (*I am, I'm not, Are you…?*)	12
2	*Be* present simple – Usage and idiomatic expressions	14
3	*There is / There are; Here is / Here are*	16
4	*It's / That's* – Impersonal usage	18
	Review 1 Units 1-4 CD-ROM	20

Present *have (got)*
Lexical theme: People and clothing

5	*Have got* present simple (*I've got, I haven't got, Have you got…?*)	22
6	*Have* and *have got* – Usage and idiomatic expressions	24
	Review 2 Units 5-6 CD-ROM	26

Present simple
Lexical theme: Weekend routines

7	Present simple – Form (1) (*I walk, I don't walk*)	28
8	Present simple – Form (2) (*Do you walk?*)	30
9	Present simple and adverbs of frequency – Usage (1)	32
10	Present simple – Usage (2)	34
	Review 3 Units 7-10 CD-ROM	36

Present continuous
Lexical theme: Hobbies

11	Present continuous – Form (1) (*I am leaving*)	38
12	Present continuous – Form (2) (*I'm not leaving, Are you leaving?*)	40
13	Present continuous – Usage	42
14	Present simple and Present continuous – Differences of usage	44
15	Action verbs and stative verbs	46
	Review 4 Units 11-15 CD-ROM	48
A	Exam preparation PET FCE CD-ROM	50

Past simple
Lexical theme: Holidays

16	*Be* past simple (*I was, I wasn't, Were you…?*)	52
17	Past simple – Form (1) (*I worked, I went*)	54
18	Past simple – Form (2) (*I didn't go, Did you go…?*)	56
19	Past simple – Usage	58
	Review 5 Units 16-19 CD-ROM	60

Used to and Past continuous
Lexical theme: Sport

20	*Used to/Would*	62
21	Past continuous – Form (*I was/wasn't playing, Were you playing…?*)	64
22	Past continuous – Usage and comparison with the past simple	66
	Review 6 Units 20-22 CD-ROM	68
B	Exam preparation PET FCE CD-ROM	70

Past participle and Present perfect simple
Lexical theme: The house

23	Past participle (*worked, sent*)	72
24	Present perfect simple – Form (*I have/haven't visited, Have you visited…?*)	74

25	Present perfect simple – with *just, already, yet, not… yet, still… not*	76
26	Present perfect simple – with *ever, never, recently, today…*	78
27	Present perfect simple – with *How long, for, since*	80
28	Present perfect simple and Past simple – Differences of usage	82
	Review 7 Units 23-28 **CD-ROM**	84

Present perfect continuous, Past perfect simple and continuous
Lexical theme: Education

29	Present perfect continuous – Form and usage (*I've been learning, Have you been learning?*)	86
30	Present perfect simple and continuous – Differences of usage	88
31	Past perfect simple – Form (*I had/hadn't started, Had you started?*)	90
32	Past perfect simple – Usage	92
33	Past perfect continuous – Form and usage (*I had/hadn't been playing, Had you been playing?*)	94
	Review 8 Units 29-33 **CD-ROM**	96
C	Exam preparation **PET FCE CD-ROM**	98

Future with *going to* and *will*
Lexical theme: Jobs

34	The future: *going to* – Form and usage (*I'm/I'm not going to apply, Are you going to apply?*)	100
35	The future: *will* – Form (*I will go, I won't go, Will you go?*)	102
36	The future: *will* – Usage (1)	104
37	The future: *will* – Usage (2)	106
	Review 9 Units 34-37 **CD-ROM**	108

Other ways to express the future, Future continuous and Future perfect
Lexical theme: Health

38	Present continuous and Present simple for the future	110
39	*Going to* / Present continuous / *Will* future – Differences of usage	112
40	Future continuous (*I will be doing*) and Future perfect (*I will have done*)	114
	Review 10 Units 38-40 **CD-ROM**	116
D	Exam preparation **PET FCE CD-ROM**	118

Imperative, Infinitive and *-ing* form
Lexical theme: Shopping and money

41	Imperative – Form and usage (*Go! Don't go! Let's go!*)	120
42	Infinitive – Form and usage (*to play, not to play, to have played*)	122
43	*-ing* form – Form and usage (*going, having gone*)	124
44	Verbs + infinitive (*I want to go*)	126
45	Verbs + *-ing* form / + infinitive (*I started reading / to read*)	128
46	Prepositions + *-ing* form; *-ing* clauses (*I'm good at skiing, Before/After going…*)	130
	Review 11 Units 41-46 **CD-ROM**	132
E	Exam preparation **PET FCE CD-ROM**	134

Modal verbs *can, could, may, might*
Lexical theme: Celebrations

47	Modals: *Can / Could* – General characteristics	136
48	Modals: *Can / Could* – Usage and alternative verbs	138
49	Modals: *May / Might*	140
	Review 12 Units 47-49 **CD-ROM**	142

Modal verbs *must, have to, need*
Lexical theme: Rules and regulations

50	Modals: *Must*	144
51	*Have to / Have got to; Be to; Mustn't / Don't have to*	146

Contents

52	*Need to / Need + -ing; Had to / Will have to; Be obliged / Be compelled*	148
	Review 13 Units 50-52 CD-ROM	150

Other modal verbs
Lexical theme: The weather

53	Modals: *Shall / Should*	152
54	*Had better; Ought to; Be due; Be bound to*	154
55	Modals: *Will / Would*	156
56	*Would like to; Want to; Would prefer to / Would rather*	158
	Review 14 Units 53-56 CD-ROM	160
F	Exam preparation PET FCE CD-ROM	162

The passive
Lexical theme: Literature, inventions, procedures

57	Passive form	164
58	Passive form – Present and past tense	166
59	Passive form – Perfect tenses and Future	168
60	Passive form – Infinitive, Modal Verbs and Conditional	170
61	Passive form – Verbs with double object; *He is said to be…*	172
62	*Make / Let someone do something; Get someone to do something; Have / Get something done*	174
63	*See someone do / doing something; See something being done*	176
	Review 15 Units 57-63 CD-ROM	178
G	Exam preparation PET FCE CD-ROM	180

Articles
Lexical theme: The natural world, geography

64	The indefinite article: *a /an*	182
65	The definite article: *the* (1)	184
66	The definite article: *the* (2)	186
67	No article vs. *the*	188
	Review 16 Units 64-67 CD-ROM	190

Nouns, possessive case
Lexical theme: Entertainment

68	Nouns	192
69	Irregular plurals; compound nouns	194
70	Nouns: countables and uncountables (1)	196
71	Nouns: countables and uncountables (2)	198
72	Collective and plural nouns; adjectives used as nouns	200
73	Possessive case (*Tom's friend, A friend of Tom's*)	202
	Review 17 Units 68-73 CD-ROM	204
H	Exam preparation PET FCE CD-ROM	206

Adjectives
Lexical theme: Famous people, music

74	Qualifying adjectives (*a big red apple / the book is new*)	208
75	Adjective formation (*surprising, surprised*); nouns used as adjectives (*a film star*)	210
76	The comparative of adjectives (1) (*cheaper than / more expensive than*)	212
77	The comparative of adjectives (2) (*as interesting as / less interesting than*)	214
78	The superlative of adjectives (*the cheapest / the most expensive / the least expensive*)	216
79	The comparative and superlative of adverbs (*faster / fastest; more quickly / most quickly*)	218
80	Comparative and superlative: irregular forms (*better / the best*)	220
81	Comparatives with nouns and verbs (*more / less … than; as much … as / as many … as*)	222

	Review 18 Units 74-81 CD-ROM	224
I	Exam preparation PET FCE CD-ROM	226

Pronouns
Lexical theme: Everyday life, countries and nationalities

82	Personal pronouns (*I, you, he… / me, you, him…*)	228
83	Possessive adjectives and pronouns (*my, your… / mine, yours…*)	230
84	Reflexive and emphasizing pronouns (*myself / yourself…*)	232
85	Demonstrative adjectives and pronouns (*this / these, that / those*)	234
86	*one / ones*	236
87	Distributive adjectives and pronouns (1) (*each / every / everyone…*); Reciprocal pronouns (*each other / one another*)	238
88	Distributive adjectives and pronouns (2) (*both / either / neither*); Correlative structures (*both… and… / either… or… / neither… nor…*)	240
89	Indefinite adjectives and pronouns (1) (*some / any / no / a little / a few*)	242
90	Indefinite adjectives and pronouns (2) (*a lot / much / many; too much / too many / enough; most / all*)	244
91	Compounds of *some, any, no* (1)	246
92	Compounds of *some, any, no* (2); Compounds with *-ever*	248
	Review 19 Units 82-92 CD-ROM	250
J	Exam preparation PET FCE CD-ROM	252

Numbers, dates, relative pronouns
Lexical theme: Technology, gadgets

93	Cardinal numbers	254
94	Ordinal numbers and dates	256
95	Relative pronouns in defining clauses	258
96	Relative pronouns in non-defining clauses	260
97	Relative adverbs *where, when, why; which, what, all that* in relative clauses	262
	Review 20 Units 93-97 CD-ROM	264

Wh- words, questions, agreeing and disagreeing
Lexical theme: Technology, communication

98	Interrogative adjectives and pronouns; Exclamations	266
99	Interrogative adverbs	268
100	Structure of *Yes / No* questions and *Wh-* questions	270
101	Asking for confirmation: question tags	272
102	Agreeing (*So do I / Neither do I / Nor do I. / I think so.*); Disagreeing (*Don't you? I do. / Do you? I don't. / I don't think so.*)	274
	Review 21 Units 98-102 CD-ROM	276
K	Exam preparation PET FCE CD-ROM	278

Adverbs, prepositions
Lexical theme: Fame, celebrities and success

103	Adverbs of manner (*quickly, slowly…*)	280
104	Adverbs of time	282
105	Adverbs of degree (*too, very, quite, rather…*)	284
106	Word order in statements	286
107	Prepositions of time (1)	288
108	Prepositions of time (2)	290
109	Prepositions indicating place and position (1)	292
110	Prepositions indicating place and position (2)	294
111	Prepositions indicating movement (1)	296
112	Prepositions indicating movement (2)	298

Contents

113	Prepositions *to* and *for*; Verbs with double object	300
114	Other prepositions	302
	Review 22 Units 103-114 CD-ROM	304
L	Exam preparation PET FCE CD-ROM	306

Reported speech
Lexical theme: Sports

115	Verbs *say* and *tell*	308
116	Reported speech (1): Reporting orders; Reporting statements in the present	310
117	Reported speech (2): Reporting statements in the past	312
118	Reported speech (3): Reporting questions	314
	Review 23 Units 115-118 CD-ROM	316

If clauses
Lexical theme: Extremes and danger

119	Conditional verb form; future in the past	318
120	If clauses – Type zero and type one	320
121	If clauses – Type two	322
122	If clauses – Type three	324
123	Conditional clauses introduced by *when, unless… I wish… / If only…*	326
	Review 24 Units 119-123 CD-ROM	328
M	Exam preparation PET FCE CD-ROM	330

Connectors and linkers, word formation, prepositions, phrasal verbs
Lexical theme: Food and drink, cooking

124	Connectors and linkers (1): coordinating, concessive	332
125	Connectors and linkers (2): reason, result and purpose	334
126	Connectors and linkers (3): time linkers and sequencers	336
127	Other connectors and linkers (4)	338
128	Word formation (1): Prefixes	340
129	Word formation (2): Suffixes	342
130	Prepositional verbs	344
131	Adjectives followed by prepositions	346
132	Phrasal verbs (1)	348
	Phrasal verbs (2)	350
	Phrasal verbs (3)	352
	Review 25 Units 124-133 CD-ROM	354
N	Exam preparation PET FCE CD-ROM	356

APPENDIX

British and American English – Main grammatical differences	358
International Phonetic Alphabet (IPA)	359
Punctuation marks	360
Modals and other verbs related to communicative functions	361
Modal verbs – tenses	362
Use of modal verbs in *if* clauses	363
Comparing quantities	364
Conjugation of a regular verb	365
Main irregular verbs	366

INDEX 370

The words of grammar – Parts of speech

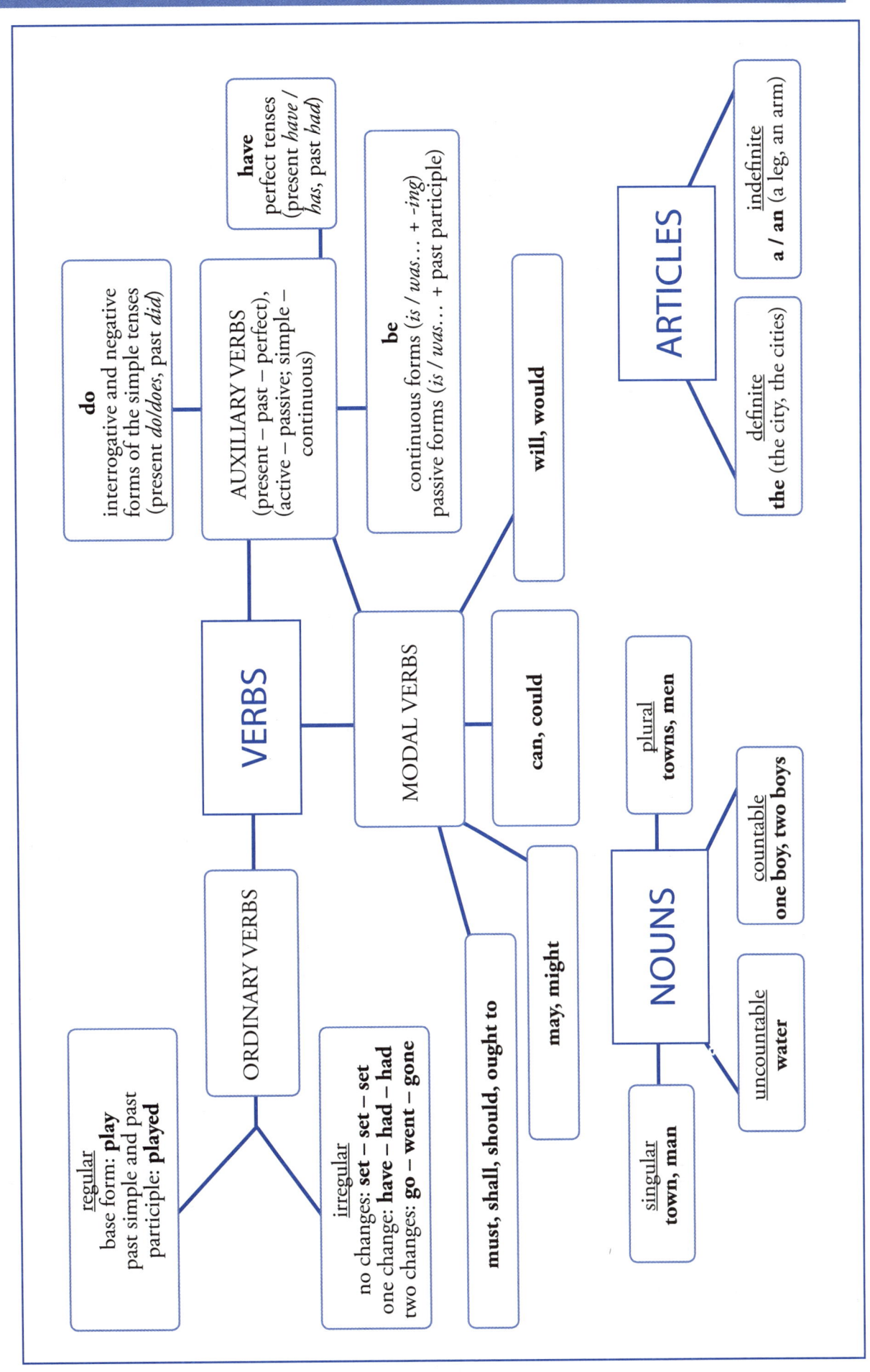

The words of grammar – Parts of speech

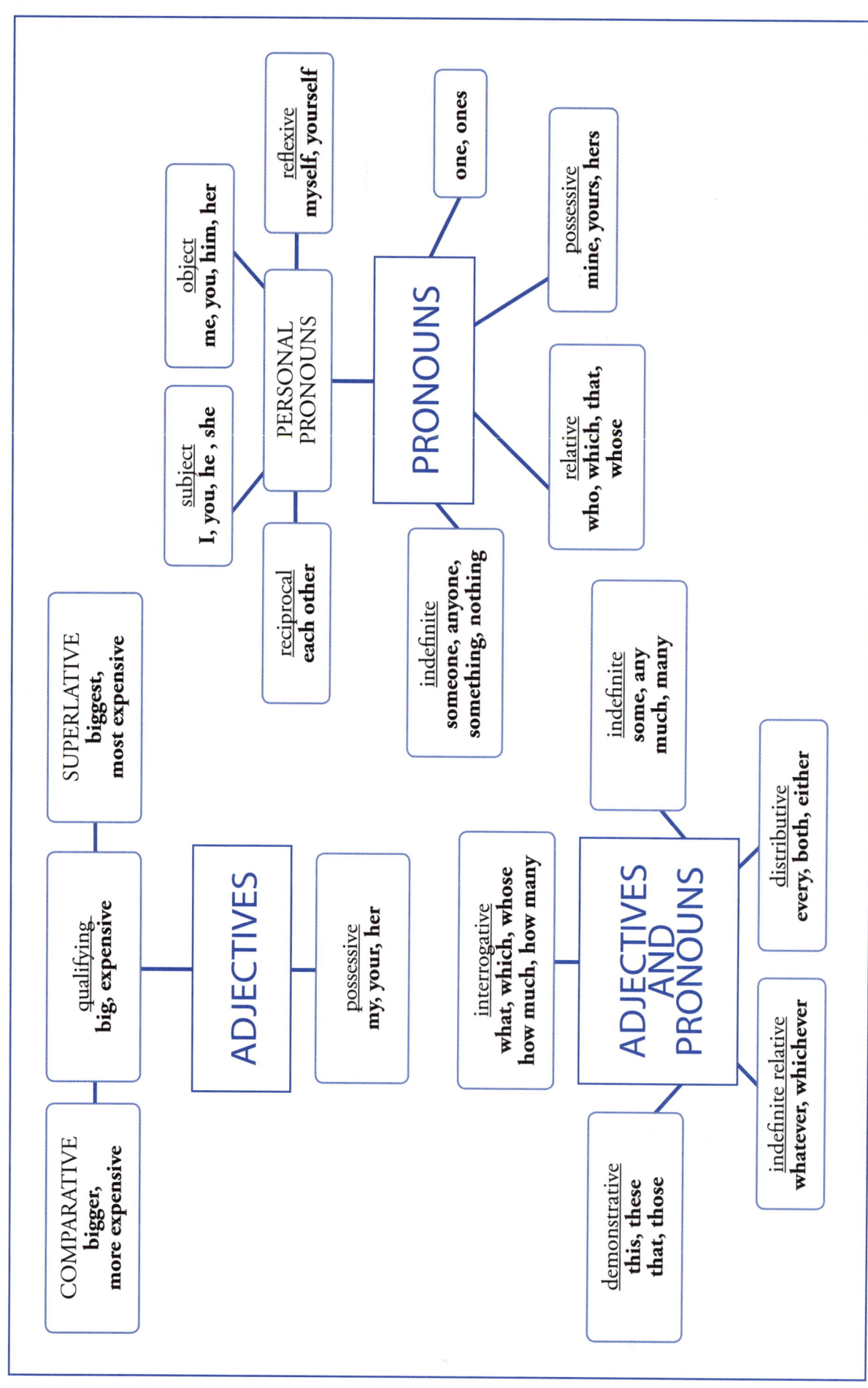

The words of grammar – Parts of speech

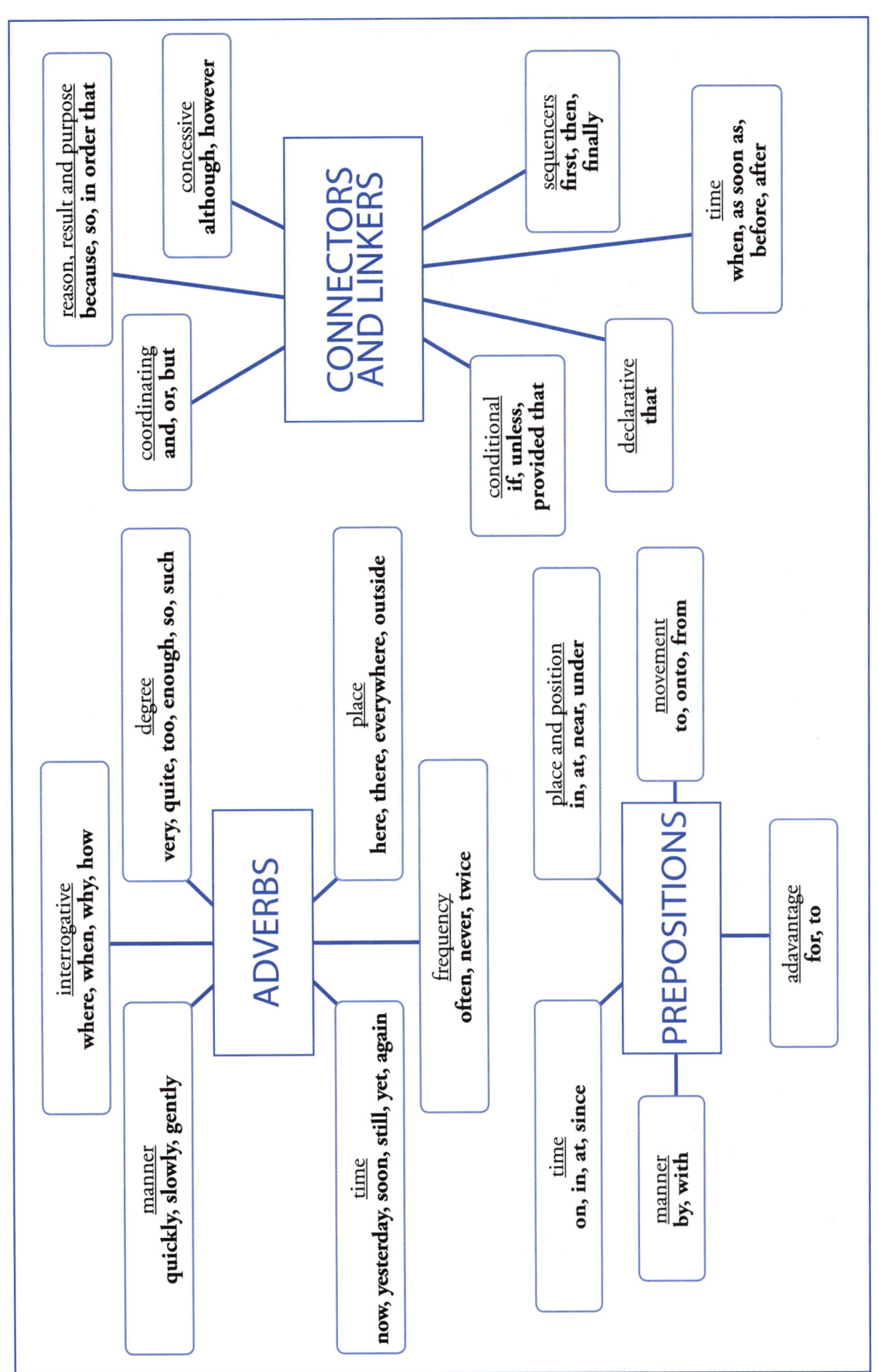

UNIT 1
Be present simple (*I am, I'm not, Are you... ?*)

A   In the present simple, the verb **be** has three forms: **am, is, are**.

Affirmative	
Full form	**Short form**
I am	I'm
You are	You're
He / She / It is	He's / She's / It's
We / You / They are	We're / You're / They're

In spoken language and in informal written language, the form most used is the **short form**. You can use it when the subject is a pronoun, a singular noun or a proper noun.
I'm sorry I'm late.
Simon's away from school today. He's ill.

B

Negative	
Full form	**Short form**
I am not	I'm not
You are not	You aren't
He / She / It is not	He / She / It isn't
We / You / They are not	We / You / They aren't

Full negative form: Subject (noun or pronoun) + **am / is / are** + **not**
We are not ready yet!

The more common short form is shown in the box. To give particular emphasis to the negation, you can use the forms **You're not, He's not, She's not, It's not, We're not, You're not, They're not**.

C

Interrogative	Negative questions
Am I... ?	Am I not... ? / Aren't I... ?
Are you... ?	Aren't you... ?
Is he / she / it... ?	Isn't he / she / it... ?
Are we / you / they... ?	Aren't we / you / they... ?

Questions are formed by swapping the positions of the subject and the verb:
Am / Is / Are + subject (noun or pronoun)
Is your brother at college? Are the students nice?

D   Short answers are formed with:
Yes, / **No,** + subject pronoun + verb **be** (affirmative or negative)
The short form is never used in short affirmative answers.
'Aren't you tired?' 'Yes, I am.' (not: ~~Yes, I'm.~~)
'Are your parents at work?' 'No, they aren't.'

E   **Wh-** questions are formed with: Question word + **am / is / are** + subject (noun or pronoun)
What's your name? When's your birthday?
Where are you from? (also possible: Where're ...)
Which is your car? (not possible: ~~Which's~~ ...)

EXERCISES

Be present simple

UNIT 1

1.1 **Complete the sentences with *am*, *is* or *are*.**

1 Carlotta ...*is*... my mother's name.
2 My best friend .... a girl called Saffy.
3 You .... a great person!
4 It .... important to have good friends.
5 Peter's aunt and uncle .... in London this week.
6 I .... Sammy's cousin.

1.2 **Rewrite the sentences using the negative form.**

1 Jessica's Conrad's new girlfriend. ...... *Jessica isn't Conrad's new girlfriend.*
2 My grandparents are very old.
3 It's fun to hang out with my brothers.
4 My mum's a brilliant cook!
5 Terry's grandmother is 99!
6 They're sorry about the argument.

1.3 **Use the words to write questions with *am*, *is*, *are*. Then complete the short answers.**

1 your / son / a teenager
   Is your son a teenager? No, *he isn't* .
2 I / your best friend
   .... Yes, ...
3 Annabel / your mum
   .... No, ...
4 Kenny and Kyle / twins
   .... No, ...
5 Jess's stepfather / nice
   .... Yes, ...
6 it / important / to be kind to your friends
   .... Yes, ...

1.4 **Write sentences about the members of this family.**

1 *Olivia and Andrew are cousins.*
2 *Alfred and Mabel are husband and wife.*
3 ....
4 ....
5 ....
6 ....
7 ....
8 ....
9 ....
10 ....

13

UNIT 2
Be present simple
Usage and idiomatic expressions

A The verb **be** indicates the existence of something, a state of being, whether it is permanent or temporary. You use it to:

- introduce yourself and say your profession
  My name's Rob Nolan. I'm a sales rep.
- introduce another person
  This is Tina. She's my neighbour.
- identify someone or something
  'Who's that?' 'It's my friend Tom.'
  'What's this?' 'It's a nutcracker.'

- ask and give personal information (age, nationality, address, telephone number, birthday…)
  'How old are you?' 'I'm 18 (years old).'
  'What's your mobile phone number?' 'It's 334 9987652.'
- talk about physical and health conditions
  'Are you hungry?' 'Yes, I'm starving!'
  'How are you?' 'I'm fine, thanks. And you?' 'I'm not very well, I'm afraid.'
- express feelings
  'Are you happy to be here?' 'Yes, I'm very happy!'
  I'm so sorry!
- indicate the characteristics of someone or something (height, personality, colour, dimension…)
  He's a very lively child.
  Tim's very tall, he's 1.95m.
  It's a large room. The curtains and the carpet are light blue.
- ask or say where someone or something is
  'Where's Peter?' 'He's in the kitchen, I think.'
  Your pen's on the desk.

The verb **be** is usually followed by a noun (**I'm Laura**), an adjective (**I'm happy**), an adverb (**I'm late**) or by a noun phrase (**She's a good student / It's in the kitchen**).

B Note the following expressions with the verb **be**.

I'm cold / warm / hot.
I'm hungry / thirsty / sleepy.
I'm afraid / ashamed.
You're right / wrong.
He's in a hurry.
She's seven years old.

C The verb **be** in the present simple is also used as an auxiliary:

- in the present continuous, followed by another verb in the **-ing form** (see p. 38)
  'What are you doing?' 'I'm trying to get in.'
- in the passive form, followed by another verb in the past participle (see p. 166)
  The film is directed by Steven Spielberg.

EXERCISES

Be present simple – Usage and idiomatic expressions

UNIT 2

2.1 Match the questions to the answers.

1 ..c.. 2 .... 3 .... 4 .... 5 .... 6 ....

1 Where's Grace?
2 Are you happy about the wedding?
3 What's this?
4 What's your dad's job?
5 Are the children polite?
6 Who's this?

a Yes, I am.
b It's our family photo album.
c She's in the living room with Dad.
d It's Jake, my brother.
e He's an engineer.
f No, they aren't.

2.2 Describe the people. Use the adjectives in the box.

| hungry sad ~~bad-tempered~~ thirsty easy-going happy |

1 Ted ......*is bad-tempered.*...... . He looks angry.
2 Rose .... She looks relaxed.
3 Joe .... with his skateboard.
4 Selina .... without her boyfriend.
5 Ros and Saskia .... They want some lunch.
6 Rocky and Fritz .... They want a drink.

2.3 Complete the paragraph with the correct form of the verb *be*.

My favourite person

My favourite person (1) ...*is*... a woman called Violetta. She (2) .... a beautiful woman. Violetta (3) .... a teenager like me – she's 39. She and her husband (4) .... both very kind, and Violetta (5) .... very easy-going too. That (6) .... one of the reasons I never fall out with her, but there (7) .... other reasons too. Violetta (8) .... funny and clever. When we (9) .... together, we always have a great time. But... the question is... who (10) .... this special person? Well, Violetta and her husband (11) .... the people I live with; Violetta (12) .... my mother!

2.4 Complete the dialogue with the words in the box.

| are |
| ~~is~~ |
| is |
| is |
| 's |
| he |
| he's |
| they're |
| isn't |
| where's |

Emily: Hey! Who (1) ...*is*... that boy over there with the brown hair?
Britney: That's Daniel. (2) .... my cousin!
Emily: Wow! He's very good-looking! (3) .... he your Aunt Hilary's son?
Britney: No, he (4) .... His parents (5) .... Uncle Pete and Aunt Iris – my dad's brother and his wife. (6) .... both teachers in Oxford. They're here visiting Mum and Dad.
Emily: (7) .... Daniel from, then? Is (8) .... from Oxford?
Britney: Yes, he (9) ....
Emily: And Oxford is 200 miles away. That (10) .... a real shame!

UNIT 3: There is / There are; Here is / Here are

A We use **There is / There are** to indicate that someone or something exists.

Affirmative		Negative
There is… (There's…)		There isn't…
There are… (also possible: There're…)		There aren't…
Interrogative	**Negative questions**	**Short answers**
Is there… ?	Isn't there… ?	Yes, there is. / No, there isn't.
Are there… ?	Aren't there… ?	Yes, there are. / No, there aren't.

There is is followed by a noun that is singular or uncountable. **There are** is followed by a plural noun. Uncountable and plural nouns can have an indefinite adjective like **some** or **a lot of** before them. In negative sentences and in questions, **any** is used instead (see p. 242).

There's a lot of traffic on the motorway today.
'Is there any butter in the fridge?' 'No, there isn't any left.'
Look! There are some stains on your jacket.

B In a list, we use **There's…** if the first thing is singular.

There's a sandwich, a bar of chocolate and two apples in my bag.

C To ask about the quantity or number of things or people, we use questions beginning with **How much… ?** and **How many… ?**

'How much flour is there?' 'There's one kilo.'
'How many boys are there in your group?' 'There're only two.'
NB: *There are three of us.* (not: ~~We are three.~~)
There are four of them. (not: ~~They are four.~~)

D **There's** and **There are** are also used as adverbs of place to indicate someone or something that is at a distance from the speaker. NB: Nouns follow the verb and pronouns precede it.

There's your mum! There she is!

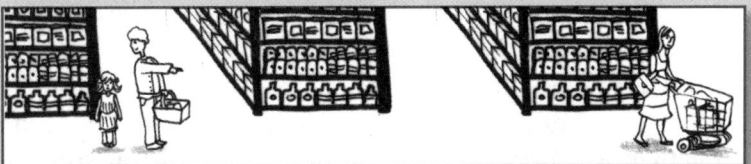

Here is used to indicate someone or something close to the speaker. When something is being handed over, we use the expressions **Here's** and **Here are**.

'Here you are… ten pounds.'
'Thanks. And here's your change.'

NB: Questions to ask if someone is there or not are formed differently:

'Is your sister there?' (not: ~~Is there your sister?~~)
'No, she isn't here.' (not: ~~No, there isn't.~~)

EXERCISES

There is / There are; Here is / Here are

UNIT 3

3.1 Complete the sentences with *There's* or *There are*.

1. *There are* five people in my family.
2. .... a girl in my class called Angelina.
3. .... a great photo of you in this album, Grandma!
4. .... lots of reasons why good friends are important.
5. .... an anniversary party tomorrow evening.
6. .... some selfish people in the world.
7. .... a present for you in the living room.
8. Look! .... your aunt!
9. .... boys in our family who love cooking.
10. .... Uncle Bill and my cousin Tom!

3.2 Complete the short answers.

1. Are there a lot of children in your family? Yes, *there are* .
2. Is there somewhere near your house where we can meet? Yes, ...
3. Is there satellite TV in every room? Yes, ...
4. Are there any letters from your parents? Yes, ...
5. Is there a teacher in your family? No, ...
6. Are there a lot of people in the living room at the moment? No, ...

3.3 Match the questions or the statements to the answers.

1. *e* 2. ...... 3. ...... 4. ...... 5. ...... 6. ...... 7. ...... 8. ......

1. Is there time for us to visit my grandparents?
2. Are there any photos of your mum as a girl in this album?
3. There are at least ten of my friends at this party.
4. There's a problem with this, Dad.
5. Are there any of your relatives in the photo?
6. Isn't there anyone in the family who takes after Mum?
7. There's someone on the phone for you.
8. There aren't any really tall people in your family.

a. Why? What's wrong?
b. Yes, there's Sheena.
c. No, but there are some of Dad as a boy.
d. No, you're right, there aren't.
e. Yes, of course there is.
f. OK, I'm on my way!
g. Really? Introduce me to them.
h. Yes, that's my uncle.

3.4 Complete the dialogue with the words in the box.

is they're aren't are (x2) there's No it's there I'm

Mia: Hi, Melanie. Is (1) *there* something wrong?
Mel: Yes, there (2) .... (3) .... not at all happy today.
Mia: Why?
Mel: I think (4) .... because I argue with my mum all the time these days.
Mia: Well, Mel, (5) .... nothing unusual about that. Lots of teenagers argue with their parents.
Mel: I know, but there (6) .... many who argue like we do.
Mia: I'm sure there are, you know.
Mel: (7) .... , you're wrong. Our arguments (8) .... different.
Mia: What (9) .... your arguments about, then?
Mel: (10) .... about the fact that Mum keeps borrowing my clothes and my make-up!

17

UNIT 4: It's / That's
Impersonal usage

A The subject personal pronouns are never omitted.

We're often abroad.
I'm usually at home in the morning.

The pronoun **it** substitutes a singular noun.

*Can you see **my house**? **It**'s the one with the red door.*

It is also used in impersonal forms, in particular to:

- introduce yourself or ask someone else who they are (e.g. on the phone) and in answer to **Who's…?**, when the question doesn't identify a person ('**Who's that?**' '**It's…**')
  'Who is it?' 'It's me. Sandra.'

Hello. It's Frank. Is that you, Steve?

- say the day, date and time
  'What day is it today?' 'It's Monday. It's 3rd June.'
  'Is it four o'clock?' 'No, it's half past four.'

- talk about the weather
  It's hot. It's 35 degrees.

- talk about distances
  It's about five miles from here.
  It's still a long way.

- ask and say the price of something
  'How much is it?' 'It's ten pounds.'

B Here are some other examples of impersonal expressions.

It's late / early.
It's a good idea.
It's all right / OK.
It's very kind of you.
It's good for you.
It's no good.
It's a shame.

It's time to wake up!

C **It's** + adjective + infinitive or verb in the **-ing** form

This sentence construction is a common alternative to sentences that have a verb in the infinitive or in the **-ing** form as the subject (see p. 122).

To feel appreciated is nice. → *It's nice to feel appreciated.*
Talking to him is useless! → *It's useless talking to him!*

D The pronoun **it** is sometimes substituted with **that**, especially when we refer to the preceding sentence or to a fact or an idea.

A trip to Miami? That's great!
'John isn't coming with us.' 'Really? That's too bad!'
'Shall we go to the beach?' 'That's fine by me.'
'Let's play cards!' 'That's OK by me / with me.'

EXERCISES

It's / That's Impersonal usage

UNIT 4

4.1 Tick (✔) the correct sentence.

1. a ☐ That's a lovely day for a picnic, Mum.
   b ✔ It's a lovely day for a picnic, Mum.
2. a ☐ Do you like Sally's hairstyle? It's new.
   b ☐ Do you like Sally's hairstyle? That's new.
3. a ☐ That's a lovely dress, Julie. Is it new?
   b ☐ It's a lovely dress Julie. Is that new?
4. a ☐ It's a long way to Simon's house.
   b ☐ That's a long way to Simon's house.
5. a ☐ That's a good idea to go and visit Granny.
   b ☐ It's a good idea to go and visit Granny.
6. a ☐ You're having a party? It's great!
   b ☐ You're having a party? That's great!

4.2 Match the questions or the statements to the answers.

1 ..d.. 2 .... 3 .... 4 .... 5 .... 6 ....

1 Mum, why must I eat an apple a day?
2 I want a haircut, Mum.
3 Look! That's Dave's mum!
4 It's only two degrees!
5 Where's Marcia's house?
6 It costs 20.

a That's good! You need it.
b That's expensive!
c It's a long way from here.
d It's good for you!
e That's cold!
f No, it's his sister.

4.3 Complete the dialogue with *it's* or *that's*.

A: Come on... get up! (1) ..It's.. a lovely day!
B: Is it? (2) .... nice. Let's do something different, then.
A: I know! (3) .... Saturday, so let's go for a picnic.
B: (4) .... a great idea. What about going to Bluebell Hill?
A: Hmm... (5) .... a long way to Bluebell Hill.
B: (6) .... OK – the exercise will do us good! And (7) .... a lovely ride out that way.
A: (8) .... true... but, just a minute... my bike isn't here... (9) .... at Don's house. I can't use it today.
B: (10) .... a shame! Never mind, we can walk instead!

4.4 Complete the second sentence so that it has a similar meaning to the first one. Use the word given without changing it.

1 In my opinion, inviting Maria to the party is not a good idea.   **IT**
  In my opinion, ...*it isn't a good*.......... idea to invite Maria to the party.
2 I think arguing with your family is very upsetting.   **TO**
  I think .... argue with your family.
3 That's Mum's favourite vase, so don't break it!   **BECAUSE**
  Don't break that vase .... favourite!
4 Yes, I agree that going to the cinema this evening is a good idea.   **OK**
  Yes, ... me if we go to the cinema this evening.
5 Mum says eating fish is good for me.   **IT**
  Mum says .... to eat fish.

REVIEW 1 EXERCISES Units 1–4

R1.1 Choose the correct alternative.
1 Families **is / are** important.
2 Sophia **not / isn't** my sister.
3 The boys in my family **are / is** all good-looking.
4 **Are / Is** Jennifer your cousin?
5 **Yes, / No,** James isn't my boyfriend … and I don't want to go out with him!
6 There **aren't / isn't** any of my friends who can beat me at chess.
7 There **is / are** nothing nicer than being with family and friends.
8 'Is there an anniversary party at the weekend?' 'Yes, **is there / there is**.'

R1.2 Complete the sentences with the correct form of the present simple of *be*.
1 Natalie ...isn't... my mum; she's my aunt.
2 .... I too late for the party?
3 There .... some interesting people in your family.
4 Selina .... my stepsister.
5 '............... you and Brian related?' 'No, we .... just good friends.'
6 One of my relatives .... a famous actor!
7 .... there anyone in your family called Mr Stopes?
8 No, I .... Linda's mum! Linda is my sister!

R1.3 Use the words to write sentences or questions with *am, is, are*.
1 David / my brother — *David is my brother.*
2 all my relatives / lovely people
3 our stepfather / 33
4 you / bad-tempered / in the mornings?
5 my cousin and I / not / like each other?
6 you and Jolene / my best friends
7 your grandfather / a funny man?
8 our parents / not / at work today

R1.4 Complete the paragraph with the correct form of the present simple of *be*, affirmative or negative.

Things (1) ...are... different in my family these days. Suddenly, I (2) .... a member of a big family instead of being an only child. You see, my mum and Steve (3) .... married now, so he (4) .... my new stepfather. And there (5) .... four children in Steve's family – Lucas, Alicia, Felix and Rosie. They (6) .... my stepbrothers and sisters now. We (7) .... all in the same house all the time – Steve's children (8) .... in a house with their mum mostly, but they (9) .... here with us every second weekend. We have a lot of fun and (10) .... all good friends now. It (11) .... great being part of a big family!

R1.5 Rearrange the words and write the sentences.
1 your – name – mother's – What's – ? — *What's your mother's name?*
2 is – girl – sister – Which – your – ?
3 mum and dad's – Today – my – wedding anniversary – is
4 help – very – kind – you – to – It's – offer – of – to
5 two – There – shopping – are – bags – full – of
6 party – you – Aren't – for – late – the – ?
7 How many – in – your – are – children – there – family – ?
8 chocolate – the – There – biscuits – are – !

REVIEW 1

R1.6 **Complete the mini-dialogue with ONE word or short form for each gap.**

1 **A:** Hi, Mishka! How are you?
   B: Sorry! I can't stop! ......*I'm*...... in a hurry!
2 **A:** Sandy .... Mark's sister; she's his cousin.
   B: Yes, you're right.
3 **A:** How old is your brother now?
   B: .... 12.
4 **A:** Are you OK?
   B: No, I'm .... I'm cold!
5 **A:** Is it time for breakfast?
   B: No, ... early.
6 **A:** This .... my new T-shirt!
   B: It's lovely!
7 **A:** Where is Richard?
   B: .... he is!
8 **A:** Let's go to the beach today.
   B: .... fine by me.

R1.7 **Choose the correct alternative.**

1 Hi! **That's / (It's)** Belinda. Is that you, Carmen?
2 **It's / That's** very kind of you to buy me this, Aunt Gloria.
3 'What's **it / that**?' 'I haven't got a clue!'
4 'Do you like this food, Claire?' 'Hmm... what is **it / that**?'
5 Hey! **That's / It's** the 6th of May tomorrow – Dad's birthday!
6 Mmm – delicious! I think **it's / that's** the nicest meal ever, Mum!
7 'Do you like the present?' 'Yes, **that's / it's** great, thanks!'

R1.8 **Choose the correct alternative.**

Today (1) **(is) / are** Saturday. (2) **There's / It's** a lovely sunny day and Jake (3) **is / it's** at home. His parents (4) **is / are** at work and his sister, Lily, (5) **is / are** at a friend's house. At ten o'clock in the morning he gets a text message on his mobile. (6) **That's / It's** from his friend Andy and it says, 'Where (7) **is / are** you? (8) **There's / I'm** in the park and (9) **there's / that's** a skateboard race at eleven. Come along!' Jake replies, '(10) **That's / There's** fantastic! I'll be (11) **here / there** in half an hour.'

UNIT 5

Have got present simple (I've got, I haven't got, Have you got... ?)

A The verb **have** in the present simple has two different forms: **have / has**. When it expresses possession, it is usually reinforced by **got** (past participle of **get**).

Affirmative

Full form	Short form
I / You have got	I've got / You've got
He / She / It has got	He's got / She's got / It's got
We / You / They have got	We've got / You've got / They've got

The short form is the most common, not only with pronouns, but also when the subject is a singular noun.

I've got lots of friends.
My teacher's got a lot of books.

NB: The short form of **is** (third person singular of **be**) and **has** (third person singular of **have**) is the same, i.e.: **'s**. The presence of **got**, helps to distinguish between **be** and **have**.

Martha's a nice girl. She's got a very good sense of humour.

B **Negative**

Full form	Short form
I / You have not got	I / You haven't got
He / She / It has not got	He / She / It hasn't got
We / You / They have not got	We / You / They haven't got

Even in negative sentences, the short form, reinforced by **got**, is the most common.

I haven't got enough money.
Jo hasn't got any brothers or sisters. She's an only child.

C

Interrogative	Negative questions
Have I / you got... ?	Haven't I / you got... ?
Has he / she / it got... ?	Hasn't he / she / it got... ?
Have we / you / they got... ?	Haven't we / you / they got... ?

Interrogatives are formed using: **Have / Has** + subject (noun or pronoun) + **got**

Have they got any relatives in England?

Negative questions are formed using: **Haven't / Hasn't** + subjects (noun or pronoun) + **got**

Haven't you got a mobile phone?

D Short answers are formed with: **Yes** + subject pronoun + **have / has.**
  No + subject pronoun + **haven't / hasn't.**

Got is never used in short answers. In affirmative ones, we always use the full form.

'Have you got a dog?' 'Yes, I have.' (not: ~~Yes, I've./Yes, I have got.~~)
'Has Simon got a brother?' 'No, he hasn't.'

E **Wh- questions** are formed using:

Question word + **have / has** + subject (noun or pronoun) + **got**

What have you got in your hand?

EXERCISES

Have got present simple

UNIT 5

5.1 Complete the sentences with *have* or *has*.

1 Eleanor ...*has*... got brown hair.
2 The twins .... got green eyes.
3 Shaun and David .... got broad shoulders.
4 My mum .... got plump legs.
5 Grandad .... got white hair now.
6 Our parents .... both got lovely personalities.
7 I .... got a big nose!
8 James's uncle .... got hazel eyes.

5.2 Complete the sentences with the negative form of *have got / has got*.

1 Don't say that! Olga ...*hasn't got*... big ears!
2 Juliette and her sister .... long noses.
3 I .... dyed hair. I'm a true blonde.
4 Eric .... muscular arms.
5 Our mum .... grey hair.
6 Gregory and Don .... aggressive personalities.
7 The people in my family .... broad shoulders.
8 It's not true! Angelina .... an ugly face!

5.3 Use the words to write questions with *have got / has got*. Then complete the short answers

1 Daniel's cousin / a pleasant personality
Has Daniel's cousin got a pleasant personality? Yes, *he has* .
2 Jason and his sister / big feet
.... No, ...
3 Aunt Mabel / dyed hair
.... Yes, ...
4 your sisters / bleached hair
.... Yes, ...
5 Sophia / big eyes
.... No, ...
6 Ronaldo / a gorgeous smile
.... Yes, ...
7 all the children in your family / long arms
.... No, ...
8 Adam / spiky hair
.... No, ...

5.4 Complete the text with the words in the box.

| we've | I've | has | haven't | ~~have~~ | have (x3) | got (x2) |

There are three of us kids in my family and we aren't the same at all. My sisters (1) ...*have*... got curly hair, but I (2) .... (3) .... got totally straight hair. And I've (4) .... green eyes, but my sisters (5) .... both got blue eyes. One of my sisters (6) .... got very long skinny legs, but my other sister and I (7) .... got short plump legs. (8) .... all got one thing the same, though. We've (9) .... wonderful personalities and we (10) .... all got very beautiful faces!

23

UNIT 6
Have and *have got*
Usage and idiomatic expressions

A The verb **have** in the present can also be used as an ordinary verb, without **got**. In this case, in negative sentences, questions and short answers, we use the auxiliary **do / does**.

Affirmative	I / You / We / They have	
	He / She / It has	
Negative	I / You / We / They don't have	
	He / She / It doesn't have	
Interrogative	Do I / you / we / they have…?	
	Does he / she / it have…?	
Short answers	Yes, I / you / we / they do.	No, I / you / we / they don't.
	Yes, he / she / it does.	No, he / she / it doesn't.

B The verb **have**, with or without **got**, indicates possession. We use it to:
- talk about things that belong to us, for example personal objects.
  I've got / I have a new mobile phone.
  My friend's got / My friend has a flat at the seaside.
- describe the characteristics of someone or something
  I've got / I have brown hair and dark eyes.
  The hotel hasn't got / doesn't have a swimming pool.
- talk about relatives and relationships.
  Mike's got / Mike has three cousins.
  I haven't got / I don't have an uncle who lives in Egypt.
- talk about illnesses and other states.
  I've got / I have a headache.
  Has she got / Does she have a sore throat?

The verb **have** (**got**) is normally followed by a noun as a **direct object**.
In American English, the use of **have** is more common than **have got**.

C Here are some common expressions with **have**.

have breakfast / lunch / dinner
have tea / coffee / a coke
have a snack / a sandwich
have a break / a holiday
have a bath / a shower
have a rest / a lie-in
have a party
have fun / a good time

What do you usually have for breakfast?
He doesn't always have tea in the morning.

D **Have to** or **have got to** followed by another verb in the base form means **must** (see p. 146).
I have to / I've got to go now.

E **Have** followed by a verb in its past participle form is used as an auxiliary in the present perfect (see p. 74).
Look! I have made a cake.

EXERCISES

Have and *have got* – Usage and idiomatic expressions

UNIT 6

6.1 Match the sentences 1–6 with the sentences a–f.

1 <u>b</u>   2 ......   3 ......   4 ......   5 ......   6 ......

1 Have you got a brother called Jack?
2 Has your sister got curly hair?
3 Look! I've got your leather jacket on!
4 Has your friend got a tattoo on his arm?
5 Have you and Matt got time to come to my house?
6 I've got a new jacket.

a Yes, we have. Thanks!
b Yes, I have.
c Yes, he has. He's got a dragon.
d It looks nice on you!
e Put it on… let me see how it looks.
f No, she hasn't.

6.2 Tick (✔) the correct sentence.

1 a ☐ Joel's got a bath every day.
  b ✔ Joel has a bath every day.
2 a ☐ They all have breakfast together in that family.
  b ☐ They have all got breakfast together in that family.
3 a ☐ Does Joanna usually have sugar in her tea?
  b ☐ Has Joanna usually got sugar in her tea?
4 a ☐ 'Do you have dinner at six?' 'Yes, I have.'
  b ☐ 'Do you have dinner at six?' 'Yes, I do.'
5 a ☐ Dad has got a rest in the afternoons.
  b ☐ Dad has a rest in the afternoons.
6 a ☐ What time do you have a break at school?
  b ☐ What time have you a break at school?

6.3 Complete the advert with the words in the box.

| have (x3)   we've got   I've got   you've got   ~~haven't got~~   don't have to   has got |

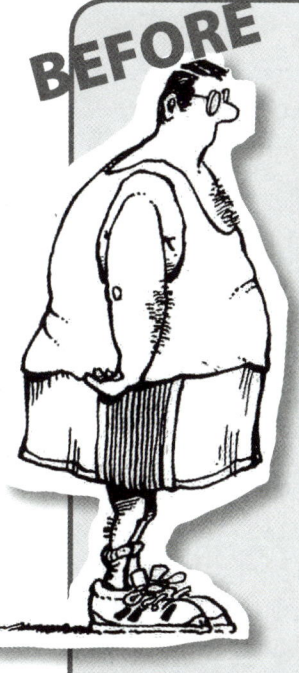

Are you bad at sport?
Do your sporty friends look down on you?

It doesn't matter if you ⁽¹⁾ <u>haven't got</u> strong muscles. You can still be good at weight lifting and other sports.
If ⁽²⁾ .... a bit of money to spare and you want to
⁽³⁾ .... bigger muscles and more strength,
⁽⁴⁾ .... the thing for you.
With our special BuildUp machine, you can ⁽⁵⁾ ....
great muscles in four weeks!
John Bentley ⁽⁶⁾ .... one of our machines.
This is what John says:
'Well, I don't need to say anything… just look at me.
⁽⁷⁾ .... great muscles now. You ⁽⁸⁾ ....
be a champion to work the machine!'

Call NOW, order your machine and ⁽⁹⁾ .... fun!
Tel: 0204 7849923

REVIEW 2

EXERCISES Units 5–6

R2.1 Complete the sentences with the correct form of *have got*.
1 Henry's mum ......*has got*...... long blonde hair.
2 .... your brother .... spiky hair?
3 No, Danny .... big ears.
4 Sandy and Mel .... beautiful blue eyes.
5 .... you .... a temperature?
6 Why .... Fritz .... such an unpleasant personality?
7 Who .... curly hair in your family?
8 '................ you .... a brother?' 'No, I haven't.'

R2.2 Rearrange the words and write the sentences.
1 breakfast – have – Let's – now
 Let's have breakfast now.
2 time – We – a – house – at – have – Sue's – great – always
 ....
3 hairstyle – amazing – Michelle – an – new – has – !
 ....
4 have – Noel – days – Does – long – these – hair – ?
 ....
5 day – have – shower – a – every – Josie – doesn't
 ....
6 Petra's – dinner – They – late – have – family – in
 ....

R2.3 Look at the table and write sentences with *has / hasn't got*.

	long hair	blue eyes	a big nose
Hilary	✗	✓	✓
Nina	✓	✗	✗

1 ......*Hilary hasn't got long hair.*...... 4 ....
2 .... 5 ....
3 .... 6 ....

R2.4 Match the sentences 1–6 with the sentences a–f.

1 ..*d*.. 2 .... 3 .... 4 .... 5 .... 6 ....

1 Look! Little Bill has got your hat on!
2 Have you got a sister called Naomi?
3 Has Maggie got wavy hair?
4 I've got a new baseball cap.
5 Has your dad got a moustache?
6 Have we got time for a game of chess?

a Yes, I have.
b Yes, we have, but let's have a snack first.
c No, he hasn't. He's got a beard.
d Tell him to take it off right now!
e Let me try it on!
f Yes, she has.

REVIEW 2

R2.5 Choose the correct alternative.

1 Marlene **hasn't got** / **don't has** straight hair.
2 Don't look down on people who **hasn't** / **haven't got** any money.
3 They **have** / **got** lunch at two every day.
4 In our family, we **don't have** / **haven't got** lunch at midday.
5 We always **have** / **have got** a great time at Tom's house.
6 Jane and Debbie **hasn't** / **haven't got** grey eyes.
7 **Do your brother have** / **Has your brother got** spiky hair?
8 Joe **has** / **got** a sore throat at the moment.

R2.6 Complete the dialogue with the words in the box.

| I   we've (x2)   you've   got (x2)   ~~haven't~~   haven't   has |

Danielle: Hey, Molly! Have you got a new hairstyle? You look great!
Molly: Thanks! No, I (1) *haven't*. Everyone in my family (2) .... got curly hair like this, you know.
Danielle: You're lucky. Nobody in my family has (3) .... curly hair. I certainly (4) ...., as you can see!
Molly: Yes, but (5) .... got lovely blue eyes. (6) .... haven't got nice eyes at all – mine are grey and boring.
Danielle: Don't be silly! You've (7) .... nice eyes.
Molly: Well, I guess (8) .... all got things we're not that happy with, and we haven't got some things we'd like.
Danielle: Yes, that's true. The best thing is to be happy with what (9) .... got!

R2.7 Complete the text with the correct form of *have (got)*.

Mitch and Bob are twins, but they aren't the same. For a start, Mitch (1) *has* got wavy hair and Bob (2) .... Bob's (3) .... straight, spiky hair. They (4) .... got black hair: Mitch (5) .... got white hair, and his brother's (6) .... brown hair. Their parents (7) .... got black and brown hair. Bob's got the same ears as his dad: they (8) .... both got big ears! Mitch and his mum (9) .... got big ears, they've (10) .... small ears, but big noses! The twins (11) .... both got skinny legs, four of them! Yes, you (12) .... got the idea … Mitch and Bob are dogs!

R2.8 Complete the information with the correct form of *be* or *have (got)*.

HOTEL PARADISO ★ ★ ★ ★

The hotel .... a heated swimming pool and a beauty spa.
There .... two restaurants and a piano bar.
Every room .... Internet and satellite TV.
There .... a Jacuzzi in all the rooms.
.... a pet? No problem! Our ground-floor rooms .... a small garden for your dog.
There .... special prices for families.
We look forward to seeing you.

27

UNIT 7

Present simple (*I walk, I don't walk*)
Form (1)

A The present simple is formed with the base form of the verb, to which you add the ending **-s** to the third person singular.

Affirmative

I walk
You walk
He / She / It walk**s**   for an hour every day.
We walk
You walk
They walk

B By adding the ending **-s**, a few spelling changes occur.

- Verbs that end in **-ss, -sh, -ch, -x**: a pronounced **e** is added before the **-s**.
  I pass → he pass**es**   /ˈpɑːsɪz/
  I wash → he wash**es**   /ˈwɒʃɪz/
  I watch → she watch**es**   /ˈwɒtʃɪz/
  I mix → he mix**es**   /ˈmɪksɪz/

  The goalkeeper passes the ball to the defender.
  My son only watches TV after dinner.

- Verbs that end in **-o**: an **e** is also added before the **-s**, but in this case the **e** isn't pronounced.
  I go → she go**es**   /gəʊz/
  I do → he do**es**   In this case, the vocal sound changes: /duː/ → /dʌz/

  She goes to art classes on Wednesdays.
  She does yoga on Fridays.

- Verbs that end in a **-y** that is preceded by a consonant: the **-y** changes to an **i** and **-es** is added.
  I stu**dy** → he stud**ies**   /ˈstʌdiz/
  I **cry** → he cr**ies**   /kraɪz/

  Jim studies in the afternoon.
  The baby cries all night.

- There is, however, no change when a **-y** is preceded by a vowel.
  I pl**ay** → she pl**ays**   /pleɪz/

  Peter plays football on Saturday afternoons.

C

Negative

Full form	Short form	
I do not walk	I don't walk	
You do not walk	You don't walk	
He / She / It does not walk	He / She / It doesn't walk	for an hour every day.
We do not walk	We don't walk	
You do not walk	You don't walk	
They do not walk	They don't walk	

Full negative form: Subject + **do / does** + **not** + base form of verb
Short negative form: Subject + **don't / doesn't** + base form of verb

Nick doesn't play tennis.
We don't eat fish very often.

EXERCISES

Present simple – Form (1)

UNIT 7

7.1 Tick (✔) the correct sentence.
1. a ✔ I do my homework on Friday evenings.
   b ☐ I does my homework on Friday evenings.
2. a ☐ Raymond go for a long walk every Sunday.
   b ☐ Raymond goes for a long walk every Sunday.
3. a ☐ Adam and I plays football in the garden.
   b ☐ Adam and I play football in the garden.
4. a ☐ Edward stays in bed until 11 on Saturdays.
   b ☐ Edward stay in bed until 11 on Saturdays.
5. a ☐ We don't get up early at the weekend.
   b ☐ We doesn't get up early at the weekend.
6. a ☐ Hannah doesn't studies on Saturday evenings.
   b ☐ Hannah doesn't study on Saturday evenings.

7.2 Complete the sentences with the present simple of the verbs in brackets.
1. Eleanor ....*tidies*.......... her bedroom at the weekend. (tidy)
2. I .... a sandwich for lunch on Saturdays. (make)
3. Sammy .... TV on Sunday afternoons. (watch)
4. Mum and Dad .... relatives at the weekend. (visit)
5. I .... my clothes on Saturday mornings. (wash)
6. Angela .... most of her homework on Sunday evening. (do)
7. Robbie .... his school friends at the weekend. (miss)
8. Joe and Bill .... computer games all Saturday afternoon. (play)

7.3 Rewrite the sentences using the negative form.
1. Nathan stays up late on Saturday nights.
   Nathan doesn't stay up late on Saturday nights.
2. Zena writes e-mails at the weekend.
   ....
3. I wear scruffy clothes on Sundays.
   ....
4. Danny gets up late on Sunday mornings.
   ....
5. They phone their friends on Saturdays and Sundays.
   ....
6. Gloria goes away for the weekend.
   ....

7.4 Complete the text with the present simple of the verbs in brackets.

Lianne (1) ....*doesn't like*.... (not like) school much, but she (2) .... (love) weekends! On Saturdays, she (3) .... (not get) up early. When she (4) .... (go) downstairs at about ten, her mum (5) .... (make) her breakfast. Then her mum and dad (6) .... (go) shopping and Lianne (7) .... (phone) her friends and (8) .... (invite) them round for coffee. They all (9) .... (listen) to music and (10) .... (talk) about the boys they (11) .... (like) at school! In the evening, Lianne (12) .... (not go) out; she stays in and (13) .... (watch) her favourite TV programmes. On Sunday, she (14) .... (do) the same again!

29

UNIT 8 Present simple (*Do you walk?*)
Form (2)

A The interrogative form of the present simple is formed using the auxiliary **do / does**.

Interrogative

Do I walk
Do you walk
Does he / she / it walk   for an hour every day?
Do we walk
Do you walk
Do they walk

Yes / No questions (questions that expect a **Yes / No** answer) always begin with the auxiliary **do / does** followed by the subject (noun or pronoun) and the base form of the main verb.

Do / Does + subject + base form of verb

Do you cycle to school?
Does Mike collect stamps? (not ~~Does Mike collects…?~~ ~~Do Mike collects…?~~)

B Short answers are formed like this:

Yes, + subject pronoun + **do / does.**
No, + subject pronoun + **don't / doesn't.**

NB: In short negative answers, the auxiliary is usually in the short form.

'Do you tidy your room every day?' 'No, I don't.'
'Does your sister work in a bank?' 'Yes, she does.'

C **Wh-** questions are formed by putting the question word first, followed by the auxiliary **do / does**, the subject (noun or pronoun) and the base form of the main verb.

Question word + **do / does** + subject + base form of verb

'Where do you live?' 'We live in Bristol.'
What does he like doing in his free time?

D **Negative questions**

Don't I walk
Don't you walk
Doesn't he / she / it walk   for an hour every day?
Don't we walk
Don't you walk
Don't they walk

In negative questions, **don't** or **doesn't** are placed before the subject:

Don't / Doesn't + subject + base form of main verb

Negative questions are often used to:

* confirm something.
  Don't they live in Yorkshire? (I think they live there)
* express surprise or astonishment
  Don't you know about that? (I'm surprised you don't know about it)

E You can also use the auxiliary **do / does** in an emphatic way, even in the affirmative form.
Oh yes, I do know!

EXERCISES

Present simple – Form (2)

UNIT 8

8.1 Match the questions with the answers.

1 ..c.. 2 .... 3 .... 4 .... 5 .... 6 ....

1 Does your dad have a lie-in at the weekend?
2 Do you do your homework on Friday evening?
3 Do your friends send you a lot of e-mails?
4 Does your mum make a traditional meal on Sundays?
5 Do you and your friends go for walks at the weekend?
6 Does the weekend seem too short?

a Yes, she does.
b Yes, it does!
c Yes, he does.
d Yes, we do.
e No, they don't.
f No, I don't.

8.2 Use the words to write questions in the present simple. Then complete the short answers

1 you / have / a picnic / on Sundays
   Do you have a picnic on Sundays? .... No, *I don't* .

2 your friends / play / computer games / at the weekend
   .... Yes, ...

3 the boys / kick / a ball around / in the park
   .... No, ...

4 your mum / go / to town / on Saturday afternoons
   .... Yes, ...

5 Simon's brother / go / skateboarding / on Saturday mornings
   .... No, ...

6 you / meet / your friends / at the weekend
   .... Yes, ...

8.3 Choose the correct alternative.

1 **(What)** / **Where** do you do in your free time?
2 **Why** / **What** does Frank stay at home every Saturday evening?
3 Where **do** / **does** Eugene go on Sundays?
4 **Who** / **What** do the kids meet in town on Saturday afternoon?
5 Why does Sheldon **get** / **gets** up early on Sundays?
6 When **do** / **does** your parents find time to relax?

8.4 Change the sentences into negative questions.

1 Susan looks tired today.
   Doesn't Susan look tired today?

2 Arthur spends his weekends at the bowling alley.
   ....

3 Jackie stays in bed on Saturday mornings.
   ....

4 Alex thinks Sunday evenings are boring.
   ....

5 Kylie and her sister have a party most weekends.
   ....

6 Your parents listen to rap music.
   ....

7 Young people wear some great clothes.
   ....

UNIT 9 Present simple and frequency adverbs
Usage (1)

A We use the present simple to:

- talk about fixed times, like departures and arrivals of buses / trains / planes, opening and closing times of shops and offices, school times…

  'What time does the train to Brighton leave?' 'It leaves at 7.15.'
  The lessons start at 8.15 a.m. and finish at 1.30 p.m.

B
- talk about habits.

  I usually get up early on weekdays.

  When talking about habits, frequency adverbs are often used with the present simple to indicate how frequently an action takes place.

Frequency adverbs

always
usually
often
sometimes
rarely/seldom
never
ever

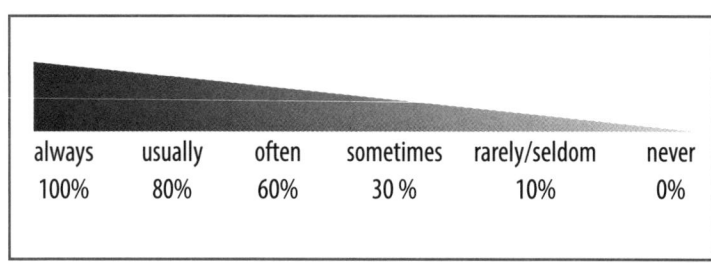

always	usually	often	sometimes	rarely/seldom	never
100%	80%	60%	30%	10%	0%

Frequency adverbs come immediately *before* the verb when the verb is an ordinary verb, but come *after* the verb when the verb is **be**.

- In affirmative sentences, we place them between the subject and the ordinary verb, or after the verb **be**.

  *We **sometimes** eat out on Saturday night.*
  *They are **rarely** at home in the mornings.*

- In negative sentences, we place them between the auxiliary **don't / doesn't** and the base form of the verb, or after the verb **be**.

  *Max doesn't **often** study in the evenings.*
  *They aren't **usually** at home on Sundays.*

- In interrogative sentences, we place them between the subject and the base form of the verb, or after the verb **be** and its subject.

  *Do you **ever** play tennis at the weekend?*
  *Is Douglas **often** at home in the evenings?*

C Other expressions of time, which we use to talk about habits, are:

- **every day, every night, every week…**

  *He comes back home from college **every week**.*

- **on Mondays, on Tuesdays, on Wednesdays** … (the day of the week in its plural form indicates that the action is repeated every Monday, every Tuesday, every Wednesday…)

  *We generally visit our grandparents **on Sundays**.*

- **once a week, twice a day, three / four… times a month / a year**

  *They are tested **once a week**.*

EXERCISES

Present simple and frequency adverbs — Usage (1)

UNIT 9

9.1 Rewrite the sentences, placing the frequency verb in the right place.
1. I sleep late at weekends. (usually) — *I usually sleep late at weekends.*
2. Mum makes breakfast on Saturdays. (never)
3. Are you lazy on Sundays? (always)
4. They are at home on Saturday evenings. (often)
5. I get up early on Sunday mornings. (rarely)
6. Dad works at the weekend. (sometimes)
7. I'm tired on Saturday nights. (never)
8. Sonya goes out on Sundays. (usually)

9.2 Choose the correct alternative
1. Eddie **sometimes tidies** / **tidies sometimes** his room on Sunday mornings.
2. Natalie stays at her friend's house **every / once** weekend.
3. Uncle Bert goes to football matches **every / twice** a month.
4. Do you **ever / once** get together with your friends on Friday evenings?
5. **Irene always / Always Irene** turns on the TV when she wakes up on Saturdays.
6. Everybody in our house **usually is / is usually** online on Sunday afternoons.
7. Mum **does often / often does** the housework early on Saturday mornings.
8. We have a takeaway on Saturday evenings three **every / times** a month.

9.3 Rearrange the words and write the sentences.
1. in – Do – Saturdays – stay – ever – on – you – ?
   Do you ever stay in on Saturdays?
2. once – dinner – Michelle – month – make – and – Grace – the – a
3. Sundays – all – Andrew – day – sleeps – on – sometimes – !
4. twice – a – go – to – cinema – the – month – They
5. boys – every – play – The – morning – in – park – the – football – Sunday
6. are – weekends – Teenagers – happy – usually – at – !

9.4 Write sentences about Giles and Geraldine. Use appropriate frequency adverbs.

On Saturdays	Giles	Geraldine
play tennis	100%	0%
surf the Internet	80%	30%
go shopping with friends	0%	100%
have a lie-in	10%	60%
feel bored	0%	10%

1. *Giles always plays tennis on Saturdays.*
2. *Geraldine never plays tennis on Saturdays.*
3.
4.
5.
6.
7.
8.
9.
10.

33

UNIT 10 Present simple
Use (2)

The present simple is also used:

A
- to talk about scientific facts and accurate data, that are always true

  The Earth rotates around the Sun.
  Water boils at 100°C.
  Birds lay eggs.

B
- to ask or give personal information about situations and conditions that are permanent or relatively stable, for example occupation, residence, likes and dislikes.

  'What does Mr Sullivan do?' 'He's the sales manager at a textile factory.'
  Jenny lives in Hampstead, an elegant suburb of London.
  My brother likes cheese, but he never eats meat.

C
- with verbs that express opinion, agreement or disagreement, like **think**, **believe**, **mean**, **agree**, **disagree**.

  I believe in friendship.
  I don't think he's right.
  I see what you mean.

D
- with verbs that express mental states, like **know**, **understand**, **remember**, **want**, **wish**.

  'Do you know Mr Hill?' 'Yes, I know him very well.'
  I want to go home now.
  I don't understand your behaviour.

E
- with verbs that indicate possession, like **have got**, **own**, **belong**.

  The flat I live in belongs to my uncle.
  My family owns a café in the city centre.

F
- with the verbs **seem**, **look like** and with verbs that refer to the five senses when used intransitively.

  He seems to be all right.
  You look like your sister.
  It smells very nice, but it tastes funny.
  It looks very interesting.
  It sounds very interesting.
  It feels so soft!

G
- to talk about the storyline of a book or a film.

  It's the story of a woman who moves to Los Angeles from a small village in the Midwest, and there...

H
- in live television or radio commentary, instead of the present continuous, to highlight the immediacy of an action

  The goalkeeper jumps... but misses the ball... Yes, Beckham scores a great goal!
  The Prime Minister reads his annual speech...

EXERCISES

Present simple – Use (2)

UNIT 10

10.1 Write F for scientific facts, P for permanent situations and O for opinions/beliefs.
1 Dad works for a mining company. ...P...
2 No, I don't think you're lazy! ....
3 The Sun rises in the east every day of the week! ....
4 My family loves life in the open air. ....
5 We change the clocks on the last weekend in March. ....
6 I believe in relaxing at the weekend. ....
7 I don't agree with you about getting up at six on Sundays! ....
8 We own a campervan and we're always on the go. ....

10.2 Find the mistakes and underline them. Then write the correct sentences in your exercise book.
1 I understand not why you laze around all day at the weekend.
   I don't understand why you laze around all day at the weekend.
2 Samantha wants always to go out on Saturday evenings.
3 All night at ten o'clock, Mum puts the cat out.
4 Ashley don't help his mum with the housework.
5 They go usually to the Internet café to go online.
6 Dad does the shopping a twice week.

10.3 Complete the dialogue with the sentences in the box. Watch out! There are two extra sentences.

Yes, I do.	Yes, they usually do.
What do you do on Saturday evenings?	My mum doesn't like me going out on school nights.
Does your mum do the housework on Saturdays?	I don't usually do anything special.
~~Do you want to come round later?~~	

Joss: Hi, Manya! (1) *Do you want to come round later?*
Manya: Hi, Joss. I can't, I'm sorry. (2) ....
Joss: Well, what about Saturday, then?
Manya: Hmm... on Saturday afternoons, I usually go out with my cousins.
Joss: (3) ....
Manya: (4) ....
Joss: Well, come on Saturday evening!
Manya: Yes, OK. That's a lovely idea.
Joss: And, do you like Chinese food?
Manya: (5) ....
Joss: We have takeaways on Saturday evenings. Mum can get one for you, too!
Manya: Fab! See you Saturday!

10.4 Complete the text with the correct form of the present simple of the verbs in brackets.

I hate Saturdays! In our house, we (1) *don't relax* (not relax) on Saturday. My sisters and I (2) .... (help) Mum with the housework every Saturday morning. Then my big sister (3) .... (tidy) our bedrooms before lunch. We never (4) .... (watch) TV and we (5) .... (not play) computer games in the afternoon. Mum (6) .... (take) us all out for a long walk with the dog. She (7) .... (say) walking is good for you! I (8) .... (not know) about that. We (9) .... (be) usually bored after the first half an hour. But Saturday evenings are OK. Mum (10) .... (not cook) – we (11) .... (get) a takeaway and we all (12) .... (sit) in the living room eating and chatting. Then Mum (13) .... (watch) TV and we (14) .... (watch) a DVD and stay up late. Luckily, Mum (15) .... (not make) us get up early on Sundays!

35

REVIEW 3

EXERCISES Units 7–10

R3.1 Choose the correct alternative.
1 **You get / Do you get** up late at the weekend?
2 James never **go / goes** out on Sunday evenings.
3 **Does / Do** your mum believe in relaxing at the weekend?
4 Mum doesn't **think / thinks** weekends are that exciting.
5 Are **you usually / usually you** tired on Saturday nights?
6 Shelley **often / ever** writes e-mails on Sunday mornings.
7 Dad **put / puts** the milk bottles out last thing at night.
8 I **enjoys / enjoy** my lazy Sunday afternoons.
9 She **don't / doesn't** get up late on Saturdays.
10 I **surf never / never surf** the Internet on weekday evenings.

R3.2 Complete the sentences with the correct form of the present simple of the verbs in brackets.
1 I rarely ......*go*...... away at the weekend. (go)
2 Simon .... skateboarding every Saturday. (go)
3 .... you .... to your friends on the phone a lot? (chat)
4 They .... early on Sunday mornings. (not get up)
5 Mum never .... breakfast on Sundays. (cook)
6 .... your friend .... at your house at the weekend? (stay)
7 William .... his smart clothes when he's at home. (not wear)
8 I .... bored when I'm on holiday. (never / be)

R3.3 Read the notes and write sentences about Judy and the twins.

Judy - Saturdays
have a lie-in - usually
go shopping - always
eat lunch in town - often
watch DVDs - never

the twins - Sundays
get up early - sometimes
play football - usually
meet Tom and Stef in town - rarely
stay up late - never

1 Judy usually has a lie-in on Saturdays.
2 ....
3 ....
4 ....
5 ....
6 ....
7 ....
8 ....

R3.4 Complete the text with the words in the box.

| stays   rings   she's   ~~do~~   don't (x2)   doesn't (x2)   visit   watches |

(1) ......*Do*...... you think Sundays are boring? A lot of people (2) .... have enough things to do on Sundays, they get bored and (3) .... enjoy the day. One person who (4) .... think Sundays are great is my grandmother. She (5) .... at home all day and she (6) .... TV. She (7) .... usually go out anywhere. She sometimes (8) .... her friends and has a chat with them on the phone. But (9) .... often lonely on Sundays. So... my cousin and I often go and (10) .... her to brighten up her day!

36

REVIEW 3

R3.5 Complete the dialogue with the affirmative form of the present simple of the verbs in brackets. Pay attention to spelling changes.

Sally (1) __likes__ (like) sports very much. She usually (2) _____ (play) hockey in her school team, so she (3) _____ (train) twice a week, on Mondays and Thursdays. She (4) _____ (go) swimming every Tuesday evening in the local swimming pool and often (5) _____ (take) part in swimming competitions on Saturdays. If you're wondering what she (6) _____ (do) on Sundays, well, she (7) _____ (watch) sports programmes on TV. She never (8) _____ (miss) a match or a tournament.

R3.6 Complete the sentences with the appropriate form of the present simple of the verbs in brackets.

play agree get work (x2) eat stay go wear do

1 My brother and I never __agree__ about whose turn it is to go online.
2 We often _____ a traditional roast on Sundays.
3 We usually _____ in bed late on Saturday mornings.
4 _____ your dad ever _____ at the weekend?
5 The kids often _____ football with their team on Saturday afternoons.
6 I _____ up quite early on Sunday mornings.
7 No, we _____ shopping on Saturdays because the shops are crowded.
8 I never _____ housework on a Sunday.
9 'When _____ Janet _____ these old scruffy jeans?'
10 'Only when she _____ in the garden.'

R3.7 Complete the e-mail with the correct form of the verbs in brackets.

Hi Steffi

I __'m__ (be) in London to improve my English. It _____ (be) great!
I _____ (go) to school every morning. I _____ (get up) at seven o'clock, _____ (have) breakfast, then _____ (walk) to the bus stop where I _____ (meet) Brigitte, my Swedish friend. We _____ (travel) to school together. Lessons _____ (start) at nine and _____ (finish) at half past twelve. I often _____ (not go) home after school. Twice a week Brigitte and I _____ (go) to the gym. I _____ (play) tennis and Brigitte _____ (do) yoga. (She _____ (not like) tennis!)
I usually _____ (get) home at seven for dinner. In the evening, I _____ (watch) TV or _____ (listen) to music. At the weekend, Brigitte _____ (come) to my house and we sometimes _____ (go) to the pub. I _____ (like) pubs, but I _____ (not drink) beer!
_____ (you/think) my English is good?
Write soon.
Martha

UNIT 11 Present continuous *(I am leaving)*
Form (1)

A The present continuous, or present progressive, is the tense used to describe an action which is happening at or around the moment of speaking. It's formed using the auxiliary **be** and the **-ing** form of the main verb.

Affirmative

I	am ('m)	
You	are ('re)	
He / She / It	is ('s)	leaving for Paris.
We	are ('re)	
You	are ('re)	
They	are ('re)	

Full form: Subject + **am / is / are** + verb in the **-ing** form
Short form: Subject + **'m / 's / 're** + verb in the **-ing** form
The short form is the most common.

Hurry up. We're waiting for you.
They're playing really well.

B The addition of the suffix **-ing** to the base form of the verb involves some spelling changes.

- We double the final consonant for:
  – verbs with one syllable that end in a single consonant preceded by a single vowel
    run → running; sit → sitting
  BUT: meet → meeting (two vowels before the first consonant)
    melt → melting (two final consonants)

  – verbs with two syllables with the stress on the second syllable, which end in a single consonant preceded by a single vowel
    refer → referring; transmit → transmitting
  BUT: suffer → suffering (the stress is on the first syllable);
    repeat → repeating (two vowels befor the final consonant);
    report → reporting (two final consonants)

  – verbs that end in **-l** preceded by a single vowel (only in British English)
    travel → travelling (Am. traveling); counsel → counselling (Am. counseling)
  BUT: feel → feeling (two vowels before the final consonant)

- The **-e** is dropped in verbs which ending with a silent **-e**.
    come → coming; leave → leaving (the **-e** isn't pronounced)
  BUT: see → seeing; be → being (the **-e** is pronounced)

- The final diphthong **-ie** becomes a **y**.
  lie → lying; die → dying

  Note: The final **y** doesn't change when adding **-ing**:
  cry → crying; study → studying; buy → buying; stay → staying

EXERCISES

Present continuous – Form (1)

UNIT 11

11.1 Complete the sentences with *am, is* or *are*.
1 Peter ......*is*...... walking the dog at the moment.
2 We .... visiting some local ancient monuments.
3 Ron .... learning how to juggle.
4 Be quiet! I .... trying to concentrate!
5 The girls .... reading in their room.
6 Quincy .... watching TV in the living room.
7 Wally and I .... going to night school to learn Japanese.
8 My friend's brother .... studying martial arts.

11.2 Rewrite sentences 1–4 from exercise 1 using the short form.
1 *Peter's walking the dog at the moment.*
2 ....
3 ....
4 ....

11.3 Complete the sentences with the present continuous of the verbs in brackets.
1 They ......*are travelling*...... around the country looking at castles. (travel)
2 Phil .... how to sail a laser dinghy. (learn)
3 Ben and I .... to music from South America. (dance)
4 We .... to trace our family history. (try)
5 Martin and his dad .... with some friends. (fish)
6 The boys .... mountain biking with their youth club. (go)
7 I .... on my bed thinking about what to do next! (lie)
8 Ellie .... at the Moon through her telescope. (look)

11.4 Complete the text with the present continuous of the verbs in the box.

| read   try   listen   cook   ~~happen~~   watch   put   have |

Lots of things (1) ......*are happening*...... in the Robinson household. Mum (2) .... an exotic meal in the kitchen and Sammy, the family's dog, (3) .... her with great interest! Dad (4) .... some new cupboards together in the living room – but he (5) .... a few problems! Rose (6) .... all about digital cameras because she wants to take up photography as a hobby. Colin and his friend Sam (7) .... to music in Colin's room. Grandma (8) .... to find somewhere quiet to sit and have a little sleep!

39

UNIT 12 Present continuous *(I am not leaving, Are you leaving?)*
Form (2)

A The negative form of the present continuous is formed by adding **not** between the auxiliary **be** and the **-ing** form.

Negative

I	am not ('m not)	
You	are not (aren't)	
He / She / It	is not (isn't)	leaving for Paris.
We	are not (aren't)	
You	are not (aren't)	
They	are not (aren't)	

Full form: Subject + **am / is / are** + **not** + verb in the **-ing** form

Short form: Subject + **'m not / isn't / aren't** + verb in the **-ing** form

In negative sentences the short form is the most used.
I'm not going out.
She isn't studying chemistry, she's studying physics.

B

Interrogative

Am I
Are you
Is he / she / it   leaving for Paris?
Are we
Are you
Are they

Interrogative form: **Am / Is / Are** + subject + verb in the **-ing** form

Are you calling Jack?
Is Simon coming home for dinner?

In negative questions, the short forms **aren't** or **isn't** come before the subject.
Aren't the children sleeping?
Isn't she doing her homework?

C Short answers are formed using: **Yes, / No,** + subject pronoun + the verb **be** in the affirmative / negative

In short affirmative answers, the verb **be** is never shortened.
'Are you joking?' 'No, I'm not.'
'Is he watching TV?' 'Yes, he is.'

D **Wh- questions** are constructed by putting the question word first.

Question word + **am / is / are** + subject + verb in the **-ing** form

What are you doing?
Where are you going?
Why aren't they listening?

EXERCISES

Present continuous – Form (2)

UNIT 12

12.1 Use the words to write negative sentences in the present continuous.

1 I / paint / any more pictures — *I'm not painting any more pictures.*
2 Shane / write / his blog
3 we / go / to the cinema
4 they / compete / in the karate competition
5 she / do / Sudoku puzzles
6 Harry and Bob / skateboard

12.2 Complete the short answers.

1 Are you learning how to rollerblade? No, *I'm not* .
2 Is Evette studying astronomy? No, .
3 Are your brothers playing ice hockey? Yes, .
4 Are you enjoying the Formula One racing? Yes, .
5 Are Jon and Dave acting in the school play? No, .
6 Are you going skateboarding on Saturday? No, .

12.3 Choose the correct alternative.

1 **Are** / **Is** Matilda learning to use a microscope?
2 **Where are** / **Are where** you going now?
3 Why **don't** / **aren't** you watching the Formula One race?
4 Are **Nathan** / **the boys** making model cars in their room?
5 **Isn't** / **Aren't** Jamie listening to music at the moment?
6 **What** / **When** are you making?

12.4 Rearrange the words and write the questions.

1 mum – drive – how – your – learning – to – Is – ?
Is your mum learning how to drive?
2 you – drama – going – group – to – the – Are – ?
3 in – reading – Ian – his – Is – room – ?
4 are – What – doing – you – ?
5 kite – fly – learning – Who – how – is – to – a – ?
6 you – are – Where – going – ?
7 they – Why – aren't – the – watching – match – ?
8 Aren't – today – in – they – band – the – playing – ?

12.5 Match the answers to the questions from exercise 4.

1 *g* 2 ..... 3 ..... 4 ..... 5 ..... 6 ..... 7 ..... 8 .....

a My brother.
b No, he isn't.
c I'm making a model plane.
d No, they aren't.
e Yes, I am.
f I'm going to the youth club.
g Yes, she is.
h Because they're having a music lesson.

UNIT 13 Present continuous
Usage

The present continuous is used:

A
- to say what is taking place in a given moment (for example, when we are talking on our mobile phones, describing a scene or picture). In this case, we often use adverbs or time expressions like **now**, **just / right now**, **at the moment**, **at present**, which usually come at the end of the sentence.

Look. It's raining hard.
I'm watching a film right now.
My father's working in the garden at the moment.

B
- to describe an action that has already begun but hasn't ended, not necessarily at the exact moment you are talking, but at that time.

I'm learning French. (at this time)
She's taking a course in business English. (and she hasn't finished it yet)

C
- to highlight, with a certain sense of annoyance, something which is done insistently, or which isn't done, but should be. We use the adverb **always** with the present continuous in this case.

You're always talking! (it irritates me)

D
- to talk about situations that are temporary or different from what one usually does.

I'm staying with an English family. (at this time, it's not my normal residence)
This week, I'm working in the morning. (not always, only for this week)
I'm teaching in a private school this year.

E
- to talk about future actions that are already foreseen or planned. In this case, we always use an adverb or a time expression like **tonight**, **tomorrow**, **next week / year**.

What are you doing next summer?
I'm going to the mountains.
I'm meeting him at the airport tomorrow at nine o'clock.
I'm starting a new school next year.

EXERCISES

Present continuous – Usage

UNIT 13

13.1 Choose the correct alternative.
1 I'm looking after my friend's pet spiders at the **moment** / **present**.
2 The kids are going bird-watching **last** / **next** weekend.
3 Be quiet! You're **always** / **never** talking about your hobbies!
4 Where are you going next **night** / **summer**?
5 Sol's going rollerblading **at** / **right** now.
6 Fred and Vera are spending a lot of time bird-watching these **days** / **moments**.
7 I'm not doing anything special **yesterday** / **tomorrow**.
8 Are you carrying on collecting Spider-Man comics **last** / **this** year?

13.2 Find the mistakes and underline them. Then write the correct sentences.
1 <u>We're meet</u> Simon at the concert at seven.
   We're meeting Simon at the concert at seven.
2 They're studying English in London last month.
   ....
3 Angela's spending always her money on stupid things.
   ....
4 Learning you how to cook Chinese food?
   ....
5 Sophie and I am collecting flowers at the moment.
   ....
6 What are you doing evening?
   ....

13.3 Simon is writing to his parents about what he will do at karate summer camp.

Saturday
10.00: train on the beach
12.00: have lunch in the hotel
14.00: meet at the sports centre
15.00: take part in the tournament
19.00: go to restaurant for dinner
Sunday
09.00: visit the town
12.00: leave on the coaches

1 *At ten o'clock on Saturday, we're training on the beach.*
2 ....
3 ....
4 ....
5 ....
6 ....
7 ....

13.4 Complete the text using the words in the box.

| They're (x2)   you're   is (x 2)   are (x 2)   ~~I'm~~   listening   writing   spending   trying |

(1) *I'm* talking to you from Camton Youth Centre. The young people are all busy. (2) .... learning new hobbies and pastimes. Some of them (3) .... making things out of pottery – they're (4) .... to use the potter's wheel that we have here, but it isn't easy! Others are painting and one boy (5) .... carving something out of wood. One group of young people (6) .... sitting in the next room. They're (7) .... to a guest speaker who (8) .... talking about writing blogs. (9) .... getting some advice and learning what not to do when they're (10) .... their blogs. If (11) .... looking for a new way of (12) .... your free time, why not come and join us?

43

UNIT 14: Present simple and present continuous
Differences in usage

The **present simple** is used to talk about:	The **present continuous** is used to talk about:
• habitual actions, not necessarily happening as you are speaking	• actions happening as you are speaking
 *I play basketball from 6 p.m. to 8 p.m. every day.*	 *It's seven o'clock. He's playing basketball.*
• actions in our daily routine	• temporary actions, which involve a change from routine
I usually get up at half past seven.	 *Today, she's getting up at five o'clock to go to the airport.*
• facts and permanent situations	• temporary situations
Joseph is an acrobat. He works in a circus.	*They are performing in Scotland at the moment.*

EXERCISES

Present simple and present continuous – Differences in usage

UNIT 14

14.1 Tick (✔) the correct sentences and correct the sentences with mistakes in them.

1. ☐ I'm going to summer camp every August. — *I go to summer camp every August.*
2. ✔ Do you collect phone cards?
3. ☐ They usually are spending their time surfing the Internet.
4. ☐ Sally and I visit Harlech Castle today.
5. ☐ You're always make a mess when you paint!
6. ☐ Darren stays in London at weekends.
7. ☐ Go away! I'm writing my blog!
8. ☐ I don't collecting anything for a hobby.

14.2 Match the two parts of the sentences.

1 _c_ 2 ...... 3 ...... 4 ...... 5 ...... 6 ......

1 Every weekend,
2 Do you
3 Are you
4 We usually
5 Sabrina's
6 I don't

a enjoying your new hobby?
b learning about astronomy.
c Steve and his mates go fishing.
d spend your free time reading?
e enjoy the same hobbies as my sister.
f go bird-watching together.

14.3 Complete the dialogue using the present simple or continuous of the verbs in brackets.

Alex: What (1) _are you reading_ (you / read), Ben?
Ben: (2) .... (I / read) about famous climbers.
Alex: Why? (3) .... (you / not climb) mountains.
Ben: (4) .... (I / know), but (5) .... (I / save up) to go to the Alps and (6) .... (I / plan) what to do when I'm there.
Alex: Hmm ... mountain climbing (7) .... (not be) a hobby that (8) .... (interest) me.
Ben: My friend Jack (9) .... (learn) how to climb and (10) .... (he / have) a great time. What (11) .... (you / do) in your free time, anyway?
Alex: (12) .... (I / sit) at my computer surfing the net or writing my blog.
Ben: Well, I think mountain climbing is a lot more fun!
Alex: Yes... and sitting at the computer is a lot safer!

14.4 Complete the sentences using the expressions in the box.

| Are you enjoying | doesn't understand | not giving up | We usually visit |
| They're all having | Bobby plays | Does your brother | spends his free time |

1. Ulla _doesn't understand_ how to do Sudoku.
2. .... the go-karting lessons?
3. Lucas .... playing the saxophone.
4. I'm .... fishing; I'm just having a break from it.
5. .... use his digital camera a lot?
6. .... a great time watching the ice hockey finals.
7. .... with his remote-control car at the weekends.
8. .... the ancient buildings in Athens.

UNIT 15 Action verbs and stative verbs

A Action verbs can be used either in the simple form or the continuous form.

He speaks English.
He's speaking to Mr Jones.

Verbs which do not express an action (**like, know, want…**), also known as stative verbs, are not usually used in the continuous form.
These include:

- verbs of perception like **see** or **hear** which are usually accompanied by the modal verb **can**.

  I can't see.
  Can you hear that noise?

- verbs that are used to talk about emotions and thoughts, like **forgive, care, like, mind, want, know, understand, believe, remember.**

  Do you understand what I'm saying?
  I don't mind cooking the dinner tonight.
  She remembers you very well and she's inviting you to the party.

- verbs of possession: **own / possess, belong, have got** (see p.34)

B Some verbs expressing feelings, preferences or sensations, like **feel, hope**, can be used in the simple form and also in the continuous form.

'How do you feel?' 'I don't feel very well.'
'How are you feeling today?' 'I'm feeling great!'
I hope you like it.
Scientists are hoping to find a clean source of energy.

C Note also:

- the verb **think** is used in the simple form when expressing an opinion, and in the continuous form when expressing an intention or reflection.

  I think it's a good idea. (expressing an opinion)
  'What are you doing?' 'I'm thinking.' (reflection)

- the verb **enjoy** is used in the simple form as a synonym of **like**, and in the continuous form when it means **to have fun**.

  I enjoy walking in the countryside.
  I'm enjoying my holiday.

- the verb **see** is used in the simple form when it means **understand**, and in the continuous form when it means **meet someone for an appointment**.

  I see what you are saying. (I understand)
  I'm seeing the doctor tomorrow morning. (I've got an appointment)

EXERCISES

Action verbs and stative verbs

UNIT 15

15.1 Choose the correct alternative.
1 I **am thinking** / **think** of taking up mountain biking in my spare time.
2 What **are you doing** / **do you do** in your free time?
3 I **hate** / **am hating** fishing!
4 I **forgive** / **am forgiving** you for taking my skateboard.
5 We **see** / **are seeing** Norman later to have a look at his DVD collection.
6 Frank **is eating** / **eats** sandwiches when he's out climbing.
7 I **don't remember** / **am not remembering** how to play the guitar.
8 Yes, I **am enjoying** / **enjoy** myself at the moment!

15.2 Use the words to write sentences using the present simple or continuous.
1 I / enjoy / this game of ice hockey
  I'm enjoying this game of ice hockey.
2 John / think / of / buy / some new rollerblades

3 they / not understand / how to write blogs

4 Jason / not like / walking the dog

5 I / think / snowboarding / be / a dangerous hobby

6 he / not believe / I can rollerblade

15.3 Find the mistakes and underline them. Then write the correct sentences in your exercise book.
1 <u>I see</u> the climbing instructor tomorrow.
  I'm seeing the climbing instructor tomorrow.
2 We're thinking it's a great idea to take up juggling!
3 I enjoy this game a lot at the moment!
4 I'm knowing how to look after tropical fish.
5 I'm not believing Stan does ballet in his free time!
6 I'm understanding all the rules of chess now.

15.4 Tick (✔) the sentence (a or b) which has the same meaning as the first one.
1 He's hating every minute of this photography lesson.
  a ☐ He hates photography lessons.
  b ✔ He is not enjoying this lesson.
2 Sarah enjoys looking for wild flowers.
  a ☐ Sarah is having a good time at the moment.
  b ☐ Sarah has a good time when she looks for wild flowers.
3 I see what you mean.
  a ☐ I understand what you're saying.
  b ☐ I am looking at you.
4 I'm seeing Martha tomorrow and we're going bird-watching.
  a ☐ I am watching Martha bird-watching tomorrow.
  b ☐ I plan to meet Martha tomorrow to go bird-watching.

REVIEW 4

EXERCISES Units 11–15

R4.1 Choose the correct alternative.
1 Clyde and I **am / are** doing some gardening this summer.
2 **Do / Are** you like watching old movies?
3 I'm **not / don't** learning about astronomy any more.
4 Neville **is / does** mountain climbing this weekend.
5 Suzy is **having / has** difficulty doing this Sudoku puzzle.
6 **Do you like / Are you liking** bird-watching?
7 Danny **is thinking / thinks** about learning to juggle.
8 I'm **dieing / dying** to see a live Formula One race.

R4.2 Complete the sentences with the correct form of the present continuous of the verbs in brackets.
1 The boys ....**are enjoying**.... fishing with their dad. (enjoy)
2 .... your friend .... exotic cookery? (study)
3 I .... all the ancient monuments in England next summer. (visit)
4 She .... to music at the moment. (not listen)
5 .... you still .... stamps as a hobby, Amy? (collect)
6 .... you .... the dog? (feed)
7 Nancy .... model aeroplanes any more. (not make)
8 .... your mates .... mountain biking tomorrow? (go)

R4.3 Match the two parts of the sentences.

1 ..**d**.. 2 ...... 3 ...... 4 ...... 5 ...... 6 ...... 7 ...... 8 ......

1 The girls are
2 Do you
3 I
4 Moira and Sam
5 Are
6 Helen
7 Are you
8 Jenny isn't doing

a they watching a DVD?
b puzzles right now.
c like mountain climbing?
d surfing the Internet.
e using the computer at the moment?
f am reading about astronomy.
g collects stamps from America.
h are collecting flowers and insects.

R4.4 Look at the picture and write what the people are doing.
1 Tracy ..**is reading about cookery.**..
2 Carl ..**is listening to music.**..
3 The cats ....
4 Mum and dad ....
5 The dog ....
6 Grandad ....
7 Grandma ....

R4.5 Complete the text using the correct form of the verbs in the box.

| stay | think | have | ~~spend~~ | show | like | write | walk | take | surf |

Kelly and her sister usually (1) ....**spend**.... Saturdays at home. They (2) .... to watch cartoons in the morning and in the afternoon they (3) .... the Internet and (4) .... e-mails to their friends. But today is different. Their cousin from Scotland (5) .... with them, so they (6) .... him London. At the moment, they (7) .... round the centre of the city, and their cousin (8) .... a lot of photographs. They (9) .... a great time, and their cousin (10) .... London is great!

48

R4.6 Present simple or present continuous? Complete the dialogue with the correct tense of the verbs in brackets. Put the adverbs of frequency in the correct position.

A: (1) *Do you often come* (you / come / often) to the office canteen for lunch?
B: No, quite rarely. I (2) ………………………… (have / usually) a sandwich or a salad in the cafeteria across the road. It's quieter.
A: So why (3) ………………………… (you / have) lunch here today?
B: Well, I (4) ………………………… (want) to see if the quality of the food is better now, as they (5) ………………………… (say).
A: And what (6) ………………………… (you / think) of today's menu?
B: The roast beef (7) ………………………… (be) good, and the vegetables (8) ………………………… (be) quite tasty. What I (9) ………………………… (not / like) are the people who (10) ………………………… (keep) talking and (11) ………………………… (not / mind) their own business.
A: Ooh!

R4.7 Present simple or present continuous? Complete the sentences with the correct tense of the verbs in the box.

| make | give | look at | look for | want | like | ~~fly~~ | serve |

1 The kids ……*are flying*…… their new kite at the moment.
2 Uncle Bill ………………………… the stars through his telescope when the night is clear.
3 Sasha ………………………… collecting wild flowers.
4 They ………………………… some really exotic meals in that restaurant.
5 Look! The children ………………………… a mess in the living room.
6 Mandy ………………………… to give up her hobby of model making.
7 Ssh! Let me listen. The teacher ………………………… us some advice about writing essays.
8 Natasha ………………………… her camera. She can't find it anywhere.

R4.8 Complete the postcard using the present simple or continuous of the verbs in brackets.

Dear Jack
Here I …*am*………… (be) in sunny California! I ………………… (have) a great time. I ………………… (stay) in a lovely hotel in Santa Barbara. Every morning I ………………… (go) to the beach, but I ………………… (not swim) every day because the water is really cold!
At the moment, I ………………… (sit) in my hotel room with Amy.
We ………………… (watch) football on the TV. Brazil and Germany ………………… (play). It ………………… (be) an exciting game!
What ………………… (you/do) these days? ………………… (you/have) fun or ………………… (you/study) as usual?
See you next week
Love Baz

A Exam preparation

A.1 PET Reading Part 5

Read the e-mail and choose the correct word(s) (A, B, C or D) for each space.

Hi George!

Thanks for the e-mail. (1) ....B.... great to have a new e-friend! (2) .... a photo of my family with this message. The woman in the middle (3) .... my mum, Alice. And of course the tall (4) .... my dad, Colin. (5) .... a teacher. The girl next to mum (6) .... Emma, my sister. She's into music, like me, and (7) .... OK. We get on with each other very well. The two little boys (8) .... Frank and Eddie, my brothers. (9) .... twins. They are funny but they (10) .... very well-behaved, I'm afraid. I fall out with them a lot! And the good-looking guy (11) .... me!

(12) .... your family like, George? (13) .... your mum and dad young or old? Any other kids in the family, or (14) .... you an only child?

Write back soon and send a photo if you can.

Will

1 A There's **B It's** C I'm D You're
2 A There's B It's C Is D That's
3 A are B be C isn't D is
4 A man B he's C man's D the man
5 A He's B It's C She's D is
6 A are B she's C she D is
7 A he's B it's C she's D I'm
8 A they B are C is D we're
9 A He's B It's C There are D They are
10 A not B aren't C isn't D am not
11 A is B are C be D am
12 A Is B What's C Are D How's
13 A Is B Are they C It's D Are
14 A aren't B are C is D am

A.2 PET Writing Part 1

Complete the second sentence so that it means the same as the first.
Use no more than three words.

1 There are five children in Mrs Roland's family.
   Mrs Roland ......*has got*...... five children in her family.
2 We can't play outside because it's raining.
   We can't play outside because the .... shining.
3 Every Friday, the children are bored.
   The children .... on Fridays.
4 Their house has got a big garden all around.
   .... a big garden all around their house.
5 My sister goes to ballet lessons, but I don't.
   I .... to ballet lessons with my sister.

A.3 PET Writing Part 2

Your English friend wants to know more about your hobbies.
Write a note to your friend (35–45 words). You should:

- say what your hobby is
- say what your hobby involves
- say how often you do your hobby
- ask about your friend's hobbies

Exam preparation

A

A.4 FCE Use of English Part 1

Read the text below and decide which answer (A, B, C or D) best fits each space.

Weekends are different for everyone!

For lots of people, weekends are the time when they (1)....C.... or have fun. They (2)................ have school and they don't (3)................ to work. But for some people, Saturdays and Sundays are the same as every other day. For example, shop assistants and people in cafés (4)................ at weekends. And what about doctors and nurses? They (5)................ a break every weekend. My father is a policeman and he (6)................ get many weekends off. When he (7)................ time off, he (8)................ to stay at home and watch some TV or (9)................ the gardening. That (10)................ like a lot of fun to me!

1 **A** relaxes	**B** are relax	**C** relax	**D** relaxing
2 **A** does	**B** doesn't	**C** not	**D** don't
3 **A** go	**B** does go	**C** goes	**D** go not
4 **A** not works	**B** works	**C** work	**D** don't work
5 **A** no get	**B** don't get	**C** get not	**D** doesn't get
6 **A** doesn't	**B** not do	**C** no	**D** does
7 **A** do get	**B** get	**C** getting	**D** gets
8 **A** like	**B** is liking	**C** do like	**D** likes
9 **A** do	**B** does to	**C** does	**D** doing
10 **A** not sound	**B** doesn't sound	**C** sound not	**D** isn't sounding

A.5 FCE Use of English Part 2

Read the text below and think of the word or short form which best fits each space.
Use only one in each space. Short forms count as one word.

Friendship

Is (1)....there.... one thing that makes a good friend? The simple answer is, no, there (2)................ . There (3)................ all sorts of people who are good friends. (4)................ the person who listens to everything you say and there's the friend who shares all their secrets with you. Then there (5)................ friends who are generous and give you things. (6)................ are other friends who disagree with you all the time, but they are still your friend. On the other hand, there (7)................ some people who aren't good friends. There are some people who are thoughtless and unkind and they (8)................ good friends. And there (9)................ many selfish people who aren't good friends either. But the main thing about friendship is that (10)................ are all sorts of people who make great friends!

A.6 FCE Use of English Part 2

Read the text below and think of the word or short form which best fits each space.
Use only one in each space. Short forms count as one word.

Hey, look! That's my friend, Morton. He's (1)..........got.......... short, spiky hair and big blue eyes and I think he's very good-looking! (2)........................... got long legs and a muscular body. He and his brother (3)........................... both got great personalities. Hold on! That's weird because the teacher said Morton (4)........................... got a temperature today, so he isn't at school. But Morton's in the chemistry lesson right now! Oh no... it isn't Morton. Morton's (5)........................... a twin brother. (6)........................... both got short, spiky hair and they're both good-looking! It's Morton's brother in the lesson!

UNIT 16 — Be past simple (I was, I wasn't, Were you... ?)

A The verb **be** in the past simple has two forms: **was, were**. There is no affirmative short form.

Affirmative
I was
You were
He / She / It was
We / You / They were
at home yesterday.

I was on holiday in June.
They were really interested in our project.

B

Negative

Full form	Short form	
I was not	I wasn't	
You were not	You weren't	at home yesterday.
He / She / It was not	He / She / It wasn't	
We / You / They were not	We / You / They weren't	

Full form: Subject + **was / were + not**
Short form: Subject + **wasn't / weren't**

The short form is the most common.

The weather wasn't very good yesterday. We weren't ready yet.

C

Interrogative	Negative questions	
Was I	Wasn't I	
Were you	Weren't you	at home yesterday?
Was he / she / it	Wasn't he / she / it	
Were we / you / they	Weren't we / you / they	

Questions with the verb **be** in the past simple are formed using: **Was / Were** + subject (noun or pronoun)

Was it a good match? Were your parents happy with your exam results?

D **Short answers** are formed using: **Yes, / No,** + subject pronoun + **was / were / wasn't / weren't**.

'Were you on the phone?' 'Yes, I was. I was speaking to Jo.'

E **Wh- questions** are formed using: Question word + **was / were** + subject (noun or pronoun)

What was the weather like? Where were you?

F The past simple of **be** is used to describe events or situations in the past.

It was a great party. But you weren't there.
Marie Curie was a great scientist.

The verb **be born** is usually used in the past as well.

'Where were you born?' 'I was born in Leeds.'

G *There was / There were...*

'Were there many guests?' 'Yes, there were a quite a few.'

52

EXERCISES

Be past simple

UNIT 16

16.1 Complete the sentences with *was* or *were*.

1 It ......*was*...... a lovely day.
2 We .... at the beach.
3 I .... under my sun umbrella.
4 The children .... all happy.
5 The sun .... hot.
6 Some people .... very red!
7 My sister and I .... relaxed.
8 The holiday .... great!

16.2 Rewrite the sentences using the negative form.

1 Paul and Judy were on holiday.   *Paul and Judy weren't on holiday.*
2 The weather was bad.
3 The staff at the airport were very helpful.
4 The travel agent was busy.
5 They were in a self-catering apartment.
6 The sea was rough.
7 The guided tour was interesting.
8 The flight attendants were friendly.

16.3 Use the words to write questions with the past simple of *be*. Then complete the short answers.

1 you / on the flight / to London
   Were you on the flight to London?   Yes, *I was* .
2 they / tired / at the end of the trip
   ....   No, ...
3 your friend / impressed / by the sights
   ....   Yes, ...
4 it / a beautiful day
   ....   No, ...
5 the tourists / annoyed / about the delay
   ....   Yes, ...
6 you / pleased / with the accommodation
   ....   No, ...
7 the hotel room / well equipped
   ....   Yes, ...

16.4 Look at the picture and write sentences with *There was / There were, There wasn't / There weren't* and with the words in the box.

| ~~bookshop~~ | baker's | policemen |
| café | firemen | clothes shop |

1 *There wasn't a bookshop in the village.*
2 ....
3 ....
4 ....
5 ....
6 ....

53

UNIT 17 Past simple *(I worked, I went...)*
Form (1)

A The past simple is the tense we use to talk about completed actions and situations that took place at a specific time in the past.

Ordinary verbs are divided into **regular** and **irregular.** The affirmative past simple of regular verbs is formed using: Subject + base form + **-ed** (play – play**ed**)

There is no general rule for the formation of the **past simple** of irregular verbs (go – **went**, know – **knew**). The list of irregular verbs is on p.376.

The past simple is the same for all persons.

*I **received** an e-mail from my brother this morning.*
*They **went** to the seaside last summer.*

Here's the past simple of the regular verb **work** and the irregular verb **come back**.

Affirmative (regular verb)		
I / You / He / She / It / We / They	worked	all day yesterday.
Affirmative (irregular verb)		
I / You / He / She / It / We / They	came back	late last night.

B The addition of the ending **-ed** has precise spelling rules.

- We add a **d** only to verbs whose base form ends in **-e**.

  live → lived; like → liked
  I liked the film very much.

- We double the final consonant of verbs with one syllable that end in a single consonant preceded by a single vowel.

  stop → stopped; sob → sobbed NB: clean → cleaned (two vowels before the final consonant)
  He stopped running after a couple of miles.

- We double the final consonant of verbs with two syllables, with the stress on the second syllable, which end in a single consonant preceded by a single vowel.

  refer → referred; omit → omitted NB: offer → offered (stress on the first syllable); repeat → repeated (two vowels before the final consonant)
  She never referred to her ex-husband.

- We double the final consonant of verbs that end in **-l** preceded by a single vowel (only in British English).

  travel → travelled (Am: traveled) NB: boil → boiled (two vowels before the final consonant)
  They travelled all over the world.

- When the base form of the verb ends in **-y** preceded by a consonant, the **-y** changes to an **i** before adding **-ed**.

  try → tried; study → studied NB: stay → stayed (there is a vowel before the **y**)
  I tried to do my best.

C The pronunciation of the ending **-ed** varies according to how the base form of the verb ends.

- If the base form ends with the sounds /t/ or /d/, we pronounce it /ɪd/:
  start → started /ˈstɑːtɪd/; land → landed /ˈlændɪd/

- If the base form ends with the sounds /p/, /k/, /ʃ/, /tʃ/ or /s/, we pronounce it /t/:
  help → helped /hɛlpt/; walk → walked /wɔːkt/; finish → finished /ˈfɪnɪʃt/;
  watch → watched /wɒtʃt/; pass → passed /pɑːst/

- In all other cases, we pronounce it /d/:
  open → opened /ˈəʊpənd/; live → lived /lɪvd/; stay → stayed /steɪd/

EXERCISES

Past simple – Form (1)

UNIT 17

17.1 Complete the sentences with the past simple of the regular verbs in brackets.

1. We ....watched.... the jet-skis whizzing over the waves. (watch)
2. The waves .... against the shore. (smash)
3. People .... about their holidays. (talk)
4. James .... to interest us in his holiday photos. (try)
5. We .... outside a small café for a break. (stop)
6. The weather .... on the second day we were there. (change)
7. The travel agent .... us a full refund. (offer)
8. I .... in Belgium for three weeks. (stay)

17.2 Write the past simple of the following irregular verbs. Then rewrite the sentences 1–8 in the past simple.

Base form	Past simple	Base form	Past simple
buy	a ....bought....	see	e ....
come	b	swim	f ....
give	c	take	g ....
leave	d	tell	h ....

1. Eleanor buys souvenirs from every destination.
   Eleanor bought souvenirs from every destination.
2. The tour operator tells passengers where to go.
   ....
3. I see some amazing sights in London.
   ....
4. We swim in the sea despite the cold!
   ....
5. He comes home from his business trip on Friday.
   ....
6. The tour guide gives us a lot of information about each place.
   ....
7. You take photos of the bridges and the canals.
   ....
8. The boat leaves early in the morning.
   ....

17.3 Complete the text with the past simple of the verbs in brackets.

When we (1) ....went.... (go) on holiday last year, it (2) .... (be) all a bit of a rush. My friend Sue (3) .... (go) to the travel agent's on the Wednesday and (4) .... (book) a holiday for the two of us. We (5) .... (set off) from home at six on the Friday morning and (6) .... (drive) to the airport, where we (7) .... (leave) our car for the week. At the airport, we (8) .... (check in) as soon as we could, then (9) .... (find) the nicest café and (10) .... (have) a coffee. We (11) .... (sit) there and (12) .... (plan) all the things we (13) ....(want) to do on our holiday in Spain. Within an hour, we (14) .... (be) in the departure lounge and by ten, we were on the plane and on our way to Spain. The plane (15) .... (land) two hours later. We (16) .... (feel) ready for our week on the beach!

UNIT 18

Past simple *(I didn't go, Did you go... ?)*
Form (2)

A The negative form of the past simple is formed by inserting the auxiliary **did** (the same for all persons) and the negation **not** between the subject and the base form of the verb.

Negative full form			
I / You / He / She / It / We / They	did not	go	to the park yesterday.
Negative short form			
I / You / He / She / It / We / They	didn't	go	to the park yesterday.

Full negative form: Subject + **did** + **not** + base form of verb
Short negative form: Subject + **didn't** + base form of verb
The short form is the most common.
I didn't like the film.
We didn't take the bus. We went by taxi.

B

Interrogative			
Did	I / you / he / she / it / we / they	go	to the park yesterday?
Negative questions			
Didn't	I / you / he / she / it / we / they	go	to the park yesterday?

Interrogative form: **Did** + subject + base form of verb
Did you take any photos of the baby?
Did the plane land on time?

In negative questions, the short form **didn't** comes before the subject.
Didn't you know the answer?

C Short answers are formed using: **Yes,** + subject pronoun + **did.**
 No, + subject pronoun + **didn't.**

'Did you sleep well?' 'Yes, I did.'
'Did they buy any souvenirs?' 'No, they didn't.'

D **Wh- questions** are formed using: Question word + **did** + subject + base form of verb

'When did your father arrive?' 'He arrived two hours ago.'
'Why didn't you wait for me?' 'Because I was in a hurry.'

E NB: In the past simple, the verb **have** (in all its meanings) requires the auxiliary **did**. **Got** is never used in the past simple.

Affirmative	Negative	Interrogative
I had a cat when I was little.	I didn't have a dog.	Did you have any pets?

He didn't have a driving licence when he was in the States. (not: He didn't have got...)
'Did you have a good time at the party?' 'Yes, we did.'

EXERCISES

Past simple – Form (2)

UNIT 18

18.1 Rewrite the sentences using the negative form. Use the short form.
1. They went to Paris on a cheap day return.
   They didn't go to Paris on a cheap day return
2. We had a good time on the voyage to Greece.
   ....
3. The travel agent gave us a brochure about the package deal.
   ....
4. The fare to New Zealand cost a lot.
   ....
5. My friend put us up at her place.
   ....
6. The passengers thought the airline was excellent.
   ....
7. I enjoyed the meal in the sushi bar.
   ....

18.2 Use the words to write questions in the past simple. Then complete the short answers.
1. you / enjoy / the flight
   Did you enjoy the flight? No, *I didn't* .
2. your mum / stay / in a bed and breakfast
   .... Yes, ...
3. the customs officials / explain / everything
   .... Yes, ...
4. they / find / the tour of the capital interesting
   .... No, ...
5. you / go / surfing in Australia
   .... Yes, ...
6. the girls / catch / fish in the rock pools
   .... No, ...
7. he / see / an alligator in the Louisiana swamps
   .... Yes, ...

18.3 Yesterday, Joan set off for her holiday. Read the list of things she needed to do and write what she did and didn't do.

- pack clothes ✔
- remember passport ✔
- give the taxi driver a tip ✗
- check in at eight ✔
- buy some perfume ✗
- have a coffee at the airport ✗
- go through customs at nine ✔
- board the plane ✔

1. *Joan packed her clothes.*
2. ....
3. ....
4. ....
5. ....
6. ....
7. ....
8. ....

18.4 Answer the questions using the correct form of the past simple.
1. What did you do yesterday afternoon?
2. Did you have a cat when you were small?
3. Where did you go for your holidays last year?
4. Who did you see last weekend?
5. What did you have for breakfast this morning?
6. Did you visit London last year?
7. What did you buy your friend for his / her birthday?

57

UNIT 19 Past simple
Usage

The past simple is used to:

A
- talk about completed actions and situations in the past, often with adverbs or expressions of time like those in the table. These expressions are generally placed at the beginning or end of a sentence.

yesterday	two hours ago
the day before yesterday	three months ago
	in 1492
last week	in May 2004
last year	in the 20th century

Yesterday, I stayed at home and worked all day.
Last summer, we went on a cruise in the Mediterranean.
The French Revolution started on 14th July 1789.

B
- ask or say when something happened

'When did the accident happen?' 'It happened early this morning.'
'What time did she get up?' 'She got up at nine.'

C
- talk about actions and events that have clearly ended and that took place at a specific time in the past, even if the speaker doesn't actually mention the specific time.

I bought this computer in Hong Kong. (I don't say when, but it's obvious that the action is completed and that it happened in a period of time that is now over: when I was in Hong Kong)

D
- tell a story or a fairytale, often with words that indicate the sequence of events like:

first
then
after that
next
finally

First, the wolf went to Little Red Riding Hood's grandmother's house and ate her up. Then he put on her nightdress and got into her bed...

E
- talk about actions and situations that happened with a certain frequency in the past, with adverbs like **always**, **sometimes**, **never**.

When I was little, my mother always helped me with my homework.
I sometimes went to the cinema with my dad.

EXERCISES

Past simple – Usage

UNIT 19

19.1 Choose the correct alternative.

1 I saw Melanie and her sister the day **ago / (before)** yesterday.
2 Did your mum and dad meet **at / in** the 1990s?
3 They had a great holiday **last / next** year.
4 We went to the south of France **in / on** July.
5 The taxi picked me up an hour **ago / last**.
6 Helen's boyfriend dropped her off at the station **at / in** ten o'clock.
7 Where did you go **before / last** summer?
8 Just think – four hours **ago / then** we were in Spain!

19.2 Match the two parts of the sentence.

1 ..c.. 2 .... 3 .... 4 .... 5 .... 6 ....

1 Why did you complain about the accommodation?
2 Where did you go last week?
3 Did your friends enjoy their city break?
4 What did the holiday rep charge you for the excursion?
5 Did you do a lot of water sports in the Caribbean?
6 When did you book the package deal?

a I went to Oxford.
b No, I didn't.
c Because we didn't have a sea view.
d About two months ago.
e Yes, they did.
f About 50 euros.

19.3 Number the sentences in the correct order to describe the Jones's first day of their holiday.

☐ After that, we wandered into the town to look for somewhere to have lunch.
☐ Finally, we had a shower and went out for the evening.
[1] First, we unpacked our suitcases at the hotel.
☐ Next, we decided to go back to the hotel for a rest.
☐ Then we went for a walk to the nearest beach and sat there for a while.

19.4 Complete the dialogue with the words in the box.

| gave | lost | swam | booked | ~~landed on time~~ | They went | didn't have | ate | swim | Did you go |

Grace: So, tell me about your holiday. How was the journey?
Andrea: It was great. The flight (1) ..landed on time.. and we (2) .... any problems at all on the way to the hotel.
Grace: What was the hotel like?
Andrea: Well, it was small but very nice. We (3) .... half board, so we (4) .... our breakfast and evening meals there every day. They (5) .... us amazing breakfasts!
Grace: Did you (6) .... every day?
Andrea: Yes, we did. The hotel had a pool, but we were near the sea, so we (7) .... all the time!
Grace: (8) .... on any organised tours?
Andrea: I didn't, but some of the others did. (9) .... to a local wine factory.
Grace: It all sounds great!
Andrea: Yes – the only problem was the airline (10) .... my luggage on the way home. So I haven't got any summer clothes at the moment!

REVIEW 5 EXERCISES Units 16–19

R5.1 Choose the correct alternative.
1 The customs officials (were) / was very pleasant.
2 There was / were some impressive sights in the centre of Barcelona.
3 The coach stoped / stopped at a local café for half an hour.
4 The kids swim / swam all day yesterday.
5 Did you see / saw the Houses of Parliament when you were in London?
6 Where you lived / did you live as a youngster?
7 Did you go on any day trips past / last year?
8 'Did they enjoy the surfing?' 'Yes, they enjoyed / did.'
9 I didn't bought / buy any souvenirs in Rotterdam.
10 I first saw the Eiffel Tower ten years ago / last.

R5.2 Complete the sentences with the correct form of the past simple of the verbs in brackets.
1 The handle on my suitcase ....*broke*.... on the way to the airport. (break)
2 At the travel agent's, we .... the brochures and found a cheap city break. (read)
3 We .... booking the camp site. (regret)
4 They .... all the sights during their stay. (not see)
5 .... you .... your money back from the tour operator? (get)
6 The pilot .... the decision to fly to a different airport because of the fog. (make)
7 We got lost several times because we .... our map with us! (not take)
8 We .... really relaxed after our week in The Seychelles. (feel)
9 The voyage .... a nightmare because of rough seas! (be)
10 Even though we .... the food was good, we still liked the hotel. (not think)

R5.3 Read the situations and write the questions. Then look for the answers in the list a–g and match them to the questions.

1 ..*e*.. 2 .... 3 .... 4 .... 5 .... 6 .... 7 ....

1 You want to know if your friend went to London last year.
   Did you go to London last year?   a By plane.

2 You want to know what your friend saw in London.   b All the major sights.
   ....

3 You want to know how your friend travelled to London.   c No, I stayed with friends.
   ....

4 You want to know if your friend stayed in a hotel.   d The night life!
   ....

5 You want to know what your friend enjoyed most about London. e Yes, I did.
   ....

6 You want to know when your friend came home.   f I got back two days ago.
   ....

7 You want to know if your friend had a good journey home.   g Yes, I did, thanks.
   ....

REVIEW 5

R5.4 **Complete the text with the correct affirmative form of the past simple of the verbs in brackets.**

When he ⁽¹⁾ ...was... (be) young, Harry ⁽²⁾ .... (live) in a seaside resort on the Adriatic Sea for five years. His parents ⁽³⁾ .... (run) an Irish pub there, and Harry ⁽⁴⁾ .... (go) to the local primary school. It ⁽⁵⁾ .... (be) a bit difficult at first, but then he ⁽⁶⁾ .... (become) fluent in Italian and he ⁽⁷⁾ .... (can) even write it quite well. He ⁽⁸⁾ .... (have) a great time during the summer when young people from Great Britain ⁽⁹⁾ .... (come) to the seaside and he ⁽¹⁰⁾ .... (talk) to them in English. But the season he ⁽¹¹⁾ .... (like) best ⁽¹²⁾ .... (be) spring. There ⁽¹³⁾ .... (be) no tourists yet, and Harry and his Italian friends ⁽¹⁴⁾ .... (play) on the beach every day after school.

R5.5 **Complete the dialogue with the appropriate form of the past simple of the verbs in the box.**

| be (x 3)   get on   ~~enjoy~~   hurt   go (x 2)   keep   can |

A: ⁽¹⁾ ...Did you enjoy... your holiday in Snowdonia?
B: Not much. It ⁽²⁾ .... a bit boring.
A: Why?
B: I ⁽³⁾ .... my foot on the second day and ⁽⁴⁾ .... walk.
A: So you ⁽⁵⁾ .... hiking with the rest of the group, did you?
B: I ⁽⁶⁾ .... just once, at the beginning.
A: ⁽⁷⁾ .... you .... well with your group?
B: Yeah. Some of them ⁽⁸⁾ .... really nice. But a couple of boys ⁽⁹⁾ .... complaining about everything in the camp.
A: What about the weather?
B: That ⁽¹⁰⁾ .... incredibly good!

R5.6 **Ms Robinson, the English teacher of an international school, asks Manuel, a Spanish student, what he did on Saturday night. Complete the dialogue with the teacher's questions.**

Ms Robinson: ⁽¹⁾ ...What did you do on Saturday night?...............................?
Manuel: I spent the evening at the local pub with some friends.
Ms Robinson: ⁽²⁾ ....?
Manuel: No, I didn't. I don't like beer. I drank tonic water.
Ms Robinson: ⁽³⁾ ....?
Manuel: Yes, we had a really good time. We played billiards.
Ms Robinson: ⁽⁴⁾ ....?
Manuel: Yes, I had a long chat with two elderly ladies.
Ms Robinson: ⁽⁵⁾ ....?
Manuel: They wanted to know everything about my country and my hometown, Cádiz. Oh, and they congratulated me on my English.

UNIT 20 *Used to / Would*

A   **Used to**, followed by the base form of the verb, is the expression used to talk about actions or habits in the past.

> **Affirmative**
> Subject + **used to** + base form of verb

This form suggests that the habit or situation has changed in the present.

I used to attend evening classes when I was in England. (now I don't any more)
We used to live on a farm back in the nineties. Now we live in a flat in town.
There used to be a fountain in this square.
She used to get up earlier then.

B
> **Negative**
> Subject + **didn't** + **use to** + base form of verb

The negative form is constructed using **didn't**, which is followed by **use to** (not: ~~used to~~) and the base form of the verb that expresses the action.

I didn't use to read detective stories, but I do now. (not: ~~I didn't used to…~~)

C
> **Interrogative**
> **Did** + subject + **use to** + base form of verb

> **Short answers**
> **Yes,** / **No,** + subject pronoun + auxiliary **did** / **didn't**.

Questions are formed using **did**, which is followed by the subject, **use to** (not: ~~used to~~) and the base form of the verb that expresses the action.

'Did you use to wear a uniform when you were in primary school?' (not: ~~Did you used to…~~) *'Yes, I did.'*

D   Another way to talk about actions and habits in the past is by using the modal **would**. With this form, we don't specify whether the situation has changed or not in the present..

> Subject + **would** + base form of verb

He would never make a decision.
They would go wherever they were needed.

Remember that a habit in the present is usually expressed using the **present simple** and a frequency adverb or an expression of time, such as **usually**, **every day**.

A habit in the past → *When I lived in the town centre, I went / I used to go / I would go to work by bus.*
A habit in the present → *Now I usually go to work by train.*

EXERCISES

Used to / Would

UNIT 20

20.1 Tick (✔) the correct sentences and correct the sentences with mistakes in them.

1. ☐ John use to play tennis for his school. — *John used to play tennis for his school.*
2. ✔ They used to live near the football stadium.
3. ☐ Molly and I used enjoy watching baseball.
4. ☐ I would never play hockey when I was at school.
5. ☐ You didn't used to watch cricket, but you do now.
6. ☐ Henry used to plays team sports more than he does now.
7. ☐ Sheridan and Tom used to be golf champions.
8. ☐ Their dad used win every boxing match.
9. ☐ I used to be thinking that rugby was great to watch.
10. ☐ Nina would play snooker all the time when we were on holiday.

20.2 Choose the correct alternative.

1. Did you **used** / **use** to play cricket?
2. Is it true that Sammy **use** / **used** to run in marathons?
3. Tina didn't **used** / **use** to like watching boxing, but she does now.
4. Dave **used** / **use** to be a Chelsea supporter when he was a teenager.
5. They didn't **used** / **use** to have a hockey team at my school.
6. Did Suzi **used** / **use** to go to kick-boxing classes?
7. 'Did you use to run a lot?' 'No, I **not use** / **didn't**.'
8. Elizabeth **didn't** / **not did** use to work out at the gym as much as she does now.

20.3 Use the words to write sentences with the correct form of *used to*.

1. Leo / be / an excellent tennis player. — *Leo used to be an excellent tennis player.*
2. Nell / ride / her bike / every day
3. Bryan / not like / volleyball
4. I / own / an expensive cricket bat
5. you / go / skiing / every winter?
6. my parents / not watch / sports on TV
7. your dad / be / a famous athlete?
8. she / play / in the tennis tournament?

20.4 Complete the text with the words in the box.

| used (x 2)   to be (x 2)   use (x 3)   ~~didn't~~ |

This is the new Gregshaw Sports Centre and it's fantastic. It (1) *didn't* use (2) .... like this, though. They didn't (3) .... to have a pool here, and the gym (4) .... to be a lot smaller than it is now. There didn't use (5) .... a basketball court at the centre either. In fact, there only (6) .... to be badminton courts, a small gym and a weight-training room. The old sports centre was originally built 30 years ago and local people didn't (7) .... to go there often. There again, 30 years ago, people didn't (8) .... to be as interested in keeping fit as they are today.

UNIT 21 Past continuous (I was / wasn't playing, Were you playing... ?)
Form

A We use the past continuous to say what was happening at a certain point in the past, when the action had not yet ended.

It is formed using the past simple of the auxiliary **be** (**was** / **were**) and the **-ing** form of the main verb. For spelling changes connected with the ending **-ing**, see page 38.

Affirmative

I was	
You were	
He / She / It was	playing with a ball.
We / You / They were	

Affirmative form: Subject + **was / were** + verb in the **-ing** form

I was listening to music in my bedroom.
We were having breakfast at this time yesterday.

B **Negative**

Full form	Short form	
I was not	I wasn't	
You were not	You weren't	
He / She / It was not	He / She / It wasn't	playing with a ball.
We / You / They were not	We / You / They weren't	

Full negative form: Subject + **was / were + not** + verb in the **-ing** form
Short negative form: Subject + **wasn't / weren't** + verb in the **-ing** form

Sorry, what did you say? I wasn't paying attention.
They weren't going to the stadium, they were going home.

C **Interrogative**

Was I	
Were you	
Was he / she / it	playing with a ball?
Were we / you / they	

Interrogative form: **Was / Were** + subject + verb in the **-ing** form

Were you leaving? Where were you going?

Negative questions: **Wasn't / Weren't** + subject + verb in the **-ing** form

Wasn't she working on her project?

D Short answers are formed using: **Yes / No** + subject pronoun + **was / were / wasn't / weren't**.

'Were you talking to Mr Brown?' 'Yes, I was.'
'Was he watching the match?' 'No, he wasn't.'

E **Wh- questions** are formed by putting the question word first.

What were you doing in my room?
Why wasn't she studying?

64

EXERCISES

Past continuous – Form

UNIT 21

21.1 Complete the sentences with *was* or *were*.

1 The girls ...**were**... playing netball.
2 Tanya .... watching the London marathon on TV.
3 The spectators .... shouting at the referee.
4 I .... taking in everything the trainer was saying.
5 We .... waiting for the Cup Final to start.
6 Jamie .... going go-karting.
7 Andrew and Alison .... wearing their cycling helmets.
8 I .... looking for a new tennis racket.

21.2 Complete the sentences with the past continuous of the verbs in brackets.

1 Terry ...**wasn't wearing**... knee pads when he had his skateboarding accident. (not wear)
2 The children .... for the ice rink to open. (wait)
3 The players .... to the umpire. (not listen)
4 Some of the crowd .... up to leave as the ref blew the final whistle. (get)
5 I .... the match until Becks scored the first goal. (not enjoy)
6 Polly .... as fast as usual. (not run)
7 The goalkeeper .... attention, so the opposing team scored! (not pay)
8 Joe .... his new football boots for the match. (wear)

21.3 Use the words to write questions in the past continuous. Then complete the short answers.

1 they / watch / the rugby on TV
   Were they watching the rugby on TV? No, ...**they weren't**... .
2 you / play / snooker
   .... Yes, ...
3 the people in the crowd / support / the national champion
   .... Yes, ...
4 Harry / go / scuba diving
   .... Yes, ...
5 the girls / play / rounders
   .... No, ...
6 the judges / smiling
   .... No, ...
7 the trainer / give / him / a telling-off
   .... No, ...

21.4 Complete the dialogue with the words in the box.

was playing	were all	were	was	was working
~~were you~~	was your	wasn't	weren't making	

Jude: What (1) ...**were you**... doing yesterday afternoon?
Matt: I (2) .... in a school football match.
Jude: (3) .... mum watching you?
Matt: No, she (4) .... She (5) ....
Jude: (6) .... your friends from school supporting you?
Matt: Yes, they (7) .... They were shouting like crazy! The kids from the other school (8) .... any noise at all!
Jude: Did your team win?
Matt: Yes, we won. The team (9) .... playing well yesterday.

65

UNIT 22 Past continuous
Usage and comparison with the past simple

A The **past continuous** is used to:
- talk about actions taking place at a certain point in the past that haven't yet ended.
  Yesterday at this time I was flying to New York.
  They were playing tennis at two o'clock yesterday.
- talk about conditions and situations as they develop in the past, often with the verb **get** (become).
  It was getting dark.
  I was getting bored.
- talk about actions in the past that happen simultaneously. The two clauses can be joined using the conjunctions **and** or **while**.
  While my mother was beating the eggs, I was peeling the apples.
- highlight, with a sense of annoyance, something in the past that was done repeatedly.
  They were always shouting!
  He was always asking for money. It was really annoying.

B The past continuous is often used in a clause that is either followed or preceded by another with a verb in the past simple. The two clauses, main and secondary, are usually joined by the conjunctions **while / as** or **when**.
The clause with the past continuous indicates an action that was happening in a certain moment, while the one with the past simple indicates an immediate or unexpected action that happened (and finished) while the other was taking place.

```
                          sudden action
                              ↓
action in progress in the past         past continuous
←─────────────────────────────────────────────────────→
                              ↑
                          past simple
```

When I rang the bell, Rob was having a shower and couldn't come to the door.

Complete action: I rang the bell ↓ **past simple**

Action taking place when the immediate or unexpected action happens: Rob was having a shower → **past continuous**

The other day, I was walking to my office when I found a wallet in the street.

The same sentence can be expressed in other ways:
I found a wallet in the street while / as I was walking to my office the other day.
When I was walking to my office the other day, I found a wallet in the street.

NB: The conjunctions **while** and **as** introduce clauses with the past continuous only, whereas **when** can introduce both the past continuous and the past simple.
When / While / As I was looking out of the window, I saw a man running in the street.
I was looking out of the window, when I saw a man running in the street.

C The past continuous is often used to describe the surrounding environment or create a background to a narrative.
Dad was working on his computer, Mum was reading and the children were already sleeping when suddenly the light went out.

EXERCISES

Past continuous – Usage and comparison to the past simple

UNIT 22

22.1 Choose the correct alternative.
1 This time yesterday, I **was playing** / **played** golf.
2 That tennis player was always **shouting** / **shouted** at the umpire.
3 I was tired by five o'clock yesterday – I **worked** / **was working** all afternoon.
4 **Did you enjoy** / **Were you enjoying** the match last night?
5 A lot of people **were turning up** / **turned up** to support the teams yesterday.
6 Ten minutes before full time, the referee **was stopping** / **stopped** the game.
7 I didn't hear the phone because I **was listening** / **listened** to the match on the radio.
8 **Were you doing** / **Did you do** your training when I phoned?

22.2 Complete the sentences with *when* or *while*.
1 What were you doing ...*when*... your friend turned up?
2 Dad was watching the football .... Mum was making the supper.
3 The referee stopped the match .... the crowd started throwing things at the players!
4 We left the stadium .... the match was still going on.
5 Jim was playing rugby .... he injured his back.
6 The goalkeeper saved the goal .... he was lying on the ground!
7 I saw the kids .... they were walking to the football pitch.
8 We never stopped talking .... we were walking round the golf course.

22.3 Complete the sentences with the past simple or the past continuous of the verbs in brackets.
1 As a teenager, ...*did*...... you ....*play*........... a lot of sport? (play)
2 While I .... round the athletics track, I was listening to my MP3 player. (run)
3 I was having a shower when my mobile phone .... (ring)
4 What .... you .... while the boxing match was going on? (do)
5 We couldn't play tennis yesterday because they .... new lines on the courts. (paint)
6 I was practising my serve when I .... my ankle! (break)
7 I wasn't watching when Simmons ...., so I didn't see how good it was. (score)
8 I think the crowd .... bored as the match was drawing to a close. (get)

22.4 Find the mistakes and underline them. Then write the correct sentences.
1 The trainer timed the players while they <u>was</u> running round the pitch.
   The trainer timed the players while they were running round the pitch.
2 I was watching a football match on TV when Dad was getting home from work.
   ....
3 Were you play golf when it started to rain?
   ....
4 I was to jogging through the park at nine this morning.
   ....
5 Dan didn't playing volleyball that afternoon.
   ....
6 Eleanor and Gemma exercising at the gym all morning.
   ....
7 The children was diving from a low diving board into the pool.
   ....
8 We watched the cricket on TV when there was a power cut.
   ....

REVIEW 6 EXERCISES Units 20–22

R6.1 Choose the correct alternative.
1. No, I didn't **used / use** to know the rules of baseball at all.
2. The badminton courts **used / use** to be more popular than they are now.
3. His opponent **was / were** looking at him in a rather unpleasant way!
4. **Did / Was** you use to have your own hockey stick?
5. I used **think / to think** running was boring.
6. **Did / Was** the goalkeeper playing well?
7. **Were you having / Did you have** a good time when I saw you?
8. What would your brother do every Sunday **when / while** you were training?
9. The umpire was talking to one of the players when it **was starting / started** to rain.
10. The children **were already sleeping / slept** when I got home from the race.

R6.2 Write about what was happening yesterday during Sports' Day at school. Use the past continuous of the verbs in the box.

| ~~play~~ talk watch jump have run shout eat |

Some students were playing football.

REVIEW 6

R6.3 **Complete the text with the past simple or the past continuous of the verbs in brackets.**

When I (1) _arrived_ (arrive) at the tennis club this morning, my friends (2) .... (have) a lesson from the club's coach. He (3) .... (show) them how to serve properly. I (4) .... (watch) for a while, then the coach (5) .... (ask) me if I wanted to have a go. Unfortunately, while I (6) .... (get) changed, it (7) .... (start) to rain. So, I (8) .... (not get) a lesson about how to serve.

R6.4 **Complete the text with the past simple or the past continuous of the verbs in brackets.**

Jane (1) _walked_ (walk) into the gym while Bruce, her boyfriend, (2) .... (do) fitness exercises and (3) .... (stare) at a beautiful girl who (4) .... (lift) weights. He (5) .... (not / see) Jane. She (6) .... (go) into the changing room, and while she (7) .... (put on) her tracksuit she (8) .... (think) about how to behave in the next few minutes. Suddenly she (9) .... (make) a decision. She (10) .... (return) to the gym hall, (11) .... (walk) straight up to Bruce and (12) .... (kiss) him. She (13) .... (look) gorgeous. She (14) .... (wear) a tight T-shirt and shorts, instead of her usual tracksuit. While Bruce (15) .... (try) to understand what (16) .... (happen), Jane (17) .... (start) chatting with the girl and (18) .... (introduce) her to one of the best-looking boys in the gym.

R6.5 **Complete the text with the correct alternative.**

Do you remember Chuck? The boy who (1) _B_ in the last row in the corner near the window? He (2) ...... a black T-shirt and jeans every single day. And his hair! He (3) ...... it for months – and I suspect he (4) ...... it either – until one day, out of the blue, he (5) ...... into the classroom with a crew cut. And then again, no cut for months, and so on. Yes, Chuck. The boy who (6) ...... so awkward that he often hurt himself in the gym and (7) ...... with an injury every time we (8) ...... rugby or hockey. Why am I talking about Chuck? Last night, while I (9) ...... dinner in town, a smart guy came up to me and said, 'Hello, Ross! How are you doing? Don't you recognise me? I'm Chuck. Chuck Denver.' Well, to cut a long story short, he is now the CEO* of a very big company, he is married to a lady who (10) ...... an actress and he leads a glamorous life.

1. **A** sits **(B)** used to sit **C** wasn't sitting
2. **A** used to wear **B** was to wear **C** used to wearing
3. **A** was cutting **B** cut **C** wouldn't cut
4. **A** was washing **B** wouldn't wash **C** washed
5. **A** was walking **B** walked **C** would walk
6. **A** wasn't **B** used to be **C** had
7. **A** was ending up **B** would end up **C** didn't end up
8. **A** playing **B** play **C** played
9. **A** had **B** used to have **C** was having
10. **A** used to be **B** was being **C** been

*Chief Executive Officer

B Exam preparation

B.1 PET Reading Part 5

Read the text below and choose the correct word(s) (A, B, C or D) for each space.

Our holiday in Venezuela (1) ...B... the most amazing holiday ever! We (2) .... for hours to get to the country by plane, then a taxi (3) .... us along tiny, winding roads until we (4) .... the small fishing village of Choroni. We (5) .... in wooden huts where there (6) .... no hot water and the showers (7) .... outside. The 'hotel' owner (8) .... all our meals every day. And we (9) .... fish for every meal! Every morning, after breakfast, we all (10) .... to one of the nearby beaches by boat and we (11) .... a huge picnic from the hotel with us. We (12) .... any other tourists there – only the people at our hotel. But we (13) .... a lot of local people. The whole experience was fantastic!

1 A were   B was   C did   D be
2 A travelled   B travel   C did travelled   D was travel
3 A drive   B drives   C drove   D to drive
4 A reach   B reaches   C reached   D reaching
5 A stays   B stayed   C staying   D not stay
6 A were   B wasn't   C weren't   D was
7 A were   B was   C wasn't   D not
8 A makes   B make   C making   D made
9 A eat   B ate   C eats   D to eat
10 A go   B was go   C did went   D went
11 A took   B take   C takes   D taking
12 A not see   B didn't saw C didn't to see   D didn't see
13 A met   B meeting   C to meet   D meet

B.2 PET Writing Part 1

Complete the second sentence so that it means the same as the first.
Use no more than three words.

1 There was only one café in the town.
   There ......*weren't*...... many cafés in the town.
2 There was a statue in the square.
   There used .... a statue in the square.
3 In France, did you see a lot of interesting sights?
   In France, ... a lot of interesting sights to see?
4 Unfortunately, the weather wasn't good while we were away.
   Unfortunately, the weather .... while we were away.
5 The water was cold so we didn't swim in the sea.
   The water .... so we didn't swim in the sea.

B.3 PET Writing Part 3

This is part of an e-mail you received from an English friend.
Write an e-mail answering her questions (about 100 words).

> Anyway, how was your weekend in Spain? What was the weather like? What was the food like? And were there lots of fun things to do? I want to hear all about it!
> Helen

Exam preparation

B.4 FCE Use of English Part 1

Read the text below and decide which answer (A, B, C or D) best fits each space.

I (1) __C__ a surprise visit to Jason's Gym yesterday, and I was delighted to find that everyone there (2) _____ a great time exercising! There were a lot of teenagers there and they (3) _____ various forms of exercise. (4) _____ I arrived, some of the kids (5) _____ with weights, and quite a few (6) _____ some of the other gym equipment. (7) _____ I was talking to Jason, the owner, a couple of girls came up and (8) _____ if they could use the swimming pool every morning at seven. They (9) _____ for the national swimming championships and needed to get some extra practice. Jason agreed right away – he (10) _____ to be a great swimmer himself at one time. I also (11) _____ about ten minutes watching some member of the gymnastics team. They (12) _____ on the gym mats, doing some incredible exercises. I really (13) _____ I was as good as them! (14) _____ I left the gym, a group of school children (15) _____ – just in time for Jason's daily keep-fit class – what a shame I had to get back to my office!

1 **A** making	**B** was	**C** made	**D** was make
2 **A** was having	**B** had	**C** having	**D** to have
3 **A** doing	**B** do	**C** were doing	**D** to do
4 **A** While	**B** What	**C** Where	**D** When
5 **A** were training	**B** trained	**C** training	**D** do train
6 **A** used to	**B** use	**C** were using	**D** uses
7 **A** Were	**B** Where	**C** While	**D** When
8 **A** were asking	**B** asked	**C** ask	**D** asks
9 **A** were train	**B** trained	**C** trains	**D** were training
10 **A** use	**B** was using	**C** used	**D** uses
11 **A** was spending	**B** spends	**C** spent	**D** spending
12 **A** were working	**B** works	**C** are working	**D** be working
13 **A** was wishing	**B** wishing	**C** am wishing	**D** wish
14 **A** What	**B** When	**C** Where	**D** While
15 **A** arrive	**B** was arriving	**C** arriving	**D** arrives

B.5 FCE Use of English Part 2

Read the text below and think of the word or short form which best fits each space.
Use only one in each space. Short forms count as one word.

At two o'clock yesterday afternoon, my friends and I (1) __were__ watching an amazing diving competition on TV. We (2) _____ plan to watch it – in fact, we (3) _____ waiting for the snooker to start, and the diving (4) _____ the programme before. My friend Daniel (5) _____ arguing with me about the programme because he did (6) _____ want to watch it, but we left it on, and I'm very glad we (7) _____ ! The contestants were (8) _____ from a huge rock into the waters below. And they (9) _____ doing twists and turns (10) _____ they dived. One man (11) _____ about six twists before he landed in the water. It was incredible – we (12) _____ sitting there holding our breath (13) _____ we were watching! At the end, (14) _____ the programme finished, we all felt quite exhausted – and somehow the snooker (15) _____ seem so exciting afterwards.

UNIT 23 Past participle *(worked, sent)*

A Regular verbs

The past participle, like the past simple, is formed by adding the ending **-ed** to the base form of the verb. For spelling and phonetic rules relative to the addition of **-ed**, see page 54.

Base form: work   Past simple: worked   Past participle: worked
Base form: express Past simple: expressed   Past participle: expressed

B Irregular verbs

The past participle is formed in different ways. Sometimes it is the same as the past simple and / or the base form, other times it has its own form, as you can see in the third column below. The list of past participles of irregular verbs is on page 376.

Base form: put   Past simple: put   Past participle: put
Base form: do   Past simple: did   Past participle: done
Base form: come Past simple: came   Past participle: come

C Usage

The past participle is used:

- as an adjective, either before a noun (attributive) or after the verbs **be**, **seem**, **look** …(predicative).
  We had a written test yesterday.
  Everybody was satisfied with the meal.
  He seemed very interested.

Note the difference between the present participle (**-ing**) and the past participle, which are both used as adjectives. The first one has an active meaning, whilst the second has a passive meaning i.e. the result of an action.

interesting	interested
boring	bored
satisfying	satisfied
relaxing	relaxed

It was a relaxing holiday. I was really relaxed.

D

- in passive forms, with the auxiliary **be** (see p.164).
  The orchestra is directed by Riccardo Muti.
  The telescope was invented by Galileo Galilei.

E

- in the compound tenses present perfect (see p.74) and past perfect (see p.90).
  I have received a lot of letters from my friends in India.
  He had worked with an insurance company before he got his present job.
  Look at a compound tense (for example, the past perfect) in the passive form. There are two past participles, one after the other.
  *He had **been employed** in an insurance company.*

EXERCISES
Past participle
UNIT 23

23.1 Write the past participle of these verbs. Write (R) if it's regular or (I) if it's irregular.

Base form	Past participle	Base form	Past participle
1 come	come (I)	11 show	
2 do		12 want	
3 drink		13 arrive	
4 give		14 buy	
5 make		15 hire	
6 move		16 eat	
7 put		17 play	
8 sit		18 sing	
9 visit		19 walk	
10 write		20 wash	

23.2 Complete the sentences with the past participle of the verbs in brackets.
1. Their ......*rented*...... flat was the largest and most expensive of them all. (rent)
2. Put all the .... glass into the dustbin. (break)
3. The police found some of the .... goods. (steal)
4. The garden in their new house was full of .... trees. (fall)
5. It was days before we found the .... cupboards in the kitchen of our new flat! (hide)
6. We had a .... agreement about the rent. (write)
7. She had some beautiful .... flowers in a vase on the table. (cut)
8. We found a .... dog sitting on our front doorstep! (lose)

23.3 Choose the correct alternative.
1. Sitting at home in the evening makes me feel **(relaxed)** / **relaxing**.
2. I am so **bored** / **boring** looking at flats!
3. Was it **interested** / **interesting** to look round their new house?
4. Being a builder is very **tiring** / **tired** work.
5. I'm **exciting** / **excited** about moving house.
6. I don't think he was very **pleased** / **pleasing** when you said how much the rent was.
7. Hearing strange noises in your house late at night can be **terrified** / **terrifying**!
8. Everyone was **amazing** / **amazed** when Carl bought his own house.

23.4 Tick (✔) the correct sentence and correct the sentences with mistakes in them.
1. ☐ We weren't interest in the plans for the housing development.
   We weren't interested in the plans for the housing development.
2. ☐ Yes, Mr Rowlands is a well-known property developer round here.
   ....
3. ☐ It's no good crying over spill milk!
   ....
4. ☐ We were freeze and wondered when she was going to turn the central heating on.
   ....
5. ☐ No, that's not where Darren lives. You must be mistaken.
   ....
6. ☐ You can't get money back that's spend.
   ....
7. ☐ I wasn't satisfied with her reply.
   ....
8. ☐ The kids were really scaring when they watched that horror movie.
   ....

73

UNIT 24 Present perfect simple *(I have / haven't visited, Have you visited... ?)*
Form

The present perfect simple is a verb tense that acts as a bridge between the past and the present. We use it to express a past action or situation which has relevance to the present.
It is formed with the auxiliary **have** and the past participle of the main verb:

Subject + **have / has** + past participle of verb

Remember that the past participle is formed by adding **-ed** to the base form of regular verbs (**started, finished**…). The list of irregular verbs is on page 366.

Subject + **have / has** + past participle

A Affirmative

I / You / We / They	have ('ve)	visited London.
He / She / It	has ('s)	

I've lost my ticket.
She has finished her project.

B Negative

I / You / We / They	have not (haven't)	visited London.
He / She / It	has not (hasn't)	

Full negative form: Subject + **have / has + not** + past participle
Short negative form: Subject + **haven't / hasn't** + past participle

I haven't been very well.
He hasn't bought the newspaper today.

C

Interrogative	Negative questions	
Have I / you / we / they	Haven't I / you / we / they	visited London?
Has he / she / it	Hasn't he / she / it	

Interrogative form: **Have / Has** + subject + past participle

Have you been to the hairdresser's?
Has Janet arrived?

Negative questions: **Haven't / Hasn't** + subject + past participle

Hasn't he answered your letter?

D

Short answers are formed using: **Yes,** + subject pronoun + **have / has.**
No, + subject pronoun + **haven't / hasn't.**

In affirmative short answers, **have** is never used in its short form.

'Have you seen Peter?' 'Yes, I have.'
'Has Anne called you?' 'No, she hasn't.'

E **Wh-** questions are formed by putting the question word first.

Question word + **have / has** + subject + past participle

Where have you been?
What has he done?

EXERCISES

Present perfect simple – Form

UNIT 24

24.1 Complete the sentences with *have* or *has*.

1. Dad ...**has**... cleaned the living room carpet.
2. Anna and Jane .... moved to a new flat.
3. Mum .... made lunch for everyone.
4. Our new dining room chairs .... arrived.
5. The Graysons .... bought a semi-detached house.
6. They .... invented a vacuum cleaner that cleans on its own!
7. Mike's car .... broken down again!
8. The flowers .... grown well this year.

24.2 Complete the sentences with the correct form of the present perfect simple of the verbs in brackets.

1. They ...**have cut**... down some trees in the village. (cut)
2. Mandy .... her bedsit. (redecorate)
3. I .... Nick's new flat; it's great. (see)
4. We .... some new bushes. (plant)
5. They .... camping. (go)
6. Tyler .... his sister in London. (visit)

24.3 Use the words to write questions in the present perfect simple. Then complete the short answers.

1. Jane / invite you / to her housewarming party
   Has Jane invited you to her housewarming party? No, *she hasn't*.
2. Dave and Ryan / repair / the hole in the roof
   .... Yes, ...
3. Henry / use / the gardening tools we gave him
   .... Yes, ...
4. the builders / finish / the work in the attic
   .... No, ...

24.4 Find the mistakes and underline them. Then write the correct sentences.

1. What <u>do you eat</u> so far today?
   What have you eaten so far today?
2. Are you washed the kitchen floor yet?
   ....
3. Has Candice moves to her new flat?
   ....
4. Where have they build their new house?
   ....
5. Olga's grandparents are living in that cottage all their lives.
   ....
6. Sorry, Mum, I not finished the housework.
   ....

24.5 Complete the text with the correct form of the present perfect simple of the verbs in brackets.

| put | do | ~~be~~ | not eat | forget | make | hang | sweep | cook | wash | tidy | clean |

It's half past one now, and Mum (1) ...**has been**... very busy in the last hour and a half! What (2) .... she ....? She (3) .... the beds and she (4) .... the dishes. She (5) .... also .... up all the leaves and she (6) .... the living room. And Mum (7) .... the clothes out and she (8) .... a meal for lunch. As well as all that, she (9) .... the fridge and, finally, she (10) .... away all the shopping! In fact, she has been so busy, she (11) .... her lunch. I think she (12) .... about it. Poor Mum!

UNIT 25 — Present perfect simple
Uses with *just, already, yet, not... yet, still... not*

The present perfect simple is used:

A
- to talk about recent actions that affect the present or that have results that are visible now, without being specific about when they took place.

  Look what I've bought. – / This T-shirt.
  (the T-shirt is visible)
  We've moved to a new house.
  (and now we live in that house)
  You've put on too much make-up.
  (the result is in front of my eyes)

B
- with the adverb **just** to indicate that an action has not long taken place.

  They've just got married.
  We've just started eating.
  I've just come back.

C
- with the adverb **already** to indicate that something is over and done with.

  I've already finished my homework.
  We have already bought his birthday present.

  In affirmative sentences, the adverbs **just** and **already** are placed between the auxiliary **have** and the past participle.

D
- with the adverbs **already** or **yet** to ask if something has been done that needed doing. **Already** is usually used when we are surprised that the action has been done, whereas **yet** is used when we are expecting the action, that needed doing, to have been done.

  Have you already had lunch?
  (It's so early, I wouldn't have thought so)

  Have you read today's newspaper yet?
  (Usually you've finished reading it by now)

  In questions, the adverb **already** is placed between the subject and the past participle, whilst the adverb **yet** is placed at the end of the sentence.

E
- with the adverbs **not... yet** or **still... not** to indicate that an action has still to happen. The use of **still** implies that the action should have taken place already.

  I haven't read this book yet. / I still haven't read this book.
  She hasn't packed her suitcase yet. / She still hasn't packed her suitcase.

  Even in negative sentences, the adverb **yet** is placed at the end of the sentence, whilst **still** is placed between the subject and the auxiliary **have**.

EXERCISES

Present perfect simple – Uses with *just, already, yet, not... yet, still... not*

UNIT 25

25.1 Look at the pictures and use the words to write sentences using the present perfect simple and *just*.

1 James / decorate / his room — James has just decorated his room.
2 they / move / into their new home
3 the kids / arrive / at the youth hostel
4 the plumber / repair / our washing machine
5 the electricity / go off
6 the last party guests / leave

25.2 Complete the sentences with *already, yet* or *still*.

1 I'm sorry. I haven't done the shopping ......yet...... .
2 It's OK, Mum's .... made breakfast.
3 Have you .... moved to the new studio?
4 Anthony has .... found somewhere to live when he goes to university.
5 Has Sandra paid for her new furniture .... ?
6 We can't invite anyone round; we .... haven't decorated the living room.
7 Melanie .... hasn't found anyone to share her flat with.
8 We've .... taken lots of photos of the palace.

25.3 Choose the correct alternative.

1 Have you found a gardener who can help you **just / (yet)**?
2 They've **yet / just** installed central heating.
3 The architect has **still / already** drawn the plans for the extension.
4 Have you paid the gas bill **yet / just**?
5 Paul's **just / still** ordered his new dishwasher.
6 I've **yet / already** met the new neighbours.
7 Dad's **already / yet** decided he needs a new garden shed when he moves!
8 I **already / still** haven't thought about what colour to paint the living room.

25.4 Match the questions to the answers.

1 ..e.. 2 .... 3 .... 4 .... 5 .... 6 ....

1 Have you already eaten?
2 Has the architect phoned you?
3 Has Sue already paid this month's rent?
4 Where have you been?
5 What present have you bought Ann?
6 Have the Blacks sold their house yet?

a No, she hasn't. Not yet.
b Yes, someone from America's just bought it.
c I've just got back from London.
d I haven't got anything yet.
e Yes, I have, thanks.
f No, he hasn't.

25.5 Complete the text with *already, yet* or *just*.

Sheena's excited because she has (1) ......just...... moved into a new flat. She hasn't found anyone to share with her (2) .... But she's put an advert in the local newspaper and she's (3) .... had a few phone calls about it. The flat's very big, but Sheena and her mum have (4) .... painted it, and Sheena's mum has (5) .... arrived with some new curtains for the living room. Sheena hasn't bought all the furniture she needs (6) .... , but she's (7) .... decided which sofa she wants. The only problem is, she hasn't saved enough money to buy it (8) .... !

UNIT 26 Present perfect simple
Uses with *ever, never, recently, today*...

The present perfect simple is also used:

A
- to talk about actions that took place in a period of time that isn't clarified, for example life experiences.

    I've been to London many times.
    (I don't say when I went)

    My father has travelled to a lot of places.
    (I don't say when he went to these places)

    Note the difference between **been** and **gone**:

    They've been to Hong Kong. (but now they're back)
    They've gone to Hong Kong. (and they're still there)

B
- with the adverbs **ever** and **never**, to ask and talk about personal experiences.

    'Have you ever had a ride on a roller coaster?'
    'No, I've never tried.'
    'Have you ever swum in a river?'
    'Yes, I have. Many times.'
    'Anyone who has never made a mistake has never tried anything new.' (Albert Einstein)

    The present perfect simple with **ever** is also found in clauses that follow a superlative.

    This is the best novel I've ever read.
    This is the most important match they've ever played.

    Ever and **never** are always placed between the auxiliary **have** and the past participle.

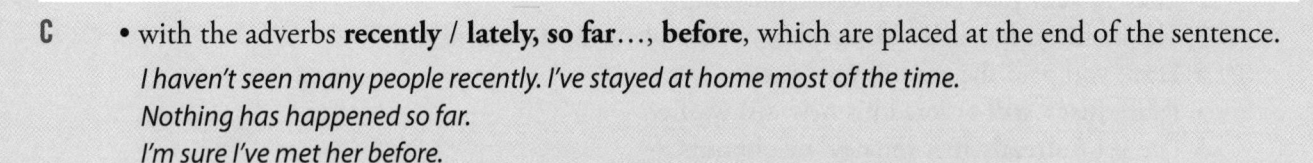

C
- with the adverbs **recently / lately, so far..., before**, which are placed at the end of the sentence.

    I haven't seen many people recently. I've stayed at home most of the time.
    Nothing has happened so far.
    I'm sure I've met her before.

D
- with the time expressions **today, this week / month..., in the last few hours / days...**, when a period of time hasn't yet finished at the time of speaking.

    I've been very busy today.
    (the day isn't over yet)

    He's only written me two e-mails this month.
    (the end of the month hasn't come yet)

    Janet hasn't been very well in the last few days.
    (including today)

EXERCISES

Present perfect simple – Uses with *ever, never, recently, today*...

UNIT 26

26.1 Tick (✔) the sentence (a or b) that has the same meaning as the first one.

1 Jess and Tanya are in New Zealand at the moment.
   a ☐ Jess and Tanya have been to New Zealand.
   b ✔ Jess and Tanya have gone to New Zealand.

2 Sandy isn't here because she's looking at a new flat today.
   a ☐ Sandy has been to look at a new flat.
   b ☐ Sandy has gone to look at a new flat.

3 Jason doesn't live here now; he moved to America last month.
   a ☐ Jason has gone to America.
   b ☐ Jason has been to America.

4 The estate agent has been here to value our property.
   a ☐ The estate agent came to our property to value it.
   b ☐ The estate agent is valuing our property at the moment.

5 Mum and Dad have gone house-hunting.
   a ☐ Mum and Dad are out looking at houses.
   b ☐ Mum and Dad went to look at houses and are back home now.

6 Eric has gone to find out about mortgages.
   a ☐ Eric is talking to someone about mortgages at the moment.
   b ☐ Eric talked to someone about mortgages some time ago.

26.2 Complete the sentences with *ever* or *never*.

1 Have you ……*ever*…… thought about moving into your own place?
2 I've ………………… seen such an amazing villa!
3 That's the smallest bedsit I've ………………… seen!
4 Robert and Vicky have ………………… shared a flat before.
5 There's ………………… been a better time to buy your own house. Prices are very low now.
6 Has your mum ………………… had the house valued?
7 They've ………………… bothered to do anything to the garden.
8 Ruth's ………………… decorated the kitchen.

26.3 Rearrange the words and write the sentences.

1 never – Sally's – before – her – own – on – lived
   Sally's never lived on her own before.
2 a – Leo and Bob – never – in – youth hostel – stayed – have
3 you – attic – looked – in – the – ever – Have – ?
4 her – invited – Has – ever – you – to – house – Nigella – ?
5 Iris – afford – been – to – never – has – a – mortgage – able
6 never – landlord – my – put up – The – has – rent
7 you – who – wondered – Have – ever – mansion – lives – in – that – ?
8 the – Jeremy – used – never – central heating – has

26.4 Complete the dialogue with the words and expressions in the box.

| ever   never   I've never   you ever done   I have   ~~have you ever~~ |

Gordon: Hey, Ken, (1) ……*have you ever*…… considered sharing a flat?
Ken: Hmm – not really. Have (2) ………………… it?
Gordon: Yes, (3) ………………… I shared with two guys when I was at college in Oxford.
Ken: How was it?
Gordon: Well, (4) ………………… met two guys who were more untidy – that's for sure!
Ken: I can imagine! How did you share things like the cooking?
Gordon: I've (5) ………………… worked out a good system for things like that, to be honest.
Ken: So, did that put you off sharing or have you (6) ………………… thought of doing it again?
Gordon: No, it hasn't put me off. In fact, if you're interested, I'm looking for someone to share with next term!

UNIT 27 Present perfect simple
Uses with *How long, for, since*

The present perfect simple is also used:

A
- to talk about situations that started in the past and are still happening now.
  I've been in England for three years.
  (I came three years ago and I'm still here)
  I've lived in London since May 2006.
  (I moved to London in May 2006 and I still live here)

- with the preposition **for**, to specify the duration of the action.
  It's six o'clock. They have been here for two hours.

  | 4 o'clock --------- 5 o'clock --------- 6 o'clock |
  for two hours

- with the preposition **since**, to specify the moment in which the action began.
  They have been here since four o'clock.

  | 4 o'clock------------------------------▶ now
  since 4 o'clock ◀-----------------------▶

B
- to ask about the duration of a certain situation. Questions start with **How long… ?**, **For how long… ?** or **Since when… ?**
  'How long have you been on holiday?' 'For a week.'
  'Since when have you had this car?' 'Since last summer.'

C
- **For** can sometimes be omitted, especially after the verbs **be** and **wait**.
  He's been away a week.
  I've waited an hour.

  For is not used before **all**.
  I've been ill all week.

D
Note the expressions **for long / for a long time** and **for ages.**
I haven't played tennis for a long time, since I broke my ankle two years ago.
I've known them for ages. We've lived next door since we were children.

As you can see in the above examples, **since** is also used as a conjunction. It introduces a secondary clause, which usually has a verb in the **past simple**.

I've lived in this town since I was born.
We've loved each other since we first met.

EXERCISES

Present perfect simple – Uses with *How long, for, since* UNIT 27

27.1 Tick (✔) the correct sentence (a or b).

1. a ☐ I haven't seen Mr Smith from next door since days.
   b ✔ I haven't seen Mr Smith from next door for days.
2. a ☐ Did you live here since you were a baby?
   b ☐ Have you lived here since you were a baby?
3. a ☐ That cottage has been there for two hundred years.
   b ☐ That cottage has been there since two hundred years.
4. a ☐ They've only had electricity in that village since 1965.
   b ☐ They only have electricity in that village since 1965.
5. a ☐ I don't see mice in the kitchen since we got the cat!
   b ☐ I haven't seen mice in the kitchen since we got the cat!
6. a ☐ Has Bill owned that studio since long?
   b ☐ Has Bill owned that studio for long?

27.2 Choose the correct alternative.

1. Film stars have lived in Hollywood **for / (since)** it became the movie capital of America.
2. Humans **don't live / haven't lived** in caves for thousands of years.
3. Architects have supported environmentally friendly housing **for / since** the last 20 years.
4. We have had the option of solar heating **since / for** the 1980s.
5. Town planners haven't been keen on high-rise flats **for / since** more than 20 years.
6. Properties in this area **are / have been** expensive since they filmed *Notting Hill* here.

27.3 Complete the dialogue using the expressions in the box.

did you   ~~have you~~   I haven't   spoken   you've   I've known   since   for

Kelly: How long (1) *have you* known Bernard?
Colin: I've known him (2) .... we were children, so that means (3) .... him (4) .... 12 years.
Kelly: And when (5) .... last see him?
Colin: Well, (6) .... seen him for over a month, actually.
Kelly: Have you seen him since you got your new car?
Colin: No, I haven't. In fact, I haven't even (7) .... to him on the phone since the weekend.
Kelly: I guess if (8) .... been friends for that long, he'll understand!

27.4 Complete the second sentence so that it has a similar meaning to the first one. Use the given word without changing it.

1. We have lived next door to the Morgans for ten years. **BEEN**
   The Morgans *have been our* neighbours for ten years.
2. I haven't seen Stella for weeks. **SAW**
   It's weeks .... Stella.
3. I met Eric ten years ago. **HAVE**
   I .... for ten years.
4. They haven't decorated the living room for five years. **SINCE**
   It's five years .... the living room.
5. When did you buy your own apartment? **HAVE**
   How long .... your apartment?

UNIT 28 Present perfect simple and past simple
Differences of usage

A
- The present perfect simple is used when there are no references to a precise period of time (**I've won!**), when an action started in the past and still continues or has a relevance to the present (**Look! I've changed my hairstyle**) or when a period of time in which an action took place isn't completely over (**I've worked hard today**).
- The past simple is used to talk about actions and experiences that have already been concluded. They took place in a defined moment in time and have been fully completed (for example, past summer holidays or something that happened yesterday). Compare:

  The girls have been here for an hour. (They arrived an hour ago and they are still here)
  They were here an hour ago. (but now they have left)
  I've seen this film twice! (I don't say when I saw it)
  I saw this film last Saturday. (I specify when I saw it)

  Look at the difference:
  I haven't seen him this morning.
  (present perfect simple because it is still morning when I say it)
  I didn't see him this morning.
  (past simple because I say it in the afternoon or evening)

B The past simple is also used:
- in questions with **When**, because it refers to a precise period of time.
  'When did you go to London?' 'I went there last summer.'
- in historical narrative, to talk about events that happened in the past or to talk about famous characters, even if the dates aren't mentioned.
  Wellington defeated Napoleon at the battle of Waterloo.

C The present perfect simple is often used when starting to recount an event or an experience, also without specifying the exact time. When the experience is put into context and details are asked or given, the story continues in the past simple.

  A: *You know, I've won a prize in a radio competition.*
     (I don't say when → present perfect simple is used)
  B: *Really? What did you win?*
     (I ask for details → past simple is used)
  A: *I won a collection of music CDs.*
     (I give details → past simple is used)

D In American English, the past simple is used more than the present perfect simple in sentences with **just**, **already** and **yet**.

  It has just started raining. (Br.E)   *It just started raining.* (Am.E)
  Have you sent her an e-mail yet? (Br.E)   *Did you send her an e-mail yet?* (Am.E)
  I've already bought everything we need. (Br.E)   *I already bought everything we need.* (Am.E)

EXERCISES

Present perfect simple and past simple – Differences of usage

UNIT 28

28.1 Match the sentences to the same meaning.

1 ..d.. 2 .... 3 .... 4 .... 5 .... 6 ....

1 She arrived at my house two hours ago.
2 She travelled to London a week ago and she isn't back yet.
3 She went to London for her holiday last year.
4 She saw the film last week.
5 She moved out of the flat last week.
6 She went to her friend's flat earlier today and she's back now.

a She's gone to London.
b She's already seen the film.
c She's left the flat.
d She's been here for two hours.
e She's been to her friend's flat.
f She's been to London before.

28.2 Tick (✔) the correct sentence (a or b).

1 a ✔ Mum swept the balcony yesterday.
   b ☐ Mum's swept the balcony yesterday.
2 a ☐ The estate agent has valued our house last week.
   b ☐ The estate agent valued our house last week.
3 a ☐ We haven't redecorated the kitchen yet.
   b ☐ We don't redecorate the kitchen yet.
4 a ☐ Shane's moved house a week ago.
   b ☐ Shane moved house a week ago.
5 a ☐ Great! The new shopping centre opened at last!
   b ☐ Great! The new shopping centre has opened at last!

28.3 Complete the sentences with the past simple or the present perfect simple of the verbs in brackets.

1 I ......painted...... my bedroom yesterday. (paint)
2 I .... Sammy's new apartment so far. (not see)
3 Mum .... already .... the balcony. (sweep)
4 They .... those houses last year. (build)
5 When .... you .... to this area? (move)
6 How long .... you .... here? (live)
7 .... you .... the rent yet? (pay)
8 Nancy's mum .... never .... a dishwasher. (have)

28.4 Complete the dialogue with the expressions in the box.

| did they hear | haven't finished | they've been | have you heard | they've won |
| chose | yesterday | they moved | haven't heard | yet (x2) | happened | won |

A: (1) ..Have you heard.. about Marcie and Dominic?
B: No, I (2) .... anything. What (3) .... ?
A: Well, (4) .... a house!
B: You're joking! How?
A: They entered a competition in one of the national newspapers last year. And they (5) .... !
B: That's fantastic! Have (6) .... in (7) .... ?
A: No, because the builders (8) .... building it (9) .... ! But they'll get the key next week! And they (10) .... lots of furniture (11) ....
B: Wow! When (12) .... about their prize, then?
A: The newspaper phoned them last week. (13) .... in shock ever since!
B: I'm not surprised!

83

REVIEW 7

EXERCISES Units 23–28

R7.1 Choose the correct alternative.
1 The decorators **hasn't / haven't** finished painting the attic.
2 Property prices **haven't been / weren't** this low for a long time.
3 **Have / Has** Walter built his garage and conservatory yet?
4 What colour have you **decide / decided** to have in the bathroom?
5 Our architect has **yet / already** drawn up the plans.
6 We've **saw / seen** a lovely semi-detached house for sale nearby.
7 Have you **ever / still** shared a flat with someone before?
8 The garden has **ever / never** looked so good!

R7.2 Complete the sentences with the correct form of the present perfect simple of the verbs in brackets.
1 *Have* the new neighbours *called* in to say hello? (call)
2 This dishwasher .... never .... properly. (work)
3 I .... the night in a mansion before! (spend)
4 Dad .... all his gardening tools in the basement. (put)
5 We .... to the building society about a mortgage yet. (speak)
6 Alan .... a new apartment. (buy)
7 Joanna .... to live in a cottage in the country since she was a girl. (want)
8 .... they ever .... camping before? (be)

R7.3 Read the table and write six sentences, as in the example.

	ten years ago	recently
Josh	only ride a bike	drive cars and motorbikes
	never make a meal	learn to cook
	share bedroom with brother	move to his own bedsit
	be at school	get job as an interior designer
Emma	only eat vegetables	start eating meat
	hate gardening	plant some bulbs and flowers
	live with parents	move to her own flat

1 *Ten years ago, Josh only rode a bike. Recently, he has driven cars and motorbikes.*
2 ....
3 ....
4 ....
5 ....
6 ....
7 ....

R7.4 Complete the text with the words in the box.

has (x 4)   have (x 3)   he's (x 2)   ~~been~~   never   ever   since   yet

Matt Renshaw has (1) *been* an estate agent for ten years. He (2) .... recently opened his own office and (3) .... found four people to work for him. Some people (4) .... been a bit rude about Matt. They say (5) .... learnt how to describe houses so they sound wonderful when they're not! But Matt says he has (6) .... told a lie about a house in his life! Well, I'm not sure about that! (7) .... you (8) .... read any of the descriptions Matt (9) .... written in the property section of the local paper? (10) .... written a few 'stories', if you ask me! But lots of people (11) .... bought properties from Matt (12) .... he started selling houses ten years ago, and nobody (13) .... asked for their money back (14) .... !

REVIEW 7

R7.5 Complete the sentences with the correct form of the present perfect simple of the verbs in the box. Use the suggestions given in the brackets.

| order | be | see | love | buy | go |

1 We *haven't ordered* yet. I'd like a banana milkshake, please.
2 Ted .... (just) out. He'll be back in half an hour.
3 .... (your dad) to Canada?
4 My cousin .... some new furniture this week.
5 .... (Charles / ever) your new flat?
6 I .... (always) this cottage.

R7.6 Complete the sentences with the past simple or the present perfect simple of the verbs in brackets.

1 *Did you speak* (you / speak) to the estate agent on Wednesday afternoon?
2 Mr Clark .... (be) born in 1929.
3 .... (you / have) your room decorated yet?
4 Jason .... (not / get up) until 11.30 last Sunday.
5 Roy .... (be) always on time when he worked with us in this office.
6 .... (you / see) Mandy last week?
7 I .... (always / like) modern houses very much.
8 My family .... (move) to the United States in 1942 and we .... (live) there ever since.

R7.7 Choose the correct alternative.

1 'Have you finished your project ...*A*...?' 'No, but I'll finish it tomorrow.'
   (A) yet   **B** ever   **C** already
2 Jim .... here since he arrived from York Hospital.
   A works   **B** worked   **C** has worked
3 Our team .... to make a correct diagnosis.
   A has ever failed   **B** has never failed   **C** never failed
4 Rick .... a diamond ring for his girlfriend yesterday.
   A has bought   **B** bought   **C** buy
5 Tim has .... got home from work. He's having a shower now.
   A never   **B** yet   **C** just
6 Have you had your coffee .... ?
   A already   **B** yet   **C** still
7 I'm really worried. Peter hasn't ....
   A ever phoned   **B** already phoned   **C** phoned yet
8 '........ have you been in England now?' 'Not long. Just two weeks.'
   A Since when   **B** How long   **C** When

85

UNIT 29 Present perfect continuous *(I've been learning, Have you been learning?)*
Form and usage

The present perfect continuous is used to express prolonged actions that started in the past and are either still going on in the present or have just been concluded.
This verb tense is formed with the present perfect of **be** and the **-ing** form of the main verb.

Subject + **have / has been** + verb in the **-ing** form

A Affirmative

| I / You / We / They | have ('ve) been | practising all day. |
| He / She / It | has ('s) been | |

I've been running for half an hour.
(and I'm still running)
She has been cooking all afternoon.
(she's just finished)

B Negative

| I / You / We / They | have not (haven't) been | practising all day. |
| He / She / It | has not (hasn't) been | |

Full negative form: Subject + **have / has not been** + verb in the **-ing** form
Short negative form: Subject + **haven't / hasn't been** + verb in the **-ing** form

I haven't been waiting for very long.
She hasn't been studying French long.

C Interrogative

| Have | I / you / we / they | been | practising all day? |
| Has | he / she / it | | |

Interrogative form: **Have / Has** + subject + **been** + verb in the **-ing** form
Short answers: **Yes, / No,** + subject pronoun + **have / has / haven't / hasn't.**

'Have you been painting the kitchen?' 'No, I haven't. I've been painting the bathroom.'
'Has she been waiting for you all this time?' 'Yes, she has. She's been very patient.'

D The **present perfect continuous** is used to:

- say what we were doing up until the moment of speaking. The action can either still be going on or just have ended, but with signs still evident in the present.
  'You're soaking wet!' 'Yes. I've been walking in the rain all the way from school.'

- highlight the amount of time a prolonged action has been going on for. In this case, we use expressions like **all day / all day long**, **all night**, **all week**, etc.
  I've been calling people on the phone all day. This is really hard work!

EXERCISES

Present perfect continuous – Form and usage

UNIT 29

29.1 Tick (✔) the correct sentence and correct the sentences with mistakes in them.

1. ✔ Miss Williams has been teaching all day.
2. ☐ I have been studied maths today. — *I have been studying maths today.*
3. ☐ You has been listening to a lecture about science. ....
4. ☐ Susan has doing her homework all evening. ....
5. ☐ David and Jackie have been trying to work. ....
6. ☐ He has been filling in his university application form. ....
7. ☐ The girls are been playing netball in the playground. ....
8. ☐ Tina has been take part in some extra drama classes. ....

29.2 Complete the sentences with the present perfect continuous of the verbs in brackets.

1. Mr Jones *has been working* at the same college for years. (work)
2. No, we .... our exam timetable. (not look at)
3. I .... for you for long. (not wait)
4. It feels like this lesson .... for ever! (go on)
5. Shelly .... a new school bag. (choose)
6. This year, my sons .... the history of art. (not study)
7. Gina .... about what the professor said. (think)
8. They .... the classrooms this month. (decorate)

29.3 Write questions in the present perfect continuous. Then complete the short answers.

1. you / read / your new chemistry book
   Have you been reading your new chemistry book? No, *I haven't* .
2. the headteacher / prepare / the new timetable
   .... No, ...
3. your English teacher / mark / the exams
   .... Yes, ...
4. Simon / have / a PE lesson
   .... No, ...
5. your mum / attend / pottery classes at night school
   .... Yes, ...
6. the children / write / on the board
   .... No, ...

29.4 Use the words given to write sentences in the present perfect continuous.

1. write / notes / from a history book
   He's been writing notes from a history book.
2. listen to / CDs / from a French course
   ....
3. read / essays / by children in her class
   ....
4. learn / drive / a very long time
   ....
5. play / in a rock band / since they were at college
   ....
6. have / swimming lessons / all morning
   ....

UNIT 30: Present perfect simple and continuous
Differences in usage

Both the present perfect simple and the present perfect continuous followed by **for** or **since** are used to express the duration of an action up to the present time.

A The present perfect simple (see p. 80) is used:
- with stative verbs (**be**, **know**, **have**, **own**...) that are not usually used in the continuous form.

Tom's been in hospital for a week.
She's known Sally since 1990.
My parents have always had a dog.
I've owned my car for three years.

B The present perfect continuous is used to express an action that is apparently uninterrupted.
It's been raining for a long time.
I've been typing for three hours

This sentence could also be expressed like this:
I started typing three hours ago and I'm still typing.

C Some verbs, for example **live**, **work**, **play**, can be used with both the present perfect simple and the continuous.
'How long have you lived / have you been living in London?'
'We've lived / We've been living here for a very long time.'
He has worked / has been working for the same firm since 1992.

It is also possible to say:
He started working for that firm in 1992 and he's still working there.

Note the difference in meaning that the continuous form can have in respect to the simple form:
They've been playing football for an hour. (without stopping)
They've played football since 2005. (they took up the sport in 2005 but they haven't been playing continuously!)

EXERCISES

Present perfect simple and continuous – Differences in usage

UNIT 30

30.1 Choose the correct alternative.
1 I have never **been going / been** to night school.
2 Peter **has been reading / has read** his geography book all afternoon.
3 Have you **finished / been finishing** your exams now?
4 I have **been trying / tried** to learn this for hours and I still don't know it!
5 She's tired because she's **taken / been taking** tests all day.
6 Joan isn't here – she's **gone / been going** to college.
7 They've **played / been playing** in the playground all morning.
8 Sally's red and sweaty because she's **been doing / done** PE!

30.2 Complete the sentences with the present perfect simple or continuous of the verbs in brackets.
1 Oscar ......*has read*...... two books today! (read)
2 Jenny .... to go to night school. (leave)
3 Molly .... all night for her exam tomorrow! (study)
4 .... Henry .... his homework since he got home? (do)
5 They .... their new secondary school for very long. (not attend)
6 How long .... you .... cookery lessons? (take)
7 I .... which university to apply to. (not decide)
8 .... the teacher .... our tests yet? (mark)

30.3 Match the two parts of the sentences.

1 ...*c*... 2 .... 3 .... 4 .... 5 .... 6 .... 7 .... 8 ....

1 The students have been   a been thinking of enrolling at technical college.
2 Have you   b studying hard this term?
3 I've   c demonstrating against the new curriculum.
4 They   d they passed their exams?
5 Have you been   e seen Professor Thomson anywhere?
6 Miranda   f haven't graduated yet.
7 Has   g hasn't been doing well at school this term.
8 Have   h Stephen been learning how to speak German?

30.4 Look at the notes and write sentences about the people.

	What have they been doing?	What have they done?
Mr Brown	teach Class 5	tell them about whales
Mal and Trevor	work on the computer	learn how to send e-mails
my friends	sit at their desks	write an essay
the students	read their history books	revise things for their exam
my mum	talk to a night-school tutor	agree to enrol for IT classes
I	think about English grammar	do this exercise

1 *Mr Brown has been teaching Class 5. He has told them about whales.*
2 ....
3 ....
4 ....
5 ....
6 ....

UNIT 31 Past perfect simple *(I had / hadn't started, Had you started?)*
Form

The past perfect simple is the tense used to talk about actions that happened before others that had already taken place in the past.
It is formed with the auxiliary **have** in its past form (**had**) and the past participle of the main verb:

Subject + **had** + past participle of verb

For the formation of the past participle, see page 72. The list of irregular verbs is on page 366.

A Affirmative

| I / You / He / She / It / We / They | had | made a mistake. |

When I arrived, Jane had already left.
(she left before my arrival)
I had just started to read my book when my mobile phone rang.

B Negative

| I / You / He / She / It / We / They | had not (hadn't) | made a mistake. |

Full negative form: Subject + **had** + **not** + past participle
Short negative form: Subject + **hadn't** + past participle

I hadn't been very well in that period.
When the teacher asked me to hand in my project, I told her I hadn't finished it yet.

C Interrogative

| Had | I / you / he / she / it / we / they | made a mistake? |

Negative questions

| Hadn't | I / you / he / she / it / we / they | made a mistake? |

Interrogative form: **Had** + subject + past participle
Negative questions: **Hadn't** + subject + past participle
Short answers: **Yes,** + subject pronoun + **had.**
No, + subject pronoun + **hadn't.**

'Had you seen everyone before you left?' 'Yes, I had.'
'Hadn't he cashed the cheque yet?' 'No, he hadn't, unfortunately.'

EXERCISES

Past perfect simple – Form

UNIT 31

31.1 Underline the verbs in the past perfect simple.
1. Colin went to Oxford University after he had left high school.
2. Natalie had finished her literature course when I last saw her.
3. The teacher hadn't gone over all our essays by the time the lesson ended.
4. When we arrived at school, the teacher had started lessons.
5. Petra hadn't finished her homework when I rang.
6. Had the nursery teacher put away all the toys by the time you left?
7. Jolene had learnt to read before she was three.
8. I had done most of my revision weeks before I sat my first exam.

31.2 Complete the sentences with the past perfect simple of the verbs in brackets.
1. The school play ......had started...... when we arrived. (start)
2. The lesson .... by ten o'clock. (finish)
3. Conrad .... most of his maths book before he went to bed. (read)
4. The bookshop .... before we got there. (close)
5. Professor Plum .... in England for ten years before he came here. (teach)
6. I fell off my bike because I .... the hole in the road. (not notice)
7. Did you see the revision programme our teacher .... for us last week? (prepare)
8. All my friends .... their English exams before I took mine. (pass)

31.3 Match the questions to the short answers.
1 ..b.. 2 .... 3 .... 4 .... 5 .... 6 ....

1. Had you met Simon before?
2. Had all the students enjoyed the lecture?
3. Had Gordon gone by six o'clock?
4. Had Miss Roberts finished the lesson?
5. Had you and your friend taken everything you needed?
6. Had the lesson been interesting?

a Yes, he had.
b No, I hadn't.
c Yes, we had.
d No, it hadn't.
e Yes, they had.
f No, she hadn't.

31.4 Choose the correct alternative.
1. **Have / Hadn't** Jack seen the new curriculum?
2. Ellie **hadn't / had** told me about the extra lesson, so I missed it!
3. We had just **sat / been sitting** down when the headteacher walked in.
4. She **hadn't / doesn't** taught at this school before.
5. None of the students had **finished / finish** the assignment.
6. **Hadn't / Has** you ever studied RE before?
7. Unfortunately, Mel hadn't **remembers / remembered** to bring the right book.
8. I had **forget / forgotten** the new teacher's name!

31.5 Use the words to write sentences in the past perfect simple.
1. the teacher / not be / very pleased with our exam results
   The teacher had not been very pleased with our exam results.
2. I / not realise / ancient Greek was so interesting!
3. you / hear / about the extra lessons?
4. the teacher / write / the results on the board
5. my parents / enrol / for an IT class at night school
6. the school / change / a lot since I went there
7. everyone / finish / writing their essay
8. Millie / attended / two different high schools in America

UNIT 32 Past perfect simple
Usage

The past perfect simple is used:

A
- for actions that took place before other actions in the past, when the past simple is the main tense of the story.

    The teacher walked into the classroom at 11 and found that the students had already finished the assignments he had given them an hour before.
    Fiona's birthday was in May, but in February her aunt had already bought her a present.

B
- to say how long an action was going on for, or how long a certain situation had lasted up until a point of time in the past. For the difference in usage between **for** and **since**, see page 80.

    When I met him, he had been in that school for two years.
    Our cousins came to see us in Italy. We hadn't seen them since they left for Argentina in 1972.

C
- in time clauses introduced by **when, after, before, as soon as, till / until** to indicate that an action happened before another. However, if the two actions took place with a short amount of time between them, it is possible to use the past simple instead.

    When he took the exam papers out, he noticed that somebody had already opened the envelope. Soon after he had received the prize, he attended a press conference.
    (also possible: Soon after he received the prize…because the actions are close to each other in time)

    Before it got dark, they had gathered all the hay in the field.
    She didn't want to leave the room until everybody had finished eating.
    He went to work for the Foreign Office as soon as he had finished university.
    (also possible: …as soon as he finished…)

D
- with **ever,** in clauses that follow a superlative introduced by a sentence in the past tense.

    That was the worst experience I had ever had.
    It was the nicest dress she had ever worn.

E
- For the use of the past perfect in indirect speech, see page 312.

EXERCISES

Past perfect simple – Usage UNIT 32

32.1 Tick (✔) the sentence (a or b) that has the same meaning as the first one.

1 Martin had studied at Cambridge before he started working here.
   a ☐ Martin came to work here before he went to Cambridge.
   b ✔ Martin went to Cambridge before he came here.
2 When I met Mary, I had got my exam results.
   a ☐ I got my exam results after meeting Mary.
   b ☐ I got my exam results before I met Mary.
3 Josh arrived at college after I had phoned him.
   a ☐ I phoned Josh before he arrived at college.
   b ☐ I phoned Josh after he had arrived at college.
4 Mum tried to ring my mobile after I had switched it off.
   a ☐ I switched my mobile off before Mum tried to ring.
   b ☐ Mum tried to ring before I switched my mobile off.
5 Billie had breakfast before she packed her school bag.
   a ☐ Billie ate breakfast after packing her school bag.
   b ☐ Billie packed her school bag after breakfast.
6 Jason had learnt to read before he started primary school.
   a ☐ Jason went to primary school, then learnt to read.
   b ☐ Jason learnt to read, then went to primary school.

32.2 Complete the sentences using the words and expressions in the box.

| had you studied | started | ~~chosen~~ | hadn't started | knew | didn't get | had |

1 David had ……*chosen*…… the university he wanted to go to before he ……………………… sixth-form college.
2 Where ……………………… before you started technical college?
3 Luckily, the school play ……………………… when we arrived.
4 The students ……………………… learnt passages from their history books before they took the exam.
5 I ……………………… the test would be difficult even before I had read the questions.
6 Jim hadn't got the right qualifications, so he ……………………… the job.

32.3 Rewrite the sentences by forming one sentence only. Use the past perfect simple and the words given.

1 I bought a new English book. Later, I enrolled for English at night school.
   (before) *I had bought a new English book before I enrolled for English at night school.*
2 Jessie studied at junior school. Then she went to grammar school.
   (before) ………………………………………………………………………………
3 The students finished their project. Afterwards, they went out.
   (after) ………………………………………………………………………………
4 The teachers had a meeting at nine. Lessons started at ten.
   (before) ………………………………………………………………………………
5 I arrived at school. The science lesson started before I arrived.
   (after) ………………………………………………………………………………
6 I studied for hours in the evening. I took the English test.
   (before) ………………………………………………………………………………
7 Jenny ate her breakfast. She met her friend and walked to college.
   (after) ………………………………………………………………………………

UNIT 33

Past perfect continuous *(I had / hadn't been learning, Had you been learning?)*
Form and usage

The past perfect continuous is used to talk about an action or a situation that had already started before a certain time but had not finished. It is formed with the past perfect of **be** and the **-ing** form of the main verb.

Subject + **had been** + verb in the **-ing** form

A Affirmative

| I / You / He / She / It / We / They | had been | reading a book. |

When I met her in the park, she had been jogging for an hour.

B Negative

| I / You / He / She / It / We / They | had not (hadn't) been | reading a book. |

Full negative form: Subject + **had + not been** + verb in the **-ing** form
Short negative form: Subject + **hadn't been** + verb in the **-ing** form

The negative form of this verb tense isn't often used. In negative sentences, it is more common to use the past perfect simple.

I hadn't been singing for a long time and my voice was a bit hoarse.
(or: I hadn't sung…)

C Interrogative

| Had | I / you / he / she / it / we / they | been | reading a book? |

Interrogative form: **Had** + subject + **been** + verb in the **-ing** form
Short answers: **Yes, / No,** + subject pronoun + **had / hadn't**.

'Had they been rehearsing since three o'clock?' 'Yes, they had.'

D

The past perfect continuous is used:
- only with action verbs, like all verb tenses in the continuous form. It is usually found when we talk about actions that are in the past simple tense, to indicate that an action was taking place before something else happened.

  He arrived at last. We had been waiting for him all afternoon.

- with **for** and **since**, to indicate the duration of an action or certain situation up to a moment in the past.

  I had been swimming for a couple of hours when my coach told me I could stop.

- with the expressions **all day**, **all afternoon…** to indicate that something took place without interruption for that period of time.

  It had been raining all day and we were looking forward to a little bit of sun.

EXERCISES

Past perfect continuous – Form and usage

UNIT 33

33.1 Choose the correct alternative.
1 Mr Watson had **been** / **be** teaching for ten hours by the end of the day!
2 When I saw Mick, he **has** / **had** been sitting in the same place for over an hour.
3 I had been **wait** / **waiting** for the teacher for ten minutes when he arrived.
4 Tessa was tired because she **has** / **had been** studying physics for four hours.
5 Paul had been **learnt** / **learning** woodwork for three years before he got his qualification.
6 **They'd** / **They've** been waiting for over an hour when the school finally opened.
7 The teacher found the RE book she **had** / **was** been looking for all morning.
8 Elsa had **to hope** / **been hoping** to pass the exam, but sadly she didn't.

33.2 Complete the sentences with the past perfect continuous of the verbs in brackets.
1 The girls *had been playing* in the playground before the teacher got there. (play)
2 Before the job offer, Nigel .... of applying to university. (think)
3 Miss Ralphs .... at my school for 20 years before she retired. (teach)
4 I .... German for two months before I took my German exam at university. (learn)
5 Sarah stood out as the best music student, which is hardly surprising, as she ....
   music since she was small. (study)
6 I .... long before my mates turned up. (not wait)

33.3 Rearrange the words and write the sentences.
This is what had been happening before school started yesterday.
1 playground – ball – the – had – The – kicking – a – been – in – boys
   The boys had been kicking a ball in the playground.
2 tests – been – Miss – marking – Brown – had
3 been – classroom – their – had – chatting – in – Some – children
4 heavily – had – raining – It – been
5 looking – The – new – curriculum – been – headteacher – at – had – the
6 lessons – The – planning – been – PE – had – extra – teacher

33.4 Complete the questions and answers by inserting one word only in each gap.
1 **A:** *Had* you been reading for long?
   B: .... , I hadn't.
2 **A:** Had Sara .... revising?
   B: Yes, she ....
3 **A:** Had .... been rehearsing for the play?
   B: No, they ....
4 **A:** .... all the teachers been marking homework since they got to school?
   B: Yes, they ....

33.5 Complete the sentences with the past perfect continuous.
1 Malcolm started studying at ten o'clock.
   By 12 o'clock, Malcolm *had been studying for two hours.*
2 The teacher started reading to us at nine o'clock.
   By half past nine, the teacher ....
3 I started writing my essay at half past two.
   By half past three, I ....
4 Olga started doing her homework at seven.
   By ten o'clock, she ....
5 Randolph started learning Spanish in 2002.
   By 2006, he ....

REVIEW 8 — EXERCISES Units 29–33

R8.1 Choose the correct alternative.
1 Class 8 **has** / is been having a pottery lesson.
2 Petra and Dana have **had / been** studying for hours.
3 I know you've been **do / doing** your best this term, so well done!
4 I **was / had** been waiting for the break so I could get a drink of water.
5 **Hadn't / Haven't** she been revising before you got home?
6 The technical college had closed **when / since** I got there.
7 Sally had been practising her violin **all / for** day.
8 'Had you met that tutor before?' 'No, I **haven't / hadn't**.'

R8.2 Choose the correct alternative.

I remember my first day at secondary school very clearly. Mum (1) **had** / has told me all about the school before I (2) **had went / went** there, of course, and we had (3) **to visit / visited** an Open Day to have a look around. We (4) **talked / had talked** to the teachers too while we were there, so I (5) **knew / had known** it was a nice school. But some of my friends (6) **did / had** decided to go to a different secondary school and I thought I'd miss them. However, once I (7) **walked / had walked** into my first class on that first day, I (8) **had known / knew** I (9) **worried / had worried** for no reason. Everyone was very nice, and before long I'd (10) **get / got** three new best friends!

R8.3 Use the words to write questions in the past perfect continuous. Then complete the short answers.

1 Sam / revise / all evening
Had Sam been revising all evening? Yes, *he had* .
2 Michaela and Josie / rehearse / for the school play
.... No, ...
3 Professor Robert Parker / prepare / the curriculum
.... Yes, ...
4 the students / have / extra lessons in science
.... Yes, ...
5 Ursula / plan / apply to Oxford University
.... Yes, ...
6 you / study / for the maths test
.... No, ...
7 Sophie and Leila / wait / for their exam results
.... Yes, ...
8 It / snow / since the weekend
.... No, ...

R8.4 Complete the sentences with the past perfect simple or continuous of the verbs in brackets.
1 By ten, the students *had been doing* their exam for two hours. (do)
2 The teacher .... the students to hand in their projects before I got to the lesson. (ask)
3 .... you .... for the teacher for long before she came? (wait)
4 No, I .... of applying to technical college until you suggested it. (think)
5 Her years at junior school .... some of the happiest of Judy's life. (be)
6 Of course Mum was tired! She .... for hours before you saw her. (work)
7 When I saw Tom, he .... his school bag yet again! (lose)
8 Everyone .... the lesson, so they thanked the tutor. (enjoy)

REVIEW 8

R8.5 **Complete the text with the correct alternative.**

Paul has never (1) ..B.. to Italy, but he (2) .... corresponding with a girl called Lorella, from Verona. She (3) .... English for five years now and is really enthusiastic about this language. Last year, Lorella (4) .... three weeks in Totnes, in the south-west of England, and (5) .... a full-immersion course. Paul and Lorella (6) .... e-mails almost every day (7) .... the past two months. He's going to Italy (8) ...., so he (9) .... a low-cost flight from Manchester to Venice. He will then take a train to Verona. It won't be Paul's first time abroad. When he was a child, he (10) .... spend every summer in Malaga with his grandparents, who (11) .... a flat there after retiring.

1 **A** gone   **(B)** been   **C** got
2 **A** has recently started   **B** started recently   **C** did recently start
3 **A** studies   **B** studied   **C** has been studying
4 **A** has spent   **B** spent   **C** has been spending
5 **A** attended   **B** has attended   **C** did attend
6 **A** exchange   **B** exchanges   **C** have been exchanging
7 **A** for   **B** since   **C** from
8 **A** at July   **B** next July   **C** last July
9 **A** has booked   **B** has been booking   **C** books
10 **A** used   **B** has used to   **C** used to
11 **A** have bought   **B** had bought   **C** have been buying

R8.6 **Complete the sentences with the appropriate tense of the verbs in brackets. Choose between: present perfect simple or continuous, past simple, past perfect simple or continuous.**

1 I ....'ve had.................... this job since last April. (have)
2 We .... Japanese for nearly six months now. (learn)
3 Colin .... in France since 2002, when he .... a job as a teacher of English in Nantes. (live / get)
4 Mary .... on this project since the beginning of the week. (work)
5 Miss Potter .... to the library for two weeks now, since the day she .... with the chief librarian. (not come / quarrel)
6 The teacher .... for over an hour when the door .... suddenly and the headmaster .... into the classroom. (talk / open / walk)
7 The students .... a long meeting at the Students' Union since eight o'clock this morning. They .... various matters for over two hours and they .... yet. (have / discuss / not finish)
8 The man .... painting the school gate when it suddenly .... to rain. (just finish / start)

C Exam preparation

C.1 PET Reading Part 5

Read the text and choose the correct word(s) (A, B, C or D) for each space.

(1) ...B... you heard that moving house is one of the most stressful things you can do? My friend Natalie has (2)............ house recently and she still (3)............ recovered from the experience! It has (4)............ her weeks to unpack all her things and find places for them in her new home. She hasn't (5)............ everything as she wants it (6)............ and she's (7)............ been in her new flat (8)............ a month. And there are some things Natalie has (9)............ found since she moved. She (10)............ paid the removal company's bill (11)............. She says they (12)............ do a good job, so she isn't going to pay them.

1	A Has	(B) Have	C Did	D Are
2	A moved	B moves	C move	D moving
3	A have	B has	C haven't	D hasn't
4	A took	B taken	C takes	D taking
5	A got	B gets	C get	D getting
6	A already	B since	C yet	D not yet
7	A yet	B already	C for	D since
8	A since	B yet	C in	D for
9	A never	B ever	C since	D yet
10	A haven't	B hasn't	C not	D didn't
11	A already	B for	C so far	D ever
12	A hasn't	B didn't	C don't	D haven't

C.2 PET Writing Part 1

Complete the second sentence so that it means the same as the first.

1. Sonya studied art at night school, then she went to university.
   Sonya ......*had studied art*...... at night school before she went to university.
2. Miss Nelson started teaching at nine and she's still teaching at three.
   It's three o'clock. Miss Nelson .... for six hours!
3. I did my homework, then Mum asked me to help her.
   I .... my homework when Mum asked me to help her.
4. I was at my desk from six until Dad got home at ten.
   When Dad got home, I .... at my desk for four hours.
5. Dicky helped Cheryl with her IT homework for two hours. Then he went out.
   Dicky .... Cheryl with her IT homework for two hours before he went out.

C.3 PET Writing Part 3

This is part of an e-mail you received from an English friend who is on a gap year in South America. Write an e-mail answering his questions (about 100 words).

> Do you know, I've been here two weeks and already home seems a distant memory. We've made friends with the village people and we've learnt a few words of their dialect. So, what's been happening back there? Have you finished your exams yet? Has everybody from our group gone on holiday or are they hanging around? How about the summer course you wanted to attend? Are you still going or have you changed your mind?

Exam preparation

C.4 FCE Use of English Part 2

Read the dialogue below and think of the word or short form which best fits each space. Use only one in each space.

Sheila: (1) ...*Have*... you visited Tom's villa in France?
Helen: (2) .... , I have. It's an amazing place! Have you (3) .... it?
Sheila: No, I (4) .... been there.
Helen: Well, it really is fabulous. And (5) .... worked hard to make it look nice.
Sheila: What (6) .... he done?
Helen: (7) .... redecorated everywhere and he's (8) .... lots of flowers and trees outside, so the gardens are lovely.
Sheila: Well, he (9) .... invited me to go over in June.
Helen: I've (10) .... some photos. I can show them to you if you like before you go.

C.5 FCE Use of English Part 3

Read the text below. Use the word given in capitals at the end of each line to form a word that fits in the space in the same line.

Fast education

I found it incredible when I realised how quickly my school years had passed. I can well remember my very first day at (1) ...*nursery*...	NURSE
school, and it only seemed like six months before I was leaving junior school and moving on to a large (2) .... school	SECOND
six miles away from home. Then, just as quickly, I had read through a college (3) .... and was busy filling in the	PROSPECT
(4) .... forms to go and study languages. And now I	APPLY
have my (5) .... and am looking for a job. How time flies!	QUALIFY

C.6 FCE Use of English Part 4

Complete the second sentence so that it has a similar meaning to the first sentence, using the word given. Do not change the word given. You must use between two and five words, including the word given.

1 It's ten o'clock, and Molly rang the estate agent five minutes ago.
   JUST
   Molly *has just rung* .... the estate agent.

2 I made my bed earlier, Mum.
   ALREADY
   I .... , Mum.

3 It's quarter past nine; the postman comes at half past.
   YET
   The postman ....

4 I don't want to read the property section of the paper; I read it before.
   ALREADY
   I .... the property section of the paper.

5 Leonie is moving into her new house tomorrow.
   HAS
   Leonie .... her new house yet.

6 I saw Miss Roberts a few minutes ago.
   JUST
   I .... Miss Roberts.

UNIT 34
The future: *going to* (I'm (not) going to apply, Are you going to apply?)
Form and usage

The future, expressed with **going to**, is mainly used to talk about our intentions.

A

> **Affirmative**
> Subject + **am / is / are** + **going to** + base form of verb
> Subject + **'m / 's / 're** + **going to** + base form of verb

I'm going to think about it.

> **Negative**
> Subject + **am / is / are** + **not** + **going to** + base form of verb
> Subject + **'m not / isn't / aren't** + **going to** + base form of verb

She isn't going to apply for that job.

> **Interrogative**
> **Am / Is / Are** + subject + **going to** + base form of verb

'Are you going to hire a bike when you get to the island?'
'Yes, I am, if it doesn't rain.'

The short forms, both affirmative and negative, are more common than the full forms.
In spoken American English, the form **gonna** (contraction of **going to**) is occasionally used.
It's gonna be a hard day.

If sentences with **going to** don't indicate a certain time, it means the action will happen in the immediate future.
You're going to work in groups of four.

Verbs of motion such as **go**, **come** or **arrive** are used more often in the present continuous, but can also have a future form with **going to**.
I'm going to university. / I'm going to go to university.

B The future with **going to** is used:
- to talk about things that we have decided to do, but that we haven't yet planned in detail.
  Mike's going to organise a welcome party.

  In comparison to the present continuous, which is used for actions that we have definitely planned (see p. 42), the future with **going to** only expresses willingness and intention of doing something.
  I'm going to give them a wedding present.
  (but I haven't decided what to get yet)
  I'm giving them a set of cutlery as a wedding present.
  (I've decided and I might have even bought the present already)

C
- to talk about long-term projects.
  'What are you going to be when you grow up?' 'I'm going to be a reporter.'

D
- to foretell an event that will happen in the immediate future, especially on the basis of what we see in the present.
  Hey, look! She's going to fall down.
  We're going to take off in just a couple of minutes.

  To talk about the immediate future, we can also use the expression **be about to**.
  Sit down, everybody. The film's about to start.
  She's about to retire from work.

EXERCISES

The future: *going to* – Form and usage

UNIT 34

34.1 Complete the sentences with the correct form of *going to* and of the verbs in brackets.

1. Ted *is going to be* a doctor when he grows up. (be)
2. They .... for jobs in the same office. (not apply)
3. I .... to get a qualification in sales and marketing. (try)
4. We .... an office party at Christmas. (have)
5. Oscar .... this weekend. (not work)
6. The students .... to the job centre and look for summer jobs. (go)
7. Irene .... with that company for much longer. (not stay)
8. The mechanic .... and look at Dad's car. (come)
9. Your boss .... very pleased when he sees that! (not be)
10. I think I .... this job! (like)

34.2 Use the words to write questions with *going to*. Then complete the short answers.

1. Henry / look for / temporary work / this summer
   Is Henry going to look for temporary work this summer?   Yes, *he is.*
2. your colleagues / organise / a surprise party / for the boss
   ....   No, ...
3. you / apply / for promotion / next year
   ....   Yes, ...
4. Sara / take over / the job of manageress
   ....   Yes, ...
5. I / get / my Christmas bonus / this month
   ....   No, ...
6. they / move / to offices closer to the city centre
   ....   No, ...

34.3 Complete the dialogue with the correct form of *going to* and of the verbs in the box.

| tell | ask | not do | take | not change | ~~be~~ |

Andy: Hey, Jane. Look busy! The boss (1) *is going to be* here in a minute!
Jane: Is he? That's good. I (2) .... him if I can see him for a few minutes.
Andy: Why?
Jane: Because I (3) .... him why we aren't happy with our jobs!
Andy: There's no point. He knows and he (4) .... anything about it.
Jane: Isn't he? Well, if nobody speaks up, things (5) ....
Andy: I think it needs more than one little chat to do that.
Jane: You're always so negative. When (6) .... you .... some action?
Andy: I like an easy life. And, Jane, I don't want to hear that you have lost your job.

34.4 Complete the sentences with the correct form of *going to* and of the verbs in the box.

| advertise | offer | employ | not retire | interview | move | ~~get~~ | not get |

1. You work very hard; you *'re going to get* ahead in this company.
2. I think they .... him the job.
3. .... to London for work?
4. They .... some new builders.
5. I'm sure Rose and Beryl .... the sack!
6. I .... until I'm 60, then I can look back on my career with pride!
7. They .... all the jobs in the local newspaper.
8. Who .... the applicants?

UNIT 35 The future: *will* (I will go, I won't go, Will you go?)
Form

A

Affirmative

Full form	Short form
I will come	I'll come
You will come	You'll come
He / She / It will come	He'll / She'll / It'll come
We / You / They will come	We'll / You'll / They'll come

Affirmative form: Subject + **will / 'll** + base form of verb

For the first person singular and plural, **shall** can be used instead of **will** (**I shall come / We shall come**). However this use is not very common.
The short form (**'ll**) is used a lot in spoken language.
It will be / It'll be sunny tomorrow.
We'll get there by noon.

B

Negative

Full form	Short form
I will not come	I won't come
You will not come	You won't come
He / She / It will not come	He / She / It won't come
We / You / They will not come	We / You / They won't come

Affirmative form: Subject + **will not / won't** + base form of verb

You won't have time to do all that work.
It won't happen again, I promise.

C

Interrogative	Negative questions
Will I come?	Won't I come?
Will you come?	Won't you come?
Will he / she / it come?	Won't he / she / it come?
Will we / you / they come?	Won't we / you / they come?

Interrogative form: **Will / Won't** + subject + base form of verb

Will it be hot at the weekend?
Won't they stay a bit longer?

D Short answers are formed using: **Yes / No** + subject pronoun + **will / won't**.

'Will you be ready by ten o'clock?' 'Yes, I will.' / 'No, I won't, I'm afraid.'
'Who will go?' 'I will.'

E The future of **be** is **will be** for all persons: **I will be / You will be…**
Note also: **There will be…**
There won't be…

There'll be hundreds of people at the conference.
The strike's been called off. There won't be any delay.

EXERCISES

The future: *will* – Form

UNIT 35

35.1 Rearrange the words and write the sentences.

1 chef – as – be – a – will – interesting – Working
   Working as a chef will be interesting.
2 will – see – manager – you – The – soon
3 be – He – busy – summer – all – will
4 Will – they – newspaper – advertise – jobs – in – the – the – ?
5 Grace – sure – get – will – I'm – promotion – the
6 a – salary – pay – you – Will – good – they – ?
7 work – I – will – enjoy – hope – you – the
8 interview – think – Do – you – well – will – I – do – at – the – ?

35.2 Rewrite the sentences using the short negative form.

1 I will be at work tomorrow. — *I won't be at work tomorrow.*
2 The doctor will have time to see you later.
3 The pay for that IT job will be very high.
4 Elizabeth will get a qualification in medicine.
5 The electrician will charge a lot for his work.
6 We will get a good pension when we retire.

35.3 Match the questions to the answers.

1 *b*   2 ......   3 ......   4 ......   5 ......   6 ......

1 Will you apply for the job?
2 Will I get six weeks' holiday a year?
3 What will the money be like?
4 Will it be a permanent position?
5 Will they advertise the job locally?
6 Will there be time to see the manager?

a Yes, you will.
b No, I won't.
c Yes, it will.
d No, there won't.
e Yes, they will.
f It will be good!

35.4 Use the words to write questions with *will*. Then complete the short answers.

1 you / look / in the job centre again
   Will you look in the job centre again?   Yes, *I will*.
2 there be / any vacancies here soon
   Yes, ...
3 he / feel / nervous at the interview
   No, ...
4 you / catch up / on your work / before the weekend
   Yes, ...
5 they / expect / me to work at weekends
   No, ...
6 Roseanne / earn / enough to live on
   No, ...

UNIT 36 The future: *will*
Usage (1)

The future with **will** is used to:

A
- make predictions about the future. In this case, adverbs can be used to indicate the level of certainty, such as: **definitely**, **certainly**, **probably**, **possibly**. These adverbs are placed between **will** and the base form of the verb.

    Don't worry! It'll be OK.
    It'll definitely end in a draw.
    The weather will probably change soon.
    Man will probably land on Mars before the end of the century.

B
- express a personal opinion as regards to what will happen. In this case, it is common to use introductory sentences like **I think, I don't think, I guess, I expect, I'm sure, I wonder**.

    I'm sure (that) we'll have a great time!
    I don't think the test will be difficult.
    I wonder who will win the rugby tournament this year.
    I expect Scotland will win. It's a very strong team.

C
- express hopes and wishes, with the verb **hope**. In this case, sentences with the modal **can** may be used instead.

    I hope you will come. / I hope you can come.

D
- talk about future actions which are certainties and have nothing to do with our intentions or willingness.

    The Sun will rise at 5.45 tomorrow.
    My mother will be 40 next month.
    Whatever will be, will be.

E
- In sentences with **will**, we often find

definite time expressions, such as:	indefinite time expressions, such as:
tomorrow	in the future
this year	in the near future
in the next few years	soon
in five days	later
in two years' time	sooner or later
in 2050	

These expressions are usually placed at the end of a sentence.

I'm busy now. I'll see you later.
The climate will get warmer and warmer in the future.

EXERCISES

The future: *will* – Usage (1)

UNIT 36

36.1 Tick (✔) the correct sentences and correct the sentences with mistakes in them.

1. ☐ I will think Jake will enjoy his retirement.   *I think Jake will enjoy his retirement.*
2. ✔ You'll definitely get the manager's job!
3. ☐ There will possibly be a vacancy here next month.
4. ☐ The committee probably promote Mr Taylor to managing director.
5. ☐ I expect Freda will have more time for sport now that she's unemployed.
6. ☐ All the staff will get an extra day off at Easter.
7. ☐ I'll to talk to you later – I'm at work at the moment.
8. ☐ His secretary won't she retire for another ten years.
9. ☐ I hope you'll to be happy in your new job.
10. ☐ What time will the office re-open after the holiday weekend?

36.2 Choose the correct alternative.

1. I'm **hope** / **(sure)** the strike will be over soon.
2. Our boss **will be** / **is being** 50 next week.
3. Ulla will **to start** / **start** work as a scientist in three days' time.
4. Joe will **probably** / **certain** get the job.
5. I **wonder** / **think** who the new boss will be!
6. I **sure** / **hope** they'll do up the offices next year.
7. I don't think the interview **will** / **won't** be too bad.
8. Mel phoned to say she will be at work **soon** / **next**.

36.3 Match the two parts of the sentences.

1 ..e.. 2 .... 3 .... 4 .... 5 .... 6 .... 7 .... 8 ....

1. The job will definitely
2. I think the boss will fire
3. I wonder who
4. The office will
5. I'll see you at work
6. Pat will probably
7. I expect
8. It'll soon

a. apply for promotion.
b. the new director will be.
c. Ralph for being late for work.
d. be time to go home.
e. be very tiring.
f. in two weeks' time.
g. be closed tomorrow.
h. it will be difficult to find a job.

36.4 Find the mistakes and underline them. Then write the correct sentences.

1. He'll probably <u>to</u> make a lot of money as a lawyer.
   He'll probably make a lot of money as a lawyer.
2. I expect Norman get the job.

3. I won't think you'll find part-time work here.

4. I will like my job, but I'll look for something different in the future.

5. I will hope my new employer will be nice!

6. Will have you time to do a full-time job and run the house?

105

UNIT 37 The future: *will*
Usage (2)

The future with **will** is also used to:

A
- make promises and express propositions for the future.

    We'll see what we can do.
    I'll come and see you in Greece, I promise.
    I'll try and work harder next term.

B
- express an immediate decision, made in that moment, to:
    – offer to do something.

    Let me help you. I'll carry the bags for you.
    Have you lost your key? I'll go and look for it!
    I'll pay!
    I'll call a taxi for you, madam!

    – say what you'd like, for example in a restaurant.

    I think I'll have roast beef and potatoes.
    I'll have fish. Yes, I'll have the grilled salmon.

C
- to refuse to do something (negative form of **will**).

    I won't play!
    She's very stubborn. She won't listen to anybody's advice.

D
- **Will** is also used to:
    – express politely a request in the present, which is usually accompanied by **please**.

    Will you help me, please?
    Will you please close the window?

    – offer something to someone (**will** followed by the verb **have**).

    'What will you have? Will you have a coffee?' 'No, thanks. I'll have a cup of tea.'
    'Will you have some chips?' 'Yes, please.'

EXERCISES

UNIT 37 — The future: *will* — Usage (2)

37.1 Complete the sentences with the correct form of *will* and of the verbs in brackets.

1. I think I ......*will ask*...... to see the manager about my position. (ask)
2. The union leader .... us decide what to do. (help)
3. .... you .... some time off at Christmas? (have)
4. Don't worry! I .... you where everything is. (show)
5. I .... any more favours for the boss! (not do)
6. What .... you .... with your wages this week? (buy)
7. He .... advice from anyone about how to do the job! (not take)
8. The manager .... for you to take a taxi home. (pay)

37.2 Complete the sentences with the correct form of *will* and with a verb in the box.

| post   have   close   ~~visit~~   work   listen   miss   show |

1. *Will* you *visit* your uncle when you are in London?
2. I .... you while you're away.
3. I .... a cheese sandwich, please.
4. I .... late again! It's the third time this week.
5. .... you .... these letters for Mr Thomson, please?
6. I .... you how to use the photocopier.
7. He's got a mind of his own. He .... to anything I say.
8. .... you .... the door, please?

37.3 Match the questions to the answers.

1 ..*d*.. 2 .... 3 .... 4 .... 5 .... 6 ....

1. What will you have to drink?
2. Will you help me with this, please?
3. Will he agree to our request?
4. Will you have lunch now?
5. When will you stop work today?
6. Will Mum be home late tonight?

a. Yes, of course I will.
b. No, she won't.
c. I'll stop when I'm tired.
d. I'll have a coffee, please.
e. No, I won't, thanks.
f. Yes, I think he will.

37.4 Write what you would say in these situations.

1. Your boss needs help carrying some files; you offer to help.
   I'll help you carry those files.
2. You want to offer your secretary a cake.
   ....
3. Your work colleague tells you he can't find his diary; you offer to help.
   ....
4. Your boss asks if you want some lunch; you decide you want a salad.
   ....
5. You go for a drink with your colleague; you decide to pay.
   ....
6. You're too cold and ask your colleague to close the window.
   ....

REVIEW 9

EXERCISES Units 34–37

R9.1 Choose the correct alternative.

Hilary: Guess what! I'm (1) **will / going to** have a job interview tomorrow – at Heel's Shoe Shop!
Hannah: Great! Who (2) **is going / will** to interview you?
Hilary: I think the manager of the shop is going (3) **to ask / ask** me some questions.
Hannah: Have you thought about what you're going to say?
Hilary: Not really. (4) **I'm / I'll** just answer the questions honestly.
Hannah: He'll (5) **going / probably** ask you why you want the job.
Hilary: Well, that's OK. I'll (6) **to tell / tell** him! I know what I'm going to say about that!
Hannah: Good! It sounds as if (7) **you're going / you'll be** fine. I'm sure (8) **you're going / you will** to get the job.

R9.2 Read Jenny's diary and write what she intends to do next weekend.

next weekend
meet Sue after work on Friday
have a lie-in
catch up on work
cook supper for my work colleagues
study the company reports

1 *Jenny's going to meet Sue after work on Friday.*
2 ....
3 ....
4 ....
5 ....

R9.3 Read Tom's notes and write full sentences on what will go on in the office next week.

next week
my office manager, Robert / go on holiday
I / have to take over / some of his work
I / use / his desk / and answer / his phone
I / get paid / overtime
my boss / oversee / my performance

1 *My office manager, Robert, will go on holiday.*
2 ....
3 ....
4 ....
5 ....

R9.4 Answer the questions on Jenny and Tom by referring to exercises 2 and 3.

1 Are Jenny and Sue going to meet on Friday? *Yes, they are.*
2 Will Tom go on holiday?
3 Will Tom work in his manager's office?
4 Is Jenny going to write the company reports?
5 Is Jenny going to cook for her colleagues?
6 Will Tom get paid less?

R9.5 Complete the text with the words in the box.

| will | be | are | ~~going~~ | won't | to |

Most of us know what we're (1) ...*going*... to do next week, next month or maybe even next year. Some of us, for example, (2) .... have a new job or a new home this time next year. But do any of us know what's going (3) .... happen in 100 years' time? The world (4) .... be the same as it is today. Things (5) .... going to change a lot. It will (6) .... very interesting to see what happens!

REVIEW 9

R9.6 Complete the sentences with the words in the box.

~~is going to~~ will be   earn   will go   is going   will charge   will get   are going to

1 Do you know what the monthly salary ……*is going to*…… be?
2 They ……………………… make ten people redundant next week.
3 There ……………………… some vacancies soon.
4 Harriet ……………………… to get a part-time job.
5 Will Dan ……………………… enough to live on?
6 How much do you think the plumber ……………………… us?
7 I think your interview ……………………… well.
8 I hope you ……………………… the promotion you applied for.

R9.7 Complete the sentences with the appropriate future (*will* or *going to*) of the verbs in brackets.

1 This year he *'s going to celebrate* ……………… his birthday with a huge party. (celebrate – *intention*)
2 I think they ……………………… these old offices. (demolish – *prediction*)
3 Joseph works hard; he ……………… definitely ……………… and do well. (get ahead – *prediction*)
4 What ……………… you ……………………… when you grow up? (do – *intention*)
5 It ……………………… me ages to catch up on all my work! (take – *prediction*)
6 Who ……………………… your job when you leave? (take over – *intention*)
7 I hear they ……………………… my old job again. (advertise – *intention*)
8 I wonder how many of the applicants ……………………… an interview. (get – *prediction*)

R9.8 You meet up with Susan and talk about what you are going to do next summer. Complete the dialogue with the appropriate future (*will* or *going to*) of the verbs in brackets.

You: What [1] *are you going to do* next summer, Susan? (you / do)
Susan: I [2] ……………………… to Cannes and I [3] ……………………… a French course. (go / attend)
You: How long [4] ……………………… in Cannes? (you / stay)
Susan: I think I [5] ……………………… three weeks there. Do you want to come with me? (stay)
You: I'd like to, but when [6] ……………………… ? (you / leave)
Susan: I don't know yet. I think I [7] ……………………… at the end of July. (leave)
You: In that case, I won't be able to come. I [8] ……………………… in August. (work)
Susan: Work? Where?
You: In a hotel in Brighton. I [9] ……………………… as a receptionist. (work)
Susan: Oh, I see. Well, I [10] ……………………… you a postcard from Cannes, then. (send)

UNIT 38 Present continuous and present simple for the future

A The future can also be expressed using the present continuous:

> Subject + **am / is / are** + verb in the **-ing** form

This type of future is used to talk about:
- actions or events that have already been planned
- personal commitments that were previously planned, for which preparations have already been made (for example, buying tickets, reserving seats, making appointments…).

The present continuous, when used for the future, is accompanied by adverbs, such as:
tonight, tomorrow, next week / next summer…, at five o'clock…

Jane's team are playing an important match next week.
(it's a fixed date)

I'm leaving Tokyo tomorrow morning at six o'clock.
(I already have a plane ticket)

I'm seeing them after the conference.
(I have an appointment with them)

B The present continuous, when used for the future, is often used with verbs of motion like **go, come, arrive, leave.**

'Are you coming with me?' 'No, we aren't coming this time.'

'What are you doing this afternoon? Are you going shopping?'
'No, I'm not. I'm going to the dentist's at half past three.'

'When's Grandma arriving?' 'She's arriving tomorrow morning.'

C Compare the present continuous to the future with **going to** (see p. 100).

I'm going to spend a couple of days in New York.
(but I haven't yet arranged anything)

I'm spending a couple of days in New York. I've booked a room in a hotel on 46th Street.
(it's already been organised)

D Even the present simple can sometimes be used for the future. This use is limited to:
- future actions that are part of a schedule, for example a holiday
- actions that take place at set times, for example arrival and departure times of train and planes.

We arrive in Barcelona at 4 p.m.. We have dinner at the hotel. We take a plane to Madrid at 2 p.m. the following day.

My train leaves at 16.04. Will you take me to the station?

The present simple for the future is also used in secondary sentences introduced by **if**, **when**, **as soon as**, when in the main sentence there is a future with **will** (see p. 320).

If his eyesight deteriorates, they will operate.
I'll talk to him as soon as he arrives.

EXERCISES

Present continuous and present simple for the future

UNIT 38

38.1 Tick (✔) the sentences that refer to the future.

1. ☐ Mum's talking to the doctor on the phone at the moment.
2. ✔ I'm seeing the nurse at four.
3. ☐ She usually gets two colds a year.
4. ☐ The next bus to the hospital leaves at 3.45.
5. ☐ Mum takes my temperature when I'm ill.
6. ☐ The doctor's calling back later.
7. ☐ He's having an operation on his knee on Tuesday.
8. ☐ Martha's suffering from chicken pox.
9. ☐ Tomorrow's Saturday, so visiting hours start at two.
10. ☐ The surgeon can't talk to you – he's operating.

38.2 Choose the correct alternative.

1. Our plane **arrives** / **is arriving** in London at seven.
2. I **see** / **am seeing** the nurse at half past nine tomorrow morning.
3. What **are you doing** / **do you do** tomorrow?
4. Mum **is spending** / **spends** a couple of days in hospital next week.
5. The train to London **leaves** / **is leaving** at ten.
6. Damien **goes** / **is going** to the Dead Sea for therapy next month.
7. The plan is that we leave here at one and **are arriving** / **arrive** at the clinic at two.
8. The nurses' meeting **starts** / **is starting** at half past seven in the morning.

38.3 Complete the sentences with the present simple or present continuous of the verbs in brackets.

1. Bob's got toothache, so he _is seeing_ the dentist at ten tomorrow. (see)
2. The bus to the surgery .... at half past the hour. (leave)
3. The nurse .... me for an X-ray in ten minutes. (take)
4. Poppy .... for physiotherapy at half past four this afternoon. (go)
5. The first-aid course .... on 7th June. (start)
6. We .... soup and sandwiches this evening. (have)
7. Tomorrow, I .... the house at ten because the train to town .... at quarter past. (leave, leave)
8. Look, read the notice! The doctor .... at his surgery at eight. (arrive)

38.4 Use the words to write sentences in the present simple or present continuous.

1. trains / to Leeds / leave every hour, on the hour
   The trains to Leeds leave every hour, on the hour.

2. I / go / to the clinic for an injection / tomorrow
   ....

3. I / not see / the heart specialist / this week
   ....

4. we / visit / Grandma in hospital / tomorrow
   ....

5. the doctor / see / her / in two weeks' time
   ....

6. my physiotherapy session / start / at two tomorrow
   ....

UNIT 39 — *Going to* / *Present continuous* / *Will* future
Differences in usage

Here is a summary of the three main ways in which to express the future.

Going to	*Present continuous*	*Will* future
• intentions • long-term projects • actions that are about to happen, predictions based on certain facts • decisions that have already been made	• planned actions • commitments made for a precise moment in the future	• predictions • promises, suggestions • decisions made at the time of speaking, without premeditation • actions that are not dependent on the willingness of the speaker

The use of one or the other of these futures often depends on the intention of the speaker. The following points show examples of these differences.

A Note the difference between the future with **will** (decision made at the time of speaking), **going to** (decision made beforehand) and the present continuous (commitment made for a certain time in the future). A friend suggests having a picnic next Saturday and I think it's a good idea:

'Why don't we have a picnic next Saturday?'
'That's a good idea. I'll buy some food and drinks.'
(it has only just been decided and I offer to buy food and drinks, it's an idea that comes to me on the spur of moment)

Then I talk about it with someone else:

'You know, we're having a picnic next Saturday.'
(it has already been planned)
'I'm going to buy some food and drinks.'
(it's a decision that I've already made)

Or else, if I've already decided when I'm going to do the shopping:

'I'm buying the food and drinks for the picnic later in the afternoon.' (commitment made for a certain time in the future)

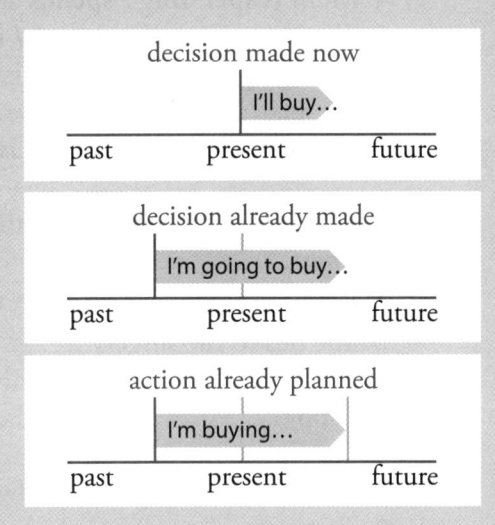

B NB: **Will** usually isn't used to talk about something that has already been decided and planned. In this case we use the present continuous or **going to**.

We're going to play tennis tomorrow. / We're playing tennis tomorrow. (it's already decided, so not: ~~We'll play…~~)
Are they going to work next Saturday? / Are they working next Saturday? (It depends on the schedule, so not: ~~Will they work…?~~)

C NB: **Will** is usually used, instead of **going to** and the present continuous, to talk about actions that are independent from our willingness.

It will be sunny tomorrow. (according to the weather forecast)
Leeds will probably win the championship. (I'm making a prediction, but it doesn't depend on me, so not: ~~Leeds is winning…~~)
However, I could say: *'Leeds are going to win the championship'* in the last few minutes of the final match, when it's obvious that they're about to win.

D **Going to** can be found instead of **will** when making predictions that are based on certain facts that we have some knowledge about.
I'm sure she's going to like our present. (it's a CD of a band that I know she really likes)

EXERCISES

Going to / Present continuous / Will future – Differences in usage

UNIT 39

39.1 Choose the correct alternative.
1 You are so stressed. When **will you / are you** going to take a break?
2 I'm uncomfortable in this hospital bed. I think **I'll ask / I'm asking** for an extra pillow.
3 You **will / are going to** probably feel dizzy the first time you get out of bed.
4 I think **I'm going to / I will** sneeze!
5 I don't know what I **'m going to / will** do with you. You're so stubborn.
6 You look a bit green! **Are you going to / Will you** be sick?

39.2 Tick (✔) the correct sentences and correct the sentences with mistakes in them.
1 ✔ I've made an appointment; I'm seeing the dentist at three o'clock tomorrow afternoon.
2 ☐ Next summer, I learn English in Oxford. *Next summer, I'm going to learn English in Oxford.*
3 ☐ I'm hungry. I think I have a bacon sandwich. ....
4 ☐ Be careful! You're going to back the car into that wall! ....
5 ☐ I'm sure you're feeling better soon. ....
6 ☐ You look as if you're going to pass out! ....

39.3 Use the words and the verbs in brackets to write sentences with the future form indicated.
1 Mum / in hospital / for three weeks (be – *going to*)
   Mum is going to be in hospital for three weeks.
2 Stay still! This / injection / at all! / (not hurt – *will*)
3 My appointment is at 9 a.m. tomorrow. I / an X-ray / on my ankle. (have – *present continuous*)
4 your temperature / probably / after the operation (go up – *will*)
5 Elsie says she is a lot better and she / in bed / for another minute (not stay – *going to*)
6 The doctor doesn't know what to say. So I / a specialist / next week (see – *present continuous*)

39.4 Complete the text with the correct form (present continuous, *will* or *going to*) of the verbs in brackets. There can be more than one answer.

Tomorrow, my sister, Phoebe, (1) *will come / is coming* (come) out of hospital, so Mum and I have agreed to organise a surprise party! I know Phoebe (2) .... (not feel) strong, so she (3) .... (not be) dancing or anything like that. But we (4) .... (invite) a lot of her friends, and they (5) .... (be) happy to sit and chat to Phoebe. In fact, I think I (6) .... (invite) two of the nurses from hospital, too! Phoebe really likes the nurses, so she (7) .... (be) pleased if they come. Now then… let's see: they (8) .... (send) her home by ambulance at four, so I think I (9) .... (ask) people to come round at about seven in the evening. In that case, I must get organised! I think I (10) .... (write) my shopping list right now… then I (11) .... (go) to the supermarket!

39.5 Complete the dialogue with the words in the box.

| I'll go | I'll | don't go | taking | starts | I'm | ~~Are you going to~~ | Are you taking |

A: (1) *Are you going to* .... visit Joshua in hospital?
B: Yes, I am. I think (2) .... tomorrow evening. I'm playing rugby in the afternoon, so I can't go then.
A: Visiting (3) .... at seven in the evening, so (4) .... before then.
B: OK, thanks. (5) .... anything for him?
A: Yes, I'm (6) .... some magazines. What about you?
B: I think (7) .... just let him borrow my MP3 player!
A: Good idea! (8) .... sure he'll like that.

UNIT 40 — Future continuous (I will be doing) and Future perfect (I will have done)

A There is also a continuous form of the future with **will**, the future continuous, that is formed using:

Subject + **will be** (**'ll be**) + verb in the **-ing** form

Sorry, I can't come to your house tomorrow night. I'll be studying for the exam all evening.

B The future continuous is a verb form that is typically used with action verbs to say what will be happening at a certain point in the future. As always for the continuous forms, it highlights the duration of the action.

I will be flying over the Pacific tomorrow at this time.
Don't call me between nine and ten. I'll be having my physiotherapy then.

The future continuous is also used for planned actions, as an alternative to the present continuous.

They're arriving tonight. / They'll be arriving tonight.
I'm not using the car today. / I won't be using the car today.

Questions with the future continuous are used to ask about other people's plans in a polite way.

What time will you be leaving tomorrow morning, Mr Smith?
Will you be working next weekend?

Compare the future continuous with the present continuous and the past continuous.

11 MAY	12 MAY	13 MAY
Tomorrow at nine o'clock I'll be watching TV.	I'm watching TV right now.	Yesterday at nine o'clock I was watching TV.

C The future perfect, is formed using:

Subject + **will have** (**'ll have**) + past participle

You will have learnt to speak Spanish fluently in two years' time.

D The future perfect is used to say that something will already be complete by a certain time in the future. It is often accompanied by time expressions such as **by five o'clock, by the time you arrive, in two weeks' time.**

You don't need to come and help us make dinner. We will have finished cooking by the time you arrive.
In two years' time I will have become very rich!
Next summer, the president will have completed his term.

Compare the future perfect with the present perfect and the past perfect.

I will have taken my degree by this time next year.
I have already taken my degree.
Before I left for Africa, I had already taken my degree.

EXERCISES

Future continuous and future perfect

UNIT 40

40.1 Complete the sentences with the correct form of the future continuous of the verbs in brackets.
1. Ian *will be having* his operation at this time tomorrow. (have)
2. Frank .... from the anaesthetic in about ten minutes. (come round)
3. The doctor .... his rounds at one o'clock. (do)
4. .... you .... in the surgery at six? (work)
5. The patients .... their lunch at 11. (not eat)
6. Your leg .... even more when the injection wears off. (hurt)

40.2 Complete the sentences with the correct form of the future perfect of the verbs in the box.

disappear   start   leave   recover   diagnose   ~~finish~~

1. The surgeon *will have finished* the operation by 12.
2. In three or four days, you .... completely.
3. Gemma's spots from the measles .... by next week.
4. I .... hospital by the weekend.
5. By the end of today, we hope the doctors .... Emily's strange illness.
6. .... the tablets .... to work by this evening?

40.3 Choose the correct alternative.
1. Will I **be feeling** / **have felt** better by this time next week?
2. The surgeons will **have used** / **be using** the operating theatre for two hours this afternoon.
3. The nurse will **be treating** / **have treated** his earache as soon as the surgery opens.
4. The doctor will **have examined** / **be examining** Gordon right now.
5. Will you **have taken** / **be taking** all your tablets by the weekend?
6. You'll **have felt** / **be feeling** a bit dizzy when you wake up.

40.4 Match the two parts of the sentence.

1 *d*   2 ......   3 ......   4 ......   5 ......   6 ......

1. Your symptoms will
2. Will you be
3. Olivia will be
4. I will have
5. The nurse
6. Will the pain

a. had lunch by one.
b. seeing the optician at four this afternoon?
c. have gone by tomorrow?
d. have gone in a few days.
e. having her physiotherapy at 11.
f. will be removing the plaster from my leg in an hour.

40.5 Complete the dialogue with the words in the box.

| be working   will have   won't have finished   will be eating |
~~have finished~~   be looking   have made   won't be

A: I'm so tired! I'm glad I'll (1) *have finished* my shift by six.
B: You're lucky! I'll still (2) .... at six. In fact, I (3) .... until nine this evening.
A: Yes, but you (4) .... working tomorrow, so that's not too bad.
B: That's true, but my husband's ill in bed at home, so I'll (5) .... after him tomorrow.
A: Well, let's hope he (6) .... recovered by the weekend, then you and I can go for our weekly evening out!
B: I'm sure he'll (7) .... a full recovery, and you and I (8) .... a nice pizza somewhere and having a good chat on Friday evening, as usual!

REVIEW 10

EXERCISES Units 38–40

R10.1 Choose the correct alternative.
1. I'm sure you **will be feeling** / **will have felt** better tomorrow.
2. Be quick, or the doctor's surgery **will close** / **has closed** before we get there!
3. Your cold **will have gone** / **is going** by the weekend.
4. I **will have had** / **am having** an X-ray on my ankle this afternoon.
5. Jason **will have started** / **will be starting** his therapy soon.
6. I know! **I'll be doing** / **I'll do** my exercises!
7. This time next year, Victoria **will have finished** / **is going to finish** her medical training.
8. Look at that cut! I think **you're going to need** / **you'll have needed** stitches!

R10.2 Use the words and the verbs in brackets to write sentences using the future form indicated.
1. your symptoms / in a few days (disappear – future perfect)
   Your symptoms will have disappeared in a few days.
2. the doctor / his rounds / at nine (start – present simple)
3. they / on Billie's leg (operate – *going to*)
4. your anaesthetic / by this evening (wear off – future perfect)
5. all the patients / physiotherapy / at four (have – future continuous)
6. this tablet / your headache to go (help – *will*)
7. I / to the dentist / at nine tomorrow (go – present continuous)
8. John / his therapy / soon (finish – future perfect)

R10.3 Find the mistakes and underline them. Then write the correct sentences.
1. The nurses <u>will having</u> a party at the weekend.
   The nurses will be having a party at the weekend.
2. Will the chemist having opened by ten?
3. The optician sees me at 11 tomorrow.
4. By ten tomorrow morning, Mitch will do his medical exams.
5. Mum, I think Ollie's going be sick!
6. I hope my tooth will to stop hurting very soon!

R10.4 Complete the text with the missing words.

By this time next week, Doctor Brown (1) *will* have seen more than 200 patients. He'll have found out what's wrong with them all and he will (2) .... given a lot of them prescriptions to make them better. In fact, (3) .... this time next week, some of them will already (4) .... feeling better! And then, next Saturday, Doctor Brown (5) .... be leaving for his holidays. That's good, because he'll probably (6) .... exhausted!

REVIEW 10

R10.5 Complete the sentences with the words in the box.

| is seeing | will be able | can't | will have | will | 'm going |

1 If you ......can't...... see well, go and ask an optician for an eye test.
2 The doctor .... give you an anaesthetic before the operation.
3 If you tell him what your symptoms are, he .... to diagnose the problem.
4 The nurse .... removed the plaster from my leg by the end of this afternoon.
5 Tomorrow I .... to the doctor's surgery to ask for a prescription.
6 Dad .... a heart specialist tomorrow about the pains he's had lately.

R10.6 Complete the sentences with the appropriate verb tense (present simple or *will* future).

1 The meeting ......will start...... (start) at eight o'clock, if Mr Green's plane ......arrives...... (arrive) on time.
2 If you .... (not read) this manual, you .... (not be able to write) the report.
3 When the school principal .... (arrive), I .... (tell) him about your problem with the class.
4 If the computer .... (break down) again, I .... (call) the technician.
5 When my son .... (be) 18, my husband and I .... (buy) him a second-hand car.
6 If the weather .... (be) still fine, we .... (go) to the swimming pool after work.

R10.7 Complete the sentences with the appropriate form of the future on the basis of the indications in brackets.

1 'There are no aspirins in the closet.' I ......'ll get...... (get) some from Dr Bride's office.' (immediate decision)
2 We .... (have) lunch with Mr Dawson next Friday. We .... (talk) about moving our offices to the new building in Cockrane Street. (definite plan/intention)
3 The doctors say Granny .... (recover), but it .... (take) some time. (prediction)
4 I promise, Doctor. I .... (not eat) so many sweet things this month. (promise)
5 Look at all the sweets the baby has eaten. He .... (feel) sick. (prediction based on present evidence)

D Exam preparation

D.1 PET Reading Part 5

Read the dialogue and choose the correct word (A, B, C or D) for each space.

A: How do you think things (1) ..D.. have (2) .... by the time our children are parents?
B: Well, I think there (3) .... going to be a lot of differences in their way of life.
A: Do you think things like houses and jobs (4) .... have changed?
B: I guess (5) .... all live in houses that save energy, for one thing. And I'm sure more people will (6) .... from home.
A: Do you think there will (7) .... more robots and things like that?
B: They're talking about robots (8) .... a lot more jobs next year, so I'm sure that (9) .... happen far more often in the future.
A: Hmm... it's (10) .... be an interesting time to live through!

1 **A** does   **B** going   **C** is   **(D)** will
2 **A** changing   **B** change   **C** changed   **D** changes
3 **A** is   **B** are   **C** does   **D** will
4 **A** will   **B** does   **C** going   **D** is
5 **A** we're   **B** we'll   **C** we   **D** we're going
6 **A** to work   **B** working   **C** are working **D** work
7 **A** are   **B** be   **C** is   **D** going
8 **A** doing   **B** do   **C** does   **D** going to do
9 **A** be   **B** to   **C** is   **D** will
10 **A** going   **B** to   **C** going to   **D** will be

D.2 PET Writing Part 1

Complete the second sentence so that it means the same as the first. Use no more than three words.

1 By this time tomorrow, he will be in hospital.
   By this time tomorrow, he *will have* .... gone into hospital.

2 This time next week, Rob will be having his plaster off.
   This time next week, the surgeon .... cutting Rob's plaster off.

3 Your temperature will have gone down to normal by this evening.
   You .... have a temperature by this evening.

4 Hopefully I will have qualified as a nurse by this time next year.
   Hopefully I will .... a qualification as a nurse by this time next year.

5 Laura knows we won't be visiting her today.
   Laura .... expect us to visit her today.

D.3 FCE Use of English Part 1

Read the text and decide which answer (A, B, C or D) best fits each gap.

From next month, life (1) ..C.. very different for Marshall Connaught. The first of June is the day he (2) .... his new job as stunt man. Marshall's excited, even though he knows it's (3) .... a dangerous job. He (4) .... his two years, specialist training by tonight and he (5) .... to do it without breaking any bones! Marshall knows he (6) .... nervous for a while once he starts work, but he is looking forward to it. Within a few weeks, he (7) .... to work on film sets – he could soon be the man you (8) .... flying through a window or jumping from an aeroplane! In August, he (9) .... in two advertisements, so you (10) .... definitely see him then. Marshall has chosen a risky career – but he hopes it's (11) .... challenging and interesting. One thing he can probably be sure of is that the job (12) .... be boring.

118

Exam preparation

D

1 **A** will	**B** is being	**C** is going to be	**D** is
2 **A** starts	**B** going to start	**C** will starting	**D** is start
3 **A** being	**B** is going to be	**C** will be	**D** going to be
4 **A** finish	**B** going to finish	**C** has finished	**D** will have finished
5 **A** will have managed	**B** manages	**C** is managing	**D** going to manage
6 **A** feels	**B** will feel	**C** to feel	**D** is feeling
7 **A** starting	**B** going to	**C** will have start	**D** will be starting
8 **A** going to see	**B** are seeing	**C** see	**D** have seen
9 **A** is going appear	**B** appearing	**C** is appearing	**D** will appearing
10 **A** do	**B** will	**C** are	**D** is
11 **A** going to be	**B** goes	**C** is being	**D** will have been
12 **A** not	**B** doesn't	**C** won't	**D** isn't

D.4 FCE Use of English Part 2

Read the text and think of the word or short form which best fits each gap. Use only one word in each gap.

It's time for the British to stop eating junk food and start eating more salads, fruit and vegetables. If not, Britain ⁽¹⁾......*will*............ be full of overweight people with health problems. And doctors ⁽²⁾.................................. going ⁽³⁾.................................... have more work than they can manage. Next year, doctors will ⁽⁴⁾.................................... another increase in the number of people who are too heavy. And those people will ⁽⁵⁾.................................... become ill by eating too much of the wrong food. The hospitals ⁽⁶⁾.................................... have enough beds for all the people who ⁽⁷⁾.................................... from illnesses connected with bad eating habits.

But it isn't too late to stop the bad habits. Hopefully, people ⁽⁸⁾.................................... soon realise that five portions of fruit and vegetables a day is good for them. It's a fact that we're all ⁽⁹⁾.................................... to feel healthier when we eat a better diet. And our doctors and nurses are going to feel better, too, because they ⁽¹⁰⁾.................................... going to ⁽¹¹⁾.................................... so many overweight people.

D.5 FCE Use of English Part 4

Complete the second sentence so that it has a similar meaning to the first sentence, using the word given. Do not change the word given. You must use between two and five words, including the word given.

1 It's nine now, and the lesson finishes at ten.
   HAVE
   The lesson ..*will have finished*............................ by ten.

2 Michael plans to have a party at the weekend.
   TO
   Michael is .... at the weekend.

3 My doctor's appointment is at 11 tomorrow.
   SEEING
   I .... at 11 tomorrow.

4 There are only ten minutes left until the end of visiting time.
   IN
   Visiting time .... ten minutes.

5 Marianne has had a headache for two weeks.
   SUFFERING
   Marianne .... from a headache for two weeks.

6 I hope John will do well with his new company.
   CAN
   I hope John .... successful in his new company.

UNIT 41 Imperative (Go! Don't go! Let's go!)
Form and usage

A The affirmative imperative of the second person singular and plural consists of the: base form of the verb. It is used to address one or more people, without expressing the subject.

Come with me!
Think about it!

Sometimes the imperative is reinforced by **Do**, which is placed before the verb:

Do sit down!

The negative imperative of the second person singular and plural is formed with: **Do not / Don't** + base form of verb.

Don't go on your own! It may be dangerous.

Don't touch! It's hot.

B The imperative of the second person singular and plural is used to:

- give orders and express bans / prohibitions.
  Stand up, everybody!
  Don't cross if the light is red.

- give instructions.
  Turn right at the traffic lights, then go straight on.
  Don't use a pen, use a pencil.

- make requests (in a polite way with **please** or **will you?**).
  Take this book to the library, will you?
  Lend me your bike, please!

- invite someone to do something.
  Come to my house after school!

- give advice.
  Eat more vegetables. They're good for you.

- offer something.
  Have a biscuit!

- wish someone something.
  Have a nice day! Enjoy your holiday!

C The imperative of the first person plural is formed with: **Let's** + base form of verb. **Let's** is the short form of **Let us**.
Let's start reading. Let's sing a song.

Negative form: **Let's** + **not** + base form of verb
Let's not run. We still have plenty of time.

The imperative of the first person plural is used to make proposals and suggestions.
Let's go for a walk.
Let's meet at the park at four o'clock.
Let's buy this jacket. It's cheaper than the blue one.

D There are also imperative forms for the third person, which are formed using:
Let + direct object + base form of verb

Let her finish her homework.
Let them go!

EXERCISES

Imperative – Form and usage

UNIT 41

41.1 Tick (✔) the sentences in the imperative form.
1. ☐ Did you put the dress back on the hanger?
2. ✔ Don't touch the items on display!
3. ☐ Take this to the checkout, will you?
4. ☐ I think that woman's trying to steal a book!
5. ☐ Will you buy a new dress for the party?
6. ☐ Remember to go to the bank when you're in town!
7. ☐ Let's walk to the shops.
8. ☐ Don't you think this colour suits me?
9. ☐ Don't use your credit card too often!
10. ☐ Let's not spend all our pocket money on CDs this week.

41.2 Choose the correct alternative.
1. Nathan, **gives / give** that to me!
2. Sit down and **doing / do** your work, please!
3. **Don't / Not** forget to call in on your aunt on your way to town!
4. Here... **have / have you** a chocolate!
5. Let's **to go / go** to the new music store.
6. Don't **looking / look** at me like that!
7. Take your time... **don't / aren't** choose the wrong thing!
8. Wrap this up for me, **please / will** you?

41.3 Rearrange the words and write the sentences.
1. want – him – manager – see – Tell – the – I – to – ! *Tell him I want to see the manager!*
2. for – ask – Let's – refund – a ....
3. it – Think – you – carefully – before – buy – ! ....
4. bring – to – Don't – money – your – forget – ! ....
5. stand – the – Don't – doorway – in – ! ....
6. to – Go – queue – back – of – the – the – ! ....
7. coffee – for – Let's – a – go ....
8. the – me – you – will – outside – Meet – bank, – ? ....

41.4 Match the two parts of the sentence.

1. *d*   2. ....   3. ....   4. ....   5. ....   6. ....

1. Wait for me outside the
2. Take my jacket
3. Don't forget
4. Remember to
5. Don't buy
6. Save

a. to the dry cleaner's, please!
b. your money for something nice!
c. anything that costs more than ten euros!
d. newsagent's, will you?
e. buy some bread!
f. to go to the greengrocer's!

41.5 Using *Let's*, write a suggestion for each situation in your exercise book.
1. You and Jo are out in town. Jo is thirsty.   *Let's go and have something to drink.*
2. Nobody at home feels like cooking supper.
3. You want to arrange to meet your friend somewhere in town later.
4. It's the end of term and you want to do something to celebrate.
5. Your brother wants to buy some new CDs.
6. You and your friend are at the shopping centre and you are both bored.

UNIT 42 — Infinitive *(to play, not to play, to have played)*
Form and usage

A Present infinitive: **to** + base form of verb

to be   **to go**   **play**
I want to be there on time.

Past infinitive / Perfect infinitive: **to have** + past participle

to have been   **to have gone**   **to have played**
It's better to have loved and lost than never to have loved at all.

The negative infinitive is formed by placing **not** first.

not to be	**not to have been**
not to go	**not to have gone**
not to play	**not to have played**

I hope not to wait long.
What a pity not to have seen the opening ceremony!

B The infinitive is used:

- after many verbs (**refuse, seem, decide…**) and adjectives (**easy, difficult, happy…**) (see p.126).
  He refused to see me.
  I'm happy to be here.

- to express an aim.
  He's saving money to buy a car.

- after the indefinite pronouns **something, anything, nothing, somebody…** (see p.246).
  I have nothing to wear to the party.
  Everybody needs somebody to love.

- in impersonal sentences with **It's** + noun or adjective (see p.18).
  It's time to go now.
  It's hard to understand why he behaved like that.

- in sentences with **too** + adjective / adverb or adjective / adverb + **enough**.
  It's too good to be true.
  Is it too late to apply for that job?
  He isn't old enough to vote.

- as the subject of a sentence, with a similar use to the **-ing** form.
  To err is human, to forgive divine.

C The continuous forms of the infinitive (continuous infinitive) are the following:

to be + **-ing** (for the present): **to be doing**
They seem to be working hard.

to have been + **-ing** (for the past): **to have been doing**
They seem to have been working hard.

EXERCISES

UNIT 42 — Infinitive – Form and usage

42.1 Choose the correct alternative.
1 I need **to go** / **go** to the supermarket.
2 Marcia is saving her pocket money **for** / **to** buy a new pair of jeans.
3 I don't think it's time **going** / **to go** to bed yet.
4 I'm 17! I'm old enough to **learn** / **learned** to drive.
5 Henry doesn't want **study** / **to study** in another country.
6 I'm going to the bank **getting** / **to get** some foreign currency.
7 I seem to **leave** / **have left** my purse at home. I'm sorry!
8 Richard promised **to phone** / **for phoning** when he got home.
9 You all seem to **work** / **be working** hard at the moment!
10 I'm going to the department store to **be looking** / **look** for a wedding present.

42.2 Complete the sentences with the infinitive of the verbs in the box.

| be | wash | get | wear | learn | ~~apply~~ | ask | go |

1 Dad is going ....**to apply**.... for a new job.
2 I haven't had time .... my hair yet!
3 Sam's going to France .... French.
4 I'm going .... the sales assistant if she can help me.
5 The prices here are too good .... true!
6 Have you bought something new .... to the party?
7 Come on! It's time .... home!
8 Is it difficult .... a job as a manager in a computer store?

42.3 Use the words to write sentences with the negative infinitive.
1 please, / try / be / late / for your appointment.   *Please, try not to be late for your appointment.*
2 he / hope / lose / his job / at the end of the summer.
3 please / tell / him / forget / his passport.
4 Simon / hope / fail / his driving test again.
5 I / must remember / call / Miss Lee by her first name!
6 we / hope / find / the house in a mess after the party!

42.4 Match the two parts of the sentences.

1 ..c.. 2 .... 3 .... 4 .... 5 .... 6 ....

1 It's hard to   a to Egypt next year.
2 It's great to know   b to shout at your sister like that!
3 They appear to have   c understand what you're saying!
4 It's not nice   d to spend my money on.
5 They're hoping to go   e been having a party in here!
6 I'm trying to decide what   f that you're my friend.

42.5 Complete the dialogue by filling in the gaps with the infinitive of a suitable verb.
A: Hi, Joss. Do you want (1) ....**to go**.... shopping with me?
B: Yes, I do! But, I'll have (2) .... home (3) .... my purse.
A: I've got some money with me. How much are you going (4) ....?
B: Oh, not much. But I want (5) .... the new Kate Nash CD.
A: OK, I can lend you the money for that.
B: Great! Let's go, then. This is going (6) .... fun!

UNIT 43 — -ing form (going, having gone)
Form and usage

A This verb form is usually formed using: base form of verb + **-ing**

go → **going**   jump → **jumping**   wear → **wearing**

However, the addition of **-ing** often involves particular spelling changes (see p. 38).

give → **giving**   dig → **digging**   die → **dying**   label → **labelling**

The **-ing** form has three main grammatical functions:
1 verb used as a noun
2 present participle
3 gerund

B The **-ing** form as a noun can be used:
- as the subject of a sentence.
  Surfing the Internet is my favourite pastime.
- as direct object after numerous verbs (**like, hate, enjoy**… see p.128).
  I enjoy dancing and playing tennis.
- as an indirect object after a preposition (**of, for, at, with, by**… see p.130).
  You're very good at skiing!

It is often found:
- in titles.
  Building a new Europe
  Sowing seeds for the new generations
- in signs for prohibited actions.
  No smoking
  No diving
- in compounds, often to indicate the function of something.
  a diving board → *a board for diving off*
  a shopping centre → *a centre for shopping*

C The **-ing** form as a present participle is used:
- as an adjective.
  What an exciting evening!
  Do the following exercises…

D The **-ing** form as a present participle is used:
- to talk about two simultaneous actions and with the verb **spend**.
  I sat quietly listening to the speech.
  They spent hours checking all the files.

E The **-ing** form is also used:
- with the verb **be** in the continuous form of all the tenses (present continuous, past continuous…).
  He is writing a new novel.
  They were going to the theatre when we met them.

F Past form of **-ing** form: **having** + past participle

Passive form of **-ing** form: **being** + past participle and **having been** + past participle
being done   having been done

EXERCISES

-ing form – Form and usage

UNIT 43

43.1 What grammatical function does the *-ing* form have? Write N (noun), G (gerund), A (adjective) or C (continuous form).

1 Smoking is not allowed in public places in England any more. ......**N**......
2 Sam spends a lot of time surfing the Internet. ....
3 I'm going to buy some new clothes at the weekend. ....
4 Have you seen Rhonda's shopping bag? ....
5 They sell everything you need for skiing in that shop. ....
6 Peter was paying for his computer when I saw him. ....

43.2 Complete the sentences with the *-ing* form of the verbs in the box.

| lose | go | change | build | ~~wait~~ | sell |

1 I'm fed up of ......*waiting*...... for you outside shoe shops!
2 We didn't enjoy .... shopping with Aunt Beryl.
3 Please don't shout at me for .... your purse!
4 Martin is going to make a career out of .... encyclopaedias.
5 Go and try it on in the .... room.
6 There's a lot of .... work going on in the town centre.

43.3 Match the two parts of the sentences.

1 ..*c*.. 2 .... 3 .... 4 .... 5 .... 6 ....

1 My grandma takes her shopping
2 I need to buy a new sleeping
3 You can put your vegetables on the
4 Uncle Ben's eyes aren't good, so he listens to talking
5 Let's go to the ice
6 Is there a waiting

a room in the station?
b scales to see what they're going to cost.
c trolley with her when she goes to the shops.
d bag for the camping holiday.
e rink after we've done the shopping.
f books instead of reading himself.

43.4 Complete the dialogue with the *-ing* form of the verbs in the box.

| write (x2) | tell | read | ~~do~~ | think | do |

A: Have you finished (1) ......*doing*...... your homework, Dan?
B: Yes, I have. It took me ages. I'm no good at (2) .... essays.
A: I used to be the same. My teacher suggested (3) .... more English books. She thought that might help.
B: And did it?
A: Well, yes, it did. These days, I find myself (4) .... an essay without even (5) .... about it!
B: Hey, thanks for (6) .... me that. I think I'll try (7) .... the same!

43.5 Choose the correct alternative.

Many people love (1) **go / (going)** to the shops to buy clothes, CDs and so on. But have you ever tried (2) **shopping / shop** online? Thousands of people have now started (3) **buy / buying** things online on a regular basis and they think it's great to be (4) **sitting / sit** at home (5) **do / doing** their shopping. Online shopping is perfect for people who don't want (6) **to walk / walking**, or for those of us who prefer (7) **avoiding / avoid** the crowds you find in shopping centres these days. Of course, there is a risk of (8) **to get / getting** something you don't like or (9) **ordering / to order** something that's the wrong size. But, for me, the biggest danger is, if you enjoy (10) **to spend / spending** money, it's too easy (11) **to buy / buying** things you don't need on the Internet!

125

UNIT 44 Verbs + infinitive (I want to go)

A Many verbs such as **want**, **ask**, **mean** can be followed by the infinitive.
She asked to leave the room.

NB: If the subject of the main clause is different from that in the dependant clause, we use:
| Subject + verb + object + infinitive |

I'd like my students to attend the conference.
Do you want me to help you?

Many verbs can be followed by object + infinitive, such as **tell**, **ask**, **remind**, **expect**, **invite**, **beg**.
I asked her to wait for me.
He reminded them to be punctual.

Sometimes it is possible to drop the infinitive and have just **to**, leaving the rest of the sentence implied.
Do you really want to go to the party? I don't want to. (implied: go to the party)
John's parents wanted him to go to university, but he didn't want to. (implied: go to university)

B Lots of other verbs are also followed by the infinitive:

agree	**expect**	**need**	**refuse**
arrange	**have (to)**	**offer**	**seem**
choose	**hope**	**plan**	
decide	**manage**	**promise**	

We had planned to join the safari, but in the end we decided not to.
He promised to give up smoking.

C After the verbs **explain, know, discover / find out**, we use the construction **how** + infinitive. After the verb **learn**, you can use **how** + infinitive or just the infinitive.
I know how to make this cake. I've got the recipe.
You should learn (how) to take care of your pets.

D The verbs **remember** and **forget** are usually followed by the infinitive.
Remember / Don't forget to bring your packed lunch.

NB: **Remember** is followed by the **-ing** form when it means 'to relive a memory'.
Forget is followed by the **-ing** form when it means 'to forget something that happened in the past'.
I remember being a very lively child.
I'll never forget crossing the Atlantic by ship.

E The verb **help** is usually followed by the infinitive, but can also be followed by the base form. This construction is more informal and more typical of American English.
He helped me (to) start the engine.

EXERCISES

Verbs + infinitive

UNIT 44

44.1 Rearrange the words and write the sentences.

1. receipt – to – Remember – keep – your — *Remember to keep your receipt.*
2. decided – Nancy – account – to – a – bank – open
3. to – grocer's – Mum – at – prefers – shop – local – the
4. to – Shall – you – help – carry – I – this – bag – ?
5. to – you – cash – have – pay – Do – by – ?
6. refused – assistant – help – The – sales – to – me

44.2 Complete the sentences with the correct form of the verbs in the box.

| remember | refuse | hope | not know | ~~invite~~ | expect | plan | want |

1. I think I'll ......*invite*...... Grace to come to town with us.
2. I hear they .... to build a new shopping centre on the edge of town.
3. .... not to tell anyone your PIN!
4. I didn't .... to find so many bargains in the sale!
5. The sales assistant .... to exchange the jeans for another pair.
6. I .... to have enough money to buy a digital camera soon.
7. Jason .... to study sales and marketing at college.
8. Olga .... how to write a cheque.

44.3 Match the two parts of the sentences.

1 ..*b*.. 2 .... 3 .... 4 .... 5 .... 6 ....

1. I haven't got time to
2. The bank manager offered to
3. I need to
4. David refused to
5. Do you know how to
6. My daughter has decided to

a. start collecting old coins.
b. walk round the shops with you.
c. give me a credit card if I opened an account with them.
d. use this ATM?
e. go shopping with his wife ever again!
f. change this cheque into foreign currency.

44.4 Complete the dialogue with the verbs in the box.

| to send | to see | remember to let | have to pay | ~~decided to do~~ |
| to pay bills | forget to do | to order | to arrange | |

A: I've (1) ..*decided to do*.. some of my shopping from a mail-order catalogue.
B: That's a good idea! Do you (2) .... every week or every month for the things you buy?
A: Every month... by credit card or cheque. It's easy for me (3) .... a cheque every month.
B: Yes, that's fine, as long as you don't (4) .... it!
A: Well, I could go to the bank and ask them (5) .... a payment every month out of my account.
B: Yes, all the banks can arrange (6) .... for their customers.
A: OK, I'll make an appointment (7) .... the manager.
B: Yes, do. Oh, and... (8) .... me see your catalogue some time! I might want (9) .... something.

127

UNIT 45 Verbs + -ing form / + infinitive (I started reading / to read)

The **-ing** form comes after:

A
- the verb **go**, when used to talk about sports and free-time activities, and the verb **do** to talk about domestic work. With the verb **do**, the **-ing** form is preceded by the article.

go dancing	**go shopping**	**go swimming**
do the ironing	**do the cleaning**	**do the washing-up**

B
- verbs that indicate a start, continuation and an end, and verbs that indicate 'intention' and 'try'.

begin	**give up**	**start**
continue	**go on / keep (on)**	**stop**
finish	**intend**	**try**

She finished writing the minute the bell rang.
They kept annoying me. I was really cross!

Start, **begin**, **continue** and **intend** can also be followed by the infinitive without changing the meaning of the sentence.
It started raining / to rain as soon as we left.
What do you intend doing / to do?

Stop and **try** can also be followed by the infinitive, but with a different meaning.
I stopped reading and went for a walk.
I stopped to let them cross the road.
Try using a different colour and see what it looks like.
I've tried to fly a kite many times, but I haven't been very successful!

C
- verbs that express preferences, such as:

like / enjoy	**prefer**	**can't stand**
love	**don't mind**	**hate**

I hate being late!
I can't stand shouting!
I don't mind doing the washing-up, but I prefer cooking.

Love, **like**, **hate** and **prefer** are followed by the infinitive when they are used in the conditional form (**I'd love to…, I'd like to…**).
I'd like to see you again.
I'd love to go with them!
I like to drive carefully.

D The **-ing** form also follows numerous other verbs and expressions, such as:

admit	imagine	suggest
avoid	miss	can't help
consider	postpone	it's no use / there's no point in
deny	practise	it's no good
fancy	risk	it's worth

EXERCISES

Verbs + -ing form / + infinitve

UNIT 45

45.1 Choose the correct alternative.
1 I want **taking / to take** some traveller's cheques abroad with me.
2 Do you fancy **coming / to come** to have a look round the new shopping mall?
3 Mum can't stand people **to push / pushing** in queues.
4 I'm sorry **to tell / telling** you that the store is about to close.
5 We try to go **to swim / swimming** every weekend during the summer.
6 I'd like **knowing / to know** more about savings accounts, please.
7 They hope **catching / to catch** shoplifters by having all those CCTV cameras.
8 Ron's given up **buying / to buy** *Superman* comics.
9 Now you've retired, do you miss **working / to work** at the bank?
10 I promise not **to spend / spending** all my pocket money in one go!

45.2 Match the two parts of the sentences.
1 ..b.. 2 .... 3 .... 4 .... 5 .... 6 ....

1 Do you like
2 We managed
3 I've finished
4 Would you like
5 Mum enjoyed
6 They stopped

a doing my homework, so let's go out now.
b going window shopping?
c to see my new mail-order catalogue?
d to find lots of bargains in the sales.
e shopping and went for a coffee.
f trying all the different hats on.

45.3 Complete the text with the *-ing* form or with the infinitive of the verbs in the box.

| get | open | shop | have | spend | write | give | see | buy |

I need (1) ..*to see*.. a bank manager very soon. I am leaving for university next month and I'd like (2) .... my money sorted out before I go. I am planning (3) .... what's called a deposit account and I want the bank (4) .... me a credit card. I think I'll need one when I go (5) .... I just hope I can control my (6) .... while I'm away! It's no use (7) .... lots of clothes and CDs and (8) .... no money left for food and electricity. I must remember (9) .... down what I spend every day.

45.4 Tick (✔) the correct sentences. Both sentences may be correct.
1 a As soon as we arrived at the mall, it started to rain. ✔
  b As soon as we arrived at the mall, it started raining. ✔
2 a Mum stopped pushing the shopping trolley to talk on her phone. ....
  b Mum stopped pushing the shopping trolley talking on her phone. ....
3 a I didn't agree paying for your new trainers! ....
  b I didn't agree to pay for your new trainers! ....
4 a I need to get some euros before I go to Spain. ....
  b I need getting some euros before I go to Spain. ....
5 a What do you intend to sell in your new shop? ....
  b What do you intend selling in your new shop? ....
6 a I've given up trying to find trendy clothes in this shop! ....
  b I've given up to try to find trendy clothes in this shop! ....
7 a I intend taking a holiday soon. ....
  b I intend to take a holiday soon. ....

UNIT 46 — Prepositions + *-ing form* (*I'm good at skiing*); *-ing* clauses (*Before / After going*)

A When a verb comes after a preposition (**about, for, at, of, to, with, like, without, besides, except…**), it is always in the *-ing* form.

What about going on a trip?
He left without saying a word.
It's like being in heaven!

B Verbs in the *-ing* form that come after a preposition are found in the following cases:
- verb or phrasal verb + preposition + *-ing* (see p.346).

accuse of	get round to	succeed in
carry on	insist on	thank sb for
feel like	look forward to	think of / about

He insisted on coming with us.
I don't feel like sleeping right now.
We're looking forward to meeting our exchange student from Australia.

C
- be + adjective + preposition + *-ing* (see p.348).

be afraid of	be good at	be tired of
be fed up with	be interested in	be used to
be fond of	be sorry for	be worried about

When I was little, I was afraid of sleeping in the dark.
I'm fed up with being picked on by those bullies!
He was sorry for behaving so badly.
I'm used to getting up early in the morning.

NB: Don't confuse **I'm used to** + *-ing* with **I used to** + base form (see p.62).
I used to get up early when I worked in London.

D
- noun + preposition + *-ing*

This is a tool for carving wood.
I had the idea of organising the party.
Is there a reason for shouting?

E The *-ing* form is also used in certain clauses (*-ing* clauses), for example:
- in time clauses, introduced by **before, after, while**, when they have the same subject as the main clause.

Before leaving, he said goodbye to everyone. (Before he left, he said…)
After playing a very hard match, they were all worn out. (After they had played…, they were…)

NB: If the subject of the main clause is different to that in the dependent clause, the *-ing* form is not used.

Before they came, we went to do some shopping.

- after the verbs of the senses **see, watch, notice, hear, feel**, when the action lasts some time.

I heard her crying.

NB: If the action does not last long, the base form is used (see p.176).
I heard him slam the door.

EXERCISES

Prepositions + -ing form; -ing clauses

UNIT 46

46.1 Complete the sentences with the correct prepositions.
1 We look forward ...._to_........ serving you again at Sampson's in the near future.
2 What .... buying a blue bag to go with those shoes?
3 We are looking forward .... seeing you again!
4 I walked out of the shop .... saying a word.
5 You're not very good .... being polite to customers, are you?
6 Harry's thinking .... opening a computer shop in town.
7 Why do you always insist .... paying with your credit card?
8 I forgive you .... dragging me round the shops for hours!

46.2 Choose the correct alternative.
1 I'm **fed / (tired)** of walking round this department store.
2 Are you **interested / good** at sorting out your old clothes?
3 Frank said he was sorry for **to waste / wasting** all his money on sweets.
4 I'm not used to **have / having** my own bank account.
5 My brother's fond **about / of** looking round computer shops.
6 He's a good manager because he isn't afraid of **to say / saying** what he thinks!
7 The kids are fed up **on / with** only getting three euros pocket money a week.
8 Do you feel **liking / like** going to the bakery for me?

46.3 Complete the sentences with the -ing form of the verbs in the box.

| rest | take | shop | pay | buy | ~~organise~~ | do | ask |

1 I'm thinking of ...*organising*..... a shopping trip to New York!
2 Can you use your mobile phone for .... pictures as well?
3 You can use your credit card for .... for flights and hotels.
4 There's a room for .... at the new shopping centre.
5 Were you worried about .... for a refund?
6 I don't like the idea of .... things online.
7 After .... for three hours, we were exhausted!
8 I'm not used to .... my banking online.

46.4 Match the two parts of the sentences.
1 _b_   2 ....   3 ....   4 ....   5 ....   6 ....

1 We watched them making   a seeing your identification before they sell you alcohol.
2 Is there a reason for   b bread in the bakery.
3 They insist on   c you being so rude to your customers?
4 I watched the cashier   d scanning my things through the checkout.
5 I'm fed up with   e becoming the most popular cake shop in town!
6 I hope your new shop succeeds in   f paying such high prices for everything.

46.5 Find the mistakes and underline them. Then write the correct sentences in your exercise book.
1 I'm looking forward <u>to wear</u> the new jeans I bought.
   I'm looking forward to wearing the new jeans I bought.
2 Look! Dad's got a new gadget for to clean the car.
3 I'm afraid we think you walked out without pay.
4 After say his goodbyes, the manager left to start his retirement.
5 I'm very fond to look at street markets.
6 I haven't got round to tidy my wardrobe yet!

REVIEW 11 EXERCISES Units 41–46

R11.1 Choose the correct alternative.
1 **To pay /(Pay)** at the cash desk over there, please.
2 **Not / Don't** write a cheque for more than you've got in your account.
3 **Call / Calling** at the supermarket and pick up some milk, will you?
4 Let's **to look / look** online for the books we need.
5 Hurry up! It's time **going / to go** to the station to get the train home.
6 Thanks for **to buy / buying** me this.
7 Oh no! I seem to **spend / have spent** all my money!
8 Do you enjoy **shopping / to shop** from a mail-order catalogue?
9 Mum's given up **looking / to look** for shoes that match her handbag.
10 I'm fed up **for / with** having to pay credit-card bills every month.

R11.2 Complete the dialogue with the correct form of the verbs in brackets.
A: Look, mum. I want (1) ...to buy... (buy) this T-shirt. What do you think?
B: Hmm ... well, I have to (2) .... (say) I don't like black much.
A: Why not? You know I love (3) .... (wear) black these days.
B: Yes, but I'm used to (4) .... (see) you in pretty clothes. And that T-shirt isn't pretty!
A: Oh, don't (5) .... (say) that, mum! I think it's really nice.
B: Well, you seem (6) .... (want) it, so buy it.
A: Great. Thanks, mum! I knew you'd (7) .... (agree) in the end.

R11.3 Complete the sentences with the correct form of the verbs in the box.

| catch | agree | find | save | look | ~~not lose~~ | open | get |

1 **Don't lose** your credit card!
2 Let's .... some fresh fruit from the greengrocer's, shall we?
3 No, I don't remember .... to buy you some new trainers!
4 The manager doesn't enjoy .... shoplifters, but it's part of his job.
5 If you want cheap clothes, go and .... in Clothes 'R' Us!
6 Sharon's not good at .... money.
7 They've had to postpone .... their new shop until next month.
8 I can't seem .... the children's clothing department.

R11.4 Complete the sentences with the *-ing* form or the infinitive of a suitable verb.
1 Would you like **to come** to town with me to help me choose some new clothes?
2 I'm not that fond of .... shopping, to be honest.
3 I can't stand .... to loud music while I'm shopping.
4 It's time you learnt .... your money instead of spending it all at once.
5 Dad refuses .... Mum shopping in the car ever again.
6 Did you remember .... your cheque book with you?
7 Do you prefer .... online or by mail-order catalogue?
8 I can't help .... about the lovely jacket I saw! I want it!

R11.5 Find the mistakes and underline them. Then write the correct sentences.
1 Don't <u>to</u> forget your change! — *Don't forget your change!*
2 We enjoy going to dance every weekend.
3 Sitting there and wait for me, please!
4 Ellen wants opening her own music store one day.
5 I think I left my bag in the change rooms.
6 Bob isn't used to be a sales assistant.

REVIEW 11

R11.6 Complete the sentences with the correct form of the verbs in brackets.
1. It's nice _to walk / walking_ round the shopping centre on a Saturday morning. (walk)
2. Take all your items to the checkout ...., please. (pay)
3. Have you got an appointment .... the bank manager? (see)
4. Make sure you keep your receipt in case you need .... it back. (bring)
5. Don't buy jeans without .... them on first. (try)
6. I watched you .... in front of that shop window for half an hour. (linger)
7. When will you get round to .... my jackets to the dry cleaner's, Mum? (take)
8. Billy, it's time .... your bedroom and pick up your clothes off the floor! (sort out)

R11.7 Tick (✔) the correct sentences and correct the ones that are wrong.
1. ✔ I'm not very good at saving, I spend all my money!
2. ☐ What about to go to the cinema tonight?
3. ☐ Even after having eaten three slices of cake, Jim was still hungry.
4. ☐ Why did you stop to paint? Your pictures were so beautiful!
5. ☐ I'm sorry, it's too late entering the competition.
6. ☐ There's no point complaining. There's nothing we can do.
7. ☐ Can you help me carrying the luggage, please?
8. ☐ I'll never forget to travel round India when I was a young child.

R11.8 Choose the correct alternative.

Yesterday, after (1) **(having)** / **to have** done my homework, I went to the new shopping centre with a couple of friends. I can spend hours (2) **wandering** / **to wander** round the shops, especially when the sales are on. There were so many bargains I couldn't decide what (3) **buying** / **to buy**. In the end, I spent £50 without even (4) **realising** / **to realise**!
When we had finished (5) **shopping** / **to shop**, instead of (6) **going** / **to go** home, we went for a hamburger. After that, I didn't even have the money for the bus home and I needed (7) **borrowing** / **to borrow** it off my mates! I should be more careful with money, because if I carry on (8) **spending** / **to spend** it like this, I risk not (9) **having** / **to have** a holiday this year!

E Exam preparation

E.1 PET Reading Part 5

Read the text and choose the correct word(s) (A, B, C or D) for each space.

I hate (1) ...B... the same thing for a long time. So last week, I gave up (2)............. in a factory because I was fed up with (3)............. so little money. Today, I started (4)............. my own business. Of course, I'm worried about not (5)............. , but if you want to control your own life, you have to risk (6)............. some money before you begin (7)............. some. I prefer (8)............. for myself. I was tired of (9)............. orders from other people, and I wanted (10)............. if I really could (11)............. my own little company. Of course, after just one day, it's too soon (12)............. if I can do it or not. But I'm looking forward to slowly (13)............. things up over the next few weeks.

1	A do	B doing	C does	D did
2	A working	B to work	C work	D worked
3	A earns	B to earn	C earning	D earn
4	A run	B runs	C to run	D ran
5	A succeeding	B success	C to succeed	D succeed
6	A lose	B to lose	C lost	D losing
7	A makes	B to make	C made	D make
8	A working	B work	C worked	D works
9	A take	B to take	C taking	D taken
10	A see	B to see	C seeing	D seen
11	A start	B starting	C to start	D started
12	A to tell	B tell	C tells	D telling
13	A build	B to build	C builds	D building

E.2 PET Writing Part 1

Complete the second sentence so that it means the same as the first. Use no more than three words.

1. I heard when she cried.
   I heard her *crying*............. .

2. I like to shop in the City Mall.
   I'm fond .... in the City Mall.

3. He said goodbye to everyone, then he left.
   Before ...., he said goodbye to everyone.

4. Can you iron these last few clothes for me, please?
   Can you finish the .... for me, please?

5. I've started playing rugby every week.
   I've started to .... rugby every week.

6. Susan forgot to take her purse with her to the shops.
   Susan didn't .... her purse with her to the shops.

E.3 PET Writing Part 3

This is part of a letter you received from an English penfriend.
Write a letter, answering your penfriend's questions (about 100 words).

> In your next letter, tell me about your favourite food and drinks. What do you enjoy eating most of all? And what kind of food do you hate eating? Do you like having snacks between your meals?

Exam preparation

E.4 FCE Use of English Part 1

Read the dialogue below and think of the word which best fits each space. Use only one in each space.

These days, I hardly seem to (1) ...*have*... any free time! I want to (2) .... dancing with my friends, but I have too much to (3) .... when I get home. I need (4) .... finish the cleaning, or wash my clothes, or… do a hundred (5) .... jobs! I'm really fed up (6) .... performing all these menial tasks, but I know that if I don't, my life will (7) .... functioning. However, I am planning (8) .... get away somewhere nice next month. I'm tired of (9) .... at home in this busy city all the time, so I'm going to (10) .... to a place I've always wanted to (11) ....: Egypt! I'm looking (12) .... to finally seeing the Pyramids and the Sphinx. It costs a lot of money, but I feel it's something that's really worth (13) ....

E.5 FCE Use of English Part 3

Read the text below. Use the word given in capitals at the end of each line to form a word that fits in the space in the same line.

Money matters

There are lots of (1) ...*wealthy*... people in the world, including	WEALTH
those who have most – the (2) .... They	MILLION
make a lot of their money through good (3)	INVEST
in companies which are on the way up. Of course, if there	
is a bad time, and the (4) .... rate is very	INFLATE
high, they lose money, but they rarely go (5) ....,	BANK
unless there is a crash on the stock market.	
I'm not one of these (6) .... rich people, but I have	EXTREME
always had enough (7) .... money in my pocket for	SPEND
the things I need. However, recently my (8)	FINANCE
affairs have become more difficult because of a series of	
late (9) .... by some of my clients. This situation	PAY
means that I need to be very (10) .... with everything	ECONOMIC
that I buy and use.	

E.6 FCE Use of English Part 4

Complete the second sentence so that is has a similar meaning to the first sentence, using the words given. Do not change the word given. You must use between two and five words, including the word given.

1 I really dislike living in this dirty city.
   STAND
   I ...*can't stand*... living in this dirty city.

2 He left and didn't say anything to me.
   WITHOUT
   He left .... anything to me.

3 When I saw her, I wanted to cry.
   FELT
   When I saw her, I ....

4 I am unable to stop myself buying new clothes.
   HELP
   I .... myself new clothes.

5 It's a great idea to raise money for charity.
   WORTH
   It's .... money for charity.

6 He gave me a kiss and then he went away.
   BEFORE
   ...., he gave me a kiss.

7 He can swim very well.
   GOOD
   He's .... swimming.

8 It's too new to throw away.
   ENOUGH
   It's .... to throw away.

135

UNIT 47 Modals: *Can / Could*
General characteristics

A Modal verbs (**can / could, may / might, must, shall / should / ought to, will / would**) have the following characteristics:
- They are followed by the base form of another verb to indicate obligation, possibility, ability, permission, etc.
- **-s** is not added to the third person singular.
- They do not have infinitives or participles.
- They do not have proper past tenses (although **could**, **would**, **should** and **might** can sometimes be used as past forms of **can**, **will**, **shall** and **may**).
- Questions and negatives are formed without the auxiliary **do**.

B **Can** is the modal verb used to express possibility and ability.

Can is the present form and **could** is the past and the conditional.

	Affirmative	**Negative**
Present	I / You / He / She / It / We / They can	I / You / He / She / It / We / They can't
Past & Conditional	I / You / He / She / It / We / They could	I / You / He / She / It / We / They couldn't

I can teach you, if you like.
She could read when she was only four.
This could be the beginning of a new story.

The full negative form is **cannot**, but this is used a lot less than the short form **can't**.
We cannot / can't go out tonight.

The full form in the past is **could not**.
They could not / couldn't tell me anything.

C

	Interrogative
Present	Can I / you / he / she / it / we / they…?
Past & Conditional	Could I / you / he / she / it / we / they…?
	Negative questions
Present	Can't I / you / he / she / it / we / they…?
Past & Conditional	Couldn't I / you / he / she / it / we / they…?

Can we start writing now?
Could you wait a couple of minutes, please?
Can't you pay a bit more attention?
Couldn't you come with me?

D

	Short answers
Present:	Yes, I can. / No, I can't.
Past & Conditional:	Yes, I could. / No, I couldn't.

'Can you ride a horse?' 'Yes, I can. / No, I can't.'

E

	Wh- questions		
Present:	What can I…?	Where can you…?	How can he…?
Past & Conditional:	What could I…?	Where could you…?	How could he…?

What can I do for you?
Where could we find a map?
How could you be so careless?

EXERCISES

Modals: *Can / Could* – General characteristics

UNIT 47

47.1 **Rearrange the words and write the sentences.**

1 well – piano – She – very – can – the – play
  She can play the piano very well.

2 party – I – tomorrow – come – your – can – to – birthday
  ....

3 Friday – the – She – finish – until – can't – work
  ....

4 could – hungry – I – eat – I'm – so – horse – a – !
  ....

5 busy – Jane's – couldn't – go – he – Mike – wedding – was – to – because
  ....

6 you – to – us – fireworks – come – Can – tonight – the – with – ?
  ....

7 to – could – the – When – prepare – they – help – decorations – ?
  ....

47.2 **Complete the answers with the appropriate form of *can / could*.**

1 Can you come to my birthday party on Saturday? Sorry, *I can't*. I'm working next weekend.
2 Can they bring some food with them tomorrow? Of course ....
3 Could Anne speak English when she was five? No, ...
4 Could he organise a party as good as Peter's? No, I don't think .... !
5 Couldn't you borrow Jim's suit for the wedding? Yes, I think .... I'll ask him.
6 Can we go to the town festival next Sunday? No, ... We're going to Sarah's wedding, don't you remember?

47.3 **Find the mistakes and underline them. Then write the correct sentences.**

1 <u>I can't to come</u> to your Christmas party next week. *I can't come*
2 Do you can ride a bicycle? ....
3 They say she cans run very fast. ....
4 Could they to go to the air show tomorrow? ....
5 We can't visit the folk dance festival yesterday. ....
6 He didn't can get to the school ball last Saturday. ....

47.4 **Match the two parts of the sentences or of the questions.**

1 *a*   2 ......   3 ......   4 ......   5 ......   6 ......

1 I can't eat any more birthday cake   a because I feel ill.
2 He's not going to the disco   b I don't understand it.
3 They couldn't meet me last night   c It's very heavy.
4 Can you help me with my maths?   d because he can't dance.
5 Could you help her carry that parcel?   e because they didn't have any flour.
6 They couldn't make the pancakes   f because the bus was late.

47.5 **Rewrite the sentences using the past tense.**

1 Tim runs fast, but he can't beat Jo. *Tim ran fast, but he couldn't beat Jo.*
2 I can't go to the garden party because it's raining. ....
3 We are asking him if he can come to the dance. ....
4 I don't play the violin, but I can play the guitar. ....
5 He says he can sing very well. ....
6 You can't play loud music there after midnight. ....

UNIT 48

Modals: *Can / Could*
Usage and alternative verbs

The modal **can / could** is used to:

A
- say that it is possible to do something.

  Yes, I'm free tomorrow, so I can come to your house.
  It's warm and sunny. We can eat outside in the garden.

B
- make a request.

  Can I / Can we / Can you…? informal
  Could I / Could we / Could you…? more formal

  Can you bring me your diary, please?
  Could we have two coffees, please?
  'Could you please call for a taxi?' 'Certainly, sir.'
  Can I have a sandwich, Mum?

C
- offer help.

  'Can I help you?' 'Yes, please. I'd like…'
  'Can I do something for you?' 'No, thanks, I'm all right.'

D
- ask permission and allow / not allow.

  'Can I invite some friends home, Mum?' 'Yes, of course you can. / Sorry, you can't. Not today.'

E
- express ability, skill.

  I can speak two languages – English and Spanish.
  I couldn't use this software, but I've learnt now.

F
- express disbelief, say that something is impossible based on the evidence.

  I can't believe that!
  She couldn't be 40. She looked much younger.

G Verbs that can substitute **can** not only in the missing tenses (infinitive, participles, etc.) but also in the present simple and past simple are:

- **be able to / be unable to**

  I'm sorry not to be able to come.
  Will you be able to get there by nine?

- **manage to**

  'Have you managed to talk to Mr Ross?' 'No, I haven't managed to talk to him yet. He's always so busy.'

- **be allowed to / be permitted to**

  You won't be permitted to come back so late.
  She wasn't allowed to bring her dog.

EXERCISES

Modals: *Can / Could* – Usage and alternative verbs

UNIT 48

48.1 **Write sentences using *can* and *could* to express possibility.**

1 Say that you are able to go to Paul's house tomorrow.
   I can go to Paul's house tomorrow.
2 Say that Steve isn't able to arrange the party room next Saturday.
   ....
3 Say that Susan was unable to finish preparing the party food last night.
   ....
4 Explain that you are unable to go dancing tomorrow because of your bad leg.
   ....
5 Say that Dan was unable to put up the Christmas tree last night because he was very tired.
   ....

48.2 **Write formal (F) or informal (I) requests using the verbs in brackets.**

1 You want a glass of orange juice. Ask your mum. (I: have)
   Can I have a glass of orange juice, Mum?
2 You want a plate of chips. Ask the waiter. (F: have)
   ....
3 You want to use your classmate's red pen. (I: borrow)
   ....
4 You need 20 euros. Your mum is out. Ask your neighbour. (F: lend)
   ....
5 You want a pizza Napoli delivered to your flat. (F: bring)
   ....

48.3 **Write what they weren't able to do in the past *(couldn't)*, but can do now *(can)*.**

1 I / ride a bike / be four — *I couldn't ride a bike when I was four, but I can now.*
2 Mike / speak English / start school — ....
3 Jane / cook / go to university — ....
4 They / play tennis / start lessons — ....
5 I / swim / go to the seaside — ....

48.4 **Rewrite the sentences by replacing *can / could* with the verb in brackets.**

1 I'm sorry I can't come to your party. I'm busy that day. (be able to)
   I'm sorry I'm not able / I won't be able to come to your party. I'm busy that day.
2 He couldn't go to the school fête last week. He had a cold. (be able to)
   ....
3 I couldn't see the exhibition. I was out of town. (manage to)
   ....
4 I couldn't park my car in front of the restaurant. It's private. (be allowed to)
   ....
5 I'm sorry, sir, but you can't smoke inside this building. (be permitted to)
   ....

48.5 **Write offers of help using *Can I…?***

1 Offer to do the shopping for your mother. — *Mum, can I do the shopping for you?*
2 Offer to carry your friend's bag. — ....
3 Offer to make your dad a cup of coffee. — ....
4 Offer to take your friend's books back to the library. — ....

UNIT 49 Modals: *May / Might*

A   **May** and **might** are modal verbs used to express possibility (not certainty) and to ask for permission.

	Affirmative	Negative
Present	I / You / He / She / It / We / They may	I / You / He / She / It / We / They may not
Conditional	I / You / He / She / It / We / They might	I / You / He / She / It / We / They might not

May does not have a short form for the negative. **Might** can have the short form **mightn't**, which is more used in spoken language.

I may work this Saturday, but I'm not sure.
You may like it or not, but that's the way it is.
I might be late tonight, I mightn't be home until 11.

	Interrogative
Present	May I…? / May we…? (only with I and we, to ask for permission)
Conditional	Might he / she / it / they…? (to ask if something could be possible)

May I use your computer?
Might your brother know my friend Janet?

B   **May** and **might** are used, in particular:

- to talk about a present or future possibility, when something isn't certain. **Might** expresses more uncertainty than **may** does.

    They may arrive any minute now.
    She may not be at home at this time.
    I might take a holiday in June.
    Take an umbrella. It might rain later on.

    Instead of **may** and **might**, it is also possible to use the adverbs **perhaps** or **maybe** and the future with **will** or the expression **it's likely**.

    Perhaps she will not be at home… / Maybe I will go to the seaside… / Perhaps it will rain…
    It's likely to snow.
    It is not likely that he will come.

- to ask, grant or refuse permission in a formal way (only **may**, not **might**).

    May I sit here?
    May I have your attention, please?
    You may go. (I'm allowing you to go – it denotes a certain authority on the part of the speaker)

    Compare with: *Can I have your attention?* and *You can go now*, which are used in a more informal way.

- to wish someone something or to express a hope.

    May you be happy!
    May your days be merry and bright…

- followed by **as well**, to suggest that someone should do something as there's nothing better to do or because there's no reason not to do it.

    I'm awake, so I might as well get up.
    Since you're here, you may as well sit down.
    He's not coming, so we might as well start without him.

EXERCISES

UNIT 49 — Modals: *May / Might*

49.1 Write sentences with *may* (possible), *may not* (unsure) or *might not* (very unsure).

1. I am unsure if my brother will arrive in time for the party.
   My brother may not arrive in time for the party.

2. It is possible that I will go to the club dinner tonight.
   I ....

3. I am very unsure if Susan will visit the Edinburgh Festival.
   Susan ....

4. I am unsure if Nadal will win Wimbledon next year.
   Nadal ....

5. It is possible that my father will have a retirement party.
   My father ....

6. I am very unsure if I will pass my maths exam.
   I ....

49.2 Rewrite the sentences with *perhaps* and *maybe*, without changing the meaning.

1. I may play football next Saturday. (perhaps)
   Perhaps I will play football next Saturday.

2. He might come with us to the New Year's Dance. (maybe)
   ....

3. Chelsea might win the Champions League. (perhaps)
   ....

4. They may invite us to their engagement party. (maybe)
   ....

5. She might go to the Easter Races without you. (perhaps)
   ....

6. We may put up the Christmas decorations tonight. (maybe)
   ....

49.3 Use *may* to ask and give the following permissions.

1. Ask Mr Brown if you can borrow his pen.
   Please may I borrow your pen, Mr Brown?

2. Ask Mrs Roberts if you can use her barbecue for your garden party.
   ....

3. Tell the guests that they can sit down now the speeches have finished.
   ....

4. Ask if you can open your birthday presents.
   ....

5. Ask Mr Smith if you can ask him a question.
   ....

REVIEW 12 EXERCISES Units 47–49

R12.1 Complete the dialogue with the correct form of *can* / *could*. Both forms may be possible.

John: Paul, what are you doing tomorrow afternoon?
Paul: Nothing. Why?
John: Because I'm going to Sarah's pool party. (1) *Can* you come with me?
Paul: I'd love to, but I'm afraid I (2) .... swim.
John: What?! You (3) .... swim at your age? I (4) .... swim when I was three years old. Why (5) .... you swim?
Paul: Well, my father (6) .... swim when I was little, so there was nobody to teach me.
John: What about at primary school?
Paul: There was no pool where I lived, so we (7) .... go.
John: Well, why don't you come to the party with me tomorrow? I (8) .... teach you.
Paul: You? (9) .... you really teach me?
John: I think so… or at least I (10) .... try!
Paul: OK then, John. I (11) .... try, too!

R12.2 Write requests with *can* (informal) and *could* (formal), depending on the situation.

1 Ask your best friend Jane to lend you her comb.
   Can you lend me your comb, please, Jane?

2 Ask a policeman to tell you what time it is.
   ....

3 Ask your mum for permission to go to Liz's party.
   ....

4 Ask your brother to help you arrange the party room.
   ....

5 Ask a teacher if it's possible for you to leave school an hour earlier today.
   ....

6 Ask a taxi driver to take you to the station.
   ....

R12.3 Complete the sentences with the correct form of *can* / *could* and of the verbs in brackets.

| ~~ride~~ | help | come | go | play | speak |

1 Danny *couldn't ride* a bicycle until he was 16.
2 .... Dave .... football with us next Sunday?
3 The girls .... to the garden party last weekend – they were ill.
4 Mike .... Spanish very well. He lived in Madrid when he was young.
5 .... you .... me with my French homework, please, Mrs Jones?
6 I'm sorry, but I .... to the dance with you tonight.

R12.4 Complete the phone conversation with the correct form of *can* / *could*.

Sandy: Hi Dick! It's Sandy. (1) *Can* you talk now?
Dick: Yes, I (2) ....
Sandy: It's about the Christmas party. Last night, when I asked Andy if he (3) .... help me put up the decorations, he said he (4) .... come at the weekend, but that he (5) .... come on Monday. That's great, because if we finished putting them up on Monday, you (6) .... come over and help me move the furniture on Tuesday.
Dick: I'm afraid I (7) .... come on Tuesday because it's the only time my parents (8) .... visit me before Christmas. But if you still needed me, I (9) .... help all day on Wednesday.

REVIEW 12

R12.5 Complete the sentences with the correct form of *(not) be allowed to* or *(not) be able to*.
1. In most countries in the world, you ......*are allowed to*...... vote when you are 18.
2. In the near future, we .... produce energy from ocean waves.
3. In the UK, you .... marry at 16 only with parental consent.
4. In the next few decades, we .... combine all sources of information into a gigantic global system.
5. In Italy, you .... buy cigarettes under the age of 16.
6. Soon we .... walk to the North Pole because the Arctic ice cap is already melting.

R12.6 Rewrite the sentences with *may* or *might* without changing the meaning.
1. Maybe I'll go to the beach party tomorrow.
   I may go to the beach party tomorrow.
2. Perhaps I'll go to the Lord Mayor's Parade on Saturday.
   ....
3. Maybe my dad will give me the money I need.
   ....
4. Perhaps they won't be able to find the way to the Festival.
   ....
5. Maybe she'll marry Paul after all.
   ....
6. Perhaps we'll finish the firework display before it rains.
   ....

R12.7 Write requests or orders using *may*.
1. Ask if you can leave the room for a minute.
   May I leave the room for a minute, please?
2. Ask if you can have another piece of Christmas cake.
   ....
3. Tell them they can go home when they've decorated the room.
   ....
4. Tell them they are not allowed to open their presents yet.
   ....
5. Ask if you can clean the party room now.
   ....
6. Ask if you can sit next to Suzanne at dinner.
   ....

UNIT 50 Modals: *Must*

A **Must** is the modal verb used to express obligation and necessity.

Affirmative	Negative
I / You / He / She / It / We / They must	I / You / He / She / It / We / They must not I / You / He / She / It / We / They mustn't

The fridge is empty. We must buy some food.
You mustn't tell anyone. It's a secret.

Interrogative
Must I / you / he / she / it / we / they…?

Questions with **must** can be used in an emphatic way to express annoyance or reluctance to do something.

Must they keep talking?
Must I really get up at five?

B **Must** is used, in particular, to:
- express an obligation imposed by the speaker (**You must…**) or felt personally as a duty (**I must…**).
  You must tidy your room, it's a real mess.
  I know I must tell the truth.
- give advice, strongly recommend something.
  You must read this book. It's such a gripping story.
  You must visit the Louvre when you're in Paris.
- say that something is forbidden or to strongly advise someone against doing something.
  You mustn't copy during the test.
  You mustn't behave like that!
- make a logical assumption or deduction based on:
  – present facts: **must** + base form
  It must be quite late. (I can see it's getting dark)
  They must be American. (I can tell by their accent)

  – on past fact: **must** + **have** + past participle
  Your grandparents must have been very rich. (they left you a lot of money)
  It must have been a very hard exam. (not many students passed it)

C The use of a different modal changes the level of certainty. Compare what someone says whilst looking for something they've lost:

It must be here! (I'm sure it's here)
It should be here. (It's likely to be here)
It may / might be here. (Perhaps it's here)
It can't be here! (I'm sure it's not here)

EXERCISES

Modals: *Must*

UNIT 50

50.1 Write the rules by completing them with *You must* (+) or *You must not* (–).
1 drive on the left in Britain. (+) — *You must drive on the left in Britain.*
2 cross the road at the zebra crossing (+) ....
3 walk on the grass (–) ....
4 smoke inside the restaurant (–) ....
5 wear a seat belt when you drive (+) ....
6 go out without your identity card (–) ....

50.2 Complete the sentences that express personal obligations. Use *must* or *must not*.
1 We ......*must*...... buy some milk on the way home.
2 You .... forget to buy a birthday card for Dad.
3 He .... be late for the concert tonight.
4 They .... win this match to stay in League 1.
5 I .... ask Paul where he keeps the keys.
6 She .... know about the party we're preparing. It's going to be a surprise party.

50.3 React to your parents' statements expressing reluctance. Use *Must…?*
1 'You're going to Grandad's with us on Sunday.' — *'Must I go to Grandad's with you on Sunday?'*
2 'Sue's coming in the car with us.' ....
3 'We're all watching *The Lion King* tonight.' ....
4 'Jimmy's playing football with us.' ....
5 'Aunt Jane's taking you to the seaside.' ....
6 'Jack's finishing his maths before he can play.' ....

50.4 Write recommendations or deductions using *must* or *mustn't*.
1 Advise someone to listen to the new Arctic Monkeys CD.
   You must listen to the new Arctic Monkeys CD.
2 Make a deduction about a woman: she's a security guard – she's watching everyone carefully.
   She must be a security guard because she's watching everyone carefully.
3 Advise someone to go to the next Chelsea match with you.
   You ....
4 Make a deduction about the time: you're hungry (you haven't eaten since breakfast)
   ....
5 Advise someone not to park their car here because it's private.
   ....
6 Make a deduction about a man: he looks very much like the boy who's with him
   ....

50.5 Complete the deductions with the past tense.
1 He has stopped competing at 25. He ......*must have been*...... very young when he won gold in the Olympics.
2 They're still together. She .... his partner for at least ten years.
3 Climbing that peak .... very hard. You look exhausted.
4 They .... a lot of money in the bank to buy that mansion.
5 They're already here. They .... very early this morning.
6 Your ring looks very expensive. It .... at least £800.

UNIT 51: Have to / Have got to; Be to; Mustn't / Don't have to

A **Have to** and **have got to** can be used instead of the modal **must** to express obligation or necessity in the present tense. For other tenses, see Unit 52.
We have to do something. / We have got to do something. / We must do something.

Affirmative	Negative
I / You / We / They have (got) to	I / You / We / They don't have to
He / She / It has (got) to	He / She / It doesn't have to

The short affirmative form is only used with **have got**: **I've got to, You've got to, He's got to**, etc. In colloquial American, it is also possible to use the contraction: **I gotta, You gotta, He gotta**, etc.
I've got to go now. → *I gotta go now.*

Interrogative *(have to)*	Interrogative *(have got to)*
Do I / you / we / they have to…?	Have I / you / we / they got to…?
Does he / she / it have to…?	Has he / she / it got to…?

The interrogative form for the first person singular (**Do I have to…?**) can have the same meaning as **must** (see p.144).
Do I have to learn all this by heart?

B **Have (got) to** in the affirmative form is usually used to express:
- duties or rules.
  I have to get up at 6.30 every morning.
- external obligations (e.g. from laws, regulations and other people's orders)
  You have to pay in advance.

Compare: *I have to read three novels before the end of the term.*
(it's an assignment that the teacher has given me)
I must read this novel. (it's me who has decided)

C To express orders or instructions, the structure **be** + infinitive can be used.
Each candidate is to show a document of identity.
The contract is to be signed on each page.

Be + infinitive can also be used to talk about plans. This construction is often found in newspapers.
The president is to arrive in Nairobi tomorrow.

D NB: The negative form **don't / doesn't have to** does *not* have the same meaning as **mustn't**.
- **Mustn't** indicates that something is forbidden.
  You mustn't put any sharp objects in your hand luggage.
- **Don't have to** indicates the absence of necessity. It has the same meaning as **don't need to** (see p.148).
  You don't have to tell me if you don't want to.
  I have to be at school by 8.30, but I live nearby, so I don't have to leave home till 8.15.

Compare: *You don't have to run.* (there's still time)
You mustn't run. (it's forbidden, e.g. in a walking race)

EXERCISES

Have to / Have got to; Be to; Mustn't / Don't have to

UNIT 51

51.1 Write sentences with the correct form of *have to*, affirmative (+) or negative (–).

1 I / + / take / the dog for a walk every night.
   I have to take the dog for a walk every night.

2 She / + / feed / her pet rabbit every morning.
   ....

3 We / – / go to school tomorrow because it's a holiday.
   ....

4 He / – / be there until four o'clock.
   ....

5 You / + / tidy your room before you go out.
   ....

6 They / – / finish their homework now; they can do it later.
   ....

51.2 Write questions with *have got to* (A) or *have to* (B).

1 (A) I / clean the car? *Have I got to clean the car?*
2 (A) she / come to our party? ....
3 (B) he / go to the police station? ....
4 (A) we / study the American penal system? ....
5 (B) you / visit them tonight? ....
6 (A) they / stay with us all week? ....

51.3 Tick (✔) the correct sentences.

1 a ✔ Notice: Deep water. You must not swim here.
   b ☐ Notice: Deep water. You don't have to swim here.

2 a ☐ Mother: You mustn't get up early tomorrow. There's no school.
   b ☐ Mother: You don't have to get up early tomorrow. There's no school.

3 a ☐ Teacher: You mustn't run in the corridors. It's dangerous.
   b ☐ Teacher: You don't have to run in the corridors. It's dangerous.

4 a ☐ Policeman: You mustn't drive so fast. It's a 50km-per-hour zone.
   b ☐ Policeman: You don't have to drive so fast. It's a 50km-per-hour zone.

5 a ☐ Classmate: You mustn't give in your essay until Friday. There's lots of time.
   b ☐ Classmate: You don't have to give in your essay until Friday. There's lots of time.

6 a ☐ Judge: I'm banning you from driving for 12 months. You mustn't drink and drive again.
   b ☐ Judge: I'm banning you from driving for 12 months. You don't have to drink and drive again.

51.4 Decide whether the following obligations are yours (*personal*) or are imposed by others (*external*).

1 That new Stephen King novel looks great. I must buy it. *personal*
2 I must buy some new trainers – these ones are worn out. ....
3 I have to complete my project by Christmas or the teacher will be angry. ....
4 I must try that new dark chocolate Magnum. I bet it tastes lovely! ....
5 I mustn't get my white trousers dirty or I'll look a mess. ....
6 I've got to get there on time or the team trainer will be mad at me. ....
7 We can't go out. No one is to leave the room during the test. ....
8 You're to go to the police station immediately. ....

147

UNIT 52 — Need to / Need + -ing; Had to / Will have to; Be obliged / Be compelled

A Besides **must** and **have to**, it is also possible to use the verb **need** to express necessity in the present. In the affirmative form **need** acts as an ordinary verb, not a modal.

You need to have your own car. The firm doesn't provide one.
He needs to be there right on time. (note the **-s** on the third person singular)

B The verb **need** need has two negative forms. One is like that of an ordinary verb and the other is like that of modal.

> I don't need to / You don't need to / He doesn't need to…
> I needn't / You needn't / He needn't…

Either form can be used. NB: If used like a modal, **need** is followed by the base form of the verb.

In the negative form, **need** indicates the absence of necessity, like **don't have to** (see p.146).

You don't need to buy all that food. There's going to be only eight of us at the party.
She needn't leave so early. It only takes an hour to get there.

C Even in questions, **need** can be used as both an ordinary verb and a modal.

> Do I need to / Do you need to / Does he need to…?
> Need I / Need you / Need he…? (this form is not as common)

Do I need to reserve a seat? / Need I reserve a seat?

D The verb **need** can also be followed by the **-ing** form when it is in the passive (something has to be done).

My bike needs to be repaired. → My bike needs repairing.
Your room needs to be cleaned. → Your room needs cleaning.

E To indicate obligation and necessity in tenses other than the present, we usually use the verb **have to**.

> **Past simple**
> Affirmative: I had to   Negative: I didn't have to   Interrogative: Did I have to…?

I had to work hard to pass my exam.
He didn't have to wait long. His friends were there in five minutes.
Did you have to wear a uniform when you were in primary school?

> **Future with *will***
> Affirmative: I will / I'll have to   Negative: I will not / I won't have to   Interrogative: Will I have to…?

We'll have to make our own costumes for the play.
You won't have to work on Saturdays.
'Will I have to book in advance?' 'No, you don't need to.'

F **Be obliged to / be compelled to / be forced to** can be used instead of **must** and **have to**. They make the obligation stronger and they can be used in all tenses.

They were obliged / forced to leave their country because of political persecution.
(stronger than: They had to leave…)

If he's proved to be guilty, he will be compelled to resign from office.

EXERCISES

Need to / Need + -ing; Had to / Will have to; Be obliged / Be compelled

UNIT 52

52.1 Complete the sentences with the correct form of *need to* (+) or *not need to* (–).
1 They (–) *don't need to* bring their dictionaries to school today.
2 On Wednesday morning, I (+) .... go to the bank.
3 She doesn't look well. I think she (+) .... see the doctor.
4 We've got enough players, so he (–) .... come.
5 My father says I (+) .... drive more carefully.
6 You (–) .... say anything to the police until your lawyer arrives.

52.2 Write the alternative negative form (*needn't / not need to*) of the underlined expressions.
1 I <u>needn't go</u> to school tomorrow. *don't need to go*
2 We <u>needn't visit</u> our grandparents on Sunday.
3 He <u>needn't come</u> with us.
4 They <u>don't need to finish</u> it now.
5 You <u>don't need to pay</u> for me as well.
6 She <u>needn't worry</u> about being late.

52.3 Complete the questions with *Do / Does… need to…?* (A) or *Need…?* (B).
1 (A) *Do* I *need to* get to the court early tomorrow?
2 (A) .... you .... speak to your lawyer again?
3 (B) .... they make so much noise when they come in?
4 (B) .... she tell everybody about the robbery?
5 (A) .... he .... ask the witnesses any more questions?
6 (B) .... the judge give her such a long prison sentence?

52.4 Complete the second sentence using the correct tense of *have to*.
1 Present: I need to study hard for my exams.
  Past simple: Last year, *I had to study hard for my exams.*
2 Present: She needs to train twice a week to stay in the team.
  Past simple: Last term, ...
3 Present: We need to prepare everything for the party ourselves.
  Future: We ....
4 Present: Does she need to bring her guitar to the party?
  Future: ....
5 Present: Do you have to go to school on Saturdays?
  Past simple: When you were a boy, ... ?

52.5 Rearrange the words and write the sentences.
1 telephone – I – Jim – evening – need – this – to
  I need to telephone Jim this evening.
2 think – now – I – pay – you – need – for – don't – it – to
  ....
3 day – go – He – to – didn't – every – there – have
  ....
4 schools – regulations – will – to – All – be – enforce – new – the – obliged
  ....
5 kitchen – tidying – needs – The
  ....
6 needn't – about – worry – You – me
  ....

149

REVIEW 13 EXERCISES Units 50–52

R13.1 Complete the sentences with the correct forms of *must* (+), *mustn't* (–) and *not have to* (–).

1. Now everyone (+) ....*must*.... wear a seat belt when they drive, but when I was young, you (–) *didn't have to* wear one.
2. You (+) .... wear a swimming cap in the pool, and you (–) .... get into the water until the instructor comes.
3. The children (+) .... go to school from Monday to Friday, but they (–) .... go on Saturday and Sunday.
4. Paul, you (–) .... smoke inside the restaurant! And you really (+) .... give up smoking altogether!
5. Cyclists (+) .... wear a helmet at all times, and they (–) .... ride without holding the handlebars with at least one hand.
6. When you're in court, you (+) .... tell the truth, and you (–) .... speak unless you are asked a question.

R13.2 Rewrite the sentences with the correct form of *have got to*.

1. Must I go to my piano lesson tonight?
   Have I got to go to my piano lesson tonight?
2. Must they come to the station with us?
   ....
3. Must you leave your books all over the floor?
   ....
4. Must she work so late at night?
   ....
5. Must we finish the project by Friday?
   ....
6. Must he keep playing that computer game?
   ....

R13.3 Find the mistakes and underline them. Then write the correct sentences.

1. I <u>don't have go</u> there tomorrow.
   I don't have to go there tomorrow.
2. You mustn't to drive so fast on this road.
   ....
3. They didn't must come here until later.
   ....
4. Do I must tidy my bedroom now?
   ....
5. Does he has to work on Friday?
   ....
6. They haven't to buy them now.
   ....

R13.4 Write five true sentences about you using the verbs in brackets.

1. (must) *I must finish my history essay by Friday.*
2. (need to) ....
3. (not have to) ....
4. (will have to) ....
5. (mustn't) ....

REVIEW 13

R13.5 Two colleagues are talking in the office. Complete the dialogue with *must*, *mustn't*, *have* or *need*. NB: At times, both *have* and *need* are possible.

Larry: Do you (1) ...have... to go to London again on Monday?
Sally: No, I (2) .... to relax a bit, so I'm taking Monday off. But the boss wants me to go to Paris on Friday, so I (3) .... prepare for that.
Larry: I've done all the photocopies. Do you need any more help?
Sally: No, it's OK, thanks. I've got enough information. All I (4) .... to do now is to go to the bank and get some euros. And I (5) .... forget to take my passport. Oh, and I also (6) .... to sign some documents before I go.
Larry: Well, I (7) .... go now. Is there anything more you (8) .... to tell me about the Paris project?
Sally: I don't think so, Larry. You don't (9) .... to worry about it any more.
Larry: That's good news! I'll go, then, because I (10) .... to make a few phone calls.

R13.6 Match the sentences to the appropriate comments.

1 ..b.. 2 .... 3 .... 4 .... 5 .... 6 ....

1 You mustn't run in the corridor.
2 Your hair is very long.
3 You don't need to finish that now.
4 Must I go to the theatre with Aunt Mary?
5 Can I talk to you for a minute, please?
6 This music is terrible!

a No, I'm afraid I have to go home now.
b Sorry. I'm late for a class.
c Yes. It will make her very happy.
d Yes, it needs cutting.
e It must be The Skeletons. I can't stand them either.
f It's OK – it'll only take a few minutes.

R13.7 Tick (✔) the correct sentences and correct the ones that are wrong.

1 ☐ When I was young, I have to wear a school uniform.
   When I was young, I had to wear a school uniform.

2 ☐ We needn't get the train last night. Mum gave us a lift.
   ....

3 ☐ You mustn't run, Jane. The train's already left!
   ....

4 ☐ What a beautiful ring! It must have been very expensive.
   ....

5 ☐ You don't have to use your mobile phone during the flight.
   ....

6 ☐ We won't need to cook tonight. We're invited to Joe's for dinner.
   ....

UNIT 53: Modals: *Shall / Should*

Shall and **should** are modal verbs that are usually used to ask and give instructions, advice and suggestions.

A

Shall is used in questions with the first person singular and plural.

Shall I / Shall we + base form of verb

It is used to:

- ask what needs doing, ask for instructions.

  'Shall I take a bus?' 'Yes, a number 32.'
  'What shall I buy?' 'Get some cheese.'

- offer to do something that we think may be useful / helpful.

  'Are you cold? Shall I get you a pullover?' 'No, thanks. I'm all right.'
  'Shall I close the door?' 'Yes, please do.'

- make suggestions.

  'Where shall we go tonight?' 'Let's go to the pub.'
  'What time shall we meet?' 'Let's meet at three o'clock.'
  'Shall we meet at the bus station?' 'All right.'

In the previous examples, it is also possible to use **should**. This use is more common in spoken American English.

Should I take a bus? / What should I buy? / Should I close the door? / Where should we go tonight?

B

Should (all forms).

Affirmative	Negative
I / You / He / She / It / We / They / Should	I / You / He / She / It / We / They should not (shouldn't)
Interrogative	**Negative questions**
Should I / you / he / she / it / we / they…?	Shouldn't I / you / he / she / it / we / they…?

It is used to:

- give or ask for advice.

  You should arrive earlier tomorrow if you want to get a better seat.
  You shouldn't drink alcohol. It's bad for your health.
  'Should I go for it?' 'Yes, I think you should.'

- say what you believe is the right thing to do.

  We should recycle glass and paper and we shouldn't waste water or electricity.

- make an assumption, i.e. say that something is probable based on the evidence (see p.144C).

  He left a long time ago. He should be there by now.
  Look at the map. It shouldn't be far.

In formal British English, **should** can also be used in **that**- clauses after the following verbs: **advise**, **insist**, **propose**, **recommend**, **suggest** and a few others.

They insisted (that) I should have dinner with them.
I suggest (that) we should cook something light.

EXERCISES

Modals: *Shall / Should*

UNIT 53

53.1 Change the sentences into questions to ask for instructions or to offer to do something. Use *Shall I / we…?*

1. I'll take my umbrella when I go to school. — *Shall I take my umbrella when I go to school?*
2. I'll catch the bus if they clear the snow. — ....
3. We'll come if it doesn't rain. — ....
4. I'll buy some winter clothes tomorrow. — ....
5. We'll go to the beach if the weather changes. — ....
6. I'll bring you some boots for when it snows. — ....

53.2 Read the answers and write questions with *shall*. Use *I* or *we* and the words in the box.

| Where | When | ~~What~~ | Which | How | Who |

1. (I) *What shall I bring to the party?*
   You can bring some juice and biscuits to the party.
2. (we) ....
   You can get there at three o'clock.
3. (I) ....
   Wear the woollen coat, not the raincoat.
4. (we) ....
   You can take the 29 bus to get to my house.
5. (I) ....
   You can ask Peter to go to the dance with you.
6. (we) ....
   You can meet me in front of the cinema.

53.3 Rearrange the words and write questions with *should*.

1. I – party – wear – to – What – the – should – ?
   What should I wear to the party?
2. we – problem – When – about – the – tell – should – him – ?
   ....
3. us – we – our – bring – clothes – with – sports – Should – ?
   ....
4. when – What – say – I – I – him – meet – should – ?
   ....
5. the – lend – ask – Should – her – I – money – to – me – ?
   ....
6. you – we – for – wait – if – Where – rains – should – it – ?
   ....

53.4 Write recommendations and assumptions with *should / shouldn't*.

1. Mick / smoke (advice) *You shouldn't smoke, Mick.*
2. Linda / get to work late (advice) ....
3. Jimmy / take more exercise (advice) ....
4. Don left for London at six o'clock. It's nine o'clock now. The journey takes two hours. (supposition) Don *should be in London by now.*
5. There was ice on the road this morning and it was difficult to drive. The ice has melted now. (supposition) Driving ....
6. There was no snow on the slopes. It's snowed for three days. You think you can go skiing now. (supposition) The slopes ....

UNIT 54 — Had better; Ought to; Be due; Be bound to

A As an alternative to **should** to give advice and make recommendations, the verb form **had better** can be used. It is the same for all persons.

Affirmative: Subject + **had ('d) better** + base form of verb

You had better start now.
We'd better hurry or we'll be late.

Negative: Subject + **had ('d) better not** + base form of verb

You had better not say a word.
You'd better not worry. I'll take care of that.

B Another verb form that can be used instead of **should** is the modal **ought to.** It has only this form and the negative form **ought not to** (short form: **oughtn't to**). The usage and meanings are identical to **should**.

You ought to eat more fruit and vegetables.
(advice)
We ought to save some money for our next trip.
(suggestion)
They've been working all day. They ought to be tired.
(assumption)
You oughtn't to get too close to the animals' cages. It might be dangerous.
(recommendation)

C The expression **be due** is used when something is expected to take place at a set time, for example arrival times of trains or other means of transport.

The train from Newcastle is due (to arrive) in half an hour.
The flight from Berlin is due (to land) at 6.55.
'When is her baby due?'
'I think it's due in a couple of weeks.'

D The expression **be bound to** is used when something is considered inevitable.

He's bound to get a pay rise. → *He's sure / certain to get a pay rise.*
You're bound to know the answer. I've told you a hundred times!
He's such a clever boy. He's bound to have a great career.

EXERCISES

Had better; Ought to; Be due; Be bound to

UNIT 54

54.1. Rewrite recommendations using *had better* (HB+) and *ought to* (OT+).

1. You should tidy your room.
   (OT+) You ought to tidy your room.
2. He should work harder.
   (HB+) ....
3. She should be more careful.
   (HB+) ....
4. They should finish the work quickly or the boss will tell them off.
   (OT+) ....
5. You should ask someone to help you or you'll never be able to hand in your project in time.
   (HB+) ....
6. We should go and see this film tomorrow.
   (OT+) ....

54.2 Use the words to write recommendations in the negative form using *had better not* (HB–) and *ought not to* (OT–).

1. you / eat so many chips
   (OT–) You ought not to eat so many chips.
2. he / go out in this thunderstorm
   (OT–) ....
3. you / use your car so much in town
   (HB–) ....
4. she / stay out so late at night
   (OT–) ....
5. we / speak to them until we decide
   (HB–) ....

54.3 Rewrite the sentences by replacing *should* with the correct form of *be bound to* or *be due*.

1. He's such a good runner he should win the race.
   He's such a good runner, he's bound to win the race.
2. Lucy's very intelligent; she should pass all her exams.
   ....
3. Jeremy's flight should land at four o'clock.
   ....
4. The train should be here in five minutes.
   ....
5. Manchester United is such a strong team that it should win the cup again this year.
   ....

54.4 Complete the sentences with the verbs in the box.

| oughtn't   due   ~~had better~~   had better   bound |

1. You ...had better... take your umbrella – it's going to rain.
2. Peter's bus isn't .... for another ten minutes.
3. Eric's .... to win the race – he's much faster than the others.
4. They .... to worry about problems before they happen.
5. You .... not go home until the snow stops falling.

UNIT 55 Modals: *Will / Would*

A **Will** and **would** are modal verbs that are usually used to express willingness. **Will** is also used to express the future (see p.102) and **would** to express the conditional (see p.318).

Affirmative	Negative
I / You / He / She / It / We / They will	I / You / He / She / It / We / They will not (won't)
I / You / He / She / It / We / They would	I / You / He / She / It / We / They would not (wouldn't)

Interrogative	Negative questions
Will I / you / he / she / it / we / they…?	Won't I / you / he / she / it / we / they…?
Would I / you / he / she / it / we / they…?	Wouldn't I / you / he / she / it / we / they…?

Short answers	
Yes, I / you / he / she / it / we / they will.	No, I / you / he / she / it / we / they won't.
Yes, I / you / he / she / it / we / they would.	No, I / you / he / she / it / we / they wouldn't.

B **Will** and **Would** (more formal) are used in questions in the second person to:

- invite someone to do something.

  'Will / Would you dance with me?' 'No, thanks.'
  'Will you go to the cinema?' 'Sure. We'd love to.'

- offer something (followed by **have**).

  'Will you have some sweets?' 'Yes, please. / No, thanks.'
  'What will you have with your tea? Biscuits or cake?' 'I'll have some cake, please.'

- make a request.

  Will you read the instructions aloud, please?
  Would you show me your passport, please?

C **Will** (present) and **would** (past) are also used to:

- express a firm intention or promise.

  'Will you marry me, darling?' 'Yes, I will!'
  I will always be at your side.

- criticise people's typical behaviour.

  They will have their own way. They just won't change their minds.
  He just wouldn't listen to me.

D **Would** is also used to express habits in the past. Its use is similar to that of **used to** (see p.62).

When I lived in Galway, I would go for a swim in the ocean every day of the year, in any weather!
He would always arrive late for classes.
My classmate would always copy my homework.

EXERCISES

Modals: Will / Would

UNIT 55

55.1 Write sentences to invite your friends to do the following things with you. Use *Will...?*
1. Steve / go / the theatre — Will you go to the theatre with me, Steve?
2. Judy / visit / the art exhibition
3. Danny / watch / the football match
4. Helen / eat / the Indian restaurant
5. Bill / come / firework display
6. Avril / fly / to Sardinia

55.2 Write formal requests. Use *Would...?*
1. show / ticket — Would you show me your ticket, please?
2. give / credit card
3. wait in the queue
4. open / suitcase
5. fasten / seat belt
6. sign / at the bottom of the form

55.3 Complete the second sentence to say that it was also a habit in the past. Use *would*.
1. He always gets up late.
   As a boy, he would always get up late, too.
2. She often falls asleep when she is reading.
   As a girl,
3. He is always ready to help other people.
   As a boy,
4. She never locks the door when she leaves the house.
   As a girl, ..., either.
5. He buys a newspaper every day.
   As a young man,
6. They sometimes cook a meal for the whole family.
   As girls,

55.4 Complete the dialogues with *Will* (I= informal) or *Would* (F= formal), the verb in brackets and *please* or *thank you*.
1. A: Would you like (like) a piece of chocolate? (F)
   B: Yes, ... I love chocolate.
2. A: .... (have) some more cake? (I)
   B: No, ...
3. A: What .... (like) to eat with your tea? (F)
   B: I'd like a biscuit, ...
4. A: What sort of tea .... (have)? (I)
   B: Can I have Earl Grey, ... ?

UNIT 56 — Would like to; Want to; Would prefer to / Would rather

A **Would** is often followed by the verb **like**. It is a conditional form that expresses willingness, wishes, etc.

Affirmative	Negative
I / You / He / She / It / We / They would like / 'd like	I / You / He / She / It / We / They would not like / wouldn't like

Interrogative	Negative questions
Would I / you / he / she / it / we / they like…?	Wouldn't I / you / he / she / it / we / they like…?

Short answers: Yes, / No, + subject pronoun + **would / wouldn't**.

Would like can be followed by a verb in the infinitive or a noun.
I would like to have another chance.
Wouldn't you like a sandwich?

Would like is used to:

- offer something (in the interrogative form).
  'Would you like something to eat?' 'No, thanks, I wouldn't.'
  'What would you like to drink?' 'Some fruit juice, please.'

  Compare the use of **Will you have…? / Would you have…?** (p.156).
  'I'd like to see those shoes, please.' 'Sure.'
  'We'd like two coffees, please.' 'Here you are.'

B In more informal situations, the regular verb **want** is used. Like **would like**, this can be followed by a verb in the infinitive or a noun.
He wants to play with you.
Do you want a cup of tea, Mum?

In spoken American, **want to → wanna**: *I wanna go home.*

C To say that you want someone to do something, the following construction is used:

I want / would like someone to do something   not: I would like that someone does something
(see p.126).
We'd like our son to become an engineer.
I'd like you to give me another chance.
He wanted me to help him, but I couldn't.

D To express preference, we use the constructions:

I would prefer to / I'd prefer to + base form of verb
I would rather / I'd rather + base form of verb (+ **than…**)

I'd prefer to go / I would rather go to the sea than to the mountains.
I'd rather walk than cycle.
She would rather stay here a bit longer than go back home right now.

EXERCISES

Would like to; Want to; Would prefer to / Would rather

UNIT 56

56.1 Use the words to write sentences with *would like (to)*.
1. I / a pineapple milkshake — I would like a pineapple milkshake.
2. She / go skiing on Saturday
3. They / roast chicken for lunch
4. We / play tennis tomorrow
5. I / visit Spain next summer
6. He / some ham sandwiches

56.2 Complete the questions with *would like to* and one verb from the box.

eat	stay	pay	meet	buy	know

1. Where ...would... you ...like to eat... this evening?
2. Who .... he .... at the party?
3. When .... they .... at our house?
4. Why .... she .... about me?
5. Which ring .... you .... for your girlfriend?
6. How .... they .... for their meal?

56.3 Someone else will do these things. Rewrite the sentences with *would like* and the suggestions given.
1. I'd like a new bike. (Dad / give)
   I 'd like Dad to give me a new bike.
2. She wants pancakes with her tea. (Mum / make)
   She ....
3. I'd like an umbrella. (someone / lend)
   I ....
4. Jane wants a beach party. (her friends / organise)
   Jane ....
5. They want a holiday in Greece. (their parents / book)
   They ....
6. We'd like a grant to study abroad. (the university / give)
   We ....

56.4 Rewrite the sentences with *would rather* or *would prefer to*.
1. I would rather go to the cinema tonight.
   I would prefer to go to the cinema tonight.
2. He would rather stay at home on Saturday.

3. Erin would prefer to eat fish than meat.

4. My brother would rather go to France for his holidays.

5. Alan would prefer not to play rugby tomorrow.

6. Denise would rather wear her red dress to the party.

REVIEW 14

EXERCISES Units 53–56

R14.1 Write the questions with *shall I ...?*

1 Ask what time to meet your friend at the leisure centre.
   What time shall I meet you at the leisure centre?

2 Ask what to wear to the fancy-dress party.
   ....

3 Offer to help your friends with the preparations.
   ....

4 Ask if you should turn right at the traffic lights.
   ....

5 Offer to go to the supermarket for your mum.
   ....

6 Ask where to hang your coat.
   ....

R14.2 Write what we should and shouldn't do to help save the environment.

1 use public transport in cities
   (+) *We should use public transport in cities.*
2 switch off the lights when we leave an empty room
   (+) ....
3 leave the tap running while we clean our teeth
   (–) ....
4 put old bottles in the bottle bank for recycling
   (+) ....
5 cut down trees in the rainforests of the world
   (–) ....
6 protect the natural environment
   (+) ....

R14.3 Match the two parts of the sentences.

1 *c*   2 ....   3 ....   4 ....   5 ....   6 ....

1 You shouldn't eat   a more exercise.
2 He should take   b early for school.
3 It's quite late. They'd better c too much chocolate.
4 Mary would always be   d catch the bus.
5 I'm sure you'd like a   e alone than with you.
6 Paul would rather go   f cup of tea now.

R14.4 Write sentences with *had better* (HB +), *had better not* (HB –), *ought to* (OT+) or *ought not to* (OT –).

1 It's snowing hard. We / drive home
   (OT –) *It's snowing hard. We ought not to drive home.*
2 It's pouring with rain. We / take our umbrellas
   (HB +) ....
3 The sun is very strong now. You / sunbathe in the morning, but not in the middle of the day
   (OT +) ....
4 It's cold in the evenings. I / forget my pullover
   (HB –) ....
5 The pavement is very icy. The children / run to school
   (OT –) ....

R14.5 Use the words to write requests with *Will you…?* (informal) and *Would you…?* (formal).

1 Your friend Paul / help you dig the garden
   Will you help me dig the garden, please, Paul?
2 Your sister / go shopping with you
3 A passer-by / tell you how to get to the station
4 A woman on the bus / close the window
5 Your dad / to drive you to the school dance
6 Your maths teacher / explain how to solve this problem

R14.6 Underline the mistakes in each sentence. Then rewrite the sentences correctly.

1 <u>You will</u> play in goal for our team?
   Will you play in goal for our team?
2 She would like go to Moscow next year.
3 They better go there by bus. It's the easiest way.
4 'What would you like to drink?' 'I like a cup of coffee.'
5 He didn't would come to the party with me.
6 They're bound do well – they're very good students.

R14.7 Complete the sentences with the verbs in the box.

| would rather | is bound | should | would | ~~would like~~ | are bound | shall |

1 I *would like* to visit Rome next year.
2 I .... drink coffee than tea.
3 .... I open the windows?
4 He .... to fail his exam. He never studied.
5 As a girl, Jenny .... always talk about school!
6 It's four o'clock, he .... be ready to start.
7 They .... to win the match – they're the best team.

F Exam preparation

F.1 PET Reading Part 5

Read the text and choose the correct word(s) (A, B, C or D) for each space.

Dave: Hi, Mike. (1) ...B... you help me carry this box downstairs, please?
Mike: I (2) .... help you, Dave, but I'm afraid I've hurt my arm.
Dave: Oh dear! How did you do it?
Mike: I (3) .... tell you really – you'll just laugh at me.
Dave: Oh, come on! I promise I (4) .... tell anyone.
Mike: Well, OK … Last Tuesday morning, since we (5) .... go to school, I stayed in bed late. Everyone else was out, and I was asleep when the doorbell rang. I decided that I (6) .... answer it. So I got up too quickly and fell over, hitting my arm on the end of the bed.
Dave: You did it last Tuesday and it still hurts?! You (7) .... see a doctor.
Mike: I saw a doctor this morning and he said I (8) .... get it X-rayed, but I (9) .... play football tomorrow, and if there's something wrong, they're (10) .... say I can't play.
Dave: That's stupid, Mike! (11) .... miss one game tomorrow, or play and risk hurting it more, so you'll be (12) .... miss the next ten games? Go and get the X-ray!!

	A	B	C	D
1	Shall	(Can)	Must	Need
2	would rather	have got to	don't need to	would like to
3	needn't	need to	shouldn't	should
4	won't	wouldn't	needn't	might not
5	had to	haven't got to	have to	didn't have to
6	ought	ought to	has to	must to
7	needn't	would like to	had better	shall
8	should	shall	need	want
9	must to	don't have to	was obliged to	want to
10	due to	bound to	ought to	need to
11	Do you have to	Are you due to	Would you rather	Need you
12	forced to	need to	have to	ought to

F.2 PET Writing Part 1

Complete the second sentence so that it means the same as the first. Use no more than three words.

1 There's no school tomorrow; it's a public holiday.
   We don't ......*need to*...... go to school tomorrow; it's a public holiday.
2 You must finish your homework by six thirty.
   You .... to finish your homework by six thirty.
3 I may go to the theatre tonight.
   Perhaps .... to the theatre tonight.
4 You ought not to do that. It's illegal!
   You'd .... do that. It's illegal!
5 When will the London train arrive?
   What time is the London train .... ?
6 Stop making so much noise!
   Don't .... so much noise!

F.3 PET Writing Part 3

**Here's part of a letter you received from an English friend.
Write a letter offering advice and suggestions. (about 100 words)**

Exam preparation F

> I'm finishing school this year. My dad says I must go straight into the family supermarket business. But I would rather go to university to study art. What do you think I should do?

....
....
....
....

F.4 FCE Use of English Part 2

Read the text below and think of the word which best fits each space. Use only one word in each space.

When I was a child, I (1) ...*had*... to eat everything on my plate before my mother let me go out and play. She said that I (2) .... to eat all the food which she cooked if I (3) .... to grow up healthy and strong. I'd (4) .... have eaten burgers and chips like my friends than eat my mother's food, but she said I (5) .... never eat such food. And so I didn't. She said my friends were (6) .... to get very fat, and I had (7) .... forget about junk food if I was to have a long and healthy life. She forgot about 'happy'! I don't (8) .... to tell you how unhappy I was eating her food – vegetable soup, porridge, cabbage and things like that. But now I am grown up, and I look at my friends, I think that they (9) .... to change their diets if they want to live to a ripe old age! They are all overweight and still eating the same stuff! And here I am, slim, fit and attractive. I (10) .... like to thank my mother for this.

F.5 FCE Use of English Part 3

Read the text below. Use the word given in capitals at the end of each line to form a word that fits in the space in the same line.

I don't know if you've ever been in an English (1) ...*courtroom*..., COURT
but they are rather strange places, almost like a theatre.
The (2) .... is brought in by the police and has DEFEND
to stand in front of an 'audience' of family, friends,
the jury and the (3) .... who will defend and LAW
prosecute him or her. The most important person in the
court, of course, is the judge, who will decide the (4) .... PUNISH
if the defendant is found (5) .... GUILT
If the verdict is 'not guilty', the defendant is set free.

F.6 FCE Use of English Part 4

Complete the second sentence so that it has a similar meaning to the first sentence, using the word given. Do not change the word given. You must use between two and five words, including the word given.

1. There's no need to go to work tomorrow.
   HAVE
   You ...*don't have to*... go to work tomorrow.

2. You ought to go and tell the police about it.
   BETTER
   You .... go and tell the police about it.

3. I would prefer not to go there on Sunday.
   RATHER
   I .... there on Sunday.

4. She must finish her project by Tuesday.
   GOT
   She .... finish her project by Tuesday.

5. Perhaps I'll visit John next summer.
   MIGHT
   I .... John next summer.

6. It's certain that he'll go to prison for it.
   BOUND
   He .... go to prison for it.

UNIT 57 Passive form

A The passive form only exists for transitive verbs. Passive structures are not possible for intransitive verbs, as they have no object that can become the subject of a passive sentence.

The passive form, for all the tenses, is formed with the auxiliary **be** followed by the past participle of the verb: Subject + **be** (in appropriate tense) + past participle

REMEMBER! The past participle is formed with the suffix **-ed** for regular verbs (**painted**, **played**…), whilst for irregular verbs, the forms are shown in the third column of the verb table (**made**, **taken**, **put**…). See page 72 and the list of irregular verbs on page 366.

Note how a sentence changes from an active one to a passive one:

Leonardo da Vinci   painted   the Mona Lisa.   →   The Mona Lisa   was painted   by Leonardo da Vinci.
subject   verb   object   →   subject   passive verb   agent

What happens in the change from active to passive?

- The subject of the active sentence (Leonardo da Vinci) becomes the agent, preceded by the preposition **by**.
- The verb **be** in the passive sentence is the same tense as the verb in the active sentence (in this case, **was** is in the past simple like **painted**), and is followed by the past participle of the main verb.

B **Negative form:** Subject + **be** + **not** + past participle
This dish is not cooked in the traditional way.

Interrogative form: **Be** + subject + past participle + …?
Short answers: **Yes,** / **No,** + subject pronoun + verb **be** (affirmative / negative).
'Are these toys made in China?' 'Yes, they are.' / 'No, they aren't. They're made in Vietnam.'
Wh- questions: Question word + **be** + subject + past participle + …?
*Where are these oranges imported **from**?*
*What is this machine used **for**?*

NB: The preposition is placed at the end of the sentence.

C The passive form is used:

- when we want to put emphasis on the action or on the result of the action, rather than who does it. In this case, the agent isn't needed.
  My wallet was found in the street.
  A lot of trout are caught in this lake.

- instead of an active sentence, when the subject is generic or not clearly identified.
  Carnival is celebrated in February.
  The active sentence would correspond to 'People celebrate Carnival…' (generic subject)

- in announcements or regulations.
  Passengers are requested to proceed to exit gate 9.
  The rooms are cleaned daily.

- in scientific texts, in descriptions of processes or experiments.
  Heated crude oil is pumped into the fractioning column and is split into separate hydrocarbons.

EXERCISES

Passive form — UNIT 57

57.1 Match the two parts of the sentences.

1 ..c.... 2 .... 3 .... 4 .... 5 .... 6 ....

1 This fairy tale was written
2 These plays were first performed
3 This short story was awarded
4 His poems were not considered
5 My aunt was given this book
6 His new novel was criticised

a first prize in the competition.
b by the author himself.
c by Oscar Wilde.
d in the 17th century.
e because of its length.
f for the new anthology.

57.2 Change the sentences from active to passive.

1 They grow a lot of oranges in Sicily.
   A lot of oranges are grown in Sicily.
2 They make Parmesan cheese near Parma.

3 People borrow lots of books from the library every day.

4 They print the books in Hong Kong.

5 They don't use artificial colouring in these sweets.

6 They wrote this poem two thousand years ago.

7 They speak English and German here.

8 They build MINI cars in Oxford.

57.3 Rearrange the words and write the questions.

1 in – ravioli – are – What – used – this – ingredients – ?
   What ingredients are used in this ravioli?
2 made – factory – What – of – this – the – in – part – is – ?

3 for – are – used – computers – these – What – ?

4 usually – time – the – delivered – What – are – papers – ?

5 fruit – from – cake – What – that – made – was – ?

6 novel – was – Who – by – this – written – ?

7 giraffes - in - Which - are - countries – found - ?

8 grapes - make - used – Where – first - to - wine – were - ?

9 played - the - was - rugby – time – When - for – first - ?

10 Who - painted - Mona Lisa - was - by - ?

UNIT 58: Passive form – present and past tenses

A Look at the table below that compares the active form and the passive form of the present and past tenses in the third person singular.

tense	active	passive
present simple	… makes	… is made
present continuous	… is making	… is being made
past simple	… made	… was made
past continuous	… was making	… was being made

Note that the verb **be** in the passive form keeps the same tense as the active verb.
They built the bridge last year.
The bridge was built last year.

B The use of tenses in passive sentences is identical to that in active sentences. For example, for habitual actions, we use the present simple for actions that have been completed, we use the past simple, and so on.
Here are a few examples using the tenses in the table.

Present simple
Gaelic football is played in Ireland. (general statement)
Breakfast is served in the cafeteria. (usually)

Present continuous
A match of Gaelic football is being played between the rival teams of Galway and Kilkenny. (the match is underway)
Breakfast is being served in the cafeteria. (in this moment of time)
The houses are being rebuilt after the tsunami. (in this period time)

Past simple
The internal structure of the Statue of Liberty was designed by Gustave Eiffel in the 19th century.
The road was repaired in three days. (the work is finished)

Past continuous
The road was being repaired, so we had to find an alternative route. (the work was in progress, they hadn't yet finished)
Our luggage was being checked while we were waiting in the security area.

C The passive form can also be formed using the verb **get** instead of **be**, in particular for actions that happened unexpectedly. This use is common in informal spoken language.
Luckily, no one got injured in the crash.
We got stuck in a traffic jam.

EXERCISES

Passive form – present and past tenses

UNIT 58

58.1 Change the sentences from active to passive. Don't use the agent.

1 They use apples to make cider.
   Apples are used to make cider.
2 They don't produce steel here any more.
   ....
3 They are clearing the rubbish at the moment.
   ....
4 Mother is cooking our lunch now.
   ....
5 They built wooden ships here in the past.
   ....
6 Europeans didn't use the printing press until the 15th century.
   ....
7 The doctors were seeing the patients when we arrived.
   ....
8 They weren't playing the match when I got there.
   ....

58.2 Change the questions from active to passive. Use the agent.

1 Did Marconi invent the telephone?
   Was the telephone invented by Marconi?
2 Did Picasso paint *Guernica*?
   ....
3 Does J K Rowling also write books for adults?
   ....
4 Is the orchestra playing Vivaldi's *Four Seasons*?
   ....
5 What did the cavemen paint on the walls?
   ....
6 When are the judges giving out the results?
   ....

58.3 Complete the sentences with the passive form and the appropriate tense of the verbs in the box.

| ~~write~~   sell   recognise   use   publish   play |

1 *The Jungle Book* ......*was written*...... by Rudyard Kipling.
2 Dickens's novels .... first .... in Victorian magazines.
3 Van Gogh's paintings .... only .... as great after he died.
4 The first blues music .... as early as 1900.
5 Papyrus .... to write on in some places even today.
6 Plastic Leaning Towers .... to tourists in Pisa.

58.4 Tick (✔) the correct sentences and correct the sentences that contain mistakes.

1 ☐ Glass bottles is made in that factory.   *Glass bottles are made in that factory.*
2 ✔ Cocoa is produced in West Africa.   ....
3 ☐ The bread is been baked now.   ....
4 ☐ The wheel was invented a long time ago.   ....
5 ☐ New laws were being introduced when I was in Egypt.   ....
6 ☐ The motor car wasn't widely use before 1950.   ....

167

UNIT 59 Passive form – perfect tenses and future

A Look at the table below that compares the active form and the passive form of the present perfect and the past perfect, and the various ways in which to express the future in the third person singular.

tense	active	passive
present perfect	… has made	… has been made
past perfect	… had made	… had been made
future (*going to*)	… is going to make	… is going to be made
future (*will*)	… will make	… will be made
future perfect	… will have made	… will have been made

B Here are a few examples using the tenses in the table.

Present perfect
Have you ever been invited to her parties?
Sorry, your car hasn't been fixed yet.

This verb tense is common in journalistic writing, when the exact moment in which something happened isn't mentioned.

An agreement has been reached between the two rival factions.
He has been proclaimed leader of his party.

Compare the use of the present perfect with the past simple:
The new sports centre has been inaugurated by the town mayor.
(when exactly isn't said)
The new sports centre was inaugurated yesterday.
(the time adverb *yesterday* indicates a specific time)

Past perfect
She had just been chosen for the main role in the school musical when she was offered a part in a film as well.
Our room had been cleaned just before we arrived at the hotel.

Future (*going to*)
He is going to be elected president of the golf club.
You are going to be asked a lot of questions.

Future (*will*)
I don't think your proposal will be taken seriously.
His book will be published next month.
The name of the winner will be announced tomorrow.

Future perfect
This tense is used to say by when a certain action will have been completed. It is followed by a time expression with **by**.
The name of the winner will have been announced by this time tomorrow.

EXERCISES

Passive form – perfect tenses and future

UNIT 59

59.1 Choose the correct alternative.
1 The arrangements **has been** / **had been** made before I arrived.
2 Their wedding **has been** / **had been** announced before I knew about it.
3 The results **have been** / **were** given last night.
4 Don't worry! Everyone **has been** / **had been** told.
5 The plan **hasn't been** / **wasn't** communicated to anyone yet.
6 The children **have just been** / **had just been** informed when the storm began.

59.2 Match the two parts of the sentences.

1 _b_   2 ....   3 ....   4 ....   5 ....   6 ....

1 Her next play will be written
2 The answers will be found
3 The sport facilities will be completed
4 His new poems will be read
5 The lecturer will be asked
6 New houses will be built

a by 2012.
b in verse.
c in front of a large audience.
d to accommodate the immigrants.
e at the end of the book.
f to speak for 50 minutes.

59.3 Change the questions from active to passive without changing the verb tense.
1 Are they going to meet him at the airport?
   Is he going to be met at the airport?
2 Are they going to make her their next leader?
   ....
3 When will they issue the next set of stamps?
   ....
4 Will they have finished the rehearsal by midnight?
   ....
5 Where will they hold the next Olympics?
   ....
6 Will they have started the new school building by the time you go there?
   ....

59.4 Use the words to write sentences with the passive form of *going to*.
1 Paul's new novel / publish / in November
   Paul's new novel is going to be published in November.
2 Jane's play / stage / at Christmas
   ....
3 Susan's poems / enter / in a poetry competition
   ....
4 Dave's short story / include / in an anthology
   ....
5 Our production of *Macbeth* / perform / at the Summer Festival
   ....
6 His next novel / illustrate / by Quentin Blake
   ....

UNIT 60 — Passive form – infinitive, modal verbs and conditional

A Transitive verbs also have a passive form in the infinitive.

Present infinitive passive: to be + past participle — **to be done**
Past infinitive passive: to have been + past participle — **to have been done**

The car needs to be washed today.
He hated not to have been informed.

B The passive form is often used with modal verbs (**can, must, may, should…**) to express deductions, permission, obligations, possibility and requests that refer to the present or the past. The structure of passive sentences with any modal verb is as follows:

Present: Subject + modal + **be** + past participle
The lift | can't | be used | by children.

Past: Subject + modal + **have been** + past participle
This movie | must | have been filmed | in Alaska.

Note the change from an active sentence to a passive one with the presence of a modal:
They might have lost your paper. → *Your paper might have been lost.*

C Here are a few examples with various modal verbs followed by the present infinitive passive.

This problem can be solved in many different ways. (possibility)
The research must be / has to be done by tomorrow. (obligation)
The ball can't be touched with the hands. (ban)
This work should be / ought to be finished before the end of the month. (request)
Only a monolingual dictionary may be used during the exam. (concession)

Here are some more examples with modal verbs followed by the past infinitive passive.

The schedule might have been changed. (it's possible but it's not certain – denotes uncertainty)
It could have been done much better than this! (there was possibility – denotes reproach)
We should have been warned of the delay. (they should have warned us – denotes dissatisfaction or reproach)
I'd like to have been given a prize. (wish that's not been fulfilled)

D Compare the active form and the passive form of the present and past conditional (see p.324).

	active	passive
2nd conditional main clause	… would make	… would be made
3rd conditional main clause	… would have made	… would have been made

The strike would be called off if an agreement was reached tonight. (there is still possibility)
The strike would have been called off if an agreement had been reached. (but it never happened)

EXERCISES

Passive form – infinitive, modal verbs and conditional

UNIT 60

60.1 **Rearrange the words and write sentences. They all have a passive infinitive.**

1 be – midday – homework – to – finished – needs – by – Your
   Your homework needs to be finished by midday.

2 ought – weekend – The – the – started – work – be – before – to
   ....

3 about – The – the – to – been – boys – told – trip – have – ought
   ....

4 repaired – to – The – needs – quickly – be – cooker
   ....

5 put – Those – have – there – boxes – not – ought – been – to
   ....

60.2 **Change the sentences from active to passive without the agent. They all have a modal verb.**

1 The police may have found your missing wallet.
   Your missing wallet may have been found.

2 We can't mend our new television at home.
   ....

3 They couldn't use their car last week – it was at the garage.
   ....

4 They must have made this furniture in India.
   ....

5 He might have found the treasure by now.
   ....

6 They would have finalised the arrangements if they had had time.
   ....

60.3 **Write questions for the following answers. Use a modal verb and the passive.**

1 *Can the machines be used when it's cold?*
   No, the machines can't be used when it's cold!

2 ....
   No, the classroom couldn't be opened earlier in the morning!

3 ....
   No, they couldn't be helped by anyone!

4 ....
   No, the onions mustn't be added after the tomatoes!

5 ....
   No, the dogs shouldn't be fed twice a day!

6 ....
   No, the door ought not to be left open during the day!

60.4 **Choose the correct alternative.**

1 The cake **can't be / ~~can't have been~~** eaten already!
2 In this game, only the feet **can be / can have been** used.
3 The house **must be / must have been** broken into last night.
4 The dog **should be / should have been** walked tomorrow morning.
5 The new carpet **ought to be / ought to have been** delivered yesterday.
6 The car **might be / might have been** stolen while we were out.

UNIT 61 Passive form – Verbs with double object; *He is said to be…*

A There are some verbs that, in the active form, are followed by a double object in the following order: **person** + **thing**, without any preposition.

I sent an e-mail to John. → *I sent John an e-mail.*

Verbs that behave in this way are: **ask, buy, bring / take, give, grant, offer, lend, pass, read, send, show, tell, write** and **teach**, as well as others.

In the passive form, the person, and not the thing, becomes the subject.

An e-mail was sent to John. → *John was sent an e-mail.*

Look at these other examples.

Active sentence	Passive sentence
They give prizes to the best students.	*The best students are given prizes.*
They offered him a big discount.	*He was offered a big discount.*
Somebody gave me a present.	*I was given a present.*
They told her a nice story.	*She was told a nice story.*

B When verbs of opinion like: **believe, consider, find, know, report, say, suppose, think**, and a few others, are used to express widely shared opinions, they can have a double passive construction:

Impersonal: **It is** + past participle + (**that**) + subject + verb in the present tense
  It is thought that he is abroad.

Personal: Subject (person) + **be** + past participle + verb in the infinitive
  He is thought to be abroad.

The second (personal) construction is the most used.
Note also that in the impersonal construction **that** can be omitted.

It was found that he was guilty. → *He was found to be guilty.*
It was known they were good actors. → *They were known to be good actors.*
It is supposed you should be studying. → *You are supposed to be studying. Why aren't you?*

If the opinion or the assumption refer to the past, the passive infinitive is used, i.e. **to have** + participle.

They are supposed to have finished by now.

Note the difference between:

People think he was a genius. → *He is thought to have been a genius.*
(it is a present-day opinion)
People thought he was a genius. → *He was thought to be a genius.*
(it was an opinion that was had in that period of time)

EXERCISES

Passive form – Verbs with double object; *He is said to be...*

UNIT 61

61.1 **Change the sentences from active to passive using the personal construction. Don't use the agent.**

1. Her mother bought her a new dress.
   She was bought a new dress.
2. He lent them his new tent.
   They ....
3. We showed him the complete range.
   He ....
4. I taught her how to swim.
   She ....
5. She asked us to get some butter for her.
   We ....
6. He granted me permission to go there.
   I ....

61.2 **Tick (✔) the correct sentences and correct those with mistakes in them.**

1. ✔ My friends were all sent a letter.
2. ☐ My dog were given a bone.
   My dog was given a bone.
3. ☐ I was taught a new song.
4. ☐ We was brought some nice cakes.
5. ☐ He was offer a high salary.
6. ☐ I was passed a secret note.
7. ☐ She were shown a pretty ring.

61.3 **Change the sentences from impersonal passive sentences into passive sentences with a personal subject.**

1. It is reported that he is in France.
   He *is reported to be in France.*
2. It is said that it is a very valuable book.
   The book ....
3. It is believed that she is a beautiful girl.
   She ....
4. It is considered that it is an important painting.
   The painting ....
5. It is known that he is a brilliant author.
   He ....
6. It is supposed that she is very intelligent.
   She ....

173

UNIT 62 — Make / Let someone do something; Get someone to do something; Have / Get something done

A Look at the following expressions, which are similar to each other but vary in meaning:

- the verb **make** + base form: **make someone do something**, which has quite a 'neutral' meaning or is used with the idea of obligation.

  Don't make me laugh!
  The boss made me stay in the office till seven last night.
  (the passive structure is also possible: I was made to stay in the office…)
  My parents made me attend this course, but I didn't really want to.
  (also possible: I was made to attend….)

- the verb **let** + base form: **let someone do something** or with the verb **allow** + infinitive: **allow someone to do something**, which are both used with a sense of permission.

  My dad let me use his computer yesterday.
  They let her go on holiday on her own.
  They allowed us to park our car in the staff car park. (also: We were allowed to park…)

- the verb **get** + infinitive: **get someone to do something**, used in the sense of convincing someone to do something.

  I'll get her to talk to him.
  We got him to sing a song at the party.

- the verbs **oblige** or **force** + infinitive: **oblige / force someone to do something** (stronger sense of obligation than 'make someone to something').

  The police obliged / forced him to surrender. (also: He was obliged / forced to surrender.)

- the verb **cause** + infinitive: **cause something to happen**, usually with negative effects.

  The frost caused the plants to die.

B Look at the following passive construction: **get / have something done (by someone)**. In this case, it's always someone else who does something for us, usually a type of service. The person isn't expressed when it's obvious who it is doing it.

Sandra got / had her hair cut very short (by the hairdresser).
Peter got his arm tattooed with a big dragon.

Note the difference between:

They're going to have the kitchen painted yellow. (by a painter)
They're going to paint the kitchen yellow. (They're are going to do it themselves)

What is done to us can also be against our will or not depend on us. Compare for example:

I got my car fixed after the accident. (it's me who decided)
I had my bag stolen. (I certainly didn't want this to happen!)

The following constructions are also common: **I need to / I want to / I must have something done.**

I need to get these photos printed.
I want to have some trees planted in my garden.
I must get this jumper dry-cleaned.

EXERCISES
Make / Let someone do something; Get someone to do something; Have / Get something done

UNIT 62

62.1 Use the words to write sentences with the correct form of *make someone do something*.

1 Peter's mother / make / him / tidy his bedroom / yesterday
   Peter's mother made him tidy his bedroom yesterday.
2 The teacher / always / make / me / stay late at school.
3 The doctor / make / Sarah / go / to see a specialist / yesterday
4 Working in the garden / usually / make / me / feel very tired
5 The film we watched last night / make / Jan / feel very frightened
6 Those big boys / often / make / Paul / cry / when he was younger

62.2 Rearrange the words and write sentences.

1 let – Mike – me – skateboard – use – yesterday – his
   Mike let me use his skateboard yesterday.
2 Jane – stay – allowed – The – in – classroom – the – to – teacher
3 was – on – sofa – the – to – Tim – sleep – made
4 to – after – him – The – two – police – go – hours – allowed – home
5 wash – me – Wendy – cut – and – hair – let – her
6 allowed – bed – James – The – to – of – get – yesterday – out – doctor

62.3 Match the two parts of the sentences.

1 _a_ 2 ...... 3 ...... 4 ...... 5 ...... 6 ......

1 My parents had their bedroom
2 My brother got his car
3 Daisy is having her teeth
4 Mrs Smith had the hedge
5 Andy is getting the computer
6 Laura had her nails

a decorated in pink last month.
b filled next week.
c upgraded tomorrow.
d manicured yesterday.
e repaired by my neighbour.
f trimmed by the gardener last week.

62.4 Use the words given and the verbs in brackets to write sentences.

1 I / get / car / washed   (need)
   I need to get my car washed.
2 My brother / have / hair / cut   (need)
3 Lucy / get / bicycle / mended   (must)
4 My mum / have / kitchen / extended   (want)
5 We / get / TV licence / renewed   (must)

175

UNIT 63 — See someone do / doing something; see something being done

A

The most common verbs of perception are: **see**, **hear**, **smell**, **taste**, **feel** and a few others such as **notice**, **listen to** and **find**. These verbs are often accompanied by the modal **can**.

You can see the cathedral on your right.
What can you hear?
I could smell something burning.

B

Perceiving active actions

Two different constructions can be used to talk about a person or a thing that actively carries out an action.

- If the action perceived is immediate or of a short duration, we use the construction:
  see / hear someone do something
  I heard him slam the door. (I perceived the entire action, from start to finish)

- If the action perceived is prolonged in time, then we use the construction:
  see / hear someone doing something
  I heard her crying. (I perceived only a part of the action, she had already been crying and continued crying)

Look at these other examples:

They got on the bus. I saw this.
→ *I saw them get on the bus.*
(action that started and finished)

They were waiting for the bus. I saw this.
→ *I saw them waiting for the bus.*
(action that extended itself in time)

NB: In sentences that contain the adverbs **always**, **never**, **often**… and in negative sentences, it is preferable to use the construction with the base form of the verb.

*I've **never** seen her smile.*
*I **didn't** hear the bell ring.*

C

Perceiving passive actions

To talk about an object (person or thing) that undergoes an action, we use the construction:
see / hear something (being) done

I saw him being chased by a dog.
I heard her name called out.
We've never seen anyone treated like that.

Perception verbs in the passive form

When a perception verb is in the passive form, the verb that follows is in the infinitive (**to** + base form) or in the **-ing** form.

*They **were seen** to leave the pub at eight o'clock.*
*He **was heard** to shout / shouting.*
*She **was** last **seen** walking around in a street market.*

EXERCISES

See someone do / doing something; see something being done

UNIT 63

63.1 Complete the sentences with a verb from the box.

| see | ~~hear~~ | smell | taste | feel | listen to |

1. I could ....*hear*.... the bells ringing at the church.
2. I can .... some lemon flavour in this cake.
3. Would you like to .... me playing my violin?
4. I could .... Andy walking towards me.
5. Can you .... our lunch cooking in the kitchen?
6. I could .... the cold wind blowing down my back.

63.2 Join the two sentences and write one sentence that has the same meaning.

1. They were coming in our direction. I saw them.
   I saw them coming in our direction.
2. They were working in the street. Paula heard them.
   ....
3. Two students left school early. I noticed them.
   ....
4. She was cooking the cabbage. I smelt it.
   ....
5. Danny came home very late last night. I heard him.
   ....
6. He was digging in the garden. Jane saw him.
   ....

63.3 Tick (✔) the correct sentences and correct the ones with mistakes in them.

1. ✔ I heard the baby being bathed.
2. ☐ I saw the dog to be taken for a walk.
   I saw the dog being taken for a walk.
3. ☐ I've never seen an animal being hunt like that.
   ....
4. ☐ I saw him being shout at by the teacher.
   ....
5. ☐ Can you hear the building being demolished?
   ....
6. ☐ I listened to the team coach interviewing on TV.
   ....
7. ☐ Did you see her being award the prize?
   ....

63.4 Complete the sentences with the words in the box.

| being (x2) | ~~sitting~~ | riding | burning | kicking |

1. At the moment, I can see my friend Paolo ....*sitting*.... at his desk.
2. Yesterday morning, we heard some vandals .... our garden gate.
3. Can't you smell the roast .... in the oven?!
4. Yesterday evening, I saw my friend .... his motorbike without a helmet.
5. He was unconscious and couldn't feel the stretcher .... shaken.
6. Last night, I listened to a rock concert .... broadcast live.

REVIEW 15

EXERCISES Units 57–63

R15.1 Write questions for the following answers. Use the passive and keep the same verb tense.

1 *Are buses still being made here now?*
   Yes, they are still making buses here now.
2 ....
   Yes, they started the factory 200 years ago.
3 ....
   Yes, they found coal and iron in the hills.
4 ....
   Yes, they still make the buses with iron from the hills.
5 ....
   Yes, they have improved production in recent years.
6 ....
   Yes, they'll produce lorries here in the future.

R15.2 Answer the questions with negative sentences in the passive form. Keep the same verb tense.

1 Does he make the pots here?
   No, the pots aren't made here.
2 Was he repairing the fridge yesterday?

3 Are they going to hold the party here tomorrow?

4 Had they started work on the flat when she left?

5 Will they have served dinner by the time we arrive?

6 Have they made any changes to the system yet?

7 Have they repaired my computer yet?

8 Will they have reached an agreement by tomorrow?

R15.3 Change the sentences from active to passive. Use the agent.

1 The teacher gave us these new books.
   We were given these new books by the teacher.
2 When did Michelangelo paint the Sistine Chapel?

3 When will Napoli next win the Italian League?

4 Carter discovered the Valley of the Kings in Egypt.

5 Our baker bakes fresh bread every morning.

6 Prince Charles is going to present the prizes.

7 Chris Thornton wrote the screenplay for the latest Thor movie.

8 Ronaldo scored the winning goal in the World Cup.

REVIEW 15

R15.4 Match the two parts of the sentences.

1 ..c.. 2 .... 3 .... 4 .... 5 .... 6 ....

1 Your homework must
2 Their car needs
3 That fish can't
4 My photos ought
5 The match may not
6 That dog should

a be played if it rains.
b to be developed by now.
c be finished by seven o'clock.
d to be cleaned.
e be kept on its lead.
f be eaten until it's cooked.

R15.5 Rearrange the words and write sentences.

1 presents – She – a – presents – given – lot – was – of
   She was given a lot of presents.

2 the – It – valuable – vases – believed – that – very – was – were
   ....

3 children – The – a – read – poem – were – beautiful
   ....

4 tribes – violent – The – very – known – be – to – were
   ....

5 said – Her – breed – very – be – dog – rare – is – a – to
   ....

6 aunt – expensive – shown – was – hats – very – some – My
   ....

R15.6 Complete the sentences with the correct form of the verbs in the box.

| make   allow   hear   ~~force~~   cause   see   need   get |

1 The guard ....*forced*.......... him to take off his belt.
2 The teacher .... the students do a test every day.
3 Sally .... her hair done in London.
4 Ben's parents .... him to stay up late at the party.
5 The heavy rain .... the river to flood the town.
6 John .... to get his hair cut tomorrow.
7 They .... leaving the town soon after the fire broke out.
8 Charlotte .... playing her favourite sonata on the piano.

G Exam preparation

G.1 PET Reading Part 5

Read this account of the life of a glass factory and choose the correct word(s) (A, B, C or D) for each space.

Glass ⁽¹⁾...*A*... made in our town today, and it ⁽²⁾............ made here when the Romans lived here nearly 2,000 years ago. The factories where glass objects ⁽³⁾............ produced are about 150 years old. They ⁽⁴⁾............ built by a Victorian businessman called Joshua Sly. In Sly's time, bottles ⁽⁵⁾............ turned out in their millions, and he ⁽⁶⁾............ made very rich by his products by the time of his death in 1912. But his son, William, was more artistic, and many products ⁽⁷⁾............ experimented with in his time: vases, bowls and drinking glasses. In the end, it ⁽⁸⁾............ decided to enter the crystal drinking-glass market. Once the machines ⁽⁹⁾............ changed, and the workers retrained, production ⁽¹⁰⁾............ finally started in 1920. Beautiful wine glasses ⁽¹¹⁾............ manufactured, and that tradition has remained. Currently, the factory ⁽¹²⁾............ managed by Andrew Sly, Joshua's great-grandson.

1 **A** is being   **B** was being   **C** has been   **D** had been
2 **A** is being   **B** was being   **C** have been   **D** will be
3 **A** was   **B** will be   **C** are   **D** have been
4 **A** was   **B** were   **C** have been   **D** are
5 **A** is   **B** are   **C** was   **D** were
6 **A** had been   **B** has been   **C** have been   **D** were
7 **A** was   **B** were   **C** is   **D** are
8 **A** is   **B** are   **C** was   **D** is being
9 **A** was being   **B** has been   **C** had been   **D** were
10 **A** was   **B** were   **C** has been   **D** will be
11 **A** was   **B** were   **C** has been   **D** are
12 **A** was   **B** were   **C** is   **D** are

G.2 PET Writing Part 1

Complete the second sentence so that it means the same as the first. Use no more than three words.

1 They produce crystal drinking glasses at Sly's factory.
   Crystal drinking glasses ....*are produced*............ at Sly's factory.
2 The company will have earned one million pounds by Christmas.
   One million pounds will .... by the company by Christmas.
3 David Beckham has started a new sports club in Los Angeles.
   A new sports club .... by David Beckham in Los Angeles.
4 You cannot use this machine today.
   This machine .... today.
5 It is thought that he died when he was 60 years old.
   He is thought .... when he was 60 years old.
6 Some painters decorated their flat for them last year.
   They .... decorated by some painters last year.

G.3 PET Writing Part 3

Use the notes to write about an imaginary football club in the past simple passive (60 words).

Strawfield Football Club: They found the club (1910). They start work on the first stadium (1915). Bill Smith manages the club (1910–1920). They build a new stadium (1952). They win promotion to League One (1952). Jack Lyons buys the club (1990). They finish the third stadium (2004).

Strawfield Football Club was founded in 1910.

Exam preparation

G

G.4 FCE Use of English Part 2
Read the dialogue below and think of the word which best fits each space. Use only one word in each space.

Danny: Have those Italian orders (1)......**been**...... completed yet, June?
June: I don't think so. The order forms need to (2) .... sent first.
Danny: What?! The forms still (3) .... been sent out?
June: I'm sorry, Danny, but they should be signed (4) .... Mr Roberts first.
Danny: And he (5) .... been seen by anyone for days, I suppose!
June: Well, he (6) .... said to be on holiday this week…
Danny: Oh is he?! Very interesting. How does he expect this office to (7) .... run efficiently if he's away all the time?
June: I could (8) .... them signed by Mrs Johnson.
Danny: They'd never (9) .... accepted by the Italian branch with her signature on them
June: Well, there's nothing else we can do, so I think a cup of tea (10) .... needed right now!
Danny: Good idea!

G.5 FCE Use of English Part 3
Read the text below. Use the word given in capitals at the end of each line to form a word that fits in the space in the same line.

These toy cars have been in (1)......**production**...... for more than	PRODUCE
45 years, and most of our (2)..................................	CUSTOM
remember them from their early (3).................................. .	CHILD
However, nobody buys them any more. Some of the	
latest (4).................................. in the toy world are much better	INVENT
than our (5).................................. products. We need ideas from	FASHION
the (6).................................. of this company if we are to survive.	MANAGE

G.6 FCE Use of English Part 4
Complete the second sentence so that it has a similar meaning to the first sentence, using the word given. Do not change the word given. You must use between two and five words, including the word given.

1. He is believed to be visiting South Africa.
   IT
   ......**It is believed that**...... he is visiting South Africa.

2. What do they use these vegetables for?
   ARE
   What .... for?

3. They might have recorded these songs in Britain.
   BEEN
   These songs .... in Britain.

4. The builders are going to build him an extension.
   HAVE
   He's .... an extension built.

5. Those boys broke the window. I saw them.
   BREAK
   I saw .... the window.

6. She was playing the guitar. I heard her.
   PLAYING
   I heard .... the guitar.

UNIT 64 The indefinite article: *a /an*

A The indefinite article has two forms, **a / an**, that are the same for all nouns.

a man   a woman   a dog   a rucksack

A is used before words that start with:
- a consonant or a semivowel (**w, y**): *a book, a girl, a car, a table, a window, a young man*
- aspirated **h**: *a house, a horse, a hand, a hot day*
- the sound /ju/: *a uniform, a university, a unit, a euro, a European country*

An is used before words that start with:
- a vowel: *an apple, an egg, an onion, an umbrella, an Italian student*
- mute **h**: *an hour, an heir, an honest person*

NB: The only words that begin with a mute **h** are: **hour, heir, heiress, honour, honest** and their derivations (**hourly, honourable, honestly**...).

B The article **a / an** is used before singular countable nouns (see p.196) to indicate:
- a thing or person amongst others (any one, not one in particular).
  Take a chair, please.
  She gave me a red rose. 
- a person or thing that is mentioned for the first time in a story.
  A good king ruled over the country at that time.
  I've never seen a man with such a long beard.
- an example that represents an entire species or category.
  A lion is a wild animal.
  An oak is a big tree.
- an object that we have or don't have.
  I've got an umbrella.
  I haven't got a watch.

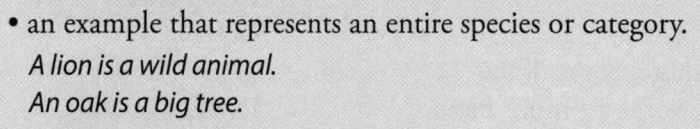

C The article **a / an** is also used before nouns that indicate:
- professions and occupations.
  He's an engineer and his wife is an interpreter.
- certain ailments or illnesses.
  I've got a cough. She's got a high temperature.

D The article **a / an** is also used:
- in expressions of
  - price: *three pounds a kilo*
  - speed: *50 miles an hour*
  - frequency: *three times a day, twice a month*
- in numeric expressions.
  a couple, a dozen, half a dozen, a hundred, a thousand, a million
- in exclamations, before a singular noun.
  What a life! What a horrible day!
- before **Mr / Ms** + surname, to indicate 'a certain someone'.
  A Mr Cox lives here, but I've never seen him.

EXERCISES

UNIT 64 The indefinite article: *a/an*

64.1 Write *a* or *an* before the words or expressions.

1. **a** man
2. .... hippo
3. .... dog
4. .... leaf
5. .... hourly bus
6. .... universal truth
7. .... walnut tree
8. .... oak
9. .... hundred
10. .... orange
11. .... iceberg
12. .... worker ant

64.2 Rearrange the words and write sentences.

1. bag – got – pear – in – a – an – and – apple – I've – my
   I've got an apple and a pear in my bag.
2. have – in – uncle – Canada – cousin – and – I – an – a
   ....
3. tiger – cat – is – big – A – a – of – sort
   ....
4. wears – soldier – A – always – uniform – a
   ....
5. present – aunt – from – of – useful – got – a – an – I – mine
   ....
6. African – ostrich – bird – is – large – a – An
   ....

64.3 Choose the correct alternative.

1. **A / (An)** education that you enjoy is **a / an** important start in life.
2. **A / An** apple a day keeps **a / an** person healthy.
3. **A / An** honest person is **a / an** useful friend to have.
4. **A / An** hyena is **a / an** horrible kind of animal.
5. **A / An** white tiger is **a / an** unusual one.
6. **A / An** interesting book is **a / an** object worth finding.

64.4 Tick (✔) the correct expressions and correct the false ones.

1. ✔ an interesting person
2. ☐ an uniform
   a uniform
3. ☐ an elephant
   ....
4. ☐ an hour and a half
   ....
5. ☐ an unique model
   ....
6. ☐ a unhappy boy
   ....
7. ☐ an Irish musician
   ....
8. ☐ a intelligent woman
   ....

183

UNIT 65 The definite article: *the* (1)

A The definite article has only one form, **the**, that is the same for all nouns.
the boy   the boys   the girl   the girls

The is pronounced /ðə/ before words that start with a consonant, and /ðiː/ before words that start with a vowel or a mute **h**.

B The article **the** is used before singular or plural nouns, to indicate:

- specific people or things.
  'Take the big chair.' 'Which one?' 'The one in the corner.'
  (not any chair, that precise one)

- people or things that are known to the speaker or listener.
  Are you coming to the concert tomorrow night?
  (the speaker and listener know which concert they mean)

- people or things that have already been mentioned before.
  I have a dog and a cat. (mentioned for the first time)
  The dog is a Dalmatian and the cat is a Persian.
  (mentioned in the previous sentence)

C The article **the** is also used before:

- nouns of which only one example can exist, for example: **the Sun**, **the Moon**, **the world**, **the equator**, **the weather**, **the sky**, **the Queen**, **the Prime Minister**, **the Pope**

- nouns that are made specific:
  – by a clause introduced by the prepositions **of**, **in**, **for**…
  Compare:
  I like the flowers in your garden. (those particular flowers)
  I like flowers. (all of them in general, therefore no article)
  The woman in the red dress is really pretty.
  The inhabitants of Morocco live mainly in the cities.

  – by a relative clause.
  I like the flowers (that) you gave me.
  The people who live next door are very nice.

- singular nouns that represent an entire category.
  The giraffe is a shy animal.
  (also possible: A giraffe is a shy animal. Or the plural with no article: Giraffes are shy animals.)

- superlative adjectives.
  John is the tallest boy in our class.
  Soccer is the most popular sport in many countries.

EXERCISES

The definite article: *the* (1)

UNIT 65

65.1 How do you pronounce *the* before the following words? Write them in the correct column, /ðə/ or /ði:/.

~~apple~~   ~~pear~~   umbrella   uniform   book   one   orange   aunt   house   insect   angel   pencil   eggs

the /ðə/	the /ði:/
pear	apple

65.2 Complete the text with the article *the* where necessary. If the article is not needed, write *0*.

(1) *The* English teacher asked (2) *0* our class if we were going to (3) .... school concert on (4) .... Saturday. I asked if (5) .... band which was playing was good or not, and she said that (6) .... music they played was (7) .... interesting music. Paul asked what time (8) .... event started, and she told us to be at (9) .... school by eight o'clock. She said that (10) .... headteacher was going to introduce (11) .... musicians to (12) .... audience and then they would start playing at (13) .... 8.30.

65.3 Write *the* before the words that indicate a unique thing. For the rest of them, write the indefinite article (*a* / *an*).

1 *the* Sun
2 .... French President
3 .... ship
4 .... Atlantic Ocean
5 .... Leaning Tower of Pisa
6 .... tree
7 .... bird
8 .... Earth
9 .... Labour Party
10 .... child
11 .... dog
12 .... North Star

65.4 Write *the* in only one of the two sentences. Where the article isn't needed, write *0*.

1 a I like *0* spaghetti.
   b I like *the* spaghetti your mother cooks.
2 a .... Italian cars are nice.
   b .... Italian cars that I saw at the fair were nice.
3 a I'd like to own .... fastest car in the world!
   b I like .... fast cars.
4 a .... boys who live next door are very noisy.
   b .... boys are often very noisy.
5 a .... man in the grey suit is very smart.
   b .... men in grey suits are very smart.
6 a .... presidents are important people.
   b .... president of the USA is an important person.

UNIT 66 The definite article: *the* (2)

A The article **the** is also commonly used:

- with names of musical instruments: *the piano, the violin, the guitar…*
  I play the trumpet and the flute.

- with ordinal numbers: *the first, the second, the third…*
  Today is the first of March.
  That's the second time you've asked me that question.

- with nouns that indicate a category of people, populations or religious groups:
  the elderly, the young, the Chinese, the British, the Americans, the Muslims, the Catholics…
  The old and the young often have different views.
  The English have a good sense of humour.

- with the plural form of surnames to indicate entire families.
  the McCabes   the Morrisons

- with abbreviations indicating various organisations.
  the UN (United Nations), the WWF (World Wide Fund for Nature), the EU (European Union)

- before names of places such as: *garden, park, cinema / movies, theatre, mountains, sea / seaside, country / countryside, office, swimming pool*, both with prepositions of movement (**to the…**) and prepositions of place (**in the…, at the…**).
  I'm going to the seaside in July.
  They're having a holiday in the mountains.
  We have a cottage in the country.
  Shall we go to the movies tonight?
  The kids are at the park, not at the swimming pool.

B The article **the** is used with geographical names indicating:

- mountain chains: *the Alps, the Highlands, the Appalachians, the Rocky Mountains* – but <u>not</u> singular summits (*Mount Blanc, Mount Everest, K2…*).
- archipelagos: *the Hawaii Islands, the Shetlands, the Maldives* – but <u>not</u> single islands (*Ireland, Malta, Sicily…*).
- rivers, seas and oceans: *the Thames, the Mississippi, the Nile, the North Sea, the Atlantic Ocean, the Indian Ocean* – but <u>not</u> lakes (*Lake Superior, Lake Garda, Loch Ness…*)
- nations with a plural name, even those expressed with an abbreviation or consisting of the words **Kingdom / Republic / Federation**: *the United States of America / the USA, the Netherlands, the Czech Republic, the United Kingdom, the United Arab Emirates, the Russian Federation* – but <u>not</u> nations with a singular name (*Italy, France, Tunisia…*).

C The article **the** is used with the pronouns **one / ones** (see p.236).
'Which book do you want?' 'The one over there.'
'Which dress do you prefer?' 'The blue one.'
Pass me the photocopies… the ones on the table, please.

EXERCISES

The definite article: *the* (2)

UNIT 66

66.1 Complete the text with the article *the* where necessary. If the article isn't needed, write *0*.

It was on (1) ...*the*... first of (2) ...*0*... September, 2008 that I started playing (3) .... bass guitar in a school band. We practised in (4) .... school music room every lunchtime and after (5) .... school on two evenings a week. We played a mixture of (6) .... pop and rock music, and wrote some songs ourselves. (7) .... first concert we played was very successful; it was in (8) .... church hall, and (9) .... 200 people came. Soon after that, we started to get (10) .... regular concerts in (11) .... clubs and dance halls of (12) .... area we lived in.

66.2 Where necessary, write *the* before the following words. If the article isn't needed, write *0*.

1 ...*the*... Industrial Revolution
2 .... Republic of Ireland
3 .... Switzerland
4 .... Sardinia
5 .... North Sea
6 .... Lake Ontario
7 .... Catholic Church
8 .... River Tiber
9 .... Pennines
10 .... Mont Blanc

66.3 Write *the* in the sentences where it is needed. If the article isn't needed, write *0*.

1 ...*The*... canal in ...*the*... park is very pretty.
2 .... Browns are going to .... mountains this weekend.
3 They went to .... countryside in .... August.
4 .... cottage we saw by .... lake was beautiful.
5 There are .... many trees on .... island.
6 .... Americans will leave .... Afghanistan later this year.
7 Is .... Prague in .... Czech Republic?
8 We're going to .... cinema with .... Smiths tonight.

66.4 Write *the* answers to these questions. Use *the* and *one / ones*.

1 Which coat are you going to buy? (red)
   I'm going to buy the red one.
2 Which film did you watch last night? (French)
   ....
3 Which bus will you catch tomorrow? (seven o'clock)
   ....
4 Which shoes have you bought? (brown)
   ....
5 Which band did you like at the festival? (first)
   ....
6 Which countries are you going to visit? (cheapest)
   ....
7 Which handbag do you prefer? (leather)
   ....
8 Which camera would you like to borrow? (digital)
   ....

UNIT 67   No article vs. *the*

A   The following cases do not require an article:
- plural nouns that are expressed in a general sense.
  Restaurants are usually crowded on a Saturday night. (all of them in general)
  But: *The restaurants of this chain are quite expensive.* (these ones in particular)
- proper nouns, even when preceded by a title: *Mark, Mr Champney, Doctor Jones, Queen Elizabeth…* and names of family members when referring to our own family: *Dad, Mum, Grandpa, Aunt Mary, Uncle John…*
- cities, countries (with singular word names), continents: *Berlin, Germany, Europe, Africa…*
- islands, mounts, lakes: *Sardinia, Mount McKinley, Lake Ladoga…*
- names of languages, areas of study, sport: *Spanish, French, maths, social studies, tennis, soccer…*
- days of the week, months, years, festivities, hours: *Monday, December, 1985, Christmas, Easter, two o'clock, half past two…*

  With the seasons, the article may or may not be used: *in the summer / in summer*
- meals: *breakfast, lunch, dinner… I have breakfast at eight o'clock.*
- colours: *red, yellow, pink… I like green.*
- uncountable nouns used in a general sense, for example names of materials or food products: *leather, wool, butter, flour*

  Compare:
  Butter is made from cream. (all butter in general)
  *Get **the** butter out of the fridge.* (that particular packet)

- abstract nouns: *peace, brotherhood, freedom, death*
- possessive adjectives and pronouns: *my sister* (not ~~the~~ my sister), *It's mine / yours…* (not ~~the~~ mine…)
- parts of the body, pieces of clothing and personal objects, which are preceded only by a possessive adjective.
  Wash your hands! (not: Whash ~~the~~ hands.)
  I usually go to school on my bike.
  It's cold. Put on your sweater.
  BUT: *Why don't you put on the sweater I gave you for your birthday?*
  (the specific sweater that was defined in the relative clause)

B   Nouns such as **hospital**, **church**, **school**, **college**, **market**, **prison**, **court** do *not* have an article when they are meant for their primary purpose (e.g. to go to church to pray). If these places are visited for a different purpose to the primary one, however, the article **the** is used.
Compare:
She went to hospital for a check-up. (as a patient)
She went to the hospital to visit her grandma.
Children go to primary school at the age of five. (as pupils, to learn)
I'm going to the school to talk to my son's teacher.
He was in prison for two years. (as an inmate)
He works in the local prison as a guard.

EXERCISES

UNIT 67 — No article vs. *the*

67.1 Write *the* only in one of the two sentences. If the article isn't needed, write *0*.

1. a I enjoyed camping by ...**the**... lake last year.
   b I enjoyed camping by ...**0**... Lake Garda last year.
2. a Mike met .... Mr Anderson last night.
   b Mike met .... Andersons last night.
3. a Linda doesn't like .... maths.
   b Linda didn't like .... maths she had for homework.
4. a She went climbing in .... mountains last week.
   b She's always been afraid of .... mountains.
5. a He always goes dancing on .... Saturday night.
   b He always goes dancing at .... weekend.
6. a We had .... dinner she had cooked at eight.
   b We had .... dinner at eight.

67.2 Tick (✔) the correct sentences and correct the ones with mistakes in them.

1. ✔ I like the green of the English countryside.
2. ☐ I like the green.   *I like green.*
3. ☐ The paper is made from wood.
4. ☐ We get wool from sheep.
5. ☐ They enjoyed the Christmas lunch I cooked.
6. ☐ He fought for the freedom all his life.
7. ☐ Can you pass me the teapot, please?
8. ☐ I can't see the my mother anywhere.

67.3 Write *the* in the sentences where necessary. If the article isn't needed, write *0*.

1. My mother works in ...**the**... hospital as a cleaner.
2. My father went into .... hospital for an operation last night.
3. .... school where my brother goes is very good.
4. Dave was late for .... school again today!
5. I went to .... market in Weston yesterday.
6. Farmers always take their goods to .... market early.
7. I go to .... church every Sunday morning.
8. I visited .... church which stands next to your house.

67.4 Which words usually require the article *the*? Write them in the correct column.

~~dates and times~~
~~musical instruments~~
categories of people
rivers
lakes
ordinal numbers
people's proper names
abstract nouns
abbreviations of organisations
materials and food
seas and oceans
meals

usually take *the*	don't usually take *the*
musical instruments	dates and times

REVIEW 16 EXERCISES Units 64–67

R16.1 Complete the story of *Little Red Riding Hood* with *a, an, the* or *0* where necessary.

Once upon (1) ...a... time there was (2) .... little girl called Little Red Riding Hood who lived with her mother in (3) .... middle of (4) .... big wood. One day, her mother asked (5) .... girl to take (6) .... cake and (7) .... bottle of (8) .... juice to her grandmother. She told Little Red Riding Hood to stay on (9) .... path. But she didn't. She stopped to pick some flowers, and then she met (10) .... wolf. She told (11) .... wolf that she was going to visit her grandmother. He ran off quickly to (12) .... grandmother's cottage. (13) .... old woman let (14) .... wolf into her cottage, and he ate her up. Then he got dressed in (15) .... grandmother's clothes and got into bed and waited.

When Little Red Riding Hood arrived, she knocked at (16) .... door. 'Come in,' said (17) .... wolf, in (18) .... voice like her grandmother's. Little Red Riding Hood gave (19) .... cake and juice to (20) .... wolf. But she noticed what (21) .... big ears, eyes and teeth her 'grandmother' had, and (22) .... wolf ate her, too. Then he lay down to have (23) .... sleep. (24) .... woodcutter who was passing looked in through (25) .... cottage window and saw (26) .... wolf asleep on (27) .... bed. He went inside, took (28) .... his axe and cut open (29) .... wolf's stomach. Grandmother and Little Red Riding Hood jumped out and thanked (30) .... woodcutter for saving them.

R16.2 Write *a* or *an* before the following words.

1 ...an... elegant woman
2 .... ugly animal
3 .... useful pot
4 .... orange ball
5 .... interesting game
6 .... untidy room
7 .... university student
8 .... Ukrainian city
9 .... artistic movement
10 .... uncrowded restaurant
11 .... unsmiling face
12 .... USB port

R16.3 Match the two parts of the sentences.

1 ...d... 2 .... 3 .... 4 .... 5 .... 6 ....

1 Gianni is an   a Abruzzi mountains.
2 He lives near the   b brown bears which live there.
3 He works as a   c few of them left now.
4 He looks after the   d old friend of mine.
5 There are only a   e list of endangered species.
6 They are on the   f warden in the National Park.

REVIEW 16

R16.4 Which words require the article *the*? Write them in the correct column.

Apennines   Lake Geneva   Colosseum   Florence   Archbishop   Argentina
Black Sea   FBI   Mount Everest   April   War of Independence   Liverpool Cathedral

with *the*	without *the*
The Apennines	

R16.5 Choose the correct alternative. *0* means that an article isn't needed.
1. He told me **the** / **an** answer to the question.
2. Last year, I spent two weeks at **the** / **a** seaside.
3. Tomorrow morning, I have **the** / **0** biology first lesson.
4. **The** / **A** Prime Minister is going to give a speech.
5. Rugby is **the** / **an** exciting game.
6. **A** / **0** flour is made from wheat.
7. I'm going skiing for **the** / **0** Christmas holidays.
8. I hate **the** / **a** way he speaks to me!

R16.6 Rearrange the words and write the sentences.
1. he – trust – man – you – kind – Is – the – of – can – ?
   Is he the kind of man you can trust?
2. reserve – I – last – visit – the – nature – to – week – went

3. in – likes – the – bird-watching – spring – go – She – to

4. school – Paul – when – started – four – was – he

5. married – World – My – after – grandparents – First – got – War – the

6. holiday – Islands – going – the – on – Shetland – We're – to

UNIT 68 Nouns

A Some nouns that refer to family members and nouns that indicate a profession have the same form for both the masculine and feminine, for example:

cousin, dancer, cook, student

Other nouns that refer to family members, however, have different forms, for example:
uncle / aunt, nephew / niece, son / daughter

Some nouns that indicate a profession end in **–er** or **–or** in the masculine but **–ess** in the feminine:
waiter / waitress, manager / manageress, actor / actress

Certain nouns for jobs that traditionally had different forms for the masculine and feminine (**policeman / policewoman, steward / stewardess…**) or had only masculine forms (**workman, postman…**), nowadays tend to be used in a neutral way as regards to the gender with words such as **officer**, **worker**, **operator**, **assistant**, **person**.

police officer, flight assistant, fire officer, factory worker, post person

B The plural of nouns is usually formed by adding **-s** to the singular noun.
building → buildings   cat → cats
poem → poems   orange → oranges

Nouns that end in **-s**, **-ss**, **-sh**, **-ch**, **-x** and some that end in **-o** (**hero, tomato, potato…**) form the plural by adding **-es**.
bus → buses   kiss → kisses   dish → dishes
watch → watches   box → boxes   hero → heroes

Other nouns that end in **-o**, usually abbreviated words or words of a foreign origin, only add **-s**.
radio → radios   zoo → zoos   photo → photos
video → videos   kilo → kilos   disco → discos

Nouns that end in a **-y** preceded by a consonant have the plural **-ies**.
city → cities   story → stories   baby → babies

BUT: *toys, rays, keys…* (only **-s**, because the **y** is preceded by a vowel)

Nouns that consist of abbreviations normally form the plural by adding **-s**.
CDs, DVDs, DJs, VJs, MPs…

C The pronunciation of the **-s** depends on the final sound of the word.

- After the sounds /k/, /f/, /p/, /t/ is pronounced /s/: *books, puffs, steps, pets…*
- After the sounds /b/, /d/, /g/, /l/, /m/, /n/, /ŋ/ and vowel sounds, it is pronounced /z/: *cabs, rods, bags, dolls, stems, cones, beginnings, boys…*
- **-es** after the sounds /tʃ/, /s/, /ʃ/, /z/ is pronounced /ɪz/: *matches, faxes, bushes, gases…*

EXERCISES

Nouns UNIT 68

68.1 Write these masculine nouns and feminine nouns in the correct column.

| steward | heir | actor | duchess | stewardess | duke | heiress | spokesman |
| aunt | bride | actress | widower | spokeswoman | widow | uncle | groom |

	Masculine	Feminine	Translation
1	steward	stewardess	
2			
3			
4			
5			
6			
7			
8			

68.2 Write the plural of these nouns in the correct column.

| ticket | country | actress | concert | ferry | pound | beach |
| bush | party | church | advert | cinema | lady | fax | fairy |

-s	-es	-ies
tickets		

68.3 Write the plural of these nouns that end in -o. Add -s or -es.

1 video — videos
2 tomato — ....
3 echo — ....
4 hero — ....
5 photo — ....
6 zoo — ....
7 Eskimo — ....
8 logo — ....
9 volcano — ....
10 potato — ....

68.4 Write the plural of these nouns in the correct column, depending on how they are pronounced.

| book | wish | theatre | piano | student | performance | shop | dance | painting | poet | stage | novel |

/s/	/z/	/ɪz/
books		

UNIT 69 Irregular plurals; compound nouns

A There are ten nouns that end in **-f** or **-fe** that in the plural end in **-ves**.

calf → calves
half → halves
knife → knives
leaf → leaves
life → lives

loaf → loaves
shelf → shelves
thief → thieves
wife → wives
wolf → wolves

Other nouns that end in **-f** or **-fe** form the plural normally, by adding **-s**.

roofs, chiefs, cliffs, proofs

B Some nouns have irregular plurals. The most common are:

man → men
tooth → teeth
mouse → mice

woman → women
foot → feet
louse → lice

child → children
goose → geese
ox → oxen

person → people (also possible: *persons,* used formally in announcements)
penny → pence (also possible *pennies,* to indicate individual coins)

Two women are jogging in the park with their children.
A lot of people turned up.
BUT: *The elevator may only carry four persons.*

Eighty-three pence, please.
BUT: *I've only got three pennies.*

C Certain names of animals have the same form for both the singular and plural.

deer (also possible: **deers**), *fish* (also possible: **fishes**),
salmon, sheep, trout

Some nouns that end in **-s** have the same form for the singular and plural.

means, crossroads, species (one or more), *series* (one or more)…

The bus is the most common means of transport among students in our school. (singular use)
You can see lots of different species of animals in the Natural History Museum. (plural use)

D Various nouns of Greek or Latin origin form the plural following the rules of Latin or Greek.

curriculum → curricula, medium → media, criterion → criteria, phenomenon → phenomena,
stimulus → stimuli, antenna → antennae, crisis → crises, thesis → theses, basis → bases

Others form the plural following the rules of English, i.e. **-s** or **-es**.

gymnasium → gymnasiums, dogma → dogmas, genius → geniuses

Some have both forms.

fungus → fungi (also possible: *funguses*), formula → formulae (also possible: *formulas*)

E Compound nouns normally add **-s** to the last word.

armchair → armchairs, teabag → teabags, weekend → weekends

Nouns that consist of a noun and an adverb or preposition only add an **-s** to the noun.

looker-on → lookers-on, passer-by → passers-by, brother-in-law → brothers-in-law

EXERCISES

Irregular plurals; compound nouns

UNIT 69

69.1 Complete the sentences with the plural of the nouns in the box.

| ~~wife~~ half life leaf shelf thief knife loaf |

1 Strangely, all three of Peter's former ....*wives*............ went to his fourth wedding.
2 In autumn, the .... turn yellow and fall to the ground.
3 These .... are not sharp enough to cut our pizzas with!
4 Thousands of .... could be saved if medicines were cheaper.
5 How many .... of bread shall I buy for the party?
6 I don't think I can reach the two top .... without a ladder.
7 Cut the peaches into .... and fill them with crumbled macaroons.
8 Fortunately, the .... were soon caught by the police.

69.2 Write the singular form or the irregular plural form of the following nouns.

1 ox   *oxen*   3 children ....   5 mice ....   7 goose ....
2 foot ....   4 tooth ....   6 woman ....   8 people ....

69.3 Decide whether the word underlined is singular (S) or plural (P).

1 There are only three <u>species</u> of big cat in our city zoo.   *P*
2 The army <u>headquarters</u> is outside the town.   ....
3 Working in a café is a popular <u>means</u> of earning money for students.   ....
4 Are you going to watch the new cartoon <u>series</u> on TV?   ....
5 Be careful! There's a very dangerous <u>crossroads</u> ahead.   ....
6 The National <u>Curriculum</u> in the UK is based on English, maths, IT and science. The <u>curricula</u> of foreign countries are sometimes based on different subjects.   ....

69.4 Write the plural of these nouns in the correct column. Two of them can go in two columns.

| ~~bacterium~~ analysis stimulus genius crisis criterion formula fungus antenna |

→-a	→-es	→-i	→-ae	+ -es/-s
bacteria				

695 Find these nouns in the picture and write their plurals.

1 calf *calves*
2 ox ....
3 child ....
4 woman ....
5 man ....
6 loaf of bread ....
7 knife ....
8 goose ....

UNIT 70 — Nouns: countables and uncountables (1)

A Nouns are:
- countable, when they refer to things, animals or people that we can count.
  one car, two cars; one dog, two dogs; one girl, two girls…
- uncountable, when they refer to things that we can't count or to abstract concepts.
  butter (not possible: ~~one butter, two butters~~…), *water, patience, freedom…*

B Countable nouns have a singular form and a plural form (apart from a few exceptions – see p.194).
- In their singular form, they can be preceded by the article **a / an**, by the number **one**, by a possessive adjective and by the article **the** or another determiner (**this, that…**).
  There's a car in the street. It's my car.
  I've only got one sandwich.
- In their plural form, they can be preceded by a number (**two, three…**), by an indefinite adjective (**some, any…**), by a possessive and by the article **the** or another determiner (**these, those…**).
  There are six eggs in the box.
  We've got some crisps left.
  Here are your biscuits.

C Uncountable nouns are those that indicate.
- substances and materials (**paper, wood, petrol, silk, cotton…**)
- many types of food (**bread, milk, salt, popcorn, spaghetti…**)
- abstract nouns (**love, beauty, education, honour, responsibility…**)
- nouns of school subjects or sport (**art, history, physics, gymnastics, athletics…**)

Usually these nouns do *not* have a plural form and are *not* accompanied by either a number or by the indefinite article **a / an**, nor by the definite article **the**, if the sense is general.
Petrol is getting more and more expensive.
I don't like vanilla ice-cream.
Education is a very important issue in the new government's policy.
BUT: *We want to give our children a good education.*

Names of substances and materials can be preceded by an indefinite adjective like **some / a little, a lot of / much** to indicate a quantity that isn't precise.
We need some flour to make the pancakes.
I have my coffee with a little milk and a lot of sugar.

See pages 242–244 for the use of the indefinites (**some, any, no…**) and 'quantifiers' (**much, many, a lot, a little…**).

D To specify the exact quantity of certain substances, expressions are used that indicate the container, the packaging, the weight or a part of the whole thing.

a bar of chocolate	a kilo of flour
a bottle of wine	a piece of cake
a can of lemonade	a pint of beer
a carton of milk	a slice of bread
a cup of tea	a spoonful of sugar
a glass of milk	a sheet of paper
a jar of jam	a tube of toothpaste

EXERCISES

Nouns: countables and uncountables (1) — UNIT 70

70.1 Choose the correct alternative.
1 Is he the new professor of **mathematics** / **the mathematics**?
2 I think this shelf is made of **a wood / wood**.
3 **Gold / The gold** is one of the most precious metals.
4 She loved **the biology / biology** at school.
5 I was sent to a famous university to get **good educations /a good education**.
6 Peter is really good at **the gymnastic / gymnastics**.

70.2 Write these nouns in the correct column.

| car   oil   economics   sugar   vegetable   health   water   poetry |
| sociology   cinema   gallery   sandwich   ballet   actor   magazine |

countable	uncountable
car,	

70.3 Complete the sentences with one of the words from the box. If nothing is needed, write *0*.

| any   your   some   a little   much   a |

1 Shall we order ....**a**........ pizza?
2 I'd like .... sugar in my tea, please.
3 Can you tell me how you got interested in .... nuclear physics?
4 We need to find a petrol station. There's hardly .... petrol left.
5 This is mine! You've already eaten .... slice of cake!
6 I'd only like .... rice with my fish, please.
7 'How much wine would you like, sir?' 'Not ...., please.'

70.4 Complete the expressions with the words in the box.

| a bottle of   a box of   beer   chocolate   a drop of   a slice of   bread   a jar of   a cup of   paper |

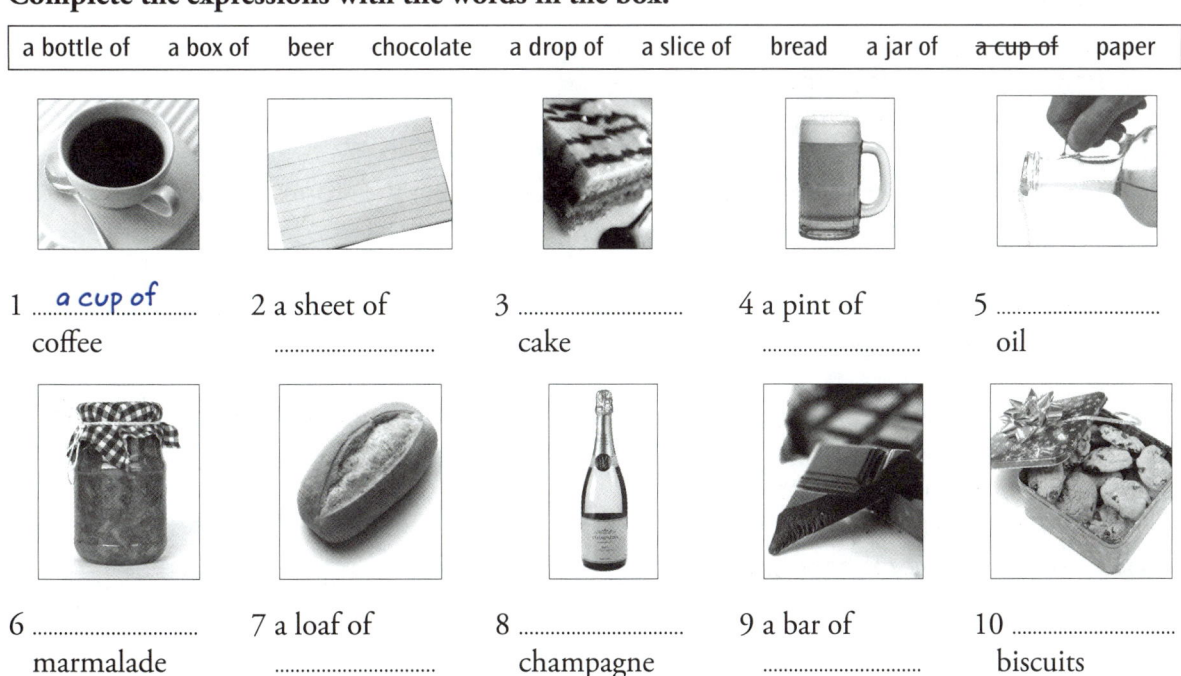

1 ....**a cup of**.... coffee
2 a sheet of ....
3 .... cake
4 a pint of ....
5 .... oil
6 .... marmalade
7 a loaf of ....
8 .... champagne
9 a bar of ....
10 .... biscuits

UNIT 71 Nouns: countables and uncountables (2)

A Some nouns can be used as uncountable nouns [U] when we refer to them as a mass, and as countable nouns [C] when we refer to them as singular units; in this case, they also have a plural form. Compare:

fruit [U], some fruit   BUT: a fruit [C]   these fruits

B Other nouns can be used as **uncountable** nouns as well as a **countable** nouns:

tea, coffee, wine, beer, cheese, cereal, noise …

Compare the different uses of some of the following nouns:

I usually have tea [U] *with milk.*
Tea [U] *is imported from India and China.*
This is a blend of selected teas [C] *from India.*
Two teas [C]*, please.* (in colloquial language, instead of: Two cups of tea.)
Can I have some cheese [U]*, please?*
French cheeses [C] *are all renowned.*
There's a lot of noise [U] *in this room.*
I heard a terrible noise [C]*.*

C Some nouns that are countable in other languages are uncountable in English. They therefore have no plural. Some of the more common nouns are:

advice   business   furniture   hair   homework
information   luggage   money   news   progress

REMEMBER: Verbs and pronouns accompanying these nouns must be singular.
Here's your luggage. It isn't very heavy.
This is today's news.
I don't have much homework today.
How much money do you have?
Give me some advice, please

Some of these nouns can be used in a singular sense, using the expression *a piece /an item of*.
a piece of news
a piece of advice
a piece/an item of furniture
a piece/an item of luggage

Other nouns, such as **business, hair** and **paper** can also be countable, but they then have a different meaning:
She set up a small business last year.
I'm allergic to cat hairs.
Could you pass me the paper, please?

EXERCISES

Nouns: countables and uncountables (2)

UNIT 71

71.1 Complete the sentences with the nouns in the box. Use the plural in *-s* where necessary.

fruit   wine   hair   paper   homework   coffee

1 Would you like fresh ......*fruit*...... for breakfast?
2 My sister has decided to grow her .... long again.
3 Is .... grown anywhere in Europe?
4 Do you think Italian or French .... are better?
5 I've got a lot of .... to do tonight!
6 I don't mind waiting. I've just bought a couple of .... to read.

71.2 Choose the correct alternative.

1 Do the English really drink **the tea / (tea)** with milk in it?
2 Have **good time / a good time** at the party!
3 I'm sorry to hear you've had such **bad luck / a bad luck** recently.
4 I just heard **a noise / noise** – let's go and see what it was.
5 I can't talk now – I haven't got **a time / time**.
6 There's **a good news / good news** about John's job.

71.3 Complete the sentences with *much, many, some* or *any*.

1 I need ......*some*...... advice about what to do next.
2 Our new maths teacher gives us too .... homework.
3 Peter doesn't seem to have .... luggage with him.
4 There are too .... problems to solve at the moment.
5 I noticed that there are .... good offers at the supermarket today.
6 How .... progress did they make in the peace talks?

71.4 Complete the pairs of sentences with the word given, in the singular if it is used as an uncountable noun or in the plural if it is used as a countable noun.

1 EXPERIENCE
   a Peter has had a lot of ......*experience*...... with this kind of project.
   b I had some wonderful ......*experiences*...... in Africa last year.

2 BUSINESS
   a It's very good to do .... with you.
   b There are a number of new .... setting up in our area.

3 DAMAGE
   a The court ordered him to pay .... to the defendant.
   b There was quite a lot of .... when he crashed his car.

4 FISH
   a This .... is very tasty. What kind is it?
   b The .... found in this river are good to eat.

5 COFFEE
   a Three ...., please.
   b Would you like some more .... now?

6 GLASS
   a The ball hit the window and the .... shattered.
   b There were numerous empty .... on the table.

UNIT 72 Collective and plural nouns; adjectives used as nouns

A Collective nouns are used to talk about a set of people, animals or things that form a group, for example:

team, government, family, army, crew, staff, swarm, flock, herd, fleet

The verb that accompanies collective nouns can usually be either singular or plural.

Our team is / are first in the championship. It's / They're a great team!

Note the plural agreement of the object with the subject.

We've all got umbrellas. (plural subject → plural object: each person has one)
They came on their bikes.

B Some nouns can only be plural. They are often preceded by **a pair of**.

(a pair of) binoculars	barracks	goods
(a pair of) glasses	cattle	outskirts / suburbs
(a pair of) pliers	clergy	people
(a pair of) pyjamas	clothes	police
(a pair of) scissors	contents	savings
(a pair of) tongs / pincers	customs	surroundings
(a pair of) trousers	earnings	youth

Note the agreement with the plural verb. **Barracks** can also be used as a singular noun.

The police <u>have</u> arrested a dangerous robber.
There <u>were</u> lots of people at the party.
Where <u>are</u> your pyjamas?
This barracks hosts / These barracks host the new recruits.

C It is possible for a qualifying adjective to function as a noun, to indicate:

- a category of people.

  the young, the old, the elderly, the rich, the poor, the living, the dead (also possible: *young people, old people, rich people*…, but not: ~~the youngs, the olds~~…). Singular: *a young man, an old man, a rich man* (not: ~~an old / a young / a rich~~).

- a population.

  the English, the French, the Dutch, the Chinese. Singular: *an Englishman, a Frenchman, a Dutchman* BUT: *a Chinese.*

- an abstract concept.

  the beautiful, the impossible, the supernatural

D There are also plural nouns that derive from adjectives:
sweets (from the adjective 'sweet'), *vegetables, valuables, criminals, the classics, the ancients, the natives*
My valuables are now safe in the bank.
I read a lot of classics when I was young.
Maori people are the natives of New Zealand.

EXERCISES

Collective and plural nouns; adjectives used as nouns

UNIT 72

72.1 Choose the correct alternative.
1 The police **has been** / **have been** looking for the thieves for a long time.
2 Could I borrow your scissors, please? Mine **don't** / **doesn't** cut very well.
3 The contents of the box **was hidden** / **were hidden** by the lid.
4 If you want to watch the news, hurry up – **it's** / **they're** just starting.
5 The local youth **are** / **is** all engaged in some voluntary work.
6 People **like** / **likes** getting free gifts from magazines.

72.2 Complete the expressions with the words from the box.

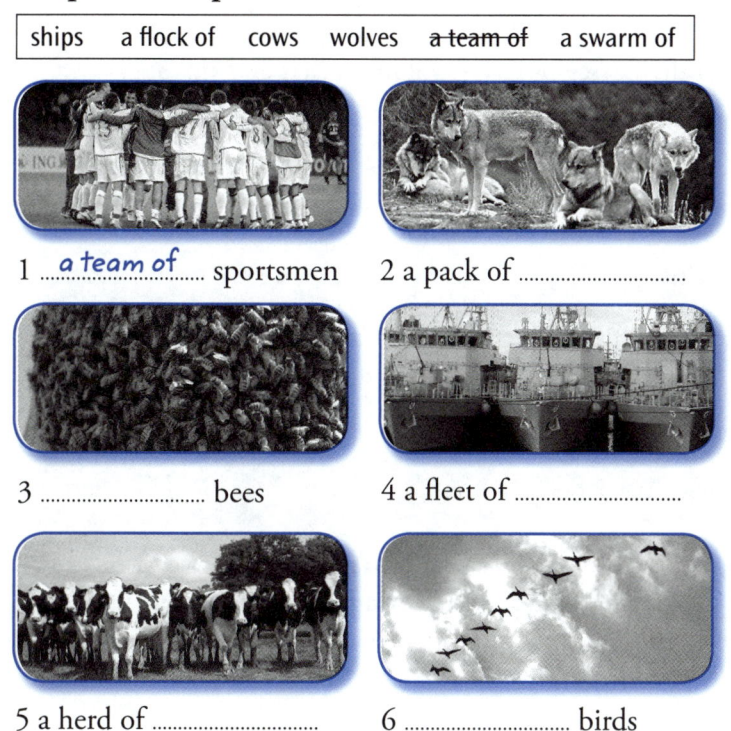

| ships   a flock of   cows   wolves   a team of   a swarm of |

1 *a team of* sportsmen
2 a pack of ....
3 .... bees
4 a fleet of ....
5 a herd of ....
6 .... birds

72.3 Complete the sentences with the nouns in the box. Watch out: there is one extra!

| trousers   congratulations   pyjamas   barracks   binoculars   savings   outskirts |

1 Skirts look very nice, but when it's cold, Alicia always wears *trousers*.
2 There are a lot of shopping malls on the .... of the city.
3 After marching on the parade ground, the soldiers returned to their ....
4 .... , Lucy, you have won first prize in the competition.
5 I've told Grandad to put his .... into a bank.
6 Pass me the .... , there's an interesting bird over there.

72.4 Write *the* before the nouns where necessary. It the article isn't needed, write *0*.
1 *The* French are proud of their cooking.
2 .... sweets are bad for your teeth.
3 Paul is reading a lot of .... thrillers these days.
4 We can't do .... impossible, but we'll try!
5 For .... Japanese, serving .... tea is an art.
6 .... vegetables and .... fruit are an important part of everyone's diet.

UNIT 73 Possessive case *(Tom's friend, A friend of Tom's)*

To indicate the possession of something, affiliation or kinship, we use the possessive case.

A The possessive case is formed by placing the noun that refers to the possessor before the object that they possess (without any article!) and by adding **'s** to the possessor when the possessor is:
- a singular noun.
  the bag of <u>the teacher</u> → <u>the teacher's</u> bag
  the garden of <u>my neighbour</u> → <u>my neighbour's</u> garden
  the twin sister of <u>Samantha</u> → <u>Samantha's</u> twin sister
- a plural noun that doesn't end in **-s**.
  <u>the children's</u> toys

Only the apostrophe is added when the possessor is a plural noun that ends in **-s**.
<u>the students'</u> dorms
<u>the Smiths'</u> flat

When the possessor consists of a proper noun or a surname that ends in **-s**, **'s** is usually added.
the diary of <u>James</u> → <u>James's</u> diary
the house of <u>Ms Jones</u> → <u>Ms Jones's</u> house

Sometimes, however, with historical names or surnames of famous characters that end in **-s**, only the apostrophe is added: <u>Jesus'</u> birth, <u>Dickens'</u> works

NB: If the same object belongs to two or more people:
Rita and Betty's room (they share the room)
BUT: *Rita's and Betty's rooms* (they each have their own room)

B The possessive case is used when the possessor is a person (**Tom's cousin**), also expressed with an indefinite pronoun (**someone's birthday**) or an animal (**the dog's kennel**). It isn't usually used when we talk about something belonging to a thing (**the pages of the book** or **the book pages**, not: ~~the book's pages~~).

C Besides indicating possession, affiliation and kinship, the **possessive case** is used:
- with names of shops, restaurants, professional studies, churches…, often only keeping the **'s** and implying the noun **shop**, **store**, **restaurant**, **surgery**, **cathedral** …

  I visited St Peter's when I was in Rome.
  Tomorrow, I'm going to the dentist's / to the doctor's. (also possible: to the dentist / to the doctor)

- to say 'at someone's house', implying **house**.
  We went to Peter's (house) yesterday.

- with expressions of time.
  today's / yesterday's newspaper, two weeks' holiday (or **a two-week holiday**), *three hours' walk* (or **a three-hour walk**)

D Look at the following construction: **a friend of Sarah's**. Also possible is: **one of Sarah's friends**, but not: ~~a Sarah's friend~~, because it isn't possible to put the article, nor other determiners, before the possessive case.

This construction is called '**double genitive**', as both the preposition **of** and **'s** are present.
Look at also: *some ties of my father's* (also possible: some of my father's ties, but not: ~~some my father's ties~~.)

EXERCISES

UNIT 73 — Possessive case

73.1 Rewrite the expressions with the possessive case.
1. the toy of the dog — *the dog's toy*
2. the guitar of the boy — ....
3. the twin brother of Paul — ....
4. the dresses of the women — ....
5. the cages of the animals — ....
6. the computer of your father — ....

73.2 Which word could be added? Complete the sentences in a logical way.
1. Are you going to your grandparents' *house* tomorrow?
2. Did you see St Paul's .... when you were in London?
3. There are lots of patients waiting at Doctor Kerry's .... today.
4. The ambulance is taking them to St Thomas's ....
5. There's a good greengrocer's .... at the corner with Lewis Street.
6. We had a great dinner at Louie Linguini's .... last night.

73.3 Choose the correct alternative (A, B or C).
1. I'm going to the ....*C*.... tomorrow.
   A doctors   B doctors'   **C doctor's**
2. I got this meat at the .... on the corner.
   A butchers'   B butcher's   C butchers
3. I visited San .... when I was in Verona.
   A Zeno's   B Zenos   C Zenos'
4. We went to .... factory yesterday.
   A Harris   B Harris'   C Harris's
5. Where did you eat last night? At .... restaurant.
   A Fausto   B Fausto's   C Faustos'
6. Did you read last .... *Observer* magazine?
   A week   B week's   C weeks'

73.4 Tick (✔) the correct expressions and correct the false ones.
1. ✔ a colleague of my mother's — ....
2. ☐ a my brother's classmate — *a classmate of my brother's*
3. ☐ some my cousin's books — ....
4. ☐ a relation of my father's — ....
5. ☐ a my sister's team-mate — ....
6. ☐ one my teacher's ideas — ....
7. ☐ an acquaintance of Paul's — ....
8. ☐ yesterday newspaper — ....

73.5 Rewrite the underlined expressions in a different way.
1. We visited <u>some relations of my wife's</u> last summer. — *some of my wife's relations*
2. Why don't you try <u>a bottle of wine of my father's</u>? — ....
3. These are <u>two of my sister's CDs</u>. — ....
4. Have you read <u>the issue of this week</u> of *Time* magazine? — ....
5. Where is <u>the newspaper of today</u>? — ....
6. Have you been <u>on holiday for three weeks</u>? — ....

REVIEW 17 EXERCISES Units 68–73

R17.1 Complete the sentences with the masculine or the feminine of the word in bold.

1 There were many famous ...*actors*... and **actresses** at the Hollywood dinner.
2 A number of European **princes** and .... attended the ball.
3 There was a .... and a **policeman** outside the building.
4 Two of my **nieces** and one .... came to visit me.
5 I got birthday cards from my **son** and my ....
6 There were **stewardesses** and .... to show people the way.
7 I want to buy some little presents for my **granddaughter** and my ....

R17.2 Complete the sentences with the plural of the nouns in the box.

| city   life   ~~dish~~   party   kiss   disco |

1 There are too many ...*dishes*... on the table.
2 They visited the Imperial .... when they went to Morocco.
3 There are three good .... in our town.
4 The .... of dead writers are fascinating.
5 The child looked at her mother and gave her three sweet ....
6 I haven't been to many .... recently.

R17.3 Choose the correct alternative.

1 Two **(oxen)** / **oxes** were pulling the old cart.
2 I've got no money left – just two **pennys** / **pence**.
3 Unfortunately, two people in my class have got head **louses** / **lice**.
4 There were about 100 **sheep** / **sheeps** in the field.
5 My brother is an artist who works in different **mediums** / **media**.
6 My **sister-in-laws** / **sisters-in-law** are visiting me next week.
7 I bought a new pair of **pyjama** / **pyjamas**.

R17.4 Complete the sentences with the words in the box.

| ~~butter~~   petrol   history   wood   wine   information   sugar |

1 I need some ...*butter*... and .... to make these cakes.
2 I'd like some .... about your hotel.
3 .... is my favourite subject at school.
4 There isn't much .... left in the cellar. Just a couple of bottles.
5 Is there enough .... in the car?
6 Please can you bring some .... to start the fire?

R.17.5 Tick (✔) the correct expressions and correct the incorrect ones.

1 ...✔... a pair of scissors
2 .... a carton of orange juice
3 .... a kilo of milk
4 .... a piece of news
5 .... a spoonful of honey
6 .... a bottle of beer
7 .... a cup of wine
8 .... a can of fruit
9 .... a jar of flour
10 .... a packet of pasta

REVIEW 17

R17.6 Rearrange the words and write the sentences.
1. afternoon – garden – I – working – neighbour's – spent – in – the – my
   I spent the afternoon working in my neighbour's garden.
2. house – match – Michael's – went – after – They – to – the
3. president's – good – He – of – friend – is – the – a
4. all – We – summer – Johnsons' – at – villa – stayed – the
5. open – hostel – round – year – The – all – is – youth
6. from – bread – Please – loaves – can – baker's – you – the – get – of – two – ?

R17.7 Four of these sentences have mistakes in them. Find them and rewrite the sentences correctly.
1. A my brother's friend came to see us last weekend.
   A friend of my brother's came to see us last weekend.
2. We saw one Picasso paintings at the exhibition yesterday.
3. Let's spend the afternoon in St James' Park. It's such a beautiful day.
4. Lillian and I had dinner at Beppe restaurant last night.
5. These are only some of my cousin's DVDs. He's got hundreds.
6. Doris's and Liam's house is opposite the playground.

R17.8 Choose the correct alternative.
1. Tamsin's going out with a friend of **Sophie / (Sophie's)**.
2. I get four **weeks' / weeks** holiday with my new job.
3. Have you read **today / today's** paper yet?
4. My **cousin's / cousin** dog is a bad-tempered animal.
5. We're invited to the **Blair's / Blair** house for dinner tonight.
6. **Katie and Emma's / Katie's and Emma's** room is very messy!
7. What do you think of **Obamas / Obama's** policies?
8. Joe's **dad's / dad** new car is awesome!
9. The **students' / student's** rooms are fine. They have lots of space.
10. One of **Tom / Tom's** friends has had a skiing accident.

H Exam preparation

H.1 PET Reading Part 5

Read the text and choose the correct word(s) (A, B, C or D) for each space.

I have received (1) ...C... to many (2) .... over the years. Some of them have been special (3) ...., such as (4) .... birthday or anniversary, and others have been for Christmas or New Year. But the strangest party I have ever been invited to was the (5) .... ball. Can you imagine the (6) .... dancing? I couldn't! But when I got there, I found it to be a very enjoyable event. There were no (7) .... in sight, and everyone was happy and smiling. The chief (8) .... speech was short and amusing, and (9) .... mood was good. There was lots of nice food, and the (10) .... were excellent. I danced with several (11) .... and they all danced beautifully.

1 **A** invitation   **B** the invitation   **C** invitations   **D** invitation's
2 **A** party   **B** parties   **C** party's   **D** partys
3 **A** occasions   **B** occasion   **C** occasiones   **D** occasion's
4 **A** someone   **B** someones   **C** someones'   **D** someone's
5 **A** policeman   **B** policemans   **C** policemen's   **D** policemens'
6 **A** police   **B** polices   **C** police's   **D** polices'
7 **A** uniform   **B** uniforms   **C** uniforms'   **D** uniform's
8 **A** detective's   **B** detectives   **C** detectives'   **D** detective
9 **A** everyone   **B** everyones   **C** everyone's   **D** everyones'
10 **A** wine's   **B** wines'   **C** wine   **D** wines
11 **A** policewoman   **B** policewomen   **C** policewomens   **D** policewomen's

H.2 PET Writing Part 1

Complete the second sentence so that it means the same as the first. Use no more than three words.

1 Janet Anderson is one of my mother's friends.
   Janet Anderson is a friend ...*of my mother's*...

2 I don't like a lot of milk in my tea.
   I only like .... milk in my tea.

3 I'd like to give you a piece of information about it.
   I'd like to give you some .... about it.

4 I'd like two teas and a piece of cake, please.
   I'd like two .... and a slice of cake, please.

5 There are several items of furniture to deliver.
   There is .... furniture to deliver.

6 That man is a colleague of my father's.
   That man is one of ....

H.3 PET Writing Part 3

These are the instructions for making a good cup of tea. Write the instructions for how to make a good cup of coffee (60–80 words).

> First, boil some water in a kettle. While it is boiling, put some black tea into the teapot. When the water has boiled, pour it into the teapot and leave it for three minutes, or longer if you like strong tea. Pour some tea into each cup, and then add some milk and some sugar.

Exam preparation

H

H.4 FCE Use of English Part 2

Read the dialogue below and think of a word which best fits each space. Use only one in each space.

Pat: Shall we make (1) *some* cakes this afternoon?
Danny: That's a nice idea, but I don't think we have the right (2)............... .
Pat: Well, there's (3)............... butter, but there isn't (4)............... flour.
Danny: We need a (5)............... of eggs and a (6)............... of jam, don't we?
Pat: Well, I'd better go to the corner shop. Can you lend me some money, because I've only got a (7)............... .
Danny: Here you are. And can you go to the (8)............... and buy some meat for dinner?
Pat: Anything else?
Danny: You could go to that tea shop – they've got some really interesting (9)............... from China, and I'd like to try some of them.
Pat: OK. Oh, and I'll get a (10)............... of toothpaste, too. I noticed we've nearly run out.

H.5 FCE Use of English Part 3

Read the text below. Use the word given in capitals at the end of each line to form a word that fits in the space in the same line.

When the famous (1) *actor* came into Paolo's restaurant,   ACT
Silvia, the young (2)..............., was very excited. But Paolo   WAIT
wasn't very happy about the two large (3)...............   POLICE
who were standing outside the door. He knew his (4)...............   TAKE
for the night would be low, because nobody likes the police
outside a restaurant. But he was an (5)............... and also a   ITALY
(6)..............., so he offered his famous guest the menu   PROFESSION
with a smile.

H.6 FCE Use of English Part 4

Complete the second sentence so that it has a similar meaning to the first sentence, using the word given. Do not change the word given. You must use between two and five words, including the word given.

1 John and I have been friends for a long time.
   MINE
   John has been *a friend of mine* for a long time.

2 We went on holiday to France for three weeks.
   A
   We had .... holiday in France.

3 I used some sports equipment belonging to my brother.
   BROTHER'S
   I used .... sports equipment.

4 I read a number of poems written by Keats.
   KEATS'
   I read a number ....

5 There were a lot of cows together in the field.
   WAS
   .... of cows in the field.

UNIT 74

Adjectives *(a big red apple / The book is new)*

A Adjectives are used to describe people and things. They have the same form for singular and plural, masculine and feminine nouns.

a nice boy   nice boys
a nice girl   nice girls

B Adjectives can be found:

- before a noun (attributive position). Note that in English, adjectives always precede nouns.
   It's a large town. (not: *It's a town large*.)
   I like green apples.
   Laura is a clever girl.

- after the verbs **be**, **look**, **feel**, **get**… (predicative position).
   Jack is new in this school.   *It's getting dark.*
   You look happy.   *I feel tired and hungry.*

   In questions, the adjective is placed after the subject.
   Is Simon lazy? (not: *Is lazy Simon?*)
   Are the children ready? (not: *Are ready the children?*)

C Possessive adjectives (**my, your**…) and the possessive case (**Mary's**) precede all other adjectives:
my red and yellow T-shirt

If there are two adjectives, the one indicating colour is usually placed next to the noun and, if there is more than one adjective referring to colour, **white** is usually placed last.
big blue eyes   a nice red skirt   a black and white photo

When several adjectives are placed before the noun, opinion adjectives, such as **interesting**, **nice**, **beautiful**…, come before fact adjectives, such as **big**, **old**, **round**… The order that adjectives are placed in is usually as follows, though it can be changed to give more emphasis to one of the aspects in particular:

| quantity – opinion – size – age – shape – colour – origin – material |

a beautiful big square wooden table
two nice blue Turkish silk scarves

D Adjectives can be modified by adverbs of degree: **too**, **very**, **rather / quite**, **a little** (see p.284). These adverbs are placed before an adjective, apart from **enough**, which is placed after the adjective.
It was too cold.
The room wasn't warm enough.
The test was rather difficult. / It was a rather difficult test.

EXERCISES

Qualifying adjectives

UNIT 74

74.1 Write sentences by placing the adjective in the right place.

1. (musical) Jane / is / a / girl — *Jane is a musical girl.*
2. (good) Mike / is / a / guitarist
3. (tired) Are / the / band / ?
4. (nice) Has / she / got / a / voice / ?
5. (loud) The / instruments / are / very
6. (interesting) It / is / an / CD
7. (beautiful) Isn't / Bach's / music / ?
8. (old) How / is / that / violin / ?

74.2 Place the adjectives in the sentence. If necessary, use *and* to join them up.

1. (red / white) Jack White has got a *red and white* guitar.
2. (fast / loud) The music they play is ....
3. (beautiful / old) He plays a .... guitar.
4. (high / clear) She sings in a .... voice.
5. (new / fresh) The songs they play are ....
6. (fast / accurate / exciting) Her piano playing is ....
7. (interesting / original) They write .... lyrics.
8. (silver / valuable) She always played a .... flute.

74.3 Put the adjectives in the right order.

1. yellow / big / plastic / oval
   a *big oval yellow plastic* table
2. black / striped / wonderful / silk
   a .... suit
3. Indian / red / long / interesting
   an .... piece of cloth
4. simple / cotton / white / new
   a .... dress
5. old / African / valuable / ebony
   a .... box
6. Asian / young / tall / handsome
   a .... man
7. 19th century / ugly / enormous / red brick
   a .... house.
8. rectangular / tall / glass / pink
   a .... vase.

74.4 Indicate (∧) where the word needs to be placed in the sentence.

1. (too) It   was ∧ cold   .
2. (too) The   disco   was   hot   .
3. (a little) The   music   was   loud   .
4. (quite) The   concert   was   boring   .
5. (enough) He   wasn't   good   to   be   in   our   band   .
6. (rather) It   was   a   embarrassing   situation   .
7. (very) The   lecture   wasn't   interesting   .
8. (enough) The   water   isn't   hot   to   have   a   bath   .

UNIT 75: Adjective formation (surprising, surprised); nouns used as adjectives (a film star)

A Many adjectives are present participles (**-ing**) or past participles (**-ed**) of regular verbs.

satisfying	satisfied	→	satisfy
relaxing	relaxed	→	relax
exciting	excited	→	excite
tiring	tired	→	tire

I've had a tiring day, so I'm very tired now.
The film I saw last night was very exciting.
I was so excited I couldn't speak.

REMEMBER: **-ing** → active meaning, **-ed** → passive meaning

Some adjectives are formed by adding the suffix **-ed** to nouns indicating parts of the body or of other objects.

a red-haired woman   *a big-nosed man*
black-eyed peas   *leather-jacketed teenagers*

Note that nouns which function as an adjective don't take **-s** in the plural form.

a 12-year-old boy (not: a twelve-years-old…)
a ten-dollar bill (not: a ten-dollars…)

For a list of adjectives formed with suffixes (see p.342).

B In English, it is common to find two nouns placed together (**noun + noun** or **compound nouns**), where the first noun functions as an adjective that defines the second one (see p.194).

the city walls
the computer keyboard
a business partner

This construction is used:

- when establishing a relation between things or affiliation to a city (it doesn't have anything to do with the possessive case, therefore there is no **'s**).

  the kitchen table   *the church choir*
  London Transport   *York Minster*

- with expressions of time or festivities.

  the winter holidays   *a weekend trip*
  Christmas carols   *a birthday card*

- to indicate the use of clothing items, equipment, vehicles…

  football boots   *a tennis racket*
  a pencil sharpener   *the school bus*

  The use of the object is often indicated by the **-ing** form of a verb.

  a frying pan   *a washing machine*
  a shopping bag   *a swimming pool*

- to indicate genres of literature, film, music, art…

  crime stories   *action films*
  disco music   *performance art*

It is also common to find three or more nouns grouped together.

the World Football Championship
the UK Energy Research Centre (UKERC)

EXERCISES

Adjective formation; nouns used as adjectives

UNIT 75

75.1 Choose the correct alternative.
1 Isn't it **surprised / surprising** that she sang that song?
2 We want to have a thousands of **satisfying / satisfied** customers.
3 People say that regular meditation makes you feel **relaxing / relaxed**.
4 Jane found it **embarrassing / embarrassed** that Suzie was wearing the same dress.
5 All the newspapers were full of the **shocked / shocking** news.
6 Bill was so **excited / exciting** that he couldn't say a word.

75.2 Complete the sentences with the correct form of the adjective (*-ed / -ing*) formed from the verbs in brackets.
1 (bore) It is very ......*boring*...... to play the same music for 30 years.
2 (annoy) We were very .... when the conductor didn't arrive on time.
3 (interest) I'm sorry, but I'm really not .... in heavy-metal music.
4 (entertain) He's really .... when he sings and dances like that.
5 (confuse) The arrangements for the concert were very ....
6 (excite) I was very .... when I met Eric Clapton last year.

75.3 Rewrite the expressions using nouns that function as adjectives.
1 the cupboard in the kitchen   *the kitchen cupboard*
2 films about science fiction   ....
3 shoes to play tennis in   ....
4 the team from the school   ....
5 a holiday in the summer   ....
6 a shelf for CDs   ....
7 a magazine about music   ....
8 the carpet in the living room   ....
9 a machine that washes your car ....
10 a garden where vegetables are grown ....
11 vegetables from the garden   ....
12 a glass for drinking wine   ....

75.4 Form new adjectives by joining the words with a hyphen and adding the suffix *-ed*.
1 Their children all have blues eyes.
  They are ......*blue-eyed*...... children.
2 That man has a long beard.
  He is a .... man.
3 Those boys have long hair.
  They're .... boys.
4 These monkeys have short tails.
  They are .... monkeys.
5 That woman's eyes are crossed.
  She's a .... woman.
6 That whale has a white back.
  It's a .... whale.

UNIT 76 The comparative of adjectives (1)
(cheaper than / more expensive than)

A To compare the qualities of two people or things, we use comparative adjectives.

- Adjectives with one syllable or those with two syllables that end in **-y** form the comparative by adding **-er**.

  small → smaller   cold → colder   light → lighter
  heavy → heavier   easy → easier   lucky → luckier

  The addition of **-er** entails a few spelling changes:
  - the **y** changes to **i**: easy → easier   dry → drier   BUT: shy → shyer
  - in one-syllable adjectives that end in a vowel + a consonant, the final consonant is doubled: big → bigger   hot → hotter, BUT: cheap → cheaper (it isn't doubled as there are two vowels)
  - **-r** is added to adjectives that end in **-e**: large → larger   wide → wider

- Adjectives with two or more syllables (apart from those that end in **-y**) form the comparative with the adverb **more**:

  useful → more useful   interesting → more interesting
  difficult → more difficult   extravagant → more extravagant

- Two-syllable adjectives that end in **-ow**, **-er**, **-le** and certain others (**quiet**, **polite**, **friendly**, **stupid**...) can have both forms.

  narrow → narrower / more narrow   clever → cleverer / more clever
  gentle → gentler / more gentle   polite → politer / more polite

B With the comparative we use the preposition **than**.

Luke is taller than his brother.
This test is more difficult than the other one.

Than can be used as a conjunction to introduce a comparative clause.

This test is more difficult than I thought.
The hotel was more comfortable than we expected.

If the second part of the comparison includes a pronoun, an object pronoun (**me, him**...) is usually used. In a more formal situation, the subject pronoun followed by the auxiliary is preferable.

My sister is taller than me. / My sister is taller than I am.
They're more organised than us. / ...than we are.
I'm luckier than her. / ...than she is.
She isn't more intelligent than you (are).

C Before comparative adjectives, it is also possible to find the adverbs **much / far / a lot** or **a little / a bit / slightly**.

Mark is a far nicer guy than Jeff.
Today's lesson was slightly more interesting than yesterday's.
Your house is much larger than ours.

"YOUR HOUSE IS MUCH LARGER THAN OURS"

EXERCISES

UNIT 76 — The comparative of adjectives (1)

76.1 Write the comparative of the adjectives in the box in the correct column. Watch out: one of the adjectives can be placed in two columns.

| ~~loud~~ | lucky | small | careful | expensive | ugly |
| old | extraordinary | clever | happy | typical | early |

adjective + -er	adjective + -ier	more + adjective
louder		

76.2 Use the suggestions to write comparative sentences.

1 Water / healthy / cola — Water is healthier than cola.
2 Peaches / sweet / apples
3 John / clever / Paul
4 A gold ring / expensive / a silver ring
5 Jane / young / Stephanie
6 Soccer / popular / hockey

76.3 Complete the sentences with the comparative of the adjective. Add *than* where necessary.

1 (nice) This dress is ...... nicer than ...... all the others.
2 (short) Linda is .... the other girls in our class.
3 (quiet) I can't hear the music. Can you be a bit .... , please?!
4 (safe) This car is expensive, but it's .... other cars.
5 (expensive) Leather shoes are cheap here. At home, they're ....
6 (comfortable) The new sofa is .... our old armchairs.
7 (careful) Try to be .... next time! You nearly broke the Chinese vase.

76.4 Write sentences using comparative adjectives. Use the adjectives in the box.

| long / short | old / young | expensive / cheap |
| warm / cold | ~~large / small~~ | high / low | heavy / light |

1 Belgium: 30,528 square km / Luxembourg: 2,586 square km
   Belgium is larger than Luxembourg. / Luxembourg is smaller than Belgium.
2 The Thames: 215 miles / The Avon: 96 miles

3 The Matterhorn: 4,478m / Mont Blanc: 4,810m

4 Madonna: 1958 / Shakira: 1977

5 My suitcase: 20kg / Jamie's suitcase: 24kg

6 everyday jeans: £39.99 / brand-name jeans: £130

7 New York: 17°C / Naples: 24°C (yesterday's temperatures)

UNIT 77

The comparative of adjectives (2)
(as interesting as / less interesting than)

A To say that people, things, etc. are equal in some way, we often use the structure: **as** + adjective + **as**
Sometimes the first **as** is reinforced by the adverb **just**.

She's just as beautiful as her sister.
The flat where I live now is about as big as the one where I lived before.

B The negative form is: **not as** + adjective + **as**
They were both very well dressed,
but he wasn't as elegant as his brother.

The first **as** can be substituted by **so**.

This road isn't so bendy as the other one.
The supermarket isn't so crowded today as it was yesterday.

today   yesterday

C To talk about inequality, we can use the adverb **less**, which is placed before the adjective.

less + adjective + **than**

The weather today is less humid than (it was) yesterday.
Grown-ups are usually less adventurous than teenagers.

This comparative isn't often used. It is more common to use:

- **more** + the adjective with the opposite meaning.
  The sales are on. Everything is <u>less expensive</u> than it was. → *Everything is <u>cheaper</u> than it was.*

- **not as** + adjective **as.**
  The sequel is <u>less exciting</u> than the original movie. → *The sequel is <u>not as exciting</u> as the original movie.*

D Particular cases of comparison

comparative + **and** + comparative (gradual increase)

It's getting darker and darker.
The book I'm reading is getting more and more gripping.

the + comparative... **the** + comparative (parallel increase)

The heavier your luggage is, the more expensive the transport gets..
The greater the challenge, the greater the reward.

the + comparative + **of**... (between two things or people)

I'll buy the larger of the two pullovers.

Compare with: *I'll buy the largest one.* (If they are more than two, the superlative is used; see p.216)

To compare two actions, the first term of comparison consists of a verb in the infinitive (**to** + base form) and the second of a verb in the base form.

It's nicer <u>to go</u> on holiday with a friend than <u>go</u> alone.
Sometimes it's quicker <u>to cycle</u> than <u>go</u> by bus.

EXERCISES

UNIT 77 — The comparative of adjectives (2)

77.1 Write comparisons with the words in brackets using *as… as…* .
1 (big) Your house is ......*as big as*...... my house.
2 (just / bad) His behaviour is .... mine.
3 (cheap) Their bags were .... ours.
4 (about / tall) Mike is .... I was at his age.
5 (just / pretty) Candy is .... Rachel is.
6 (about / good) This computer is .... my old one.

77.2 Using *not as* or *not so*, change these terms of comparison into the negative form.
1 My house is less comfortable than his house. — *My house isn't as comfortable as his house.*
2 Your guitar playing is less intricate than Paul's.
3 The weather yesterday was sunnier than today.
4 Julie is more intelligent than Pauline.
5 Spielberg's films are less influential than Scorsese's.
6 Elephants are more dangerous than rhinos.

77.3 Match the two parts of the sentences.

1 ...*e*... 2 .... 3 .... 4 .... 5 .... 6 .... 7 ....

1 His writing is getting neater
2 Their English is becoming clearer
3 The more complicated your task is,
4 The nicer you are to people,
5 This is the more interesting
6 Don is the cleverer
7 Can I have the smaller

a of the two brothers.
b of his two books.
c the more people like you.
d and clearer.
e and neater.
f of the two coats?
g the happier you are when you do it successfully.

77.4 Write sentences with *as… as…* using the adjectives in brackets.

1 Both Julie and Helen are 1.65m tall. (tall)
   ....*Julie is as tall as Helen.*............

2 Both the watch and the ring are £120. (expensive)
   ....

3 Both the sweater and the cardigan are size 12. (big)
   ....

4 Both the Boeing 747 and the Airbus A380 can fly at 890km per hour. (fast)
   ....

5 Both the dictionary and the novel have got 300 pages. (long)
   ....

6 Both Robert and Samira are 14 years old. (old)
   ....

UNIT 78: The superlative of adjectives
(the cheapest / the most expensive / the least expensive)

A To compare a person or thing with a group, the superlative of adjectives is used.

- Adjectives with one syllable or those with two syllables that end in **-y** form the superlative by adding **-est**.

    the youngest   the oldest   the busiest

    The addition of **-est** entails the same spelling changes as the addition of **-er** in the comparative does:
    - the **y** changes to **i**: *easy → the easiest   dry → the driest*   BUT: *shy → the shyest*
    - in one-syllable adjectives that end in a vowel + a consonant, the final consonant is doubled.
        fat → the fattest, thin → the thinnest, BUT: *deep → the deepest* (it isn't doubled, as there are two vowels)
    - **-st** is added to adjectives that end in **-e**.
        large → largest, pale → palest

- Adjectives with two or more syllables (apart from two-syllable ones that end in **-y**) form the superlative with the adverb **most**.

    the most famous   the most common   the most popular

- Two-syllable adjectives that end in **-ow**, **-er**, **-le** and certain others (**quiet, polite, friendly, stupid…**) can have both forms.

    the cleverest / the most clever   the quietest / the most quiet

    Superlative adjectives are nearly always preceded by the definite article (**the**) or by a possessive (**my, your, his, Lucy's…**).

    Tim is <u>the</u> most popular student in his class.
    That was <u>his</u> greatest success.

B The object that follows the superlative is introduced by the preposition **in** if it's a place (**in the world, in Europe…**) or by the preposition **of** when the term of comparison is a group of elements or an expression of time (**of all my friends, of all times…**).

Chicago is one of the largest cities <u>in</u> the USA.
February is the shortest month <u>of</u> the year.

The comparison can also be expressed by a relative clause with a verb in the present perfect or past perfect, which is sometimes accompanied by the adverb **ever**.

It's one of the funniest films (that) I've seen.
He was the most generous person I had ever met.

C To emphasise a superlative, the adverbial expression **by far** can be used.

He's by far the most talented musician in the orchestra.

D The superlative of **less** is **least**.

This bag was the least expensive they had in the shop.
It's the least relevant thing I've ever heard.

EXERCISES

UNIT 78 — The superlative of adjectives

78.1 Write the superlative of these adjectives.
1. tall — the tallest
2. narrow — ....
3. nice — ....
4. easy — ....
5. exciting — ....
6. hard — ....
7. heavy — ....
8. pale — ....
9. dark — ....
10. comfortable — ....

78.2 Use the words to write sentences with the superlative.
1. Paul / tall / boy / I / ever / meet — Paul is the tallest boy I've ever met.
2. It / funny / play / I / ever / see — ....
3. They / loud / band / we / hear — ....
4. It / pretty / village / he / visit — ....
5. That / amazing / concert / I / attend — ....
6. It / dangerous / place / I / be to — ....

78.3 Rearrange the words and write questions with the superlative.
1. man – fastest – Who – on – is – the – Earth – ?
   Who is the fastest man on Earth?
2. Italy – is – mountain – What – highest – in – the – ?
   ....
3. city – world – in – biggest – Where – the – is – the – ?
   ....
4. tall – tallest – is – man – How – the – ?
   ....
5. supercar – Which – the – Italian – is – fastest – ?
   ....
6. the – world – is – diamond – Which – valuable – the – in – most – ?
   ....

78.4 Complete the sentences with the words in brackets. Use *the least* + adjective + noun.
1. (book / interesting) It's the least interesting book I've ever read.
2. (invention / useful) It's .... I've ever seen.
3. (guide / helpful) He's .... we've ever had.
4. (match / exciting) It was .... he had ever watched.
5. (comedian / amusing) He's .... I've ever heard.
6. (person / patronising) She's .... I've ever met.

78.5 Complete the interview with the superlative of the adjectives in the box.

| likely | ~~famous~~ | exciting | annoying | shy |

A: How does it feel to be (1) the most famous comedian on the showbiz scene these days?
B: Well, it's one of (2) .... feelings I've ever had. Everyone recognises me wherever I go. But this has also its negative side.
A: Do you mean you haven't got any privacy any more?
B: Yes, that's exactly what I mean. That's (3) .... aspect of my being so popular. The funny thing is that I was (4) .... boy in my class when I was at school and I was (5) .... to make people laugh. I wonder what my teachers would think of me now.

217

UNIT 79 — The comparative and superlative of adverbs
(faster / fastest; more quickly / most quickly)

A The comparative of adverbs is formed in the same way to that of adjectives. In particular:

- **-er** is added to adverbs that have the same form as adjectives, following the same spelling rules.
  fast → faster
  high → higher

  Compare the sentences that use an adjective to those that use an adverb.
  This is a faster car.   *It goes faster.*
  This peak is higher.   *This plane flies higher.*

- adverbs that end in **-ly** are preceded by **more** in the comparative.
  slowly → more slowly
  quickly → more quickly
  Speak more slowly, please. I can't follow you.

B With the comparative, we use the preposition **than**.

Yesterday, we got up earlier than you.
He arrived later than me.
My mother drives more carefully than my father.
It took much longer than I expected.

C We use the structure: **as** + adverb + **as.**

I can run as fast as you.
He hasn't trained as hard as the rest of the team.

D To form the superlative, adverbs follow the same rules as adjectives. Adverbs are preceded by **the** and are modified by:

- adding **-est** to adverbs that have the same form as an adjective: long → the longest

  The turtle is one of the animals that live the longest.

- adding **the most** before adverbs that end in **-ly**: quickly → the most quickly

  She works the most quickly when she is alone and not under pressure.

In formal English, sometimes **most** is used before adverbs. Its meaning is stronger than **very**. In this case, **the** is omitted.

Please drive most carefully, there's a baby in the car.
They behaved most stupidly.

EXERCISES

The comparative and superlative of adverbs

UNIT 79

79.1 In each sentence, circle the comparative of the adverb.
1 This is a faster car than yours; in fact, it goes (faster than) everybody's car.
2 Mike works harder than everyone; he's the most hard-working of all my employees.
3 He's a more careful driver than anybody I know. He drove more carefully than his instructor along that road.
4 Summer arrived later this year – it was a later summer than usual.
5 It was a higher climb than we'd done before – we went higher than ever before.
6 He spoke lower than other men, with such a low voice that he was hard to hear.
7 Eat more slowly – a slow eater is a healthier person.

79.2 Complete the sentences with the comparative of the adverb formed from the adjective in brackets.
1 (slow) The bus went *more slowly* than it usually did.
2 (expensive) The film star was dressed .... than anyone else.
3 (loud) The Crazy Four played .... than all the other rock bands.
4 (late) Don't worry – you can arrive .... than the other guests.
5 (happy) The children danced .... than their parents.
6 (sweet) She kissed him .... than ever before.
7 (convincing) In the last debate, she spoke .... than ever before.

79.3 Complete the sentences with as... as... and the adverb formed from the adjective in brackets.
1 (neat) I can't draw *as neatly as* you can.
2 (quick) I'm sure Diana can run .... Sally.
3 (clear) I know I can't speak .... him.
4 (just; nice) He knows how to sing .... me.
5 (careful) They drive .... we do.
6 (deep) She doesn't sleep .... Mary does.
7 (hard) This term, you haven't studied .... last term.

79.4 Rearrange the words and write sentences.
1 played – the – Paul – all – quietest – children, – Of – the
Of all the children, Paul played the quietest.
2 race – in – Hamilton – last – fastest – the – drove – the

3 behaved – during – sensibly – the – school trip – most – The – children

4 Try – nine o'clock – by – here – be – latest – to – the – at

5 thoughtfully – He – most – mother – helped – sick – his

6 at – lessons – diligently – They – most – Italian – worked – their

7 to – church – the – They – generously – most – gave

219

UNIT 80

Comparative and superlative: irregular forms
(better / the best)

A Certain adjectives and adverbs have irregular comparative and superlative forms.

adjective	adverb	comparative	superlative
good	well	better	the best
bad	badly	worse	the worst

Her French is better than mine.
She speaks French better than me.
He's a good friend. Actually, he's my best friend.
Yesterday, the weather was bad, but today it's even worse.
I think I did worse in this exam than in the other one.
What was your worst experience ever?

B Other adjectives and adverbs with irregular comparative and superlative forms are:

- far farther / further the farthest / the furthest

   For distances, either the first or second form can be used.
   York is farther / further from here than Newcastle.
   The road was blocked, so they couldn't go any farther / further.

   Further also has the meaning of 'additional'.
   Furthest means 'extreme'.
   Ask for any further information you should need.
   North Cape is the furthest northern point in the European continent.

- old older / elder the oldest / the eldest

   The irregular form **elder / the eldest** is used when talking about people only, primarily to compare the ages of brothers and sisters within a family.
   John is my elder brother. (there are two sons, therefore the comparative is used)
   My sister is the eldest, I'm the youngest in the family. (there are more than two children, therefore the superlative is used)

- late later the latest / the last

   The latest indicates the last in order of time, the most recent. **The last** indicates conclusion.
   This is the latest issue of Science Magazine. (there will be other issues)
   This is my last day in London. (I leave tomorrow)

- much / many more the most
  little   less   the least

   I have more students this year, about 30, but my colleague James has got the most: 52 students have enrolled in his course!
   Peter has got the least baggage of all, just a small backpack.

   Most (without **the**) before a plural noun means 'the majority of…'.
   Most people left the room before the conference was over.

EXERCISES

Comparative and superlative: irregular forms

UNIT 80

80.1 Complete the sentences with the comparative of the irregular adjectives and adverbs from the box.

little ~~good~~ far much bad old

1 This flute is ...**better**... quality than that one.
2 His voice sounds really bad – it's a lot .... than mine.
3 That guitar is very expensive; it costs £500 .... than a Fender!
4 If you want .... information about the concerts, please phone.
5 If you pay .... for your festival tickets, you'll get bad seats.
6 My .... sister now lives in Canada.

80.2 Choose the correct alternative.

1 This new CD is (**better**)/ **best** than their first one.
2 Paul is the **elder / eldest** of the four musicians in the quartet.
3 It's the **worse / worst** musical I've ever seen in my life!
4 His singing career has taken him **further / furthest** than he imagined.
5 He has the **less / least** musical ability of all the *Pop Idol* contestants.
6 The **more / most** he plays saxophone, the **better / best** he gets.

80.3 Complete the sentences with the superlative of the adjectives in brackets.

1 (good) It was ...**the best**... show I've ever seen.
2 (far) He swam .... of all the swimmers in the last competition.
3 (old) His .... sister didn't come to the performance.
4 (bad) This is .... party I've been to for years.
5 (much) We all sang last night, but Jane sang .... songs of all.
6 (little) Finding the house is .... of our problems!

80.4 Rearrange the words and write sentences.

1 is – you – school – home – after – best – It – quickly – come – if
   It is best if you come home quickly after school.
2 schoolwork – better – is – John's – week – better – every – and – getting
   ....
3 could – I – least – the – do – was – That
   ....
4 to – I – Eric Clapton's – been – have – CD – listening – latest – just
   ....
5 More – more – and – people – sending – prefer – e-mails – to – letters
   ....
6 in – is – Europe – one – Stonehenge – constructions – the – of – oldest
   ....

80.5 Complete the message with the comparative or superlative of the adjectives in brackets.

The gig tomorrow

The .... (good) local heavy metal bands will be performing their .... (late) hits. My .... (old) brother is coming with us, but the .... (young) one can't come because he's got a football match. Meet me there at 8. Don't be late. The .... (late) we arrive, the .... (long) the queue for tickets will be. They say it'll be the .... (awesome) gig of the year!

UNIT 81 — Comparatives with nouns and verbs *(more / less... than; as much / as many... as)*

A The comparative of nouns is expressed using:

more + noun (+ **than**)

I have more free time now I've retired from work.
This year, I'm getting more good marks than I did last year.

To strengthen the comparison, we use:

much / a lot more with uncountable nouns

I'm spending much more money than I usually do.

many / a lot more with plural nouns

Janet has got a lot more music CDs than I have.
I've got many more friends in my new school.

(not) as much + uncountable noun + **as**

I'm much busier now. I don't have as much free time as I had last year.

(not) as many + plural noun + **as**

They have as many friends in London as they have in New York.

less + uncountable noun + **than**
fewer + plural noun + **than**

In spoken language, **less** is used more often, even when referring to plural nouns.
These biscuits contain less sugar and fewer (less) fats than most other cookies.

B The comparative of verbs is expressed using:

verb + **(a lot) more** + **than**

She talks a lot more than her mother. She's a real chatterbox!

verb + **as much as**

I'm not spending as much as you. I'm saving a little money.

verb + **less** + **than**

This week, I've been spending less than usual.

With the verbs **like** and **enjoy**, both **more** and **better** (and both the superlatives **most** and **best**) can be used.

I like this song more than / better than the other one.
I like this one most of all / best of all.

With the verbs **study** and **work**, the adverb **harder** (superlative **hardest**) is usually used rather than **more**.
My son's studying harder this year.
He's working the hardest he possibly can.

EXERCISES

Comparatives with nouns and verbs

UNIT 81

81.1 Choose the correct alternative.

1 Last week, I earned ....*B*.... all my colleagues at work.
   A as many money as   **(B)** as much money as   **C** as much money than
2 He has got .... DVDs than my brother and me.
   A much more   **B** a lots more   **C** many more
3 He works .... than the other people in the office.
   A much harder   **B** many harder   **C** a lot hardest
4 Have I got a lot of jeans? No, Lisa's got .... me.
   A much more than   **B** many than   **C** more than
5 I enjoy Harry Potter books ....
   A better than all   **B** best of all   **C** best than all
6 My sister has got .... me.
   A much patience as   **B** much patience than   **C** more patience than
7 There were .... people than we expected.
   A much   **B** more   **C** many
8 He knows .... songs than we do.
   A a lot more   **B** much more   **C** more than

81.2 Complete the sentences with the comparative of the adverbs in brackets.

1 I like this dish ....*better than*.... the other one. (good)
2 I enjoy Madonna's music .... Anastacia's. (much)
3 They spent a lot .... they could afford. (much)
4 Janet is studying .... she did last term. (hard)
5 He goes to the disco a lot .... his brothers do. (often)
6 We like reading comics .... listening to music. (much)

81.3 Match the two parts of the sentences.

1 ..*c*..   2 ....   3 ....   4 ....   5 ....   6 ....

1 I have less free time
2 Mummy, why did the Tooth Fairy
3 Although this laptop is new,
4 My brother's not up yet –
5 Look at this ad! This mobile
6 Listen, guys, I'll need

a much more help from everyone.
b he sleeps a lot more than I do.
c since I started my new job.
d I have more problems than before.
e bring Alison more money than me?
f has a lot more ring tones than ours.

223

REVIEW 18

EXERCISES Units 74–81

R18.1 Underline the adjectives and circle the adverbs in the following sentences.
1. He was a (very) nice boy and he did (very well) at school.
2. Maria is a beautiful dancer. She dances beautifully!
3. He shouted angrily at me, and I felt very angry about it.
4. I bought a French car last year. Its seats are very comfortable.
5. Our new neighbours are quite friendly.
6. Rhinos are dangerous animals. Our guide drove very carefully when we approached them in Kruger Park.
7. He goes to bed very late on Saturday nights.
8. They drove fast because they wanted to get to the stadium early.

R18.2 Complete the sentences with the correct form of adjective (-ed / -ing) formed from the verbs in brackets.
1. (excite) It was an ......*exciting*...... match, and Paul felt very ......*excited*...... .
2. (interest) It was an .... story, and I was .... to hear more.
3. (frighten) It was a .... film, and I felt very .... by it.
4. (shock) He had a .... accident, and everyone was ....
5. (surprise) The book had a .... ending – I was .... by it.
6. (exhaust) I had an .... day at work – I'm completely ....

R18.3 Match the two parts of the expressions.

1 sports	a dress	1	...*d*...
2 wedding	b pie	2	....
3 Easter	c hotel	3	....
4 apple	d kit	4	....
5 three-star	e tree	5	....
6 four-wheel	f egg	6	....
7 seaside	g drive	7	....
8 Christmas	h resort	8	....

R18.4 Read the text and write the names of the four people in the correct boxes. Then complete the description of them with the comparative or the superlative of the adjectives in brackets.

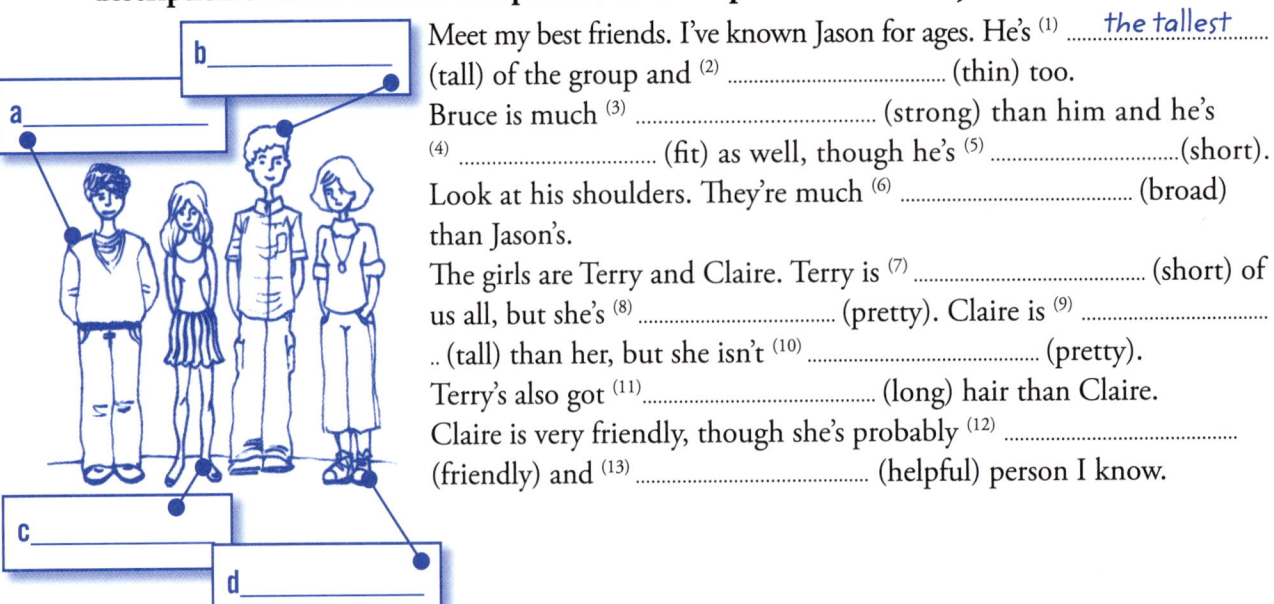

Meet my best friends. I've known Jason for ages. He's (1) ......*the tallest*...... (tall) of the group and (2) .... (thin) too.
Bruce is much (3) .... (strong) than him and he's (4) .... (fit) as well, though he's (5) ....(short).
Look at his shoulders. They're much (6) .... (broad) than Jason's.
The girls are Terry and Claire. Terry is (7) .... (short) of us all, but she's (8) .... (pretty). Claire is (9) .... (tall) than her, but she isn't (10) .... (pretty).
Terry's also got (11) .... (long) hair than Claire.
Claire is very friendly, though she's probably (12) .... (friendly) and (13) .... (helpful) person I know.

224

REVIEW 18

R18.5 Complete the table with the missing forms.

Adjective	Comparative	Superlative
1 nice	nicer	nicest
2 big		
3	happier	
4 exciting		
5 shallow		
6		best
7	heavier	
8 patient		
9 far		
10		whitest

R18.6 Complete the sentences with the comparative of the adjectives in brackets.

1 (nice) I think Lincoln is ......nicer than...... Manchester or Leeds.
2 (easy) I find English .... maths and physics.
3 (tiring) For me, working out in the gym is .... jogging.
4 (exotic) Mangoes are .... fruits .... apples.
5 (handsome) I think George Clooney is .... Brad Pitt.
6 (bad) James's behaviour is .... Ewin's.

R18.7 Complete the sentences with the comparative of the adverbs formed from the adjectives.

1 He's a quick walker. He walks ......more quickly...... than everyone else.
2 She's a slow learner. She learns .... than most of her classmates.
3 They're good cooks. They cook .... than the chef at the Grand Hotel!
4 He's a hard worker. He works .... than most of the other employees.
5 This is really loud music. They're playing it .... than usual.
6 Peter's a careful biker. He rides his motorbike .... than his friends.

R18.8 Complete the email with the comparative or superlative of the adjectives in brackets.

I'm writing from the Internet point in the hotel where I'm spending ......the best...... (good) holiday of my life! I hang out every night with George, who is .... (sweet) guy I've ever met. Yes! I've finally got over Mike. George is much .... (nice) then Mike and he plays the guitar brilliantly. He has .... (strange) guitar I've ever seen – star shaped and covered in flowers! He always has it with him! There's a lovely beach here. It's .... (wide) and .... (clean) than the one we usually go to. The hotel is great. It's not .... (big) as the one we went to last year - the rooms are .... (small) and .... (cosy), but I want to stay here forever.
Love T

I Exam preparation

I.1 PET Reading Part 5

Read the text and choose the correct word(s) (A, B, C or D) for each space.

Life is much ⁽¹⁾ ..A.. when people are ⁽²⁾ .... and behave ⁽³⁾ .... to each other. But too often people are ⁽⁴⁾ .... because everyone's life is ⁽⁵⁾ .... than in the past. The pace of life is getting ⁽⁶⁾ .... every day, and nobody seems able to live ⁽⁷⁾ .... any more. Even children don't seem to be ⁽⁸⁾ .... they were. They watch ⁽⁹⁾ .... television and eat ⁽¹⁰⁾ .... food than previous generations, and generally live ⁽¹¹⁾ .... We need to find a way to make everyone ⁽¹²⁾ ....

1	**A** nicer (circled)	**B** nicest	**C** nice	**D** nicely
2	**A** less happy	**B** happy	**C** more happy	**D** happily
3	**A** good	**B** best	**C** well	**D** goodly
4	**A** aggressive	**B** aggressively	**C** aggressiver	**D** most aggressive
5	**A** difficult	**B** difficulter	**C** difficulty	**D** more difficult
6	**A** fast	**B** faster	**C** fastly	**D** more fast
7	**A** calm	**B** calmer	**C** calmly	**D** calmest
8	**A** as carefree as	**B** so carefree than	**C** carefreer than	**D** carefreest as
9	**A** most	**B** much	**C** more	**D** the most
10	**A** badder	**B** worse	**C** worst	**D** baddest
11	**A** unhealthy	**B** unhealthiest	**C** unhealthier	**D** unhealthily
12	**A** more contented	**B** as contented as	**C** less contented	**D** most contented

I.2 PET Writing Part 1

Complete the second sentence so that it means the same as the first. Use no more than three words.

1 Danny thought that chemistry was more boring than biology.
   Danny thought that biology was ...*more interesting than*... chemistry.
2 Peter was seven centimetres taller than Mike.
   Mike was seven centimetres .... Peter.
3 Suzie is a faster runner than Liz.
   Liz runs .... Suzie.
4 Johnny works harder than Pete.
   Pete doesn't work .... Johnny.
5 Angela has less money than me.
   I have .... Angela.

I.3 PET Writing 3

This is part of an e-mail you received from an English friend who has just moved to a new town and school. Write an e-mail asking for more details about why things are like he says. (80 words)

> This town is bigger than where I lived before, but it isn't nicer. It's a worse place to live. And the school is less interesting than the old one. I've made one or two friends, but they're not as good as the ones I left. The worst thing is the smell in the town – everywhere you go it's terrible. Is there anything good about this move? Well, I've met a rather beautiful girl who I like a lot. And my bedroom's better. But that's about all.

Exam preparation

I.4 FCE Use of English Part 2

Read the text below and think of the word which best fits each space. Use only one in each space.

The (1) ....*most*.... beautiful place I've ever been to is Oxford. It's a (2) .... famous old university city, full of the (3) .... amazing buildings you have ever seen. The stone they are built out of is (4) .... yellow as gold, and none of them are the same – they're all built in (5) .... styles of architecture.
For me, (6) .... most interesting college was New College, which has a section of the old city walls running through it. Each area has a special atmosphere to it, which isn't like the others. The (7) .... beautiful part (8) .... the city is the shopping centre – it's terrible! The modern buildings there aren't designed well (9) .... to match the old buildings which surround them.

I.5 FCE Use of English Part 3

Read the text below. Use the word given in capitals at the end of each line to form a word that fits the space in the same line.

Last night, I went to the (1) ....*loudest*.... rock band concert I have ever   LOUD
heard. The whole concert was (2) .... ! I actually think it was   DEAF
probably very (3) .... for the band who were playing, as   DANGER
they could (4) .... damage their ears doing that night   EASY
after night. And it wasn't (5) .... for the audience, either   ENJOY
– my ears were ringing all day!

I.6 FCE Use of English Part 4

Complete the second sentence so that it has a similar meaning to the first sentence, using the word given. Do not change the word given. You must use between two and five words, including the word given.

1. I have never walked farther than I did yesterday.
   FARTHEST
   It was ....*the farthest I have ever*.... walked.

2. I am leaving Rome tomorrow.
   LAST
   Today is .... in Rome.

3. Nobody is such a beautiful dancer as Julie.
   MOST
   Julia dances ....

4. I got lots of nice presents for my birthday.
   MANY
   I got .... presents.

5. Nobody walks as slowly as you do.
   THE
   You are .... of all.

6. Their kitchen is large and bright.
   A
   They have .... kitchen.

UNIT 82 Personal pronouns (I, you, he.../me, you, him...)

A Subject pronouns are placed before the verb in affirmative and negative sentences and after the auxiliary in interrogative sentences.

I	→	is always written with a capital letter
you	→	is used both with the second person singular and the second person plural
he	→	substitutes the name of a male person
she	→	substitutes the name of a female person
it	→	substitutes the name of a thing or animal
we	→	refers to the speaker and to one or more other people
they	→	substitutes plural names, both of people and animals or things

B Subject pronouns are usually always expressed. They can be implied only in certain cases, for example in two-part sentences with **and** or **but**, or when the subject of the second part of the sentence is the same.

They start work at 8 a.m. and (they) finish at 5 p.m.
She loves cooking, but hates washing up.
In the evenings, he listens to music or surfs the net.

C
- **You** is also used as the subject of sentences that refer to everyone in general.
  You can visit a lot of castles in Scotland.
  You must respect the school rules.

- For animals, we usually use the pronoun **it**, but for domestic animals and pets we can use **he** or **she**. For a baby, we use **it** (unless we know the gender).
  The panda is a lazy animal. It sleeps most of the time.
  I've got a German shepherd. He's called Rusty.

- **It** is also used in impersonal sentences: **It's** + adjective + verb in the infinitive (see p.18)
  It's nice to be here.
  It's too good to be true.

- **She**, other than for females, can also be used for ships and, sometimes, nations.
  The Queen Elizabeth is a big cruise ship. She carries thousands of passengers.

D Object pronouns are either found after a verb (direct object) or after a clause (indirect object).

me	→	He loves me.	Come with me.
you	→	I love you.	Can I talk to you?
him	→	I love him.	Go with him.
her	→	I love her.	Go with her.
it	→	I like it.	Can I use it?
us	→	Send us an e-mail.	Is it for us?
them	→	Take them away.	Have you talked to them?

EXERCISES

Personal pronouns

UNIT 82

82.1 Complete the sentences with the correct subject pronoun.
1 Get ready now, children, then ......*you*...... can go to the Christmas party.
2 Bob is in Greece. .... won't be back until Monday.
3 My sister can't find her Italian bag. I'm sure .... is on her bed, as usual.
4 My name is Irina. .... used to be in the Russian Ballet Company.
5 Those Americans look angry. .... have already complained once.
6 Which one is the Spanish lady? Is .... the one in the blue dress?
7 Did we tell you about our holiday? .... went to the USA.

82.2 Match the two parts of the sentences.

1 ...*b*... 2 .... 3 .... 4 .... 5 .... 6 ....

1 We have been invited, but
2 Lily watches TV or
3 The film starts at 8.30 and
4 Mike enjoys being with friends, but
5 In my spare time, I play tennis or
6 I adore Indian food, but

a can't stand Chinese cooking.
b probably won't be able to go.
c reads a book in her spare time.
d go swimming.
e dislikes meeting strangers.
f ends at 11.00.

82.3 Complete the sentences with the correct subject pronoun.
1 My cat is called Toffee. ......*She*...... loves drinking milk.
2 The *Titanic* sank after hitting an iceberg. .... was a huge ship.
3 .... can eat very well in the little restaurants by the sea.
4 The koala bear lives in Australia. .... eats eucalyptus leaves.
5 .... is a lovely day today.
6 .... must do as the teacher says, Robert!
7 Shall I take an umbrella? .... looks as if .... is going to rain.

82.4 Complete the sentences with the correct object pronoun.
1 Tim never lets anyone tell ......*him*...... what to do.
2 My boyfriend loves blues music. If he sees a good CD, he always buys ....
3 I really like Jessica. Do you think she'd go out with .... ?
4 We're going to raise money for charity. Do you want to help .... ?
5 Sarah's so bossy! I really don't like ....
6 What happened to my keys? Has anyone seen .... ?
7 You're always so stupid! I don't want to listen to ....

82.5 Complete the dialogue with the correct personal pronouns.
Jackie: Hi Barbara! I haven't seen (1) ......*you*...... for ages!
Barbara: (2) .... was on holiday in Greece for three weeks.
Jackie: Lucky (3) .... !
Barbara: What have (4) .... been doing?
Jackie: Nothing much. The kids are back into their routine. I'm driving (5) .... to school every morning. Bill is at the bank all day. I hardly ever see (6) ....
Barbara: What happened to your job?
Jackie: (7) .... made (8) .... redundant a month ago. Didn't (9) .... know?
Barbara: Oh dear! (10) .... didn't know about that.

UNIT 83 Possessive adjectives and pronouns (my, your… / mine, yours…)

A Possessive adjectives have a single form for the masculine and feminine and singular and plural.

> my…
> your…
> his…
> her…
> its…
> our…
> their…

B Possessive adjectives are placed before the noun that they refer to. They are *never* preceded by an article, nor by an indefinite adjective or by other determiners.

my friend (not: the my friend)
my friends (not: the my friends)
one of my friends (not: a my friend) (also possible: a friend of mine)
some of my friends (not: some my friends) (also possible: some friends of mine)
this friend of mine (not: this my friend)

C The possessive adjective of the third person singular refers to the possessor, not to the thing owned by the possessor.

John's book → his book   Janet's book → her book   the dog's kennel → its kennel
<u>Brian</u> must be at home. That's <u>his</u> car.
<u>Linda</u> has cycled to work today. This is <u>her</u> bike.
So you've got <u>a hamster</u>. Do you clean <u>its</u> cage?

WATCH OUT! Don't confuse:
- **it's** with **its**, which are pronounced in the same way;
- **he's** with **his**, which are pronounced in a similar way.

  'Here's your pen… but where's <u>its</u> cap?' '<u>It's</u> here, under the chair.'
  <u>He's</u> a cool guy and <u>his</u> friends are cool, too.

D Possessive adjectives can be reinforced by the adjective **own**.

I've got my own room. (all to myself, that I don't share with others)
They've made their own fortune.

E Possessive adjectives are usually used before personal objects (**my watch**, **my diary…**), parts of the body (**my head**, **my hands…**) and items of clothing (**my sweater**, **my jeans…**).

My head is aching.   Did you take your umbrella?

F Possessive pronouns are invariable. The pronoun that corresponds to the possessive adjective **its** is very rarely used.

> mine   yours   his   hers   ours   theirs

Like adjectives, possessive pronouns are not preceded by an article, nor by an indefinite adjective or by other determiners.

'Whose bag is this?' 'It's mine.'
This isn't Lara's bag. Hers is black.

Note the difference between the use of the adjective (followed by a noun) and the pronoun (not followed by a noun).
Is that your **racket**?   Is that racket **yours**?

EXERCISES

Possessive adjectives and pronouns

UNIT 83

83.1 Complete the sentences with the correct possessive adjective. Indicate in which sentences the adjective can be reinforced by *own*.

1 Daddy! Jack won't lend me ......*his*...... blue crayon!
2 Carol is a great actress, and tonight .... performance was marvellous.
3 The dog wants to go out. Can you pass me .... collar, please?
4 Why are you whispering? Is there a problem with .... voice?
5 My grandparents live in the French capital. .... flat is beautiful.
6 Michael has lost .... copy of the Polish national anthem.

83.2 Choose the correct alternative.

1 Take the rabbit out of **it's / its** (cage) – we need to clean it.
2 Where's Robert? **His / He's** mobile phone is ringing.
3 Listen! I can hear **there / their** car coming up the drive.
4 Simona is my Italian exchange student. I really envy **her / hers** stylish clothes.
5 **Its / It's** a very good time of year to visit South Africa.
6 Here come the guests – **they're / their** all from Norway.

83.3 Complete the second sentence with the correct possessive pronoun.

1 Is this your laptop? Is this laptop ......*yours*...... ?
2 This is Maria's handwriting. The handwriting is ....
3 That's my schoolbag! That schoolbag is ....
4 This was his watch. This watch was ....
5 This is our classroom! This classroom is ....!
6 Was it their idea? Was the idea .... ?

83.4 Complete the text with possessive adjectives or pronouns.

A crofter's cottage

We visited some friends of (1) ......*ours*...... in Scotland last September. (2) .... house in the Highlands was very small, but warm and comfortable. Andrew is a teacher in the village primary school. Most of (3) .... students are the children of farmers – called crofters in this region. (4) .... wife Fyfa doesn't go to work. (5) .... main job is looking after (6) .... children. There are three of them, all under five, and (7) .... chief occupation is running around (8) .... grandad's croft. (9) .... grandma is a very good cook. (10) .... are the best cakes in the village. She has won lots of cooking competitions so far.

231

UNIT 84 Reflexive and emphasising pronouns (myself / yourself...)

A The reflexive pronouns are:

myself	ourselves
yourself	yourselves
himself	themselves
herself	
itself	

Oneself is the impersonal form of the reflexive pronoun.

B Reflexive pronouns are used as direct or indirect objects of certain verbs, when the action refers to the subject itself, for example: **hurt oneself, enjoy oneself, wash oneself, cut oneself, think to oneself.**

They enjoyed themselves a lot at the party.
Behave yourselves!
Don't make a fool of yourself!
I said to myself I shouldn't get angry.

C When the direct object is a noun referring to a part of the body, we use a possessive adjective, not the reflexive.

I'm washing myself. BUT: *I'm washing <u>my hands</u>.* (not: I'm washing myself the hands)
He cut himself with a knife.
He cut <u>his finger</u> with a knife.
She hurt herself.
She hurt <u>her knee</u> while she was skating.

E Reflexive pronouns are also used in an emphatic way. In this case, they can also refer to the object of the verb instead of the subject.

Did you make it yourself?
The Queen herself gave the cup to the winning team.
She'll go and ask the manager himself if you don't tell her.

F Expressions with **by** + reflexive pronoun (**by myself, by yourself**...) can also be expressed using **on** + possessive adjective + **own** (**on my own, on your own**...).

They're often at home by themselves / on their own.
I'd like to live by myself / on my own.
She likes being on her own.

EXERCISES

Reflexive and emphasising pronouns

UNIT 84

84.1 Match the two parts of the sentences.

1 ..d.. 2 .... 3 .... 4 .... 5 .... 6 ....

1 Paul saw   a hurt themselves when they crashed.
2 The girls   b myself shaving this morning.
3 I cut   c ourselves in Turkey.
4 You mustn't   d himself in the mirror.
5 We enjoyed   e cut itself on some broken glass.
6 The dog   f fool yourself that she loves you.

84.2 Rearrange the words and write sentences.

1 for – This – themselves – students – course – to – teaches – think
   This course teaches students to think for themselves.

2 yourselves – will – afternoon – You – this – amuse

3 cooked – camping – when – ourselves – for – We – we – went

4 table – and – to – the – food – He – himself – helped – the – to – walked

5 how – herself – Nobody – hurt – Sandra – understands

6 stand – themselves – talk – people – I – can't – about – who – always

84.3 Rewrite the sentences using reflexive pronouns without changing the meaning.

1 He likes to spend time alone.
   He likes to spend time by himself.

2 She was on her own all week.

3 They did it without any help.

4 You can work on your own today.

5 We travelled around Spain alone.

6 I've made a wonderful cake without my mother's help.

7 You can't leave a baby alone in the house.

8 He was able to run the firm single-handed.

UNIT 85 Demonstrative adjectives and pronouns *(this / these, that / those)*

A The demonstratives are:

| this | these | to indicate someone or something near the speaker |
| that | those | to indicate someone or something far from the speaker |

They can be used as both adjectives (followed by a noun) and pronouns.

This handbag is really nice!
This is a good bargain!
Look at these boots. Aren't they funny?
These are my boots. They're not on sale.

That boy at the bus stop is Sheila's brother.
That's my car over there!
What are those boys doing?
Those aren't my suitcases. Mine are smaller.

Demonstratives have singular and plural forms, but are the same for all genders.

singular	plural
this man	these men
this woman	these women
that actor	those actors
that actress	those actresses

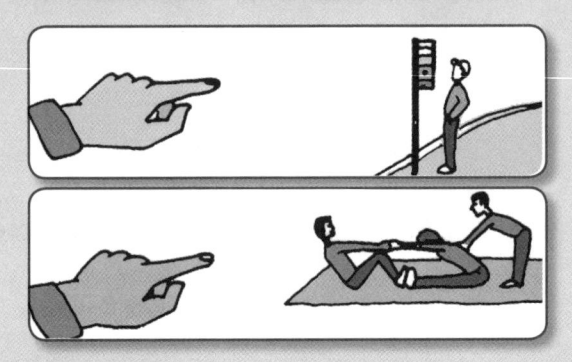

B
- The demonstrative pronouns **this** and **these** are often used to introduce someone.

  This is Mr Durrell, our sales manager.
  These are Paul and Josh, our friends from Canada.

- **This** can also be used to introduce yourself on the phone or to ask who's speaking.

  Hello! This is Sheila Ross. (also possible: Hello! Sheila Ross speaking.)
  Is that you, John?

- **This**, **these**, **that** and **those** are often matched with the pronouns **one** and **ones** (see p.236).

  Which is your bag? This one or that one?
  Which are your boots? These ones or those ones?

- **That** is frequently used as the subject of impersonal sentences (see p.18), or as the object of a verb, with the meaning of 'what was said or done' or 'the thing that is being spoken about'.

  That's incredibile!
  I can't believe that! (what you said)
  I don't like that. (what you did)
  Don't do that!

EXERCISES

Demonstrative adjectives and pronouns

UNIT 85

85.1 Rewrite the sentences in the plural.

1 This boy is from Namibia. — *These boys are from Namibia.*
2 This is a foreign visitor. — ....
3 That is a photo of our capital city. — ....
4 Is this your map? — ....
5 Where's this family from? — ....
6 What's that flag? — ....

85.2 Read the information and then write the orders.

You are sitting at the table with a friend. The table has a number of objects on it. At the other end of the room, there are some shelves which have other objects on them. Tell your friend what to do.

1 **Place:** table **Object:** red book (open)
   Open this red book, please.

2 **Place:** table **Objects:** three glasses (take)
   ....

3 **Place:** shelves **Objects:** two vases (bring me)
   ....

4 **Place:** shelves **Object:** small box (close)
   ....

5 **Place:** table **Object:** new umbrella (take)
   ....

6 **Place:** shelves **Objects:** photographs (give me)
   ....

85.3 Complete the sentences with *this* or *that*.

1 ......*That*...... is my new house over there!
2 What?! No, I'm afraid I don't believe .... !
3 Good morning. .... is Peter Williams speaking.
4 Can I introduce you? Mike, ... is Steve Hope from IBM.
5 Which is your bike? This one or .... one?
6 Who is .... tall woman over there by the window?

85.4 Complete the text with *these* or *those*.

We use the word (1) ......*these*...... to talk about more than one object or person which is near us, while we use (2) .... to talk about the same things when they are distant from us. (3) .... often collocates with the word *there*, and (4) .... collocates with *here*. For example, we say: '(5) .... are my clothes here' and '(6) .... are my friend's over there'.

235

UNIT 86 one / ones

A The pronouns **one / ones** are used instead of nouns that have already been used, to avoid repetition. **One** substitutes a singular noun; **ones** substitutes a plural noun.

They are usually preceded by:
- the definite article (**the one / the ones**)
- demonstratives (**this one / that one; these ones / those ones**)
- the expression **the other** (**the other one / the other ones**)
- the interrogative **which** (**which one? / which ones?**)

One can be preceded by:
- indefinite article + qualifying adjective (**a red one**)

Ones can be preceded by:
- indefinite adjective + qualifying adjective (**some good ones**)

B **One** and **ones** are used when there is a choice of one or more things.

This T-shirt is quite nice, but I prefer the other one.
These rooms are larger than the ones on the second floor.

Look at these short dialogues and note the words in bold to understand the use of these pronouns.

	A: I'd like **a cake**, please. B: A big **one** or a small **one**? A: Er… I think I'll have a big **one**, please. The chocolate **one**.
	A: Could I try this **jacket** on, please? B: Which **one** do you mean? A: This blue **one** here.
	A: I'd like to see those **trousers**, please. B: These **ones**? A: No, the white **ones** on the left.
	A: Which **dress** do you prefer? This **one** or that **one**? B: The cheaper **one**!
	A: Which is David's **girlfriend**? B: I think she's the tall **one** with long black hair.

EXERCISES

one / ones

UNIT 86

86.1 Match the questions to the answers.

1 _c_   2 ....   3 ....   4 ....   5 ....   6 ....

1 Can you pass me those books, Dad?
2 I'm looking for size 5 black boots, please.
3 Could you lend me an umbrella, please?
4 Which coat shall I put on, Mum?
5 What sort of wine is that?
6 Which cake shall I give you, Suzie?

a I want the one with pink icing.
b I'm sorry, I haven't got one.
c The ones on the floor?
d It's a dry, white one.
e Try these high-heeled ones.
f The thick, waterproof one.

86.2 Answer the questions using the words in brackets and *one / ones*.

1 What cheeses do you prefer? (French / Italian)
   I prefer Italian ones.
2 What paper do you usually read? (a daily / a weekly)
   ....
3 What clothes do you wear? (Italian / British)
   ....
4 Which football team do you support? (a British / an Italian)
   ....
5 What dogs do you like? (small and sweet / large and fierce)
   ....
6 What holidays do you choose? (active / relaxing)
   ....

86.3 Complete the sentences using the words from the box. Add *a / an* where necessary.

| ~~my latest one~~   another one   new one   which one   French one   blue one |

1 **A:** What did the critics say about your novels?
  B: They all said they like _my latest one._
2 **A:** My watch has stopped working.
  B: Don't worry. I'll buy you ....
3 **A:** Do you know what kind of cheese this is?
  B: I think it's ....
4 **A:** .... is your toothbrush?
  B: I don't know. They both look the same!
5 **A:** Take another Vitamin C tablet, love.
  B: I'm better now, Mum. I don't need ....
6 **A:** Would you like a blue balloon, Joanna?
  B: No thanks. I've already got ....

86.4 Choose the correct alternative.

1 **The one /(The ones)** on the shelf are difficult to reach.
2 The children all took **one / ones** each.
3 **Which one / Which ones** is your new rabbit?
4 **The one / The ones** in the garden next door have more flowers.
5 Don't eat the other **one / ones** ! It's gone bad!
6 Do you prefer these Italian **one / ones** or the English ones?

UNIT 87 — Distributive adjectives and pronouns (1) (each / every / everyone…); reciprocal pronouns (each other / one another)

A The most common distributive adjectives and pronouns are:

> each
> every
> everyone / everybody
> everything

B **Each** and **every** are practically synonyms. **Each** can be used as both an adjective and pronoun, whilst **every** is only an adjective and isn't usually used with small numbers.

Each candidate must have an identification card.
Each of the three finalists was given a prize.
There's an Internet connection in every room.

These souvenirs cost three pounds each.

Note the difference between the expressions **every day** and **all day**.

I used to see them every day.
I worked all day yesterday.

C **Everyone** and **everybody** are synonyms. The verb that follows is in the third person singular. Note the expressions: **all of us / of you / of them** (see p.240).
Everything is also followed by a verb in the third person singular.

Everyone says it's a real bargain. (also: They all say…)
Everybody, clap your hands!
Everything was ready for the show. (also: All was ready…)
Money is not everything.

D Another compound of **every** is the adverb **everywhere**.

I've looked everywhere, but I still can't find my car keys.

E The reciprocal pronouns are:

> each other / one another

One another is used to talk about people in general, not a specific person.

Rob and Jasmine were madly in love with each other.
We live in a community where people help one another.
When the three friends met at the station, they gave each other a big hug.

EXERCISES

Distributive adjectives and pronouns (1); reciprocal pronouns

UNIT 87

87.1 Complete the sentences using *everybody / everyone, everything* or *all*.
1 *Everyone* I know likes travelling to different countries.
2 .... of us thought the food in the Mexican restaurant was great.
3 Whatever shop we go into, my wife always wants to buy ....
4 .... Swedish children seem to have fair hair and blue eyes.
5 .... we did in China was interesting.
6 She knew most people at the party, but she didn't recognise ....

87.2 Choose the correct alternative.
1 Come on **everything / (everyone)** let's start work!
2 **Everyone of / Each of** the British sportsmen wore a tracksuit.
3 Please will you two stop quarrelling with **each other / every other.**
4 Each **applicant / applicants** must hand in a photo with the form.
5 Ken goes to work very early **all / every** day.
6 It was terrible! The guests all looked angry and refused to talk to **one another / one each other**.

87.3 Complete these famous sentences and proverbs using the words in the box.

| all   everything (x 2)   every (x 2)   everybody |

1 *All* *you need is love* is the title of a famous song by The Beatles.
2 .... cloud has a silver lining.
3 .... men are created equal.
4 .... in its place and a place for everything.
5 .... dog has its day.
6 If you want ...., you may end up with nothing.
7 .... needs somebody to love.

87.4 Complete the second sentence so that it has the same meaning as the first one.
1 On Monday, Tuesday, Wednesday, Thursday, Friday, Saturday and Sunday morning, Daniel gives up smoking, but by noon he has started again.
Daniel gives up smoking *every* morning, but by noon he has started again.

2 A weekend away together would be an excellent opportunity for everyone who works here to get to know their colleagues well.
A weekend away together would be an excellent opportunity for us to get to know ....
3 Tim had a beer, Mark had a beer and Tony had a beer.
The three friends .... had a beer.
4 The witness told the jury about all the events that had happened.
The witness told the jury about .... that had happened.
5 All the people want to be happy.
.... wants to be happy.
6 He went to all the possible places when he was travelling in Australia.
He went .... when he was travelling in Australia.

239

UNIT 88 — Distributive adjectives and pronouns (2) (both / either / neither); correlative structures (both... and... / either... or... / neither... nor...)

A Other distributive adjectives and pronouns are:

both
either
neither

All three can be used as both adjectives and pronouns.
It can be done both ways. (**both** used as an adjective)
'Did they both go?' 'No, just John.' (**both** used as a pronoun)

B **Both** indicates 'both the two things or people', **either** indicates 'one or the other of the two', **neither** indicates 'none of them'.

Do you like the two kittens? Well, you can have both.
You can have either of them.
(one or the other, it's your choice)
'Which one do you prefer?' 'I don't mind either.'
'Which one do you like?' 'Neither. You know I don't like cats.'

C Look at the two possibilities: **neither** + affirmative verb = **either** + negative verb

'Did you like both novels?'
'Actually, I liked neither of them. / I didn't like either.'

D The pronouns **both**, **neither**, **either**, but also **each**, **most**, **all** and **none**, are often followed by the preposition **of** and by a noun or personal object pronoun (**us / you / them**).

Be quiet! Both of you!
My parents were involved in a car accident, but luckily neither of them was hurt.
Could you please help me? Either of you!
Most of the people in the audience were clapping.
All of my friends were happy with the results.

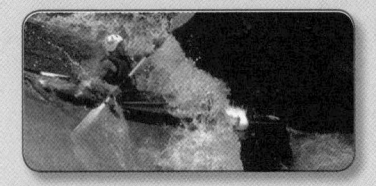

None of us should go. It may be dangerous.

E Note the correlative structures, in which **both**, **either** and **neither** can also be used as conjunctions.

both... and...
either... or...   (in a sentence with a negative verb)
neither... nor...   (in a sentence with an affirmative verb)

Both Peter and John came to my party.
You can either leave today or early tomorrow.
It's a funny colour. It isn't either brown or grey. / It's neither brown nor grey.

F Note that **neither** is followed by the verb in the singular.
Neither Lucy nor Jane has a big house.

EXERCISES

Distributive adjectives and pronouns (2); correlative structures

UNIT 88

88.1 Complete the sentences with *both*, *either* or *neither*.

1 I know it's extravagant, but I want to buy them ......*both*...... .
2 'Which one shall we go to for our holiday: Thailand or Vietnam?' 'I don't mind – ....'
3 'Shall we go to the pub or the cinema?' '........................... . I'm too tired to go out.'
4 The two paintings are similar: .... are 18th-century Dutch portraits.
5 'Shall I come on Saturday or Sunday?' '........................... . I'm away all weekend.'
6 'Can .... of you speak Danish?' 'No, but we can speak Norwegian.'

88.2 Complete the second answer so that it has the same meaning as the first one.

1 Did you enjoy these last two wines?
Actually, I didn't like either of them. They were too acidic.
Actually, I ......*liked neither of them*...... . They were too acidic.

2 Two for a pound! Do you want two melons for a pound?
I'm afraid I can't take either of them. My shopping's already too heavy.
I'm afraid I .... My shopping's already too heavy.

3 Can you tell me Jason's mobile number, or his e-mail address, please?
I'm afraid I can remember neither of them at the moment.
I'm afraid I .... at the moment.

4 Which club shall we go to? There's one called Flash and one called Moon.
We can't go to either. We're under 18 and they won't let us in.
We .... We're under 18 and they won't let us in.

5 Do you want to watch *Terminator* or *The House* tonight?
I want to watch neither. I want to go to bed early!
I .... I want to go to bed early!

88.3 Choose the correct alternative.

1 You can borrow **either / (either of)** my two CD players for the weekend.
2 When the two branches fell, **neither of / either of** them injured Mr Green, luckily!
3 Our baby tried to stand up twice, but he fell down **both / both of** times.
4 **Neither / Neither of** Alice's parents is Welsh. They're both Scottish.
5 My father can speak **both / both of** Japanese and Chinese.
6 If anyone saw us now, they wouldn't think **either / either of** us is normal!
7 **Both of / Both** Pat and I are interested in Irish folk dancing.

88.4 Complete the sentences with *both… and*, *either… or* or *neither… nor*.

1 It was ......*either*...... the place ......*or*...... the music which made her feel so good. She couldn't tell which.
2 .... the group of tourists .... the guide were late for the bus, so they left on time.
3 I'm afraid .... the blue .... the purple dress suits you. I would try the pink one.
4 You can have .... this one .... that one, but not both!
5 She was .... tearful .... exhausted when she finally got home.
6 I'm sorry, but I have .... the time .... the money to help you.
7 The school trip could be .... to a location in Britain .... to France.

UNIT 89 — Indefinite adjectives and pronouns (1) (some / any / no / a little / a few)

A To talk about a quantity that isn't well defined, we use various adjectives and pronouns called **quantifiers** or **indefinite adjectives and pronouns**. The most common are:

> **some** (in affirmative sentences and in offers and requests)
> **any** (in interrogative and negative questions)
> **no** (adjective) / **none** (pronoun) indicate 'zero quantity' (in sentences with an affirmative verb)

As adjectives, they are used before:
- uncountable nouns (**some fruit**, **any cheese**, **no money**…)
- plural nouns, when the exact number isn't known or isn't relevant (**some roses**, **any books**…).

As pronouns, they substitute the noun.

B **Some** is used:
- in affirmative sentences.
  There's some fruit on the table.
- in offers and requests.
  Do you want some biscuits? / Do you want some?
  Can I have some chips? / Can I have some, please?
- in questions that expect an affirmative answer and in negative questions that presume agreement.
  Don't we need some butter for the cake? (I think so and I'm expecting an affirmative answer)

C **Any** is used in questions for asking for information and in negative sentences.
'Is there any milk?' 'Yes, there's some in the fridge.'
'Are there any free seats?' 'Sorry, there aren't any left.'
There weren't any cars in the 19th century.

It is also possible to use **any** in affirmative sentences.
Come at any time! I'll be waiting for you.

D **No** and **none** are used in sentences with an affirmative verb, as an alternative to **not… any**. Remember, in English you can't use two negations in the same sentences, as, logically, two negations would render the sentence affirmative: **not… any…** → **no… / none**

I haven't got any money. → *I've got no money.* (not: ~~I haven't got no money.~~)
'Are there any peppers?' 'No, there aren't any.' → *'There are none.'*

E To indicate small quantities, we use:

a little / a bit / a little bit (of…)	a few
little	few
very little	very few

'How much sugar do you want?' 'Not much. I just want a little bit.'
I've bought a few bottles of mineral water.
We need to buy some more wine. There are only a few bottles left.
He knows very little about me.
Very few people know that.

EXERCISES

Indefinite adjectives and pronouns (1)

UNIT 89

89.1 Complete the sentences using *some* or *any*.

1 'Mum, can I have ......*some*...... money to go to the cinema?' 'No, you can't have .... today. I gave you .... money yesterday and that's enough.'
2 'Excuse me, are there .... trains to Venice late this afternoon?' 'Yes, there's one at 5.30.'
3 'Are there .... students who didn't bring the money for the school trip?' 'No, there aren't .... Everybody has paid.'
4 'Would you like to visit .... other places in the city today?' 'Yes, please. It would be very nice if you could show me around again.'
5 'Have you got .... free tickets for the concert?' 'Yes, we still have ....'
6 'Are you carrying .... identification with you, madam?' ' I've got my driving licence, officer.'
7 'Have you got .... free rooms left for tonight?' 'Yes, sir, we still have ...., but they're all single rooms.'

89.2 Use the words to write interrogative or negative sentences with *any*.

1 we / have got / milk / ?   *Have we got any milk?*
2 you / spend / money / yesterday / ?
3 he / not do / work / this morning
4 there / not be / apples / in the shop
5 she / find / new clothes / last Saturday / ?
6 they / not like / of the flats / see / last week

89.3 Complete the second sentence with *no / none* or *not… any* so that it has the same meaning as the first one.

1 There aren't any good clothes shops in our town.
   There ......*are no*...... good clothes shops in our town.
2 There aren't any places left on the trip to Algeria.
   There .... places left on the trip to Algeria.
3 There are no nice people in the yoga class I go to.
   There .... nice people in the yoga class I go to.
4 Aren't there any holidays available in New Zealand?
   .... there .... holidays left in New Zealand?
5 They told me that there weren't any left.
   They told me that there .... left.
6 Haven't you had any yet?
   .... you .... yet?

89.4 Match the two parts of the sentences.

1 ..*b*.. 2 .... 3 .... 4 .... 5 .... 6 ....

1 There is only a little   a people in the town square.
2 I've only got a few   b cheese left.
3 You will get little   c milk in my coffee, please.
4 There were few   d help from Mr Jones.
5 I'd just like a little   e hope left for the survivors.
6 There is very little   f pounds in my pocket.

UNIT 90 — Indefinitive adjectives and pronouns (2)
(a lot / much / many; too much / too many / enough; most / all)

A To indicate large quantities, we use the following indefinites, which can be used as both adjectives and pronouns:

a lot / lots (of…), plenty (of…)	used mainly in affirmative sentences
much	used mainly in negative sentences and questions
many	used mainly in negative sentences and questions

REMEMBER: **much** is used only with uncountable nouns, **many** only with plural nouns, whilst **a lot of** and **plenty of** can be used in both cases.

Don't hurry. We still have plenty of time!
Hurry up. We don't have much time. (also: *We have little time.*)
We had a lot of homework to do yesterday, but today we don't have much.
'Were there many people on the bus?' 'No, there weren't many.' (also: *…there were just a few.*)

Look at:

> not much = little
> not many = few / just a few

There were a lot of people at the bus stop.

B Other adjectives and pronouns which indicate quantity are:

too much	(with uncountable nouns)
too many	(with plural nouns)
enough	
most	
all	

There's too much noise in this room.
Too many cooks spoil the broth.
Most people enjoyed the concert.
I knew most of the answers in last night's quiz show.
All the students from my school will take part in the sports competitions next week.

C **Enough** can have different places in a sentence. It can:

- precede a noun.
  We didn't have enough food.
  There were enough chairs for everybody.

- follow an adjective.
  Is the room large enough?

- be used on its own.
  I've had enough, thank you.

D Note the difference in usage between **all** and **the whole**.
He ate all the biscuits.
He ate the whole cake.

EXERCISES

Indefinitive adjectives and pronouns (2)

UNIT 90

90.1 Complete the sentences with *much* or *many*.

1 There were ....*many*........ things about living in Brazil which I liked.
2 There aren't .... people who have been to Fiji.
3 We don't have .... money left in our account.
4 There was .... to do when the Chinese delegates arrived.
5 I don't think .... Hungarians visit Australia each year.
6 They haven't grown .... rice in Myanmar since the tornadoes.
7 We were late and we didn't have .... time.
8 Did you drink .... coffee yesterday?

90.2 Complete the sentences with the words in the box.

| ~~too much~~   too many   enough   most   all   too much |

1 There was ....*too much*........ food wasted in this country last year.
2 There aren't .... people here for us to complete the job.
3 I think that .... my Asian friends will come to my party.
4 There are .... good books published each year to read.
5 I heard that .... Americans think carrying guns is OK.
6 There is .... violence in Britain today.

90.3 Indicate (∧) where you would place *enough* in the following sentences.

1 I haven't got ∧ money to pay for it .
2 There aren't sandwiches for everybody to have one .
3 Are there people here for us to start ?
4 Do you think this box is big ?
5 We've seen of this film , thank you .
6 He isn't clever to pass the exam .
7 Have you had to eat ?
8 Did they room in the car for the dog ?

90.4 Complete the second sentence so that it has the same meaning as the first one.

1 There isn't much bread left. We should buy some more
    There's ..*not a lot of / little*.. bread left. We should buy some more.

2 We've got just a few friends here.
    We haven't got .... friends here.

3 The majority of our guests enjoyed the food.
    .... of our guests enjoyed the food.

4 I got a hundred per cent of the answers right.
    I got .... the answers right.

5 I've been doing plenty of work.
    I've been doing a .... of work.

6 Don't eat so many sweets. They're bad for your teeth.
    Don't eat .... those sweets. They're bad for your teeth.

245

UNIT 91 Compounds of *some, any, no* (1)

A The indefinites **some**, **any** and **no** have the following compound forms:

	affirmative sentences	interrogative sentences	negative sentences	
people	somebody / someone	anybody / anyone	not… anybody / not… anyone	nobody / no one
things	something	anything	not… anything	nothing
places	somewhere	anywhere	not… anywhere	nowhere

B These compound pronouns follow the rules of usage of **some**, **any** and **no**, depending on the type of sentence (affirmative, interrogative or negative see p.242).

You must tell someone. (affirmative sentence → compound of **some**)
Did anything happen? (interrogative → compound of **any**)
They didn't go anywhere last summer. (sentence with negative verb → compound of **any**)

REMEMBER:
- two negations in the same sentence aren't possible.
  I did<u>n't</u> meet anybody I knew. → *I met <u>nobody</u> I knew.*
  He does<u>n't</u> know anything about that. → *He knows <u>nothing</u> about that.*
- the compounds of **some** aren't only used in affirmative sentences, but also in questions and in general when an affirmative answer is expected.
  Would you like something to drink? (offer)
  Can I have something to eat, please? (request)

C Compounds with **-body** and **-one** can be used indifferently, as their meaning is identical.
Somebody / Someone must have told him.
'Did anybody / anyone come with you?' 'No, nobody did.'

D The compounds of **any** can also be used in affirmative sentences.
He was very sociable. He would talk to anybody.
'What would you like to eat?' 'Anything! I don't mind.'
Anywhere you go, you'll find nice people.

The conference is open to anyone who is interested in economics.

EXERCISES

Compounds of *some, any, no* (1)

UNIT 91

91.1 Complete the sentences using *someone / somebody*, *something* or *somewhere*.
1 Look! ......*Somebody*...... is walking up to our front door!
2 When I got to class, ... was sitting in my place.
3 Let's go out .... nice at the weekend.
4 Julie told me .... terrible about Paul yesterday.
5 Mike told me he was going to work .... in Africa next month.
6 .... is wrong with the computer – it won't start up!

91.2 Rearrange the words and write the questions.
1 you – Are – holiday – going – exotic – anywhere – summer – your – for – ?
   Are you going anywhere exotic for your summer holiday?
2 knew – see – conference – anybody – Did – at – you – the – you – ?
   ....
3 you – Have – given – anything – him – birthday – his – for – ?
   ....
4 my – you – seen – Have – office – anywhere – keys – ?
   ....
5 bring – could – Japan – anything – Is – from – you – I – there – ?
   ....
6 scarf – Friday – Did – by – last – take – anybody – my – home – mistake – ?
   ....

91.3 Change the sentences with *not… any-* into sentences with *no-*, and vice versa.
1 There wasn't anybody in the office when I got there.
   There ......*was nobody*...................... in the office when I got there.
2 There isn't anything in the fridge to eat tonight.
   There .... in the fridge to eat tonight.
3 There's nowhere nice to eat in this part of town.
   There .... nice to eat in this part of town.
4 Marina told me nothing about what happened last night.
   Marina .... about what happened last night.
5 Susan didn't go anywhere with Mark at the weekend.
   Susan .... with Mark at the weekend.
6 Whenever I have a problem, there's no one around to help me.
   Whenever I have a problem, there .... around to help me.

91.4 Match the two parts of the sentences.

1 *e*   2 ......   3 ......   4 ......   5 ......   6 ......

1 I've found someone   a that I like here.
2 There's nothing   b you want to go tonight?
3 Is there anywhere   c good to stay in this town.
4 There isn't anyone   d I have to tell you.
5 There is something   e who can help with my computer.
6 There's nowhere   f who knows how to do it.

247

UNIT 92: Compounds of *some, any, no* (2); compounds with *-ever*

A As already mentioned on page 246, **nobody / no one**, **nothing** and **nowhere** are used in sentences with an affirmative verb, whereas the compounds of **any** require a negative verb instead.

I told nobody! / I didn't tell anybody. (not: I didn't tell nobody.)
There was no one in the room. / There wasn't anyone in the room.
She said nothing. / She didn't say anything.

In subject position, however only **nobody**, **nothing** and **nowhere** are used.

Nobody was worried about the exam. (not: Not anybody was worried…)
Nothing is wrong with me.
Nowhere is like home.

B WATCH OUT! When indefinites are followed by a noun or pronoun, the forms **some of…**, **any of…** and **none of…** are used. In these cases, the verb is usually used in the plural form.

None of them were wearing a jacket. (not: Nobody of them…)
Did any of the boys qualify for the finals?
Some of you should talk to the teacher.

C When an indefinite pronoun is followed by an adjective, no preposition is placed between them.

You can always learn something new. (not something of new)
We haven't seen anything interesting at the fashion show.
She was sure that nothing good would come of it.

D The adverb **else** is often used after indefinite pronouns.

Does anyone else know the answer? (not: …anyone other…)
'Anything else?' 'No, thanks, nothing else for today.'

E Compounds with **-ever** are used as conjunctions, sometimes as an alternative to the compounds of **any**.

- whoever
- whatever
- whichever
- wherever
- whenever
- however

They were great leaders. Wherever they went, they would find lots of supporters.
(also: Anywhere they went…)

Come whenever you like.
(also: …anytime you like.)

They will give you whatever you like.
(also: …anything you like.)

I'll give my girlfriend this ring, however much it costs.
(also: …whatever it costs.)

EXERCISES

Compounds of *some*, *any*, *no* (2); compounds with *-ever*

UNIT 92

92.1 Rewrite the sentences using *nobody / no one*, *nothing* or *nowhere*.

1 There are no people who are as brave as Michael.
   Nobody is as brave as Michael.
2 There are no people who sing as well as Patsy.
   ....
3 There are no places in the world that are like Venice.
   ....
4 There are no things which are as interesting as nature.
   ....
5 There isn't a place that is as exciting as London.
   ....
6 There are no things which are as important to me as my wedding ring.
   ....

92.2 Match the two parts of the sentences.

1 *f*   2 ......   3 ......   4 ......   5 ......   6 ......

1 Some of my   a watch the match last night?
2 None of the   b paintings displayed there?
3 Did any of you   c relations were there.
4 Some of his   d people I asked knew about it.
5 Were any of her   e were any good.
6 None of them   f friends came round last night.

92.3 Tick (✔) the correct sentences and correct those with mistakes in them.

1 ✔ Nothing exciting happened last night.
2 ☐ Did you buy something of good to eat?   *Did you buy anything good to eat?*
3 ☐ Nothing of value was found at the site.
4 ☐ Nobody of famous came to the opening.
5 ☐ Not anyone turned up on time.
6 ☐ I didn't find anybody nice in the hotel.
7 ☐ No one witnessed the robbery.
8 ☐ Nothing of unusual was seen there.

92.4 Complete the sentences using the words from the box.

~~whoever~~   whoever (x 2)   whatever (x 2)   wherever   whenever   however

1 *Whoever* .... dismissed her must have had a reason.
2 You can cook this chicken .... you want: roasting, boiling or frying.
3 They said we could visit them .... we had time.
4 I take my laptop with me .... I go.
5 I will do it .... the consequences.
6 .... takes over as president, it will be a disaster.
7 .... calls me, please say I'm busy.
8 Here's some money for your birthday. Buy .... you like.

REVIEW 19 EXERCISES Units 82–92

R19.1 Complete the text with the correct personal pronouns and possessive adjectives.

Paul got up late yesterday morning because ⁽¹⁾ ....*he*.... had forgotten to set ⁽²⁾ .... alarm clock to school time. Paul's parents were eating ⁽³⁾ .... breakfast in the kitchen, and his mother shouted at ⁽⁴⁾ .... for being late. There was no time for ⁽⁵⁾ .... to eat breakfast, so he and ⁽⁶⁾ .... sister got on ⁽⁷⁾ .... bikes and got ready to cycle to school. 'Don't be late for ⁽⁸⁾ .... dinner tonight, ⁽⁹⁾ .... two!' shouted ⁽¹⁰⁾ .... mother as ⁽¹¹⁾ .... cycled down the drive. 'I can't stand Mother shouting at ⁽¹²⁾ ....!' said Paul to ⁽¹³⁾ .... sister as ⁽¹⁴⁾ .... rode to school.

R19.2 Complete the sentences with the correct possessive pronoun.

1. I used my paints and Andrew used ....*his*..... .
2. My family and the family next door have both bought new cars this week. I like the one we bought, but I don't like ....
3. Lucy and I have similar skis; these are my skis and those are ....
4. We've got the presents we were given, and you've got ....
5. Have you got your ticket? I've got ....
6. They showed us their holiday photos, but we didn't have time to show them ....

R19.3 Complete the sentences with the correct form of the verbs in brackets and a reflexive pronoun.

1. (cut) David ....*cut himself*.................... on the broken window this morning.
2. (enjoy) Good night and thank you! We really .... at your party!
3. (wash) The dog .... in the river when we went for a walk.
4. (buy) I .... a nice winter jacket when I went to Canada.
5. (ask) .... if you really want to take this exam.
6. (find) They .... stranded at the airport.

R19.4 Complete the sentences with *this*, *that*, *these* or *those*.

1. ....*This*........ is the book I was looking for; it was right here all the time!
2. Look at .... boy over there; he can juggle very well!
3. .... girls are very badly behaved. Go and tell them to be quiet.
4. I'm sorry, but I really don't like .... soup. It's too salty.
5. .... motorbikes in the shop over there are very cool.
6. Look! .... is a picture of me when I was a baby!

R19.5 Choose the correct alternative.

1. Don't be sad. **Anybody / (Somebody)** somewhere loves you.
2. **Someone / Everyone** knows that you can't smoke in the office.
3. I don't like **neither / either** rap or heavy metal.
4. **Nobody / Anybody** was home when the postman came.
5. You can wear **however / whatever** you like to the party.
6. Is the soup **hot enough / enough hot** for you?
7. **Neither / Either** of us are going out tonight. We've got too much homework.
8. I didn't do it! I have nothing **else / other** to say!

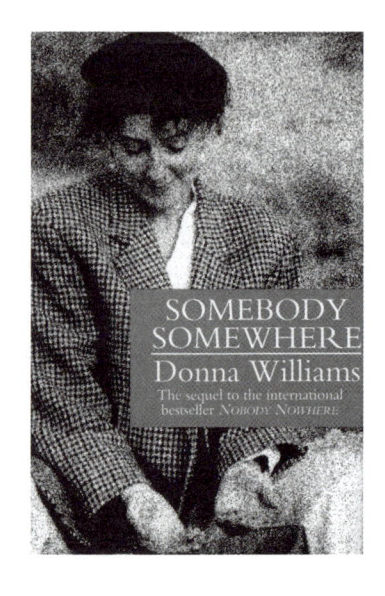

R19.6 Match the questions to the answers.

1 ..*a*.. 2 .... 3 .... 4 .... 5 .... 6 ....

1 Which trousers do you want?
2 Do you want this bag?
3 Which of his brothers did it?
4 Shall we take these books?
5 Have you already got a ticket?
6 Which shoes can I have?

a The ones with the blue belt.
b The elder one.
c Whichever ones you like.
d No, I'll buy one at the door.
e No, I want the other one.
f Yes, if they're the right ones.

R19.7 Complete the sentences using the pronouns from the box.

everything nothing ~~something~~ anything anything something

1 There's .....*something*..... I don't like about him.
2 Do you want me to get you .... from the shops?
3 Unfortunately, there's .... we can do about it now.
4 It was terrible for them. .... was destroyed in the fire.
5 I've got .... very important to tell you.
6 There isn't .... I'd rather do than be with you.

R19.8 Choose the correct alternative.

1 She drinks ..*B*.. coffee and is very nervous.
 A enough (B) too much C too many D too

2 There's .... sugar in this fruit salad. Could I have some more, please?
 A too much B too many C enough D not enough

3 Oh dear! Let's stop at the petrol station. We've got .... petrol.
 A hardly little B hardly C plenty of D hardly any

4 We can't make a cheesecake. There isn't .... cottage cheese in the fridge.
 A too much B many C any D some

5 Venice is a unique city, so .... tourists visit it every year.
 A not enough B a lot C lots of D few

6 I'm quite happy to live in this new neighbourhood. I have already made .... friends here.
 A a little B a few C few D lots

7 So you know Paul Ramsey. I like him so much. Tell me.......... about him.
 A enough B much C either D everything

8 Sheila was so sad. .... phoned her on her birthday.
 A Neither B Not much C Nobody D Someone

J Exam preparation

J.1 PET Reading Part 5

Read the text and choose the correct word (A, B, C or D) for each space.

I had (1) .....**A**..... important to do on Monday after school; I was meeting (2) .... from the local council because they had done (3) .... about putting the recycling bins in our street yet. I complained that (4) .... was still throwing (5) .... into the same bin. I was angry that (6) .... from the council seemed to care about green issues. The man explained that they hadn't received the money they needed and so couldn't do (7) .... yet, but that next month they would start putting the bins (8) .... in the town. I asked whether (9) .... had made plans about where to send the glass, paper, plastic and tins. The man told me that the things would be sent to a recycling factory (10) .... in the south of England. I said I hoped that (11) .... from the council had checked the factory, and he told me that (12) .... about it was all right.

	A	B	C	D
1	(A) something	B someone	C anything	D anywhere
2	A something	B someone	C anything	D anywhere
3	A something	B somewhere	C anything	D nothing
4	A everyone	B nothing	C somewhere	D anybody
5	A everyone	B nothing	C everything	D somewhere
6	A nothing	B nobody	C nowhere	D anyone
7	A nothing	B somebody	C somewhere	D anything
8	A everywhere	B nowhere	C somebody	D anything
9	A anything	B everyone	C anyone	D somewhere
10	A anything	B somewhere	C anywhere	D something
11	A something	B anyone	C someone	D anywhere
12	A anything	B everyone	C somewhere	D everything

J.2 PET Writing Part 1

Complete the second sentence so that it means the same as the first. Use no more than three words.

1. Paul has been everywhere in Italy.
   There .....*isn't anywhere*..... Paul hasn't been in Italy.
2. Julie knows everyone who works here.
   There .... who works here that Julie doesn't know.
3. There isn't anything my father doesn't know about car engines.
   My father .... about car engines.
4. Vicky studies all the things you can study about painting.
   Vicky studies .... about painting.
5. There are no people who know what happened last night.
   .... what happened last night.
6. It's no use running away because there isn't anywhere to hide.
   It's no use running away because there's .... to hide.

J.3 PET Writing Part 3

This is part of a menu for a school canteen. Write an e-mail to a new student explaining about how the system works. Use *either… or*, *both… and* and other suitable connectors. (60 words)

SCHOOL CANTEEN MENU – MONDAY	
• Tomato soup *or* Cheese salad	£ 1
• Roast beef with carrots and potatoes *or* Fish with chips and peas	£ 2.50
• Chocolate ice-cream *or* Apple pie	£ 1
Any two courses £ 3 All three courses £ 4	

On Monday, you can have ....

Exam preparation

J.4 FCE Use of English Part 2

Read the text and think of the word which best fits each space. Use only one in each space.

I know that (1) *everyone* always thinks I have a great time (2) .... I go to Italy on business, but actually I don't! It's very hard work – I am (3) .... on a train or a plane going somewhere or in an office having a meeting. And I can tell you that there is (4) .... more frustrating than discussing work when you know there is (5) .... beautiful to see just in the next street! The problem is that you can't (6) .... work and play at the same time. However, there isn't (7) .... nicer than sitting (8) .... in a nice square after work has finished and enjoying the view. (9) .... once told me that Italy is the best country to watch the world go by in, and (10) .... could disagree with that. Especially after a hard day's work!

J.5 FCE Use of English Part 3

Read the text below. Use the word given in capitals at the end of each line to form a word that fits in the space in the same line.

When I spoke to the (1) *manager* about the post, he told me	MANAGE
to contact the (2) .... office who dealt with everything	PERSON
connected with (3) .... So I got in touch with	APPOINT
them and they said they hadn't put an (4) .... in the paper	ADVERTISE
yet, but would be doing so in the next week. However, they also	
told me that any (5) .... who expressed an interest in the	EMPLOY
job before that would be given immediate (6)	CONSIDER

J.6 FCE Use of English Part 4

Complete the second sentence so that it has a similar meaning to the first sentence, using the word given. Do not change the word given. You must use between two and five words, including the word given.

1. There isn't anything I wouldn't do for you.
   IS
   There ....*is nothing*........ I wouldn't do for you.

2. I've got no suitable clothes to wear to the party.
   HAVEN'T
   I .... clothes to wear to the party.

3. I like both English Cheddar and French Brie.
   MIND
   I don't .... or French Brie.

4. The cinema is almost empty.
   LOT
   There are .... seats left in the cinema.

5. He ate all of the chocolates in that box!
   WHOLE
   He ate .... chocolates!

6. The car was too small for all of us to get in.
   ENOUGH
   There .... for all of us to get into the car.

UNIT 93 Cardinal numbers

A The cardinal numbers are: *one, two, three, four, five, six, seven, eight, nine, ten, eleven, twelve.*
The next seven numbers all end in **-teen**: *thirteen, fourteen, fifteen, sixteen, seventeen, eighteen, nineteen.*

The tens end in **-ty**: *twenty, thirty, forty, fifty, sixty, seventy, eighty, ninety.*
To join units to the tens, a hyphen is used: *35 thirty-five   89 eighty-nine*

100	a hundred / one hundred	200	two hundred ...
1,000	a thousand / one thousand	2,000	two thousand ...
10,000	ten thousand	100,000	a hundred thousand ...
1,000,000	one million	2,000,000	two million ...
1,000,000,000	one billion	2,000,000,000	two billion ...

B Note that:
- when a number is expressed in words, the hundreds are joined with the tens and the units with the conjunction **and**.
  521 *five hundred <u>and</u> twenty-one*   305 *three hundred <u>and</u> five*
  4,620 *four thousand, six hundred <u>and</u> twenty*

- when a number is expressed in figures, the thousands are separated by a comma, and not by a dot.
  10,600 *ten thousand, six hundred*   300,000 *three hundred thousand*   8,000,000 *eight million*

- the dot is used for decimal numbers, to separate the tenths, hundredths, etc. from the units. Decimal figures are read out separately.
  3.5 *three point five*
  65.72 *sixty-five point seven two*

- the hundreds and thousands preceded by a number do not add **-s** to the plural form. The **-s** is only added in indefinite expressions such as **hundreds**, **thousands**, **millions**.
  About two thousand people were at the concert.
  Thousands of people were cheering the rock star.

C **0** can be indicated in different ways:
- for temperatures, we use **zero**.
  −12 °C = *twelve degrees below zero*

- in mathematics, we use **nought** or **zero** (in American English).
  0.65 = *nought point six five*

- for telephone numbers, we say either **zero** or **oh**, pronounced [oʊ] or [əʊ].
  My phone number is three-four-seven six-double oh-five (347 6005).

- for sports results, we usually use **nil**.
  Arsenal's in the lead, three goals to nil.

- in tennis, we say **love**.
  The score in this game is thirty love (30–0).

D Look at the sentences with percentages and other expressions with numbers.
three <u>out of</u> five / three <u>in</u> five
33% = thirty-three <u>per cent</u>
His score was ten out of ten, he got all the answers right.
There was a 30-per-cent discount on every item.

EXERCISES

Cardinal numbers

UNIT 93

93.1 Solve the anagrams. Then write the numbers in ascending order.

1 eon ....one..........
2 levtew ....
3 ddhrneu ....
4 gehti ....
5 yttnew ....
6 ttyihr-hreet ....
7 wot ....
8 eeeenntvs ....

one, ...

93.2 Write the numbers and symbols in full.

1 14m people — fourteen million people
2 1,000km
2 £52
3 39.5°C
4 78%
6 tel: 559 8026
7 €1,376
8 $10,640

93.3 Write how you would say 0 in the following cases.

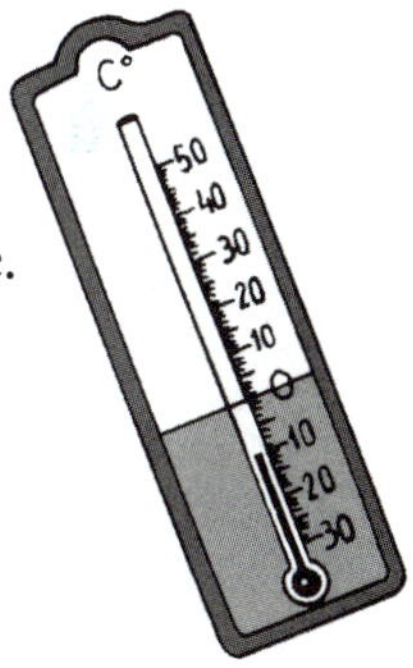

1 –10°C — ten degrees below ....zero..........
2 It's 30–0 to Federer in this game. — It's thirty .... to Federer in this game.
3 It's 2–0 to Juventus. — It's two .... to Juventus.
4 James Bond, 007 — James Bond, double .... seven.
5 I got 0/10 in the test. — I got .... out of ten in the test.
6 The answer's 0.15. — The answer's .... point one five.
7 Your room number is 507. — Your room number is five .... seven.
8 The diameter of the circle is 0.87cm. — The diameter of the circle is .... point eight seven centimetres.

93.4 Choose the correct alternative.

1 Shhh… I'm counting!… **three hundred eleven** / **(three hundred and eleven)**.
2 Nobody would dare to ask for a pay rise of **several hundreds** / **several hundred** pounds.
3 **Fourty-four** / **Forty-four** isn't old for a man to have children.
4 Nearly two **thousands** / **thousand** people have bought laptops this week.
5 The highest score in the exam was only 61 **on** / **out of** a hundred.
6 **Million** / **Millions** of people have visited St. Peter's in Rome.
7 Only 40 per **hundred** / **cent** of the visitors were satisfied with the new location of the trade fair.
8 I paid **four thousand and five hundred** / **four thousand five hundred** pounds for this motorbike.

93.5 Match the price tags to the correct words.

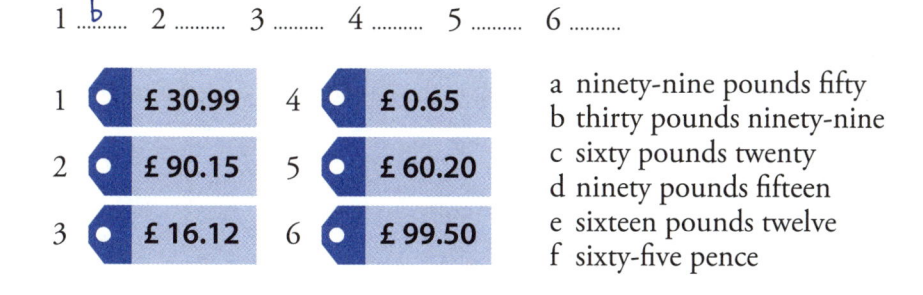

1 ..b.. 2 .... 3 .... 4 .... 5 .... 6 ....

1 £ 30.99
2 £ 90.15
3 £ 16.12
4 £ 0.65
5 £ 60.20
6 £ 99.50

a ninety-nine pounds fifty
b thirty pounds ninety-nine
c sixty pounds twenty
d ninety pounds fifteen
e sixteen pounds twelve
f sixty-five pence

UNIT 94 Ordinal numbers and dates

A Ordinal numbers are used to indicate the order of sequence, for example a ranking. They can be written in full (**second**), abbreviated (**2nd / 2ⁿᵈ**) or expressed with a Roman numeral (**II**).

She was third in the race.
Today is the 4th of October.
Queen Elizabeth I (the first) was Henry VIII's (the eighth's) daughter.

B They are formed by adding **-th** to the cardinal number. For example:

four	→	4ᵗʰ	the fourth
six	→	6ᵗʰ	the sixth
seven	→	7ᵗʰ	the seventh
eleven	→	11ᵗʰ	the eleventh
hundred	→	100ᵗʰ	the hundredth

the hundredth

There are, however, some exceptions. The first three ordinal numbers have their own forms:
1ˢᵗ the first   2ⁿᵈ the second   3ʳᵈ the third

And so do the first three of every ten, for example:
21ˢᵗ the twenty-first   22ⁿᵈ the twenty-second   23ʳᵈ the twenty-third   31ˢᵗ the thirty-first…

WATCH OUT! The following add **th**:
11ᵗʰ eleventh, 12ᵗʰ twelfth, 13ᵗʰ thirteenth

Note also the following spelling changes that occur when a cardinal number becomes an ordinal number.

five	→	the fifth
eight	→	the eighth
nine	→	the ninth
twelve	→	the twelfth
twenty	→	the twentieth

Henry VIII (the eighth)

It is the same for all the tens:
the thirtieth, the fortieth, the fiftieth…

C Ordinal numbers are used for dates and can be placed before or after the month.
10ᵗʰ March, 2009 → the tenth of March, two thousand and nine (also: 10.03.09, Br.)
March 10ᵗʰ, 2009 → March the tenth, two thousand and nine (also: 03.10.09, Am.)

The year can be expressed in various ways.
320 BC → three hundred and twenty before Christ
112 AD → one hundred and twelve anno Domini
1900   → nineteen hundred
1904   → nineteen hundred and four / nineteen-oh-four
1999   → nineteen ninety-nine
2005   → two thousand and five / twenty-oh-five

D In a fraction, the numerator is expressed with a cardinal number and the denominator with an ordinal number, singular or plural. It is also possible to use the preposition **over** between the two numbers.

¼ one fourth (or: **one** quarter)
⅔ two-thirds
⅗ three-fifths
BUT: ½ one-half

EXERCISES

Ordinal numbers and dates

UNIT 94

94.1 Complete the song *The Twelve Days of Christmas* using ordinal numbers.

On the (1) **first** day of Christmas my true love sent to me
a partridge in a pear tree.
On the (2) .... day of Christmas my true love sent to me
two turtle doves and a partridge in a pear tree.
On the (3) .... day of Christmas my true love sent to me
three French hens, two turtle doves and a partridge in a pear tree.
On the (4) .... day of Christmas my true love sent to me
four calling birds, three French hens, two turtle doves, and...
On the (5) .... day of Christmas my true love sent to me
five gold rings, four calling birds, three French hens, two...
On the (6) .... day of Christmas my true-love sent to me
six geese a-laying, five gold rings, four calling birds, three...
On the (7) .... day of Christmas my true love sent to me
seven swans a-swimming, six geese a-laying, five gold rings, four...
On the (8) .... day of Christmas my true love sent to me
eight maids a-milking, seven swans a-swimming, six geese a-laying
On the (9) .... day of Christmas, my true love sent to me
nine ladies dancing, eight maids a-milking, seven swans a-swimming...
On the (10) .... day of Christmas, my true love sent to me
ten lords a-leaping, nine ladies dancing, eight maids a-milking...
On the (11) .... day of Christmas, my true love sent to me
eleven pipers piping, ten lords a-leaping, nine ladies dancing...
On the (12) .... day of Christmas, my true love sent to me
twelve drummers drumming, eleven pipers piping, ten lords a-leaping...

94.2 Write the underlined ordinal numbers in words.

1 Elizabeth II was born in 1926. Elizabeth **the second**
2 We live in the 21st century. .... century
3 You're a teenager after your 13th birthday. .... birthday
4 20th Century Fox is a famous film company. .... Century Fox
5 Congratulations! You're our 1,000,000th customer. .... customer
6 A penny is a 100th of a pound. .... of a pound
7 Barack Obama is the 44th President of the USA. .... President of the USA

94.3 Write the dates in figures.

1 ten sixty-six   **1066 AD**
2 the twenty-fourth of March, 2008   ....
3 fifty-five before Christ   ....
4 the eighteenth of December, 1834   ....
5 nineteen-oh-eight   ....
6 two thousand and one   ....
7 thirty-three before Christ   ....

94.4 Write the fractions in figures.

1 one-quarter = **1/4**   4 one-half = ...   7 seven-fifteenths = ...
2 two-ninths = ...   5 five-eighths = ...   8 three-fifths = ...
3 four-sevenths = ...   6 three over a hundred = ...   9 two-thirds = ...

257

UNIT 95 Relative pronouns in defining clauses

A A defining clause tells us what kind of person or thing the speaker means. It forms the answer to the questions 'Which person or thing? What kind of person or thing?'.

Relative clauses are joined to the main clause by pronouns (**who**, **which**, **that**...) to make the conversation flow and to avoid repetition. The following shows you how two clauses can be joined with a relative pronoun:

The waiter was nice.   **He** served us last night.   → The waiter **who** served us last night was nice.
Show me the photos. You took **these photos** in Kenya.   → Show me the photos **that** you took in Kenya.

REMEMBER: a defining clause is essential for identifying the person or thing that is being spoken about. In the above sentences, for example, if you were to omit the underlined relative clauses, you would not be able to understand which waiter or which photos were being talked about.
As a defining clause is closely tied with the main clause, they are never separated by a comma.

B The relative pronouns that are used in defining clauses are:

	referring to people	referring to animals or things
subject	**who** or **that**	**which** or **that**
direct object	(**who**) or (**whom**) or (**that**)	(**which**) or (**that**)
possession	**whose**	**whose**

C A relative pronoun can function as a subject, a direct object or an indirect object (if accompanied by a preposition), and can express possession.

- When a pronoun is the subject of a relative clause, it has to be expressed.

    Simon is the boy **who** lives next door.
    The cheetah is the animal **which** runs fastest.

- When a pronoun functions as a direct object, it is usually implied, as the brackets indicate in the table above.

    The man **who / that** you met at my house is my uncle. → The man you met...
    (also possible: ...**whom** you met..., in formal written language)
    The car **which / that** we bought last month is a hybrid car. → The car we bought ...

- A relative pronoun can also be omitted when it functions as an indirect object, whilst the preposition is moved to the end of the relative clause.

    The magazine **for which** you're looking is on the table.
    The magazine **X** you're looking **for** is on the table.

    A relative pronoun, however, doesn't always have to be omitted. It can stay in its place whilst the preposition is moved (**The magazine which you're looking for is on the table**) or, in formal English, it is also possible to place the preposition before the relative pronoun (but only before **which** and **whom**, not before **who** and **that**).

    Is that the film **in which** he robs a bank?

- To express possession in a relative clause, we use the pronoun **whose**, which can't be omitted.
    That's the lady **whose** son works with my husband.

EXERCISES

Relative pronouns in defining clauses

UNIT 95

95.1 Complete the sentences using *which* or *who*.

1 My friend has a computer game *which* can take days to finish.
2 There are meeting places on the Internet .... are called chat rooms.
3 This is the lady .... gave me her old laptop.
4 I'll call that friend of mine .... can fix most computer problems.
5 I bought some software .... is the most recent on the market.
6 Paul is the programmer .... designed my website.

95.2 Rewrite the sentences by placing the preposition at the end of the relative clause and omitting the relative pronoun.

1 The holiday to which he was looking forward was cancelled.
The holiday *he was looking forward to* was cancelled.

2 The text with which I was working suddenly vanished from the screen.
The text .... suddenly vanished from the screen.

3 The book about which we were talking got an important award.
The book .... got an important award.

4 Who are the people for whom you are waiting?
Who are the people .... ?

5 The boat in which he rowed across the Atlantic has been preserved.
The boat .... has been preserved.

6 The women with whom he went to the party soon left.
The women .... soon left.

7 The house in which he lived as a boy was burnt to the ground.
The house .... was burnt to the ground.

95.3 Join the two sentences with *whose*.

1 That is the boy. His father was on TV.   *That is the boy whose father was on TV.*
2 She is the girl. Her mother is a famous painter.   ....
3 We are the students. Our bags were stolen.   ....
4 I am the man. My music was played at the wedding. ....
5 They are the people. Their house caught fire.   ....
6 You are the one. Your essay was brilliant.   ....

95.4 Tick (✔) the sentences that you can omit the relative pronoun from.

1 ...✔... The language **that** they speak must be Urdu.
2 .... I've never met the boy **who** is going out with Julia these days.
3 .... It's the kind of film **which** I don't really like.
4 .... He's the man **whom** you saw at the theatre last night.
5 .... He's an artist **whose** work has been greatly praised.
6 .... Have you ever been to the house **which** the Seymours bought in Blackpool last year?

95.5 Join the two sentences with a suitable relative pronoun. Omit it where possible.

1 This is the man. He stole my bag.   *This is the man who stole my bag.*
2 The dog was found in the park. It is Mr Ross's dog. ....
3 This is the girl. I gave the flowers to her. ....
4 The phone call arrived too late. I was waiting for it. ....
5 This is the new car. I'm going to buy it.   ....
6 That's the teacher. He gives us lots of homework. ....

UNIT 96 Relative pronouns in non-defining clauses

A Non-defining clauses provide additional information, but are not essential for identifying the thing or person that the speaker means. For this reason, they are also called 'extra-information clauses'.

Look at, for example:
The Porters, who live next door, have three children.

If you were to eliminate the relative clause, we would know who is being spoken about (**the Porters**) and the main clause would still make sense: **The Porters have three children.** It is therefore a non-defining clause.

Now look at this sentence:
The people who live next door have three children.

In this case, by omitting the relative clause, we wouldn't know who the speaker means (which people have children?). It is therefore a defining clause (see p.258).

B The relative pronouns used in non-defining clauses are:

	referring to people	referring to animals or things
subject	who	which
direct object	who or whom	which
possession	whose	whose or of which

Note that:
- a non-defining clause is always contained between commas or between a comma and a full stop.
- in these kind of sentences, **that** isn't used.
- in non-defining clauses, relative pronouns <u>are always expressed</u>, even when they function as an object.

*Yesterday, I met John Simmons, **who** used to work in my office.*
*Our friends George and Linda, **who(m)** you met last year, are now in the USA.* (**whom** is typical in formal written language)
*This science book, **which** I borrowed from the library, is really interesting.*
*King Alfred the Great, **whose** statue is in Winchester, lived in the 9th century.*

In the case of an indirect object, the preposition can precede the relative pronoun (**to whom**, **with whom**, **for which**, **about which**...) or it can be moved to the end of the relative clause but, as opposed to defining clauses, the pronoun can't be implied.

The Danes, <u>with whom</u> King Alfred made peace, settled in the north of England.
Last week, I visited the National Gallery, <u>which</u> I had never been <u>to</u> before.

The use of commas is very important, as it can change the meaning of the sentence. Look at, for example, the difference between a defining clause (without commas) and a non-defining clause:

The passengers who hadn't been informed of the delay waited at the airport for six hours. (only those that weren't informed)
The passengers, who hadn't been informed of the delay, waited at the airport for six hours. (all of them!)

EXERCISES

Relative pronouns in non-defining clauses

UNIT 96

96.1 Decide whether the underlined relative clauses are defining (D) or non-defining (ND). If it is non-defining, add the necessary punctuation.

1. ...D..... The man who I met last week was very nice.
2. .... Doctor Johnson who I know very well helped me a lot.
3. .... Peter who sits next to me in class can run very fast.
4. .... The woman who lives over the road is called Mrs Jones.
5. .... My French dictionary which I use every day got wet in the rain.
6. .... The computer that you are using isn't very good.

96.2 Complete the sentences with the correct relative pronoun: *who*, *whom*, *which* or *whose*.

1. Our teacher, ...who...... is a good tennis player, is a very kind person.
2. My neighbour, ... I asked for help with my iMac, works in a computer shop.
3. This iPod, ... I bought last week, doesn't seem to work properly.
4. Your cousin, ... results in the exam were excellent, has joined my class.
5. Those headphones, ... were reviewed in *Music World*, are excellent.
6. Her father, ... recently ran a marathon, seems to be quite ill.

96.3 Choose the correct alternative, *who* or *whom*. In certain cases, both are possible.

1. My friend, (who)/ whom is at university, played rugby for Wales.
2. My girlfriend, **who / whom** works in a bank, is trying to change jobs.
3. My granny, **who / whom** you met last year, is now living in Spain.
4. Mr Rogers, **who / whom** I often played tennis with, died last week.
5. Your dad, **who / whom** likes to eat and drink, should lose some weight.
6. Lucy, **who / whom** is best in our class at English, failed her exams.

96.4 Join the two sentences with a suitable relative pronoun.

1. Mr Driscoll is my father's boss. He has got a huge collection of old stamps.
   Mr Driscoll, who has got a huge collection of old stamps, is my father's boss.
2. Mrs Sarandon returned from the USA two weeks ago. Her daughter was in the same class as my sister.
   ....
3. My boss is going to retire next December. I've worked for him for 20 years.
   ....
4. Malindi is in Kenya. It is a popular holiday resort.
   ....
5. Nicole Kidman was born in Australia. She has made a lot of Hollywood movies.
   ....
6. The Beatles first played together at the Cavern Club. Their name then was The Silver Beatles.
   ....
7. *Crypto* is a novel based on the world of computers. Its author is Dan Brown.
   ....
8. The Eiffel Tower is the most famous landmark in Paris. It was built between 1887 and 1889.
   ....
9. The Olympic Games were first revived in Athens in 1896. They were held at Olympia in ancient times.
   ....
10. The Smiths are buying a house in Chicago. They have just sold their house in the UK.
    ....

UNIT 97 Relative adverbs *where, when, why;* *which, what, all that* in relative clauses

A To talk about places in a relative clause, we usually use the adverb **where**, which can be substituted by the expressions **in which / at which**....

*The town **where** I was born is in the north of Belgium.* (also: *The town **in which** I was born...*)
*This is the hotel **where** / **in which** we spent our honeymoon.*

B To talk about a period of time, we usually use the adverb **when**, which can substitute **in which / on which / at which**...

*Halloween is the festival **when** children play 'trick or treat'.*

With the expressions **the year...**, **the day...**, **the time...**, you can find both **when** and **that** or no adverb at all.

*This is the time (**when**) we usually meet.*
*The year (**that**) they got married was 1992, I think.*

C To talk about the motive for something happening, we usually use **the reason why...** or even just **the reason...**, instead of **the reason for which**.

*I don't know **the reason why** she left.*
***The reason** I went to the party was that I wanted to meet Marion.*

D Other relative clauses can be introduced by:

- **which**, referring to all the previous sentence, not just the last part. Note that a comma separates the main clause from the relative one.
  *Sandra passed her exam, **which** she didn't quite expect.*
  *They didn't come to the concert, **which** was such a pity.*

- **what**, instead of **the thing(s) that...**
  *Tell me **what** you know.*
  *Did you hear **what** I said?*

- **all (that) / everything (that)** WATCH OUT! Not: ~~all what~~
  *Tell me **all that** you know.*
  *This is **all** we need.*
  *She could have **everything** she wanted.*

E At times, instead of a relative clause, we can use the present participle of the verb (**-ing** form) if the action described is underway. Or we can use the past participle of the verb if it has a passive meaning.

There are a lot of people jogging in the park this morning. (instead of: *There are a lot of people who are jogging...*)
The Mona Lisa, painted by Leonardo da Vinci, is one of the most famous paintings in the world. (instead of: *The Mona Lisa, which was painted...*)

EXERCISES

Relative adverbs *where, when, why; which, what, all that* in relative clauses

UNIT 97

97.1 **Complete the sentences with *where* or *when* instead of the expressions *in / at which*.**
1 This is the flat (in which) ...*where*... I lived as a student.
2 This is the desk (in which) .... I used to sit in Class 1.
3 Nine o'clock was the time (at which) .... we always went to bed as children.
4 It was a period of my life (in which) .... I was very happy.
5 That was the B&B (at which) .... we always stayed on holiday.
6 It was the day (on which) .... all the students met in the Hall.

97.2 **Write *that* in the sentences where it's possible to use it as an alternative to *when* or *which*.**
1 This is the dress which / ...*that*... I spilt tomato sauce on.
2 Here's the book which / .... I wanted to tell you about.
3 It's the time when / .... I usually take my medicine.
4 I didn't see them last night, which / .... made life difficult.
5 They didn't come in when / .... I called them.
6 It's at Christmas when / .... I usually have a big party.

97.3 **Match the two parts of the sentences.**

1 ...*c*... 2 .... 3 .... 4 .... 5 .... 6 ....

1 I don't understand
2 She disappeared last week,
3 I want to read
4 I'm not listening to
5 This is
6 She couldn't decide

a where to go.
b everything that he writes about it.
c why you did it.
d all that was left when he died.
e which is very surprising
f what you're trying to say.

97.4 **Change the present or past participle into a relative clause.**
1 The café was full of people eating their lunch.
   The café was full of people ...*who were eating*.................... their lunch.
2 This is the book illustrated by my father.
   This is the book .... by my father.
3 There were lots of children playing on the beach.
   There were lots of children .... on the beach.
4 We saw their dog eating a bone on the carpet.
   We saw their dog .... a bone on the carpet.
5 I met Lynda taking a walk in the main street.
   I met Lynda .... a walk in the main street.
6 There was a dark cloud covering the sun.
   There was a dark cloud .... the sun.
7 Where's the portrait painted in Paris?
   Where's the portrait .... in Paris?
8 Have you seen the men digging the road?
   Have you seen the men .... the road?

263

REVIEW 20

EXERCISES Units 93–97

R20.1 Match the ordinal numbers in words to the ones written in figures.

1 _d_ 2 .... 3 .... 4 .... 5 .... 6 .... 7 .... 8 ....

1 forty-seventh   a 3rd
2 third   b 80th
3 twenty-eighth   c 99th
4 ninety-ninth   d 47th
5 eighteenth   e 100th
6 eightieth   f 88th
7 eighty-eighth   g 28th
8 one hundredth   h 18th

R20.2 Write these numbers in full.

1 21   _twenty-one_
2 357   ....
3 17.4   ....
4 8,926   ....
5 0.34   ....
6 425,000   ....
7 50,000   ....
8 10,873   ....

R20.3 Complete the sentences with the correct relative pronoun. Put it in brackets if it can be implied.

1 I quite like the painting ......_(which)_...... you bought at the auction.
2 She didn't finish in time, ... was quite unusual for her.
3 I talked to the woman .... you met last week.
4 I can tell you .... bag that red one is. It's Sandra's.
5 I didn't hear .... he was saying.
6 There's the boy .... brother is a footballer.
7 You didn't tell her the truth, ... is very serious.
8 The match .... they played yesterday ended with a nil–nil draw.

R20.4 Write the numbers in full.

1 The Eiffel Tower is 324 metres high.
   three hundred and twenty-four metres

2 The lowest temperature registered in Antarctica was -89.2°C.
   ....

3 The average African elephant weighs about 5000 kilos.
   ....

4 The Sahara desert is about 9,000,000 square kilometres.
   ....

5 It costs $1,700,000 to buy a Bugatti Veyron car.
   ....

6 The average annual income in the poorest country in the world is about $470.
   ....

7 2/3rds of the class are on Facebook.
   ....

8 Temperatures have reached 57.8°C in Libya.
   ....

R20.5 **Join the two sentences with a suitable relative pronoun.**

1 The Smiths have moved to Spain. They bought our old car.
   The Smiths, who bought our old car, have moved to Spain.

2 The old oak tree fell down last night. It was in our garden.

3 The footballers celebrated after the game. They all played well.

4 My friend gave me a CD. His sister is a dancer.

5 Captain Caldwell sailed to Australia. I met him last summer.

6 Arthur lives next door. He is very good at chess.

7 My car is painted green. It is getting rather old.

8 Your sister is very pretty. She is tall for her age.

R20.6 **Tick (✔) the sentences in which you can use *whom* instead of *who*.**

1 ✔ That's the boy who I played with last Monday.
2 ...... Where are the girls who I talked to this morning?
3 ...... I met Paul, who happened to be on the same bus as me.
4 ...... Is this the athlete who won the marathon last night?
5 ...... He's a writer who I haven't heard of before.
6 ...... I was so frightened and he was the person who I turned to for help.
7 ...... There are plenty of people who like to make easy money.
8 ...... I don't mind who I travel with tomorrow.

R20.7 **Complete the sentences using the words from the box.**

| ~~of whom~~ | with whom | without whom | under whom | to whom | for whom | in whom | about whom |

1 He is a teacher ...*of whom*... I have heard wonderful things.
2 She is someone .... I have the greatest trust.
3 He's the kind of person .... nothing is too much trouble.
4 Paul is the one person .... I would go anywhere!
5 She's a painter .... I have read much in the press.
6 He's the kind of man .... nothing could have been achieved.
7 He's a leader .... it is a pleasure to serve.
8 Patricia is the girl .... I wrote many letters.

UNIT 98 — Interrogative adjectives and pronouns; exclamations

A

The main interrogative adjectives and pronouns are:

	to ask questions...
who (pronoun only)	relative to people
what	relative to things or occurrences
which	that imply a choice
whose	on possession or family relations

- Interrogatives always take first place in a question. When they are accompanied by a preposition, the preposition is placed at the end of the question.
  Who are you waiting for?
  What was the weather like?
  What are you thinking about?

- Note the difference between the sentences in which the interrogative pronoun functions as subject...
  Who talked to you? (**who** is the subject)
  What happened? (**what** is the subject)
  Which tennis player won? (**which** accompanies the subject)

  and those in which the pronoun is the object.
  Who did you talk to? (the subject is **you** and **who** is the object)
  What does he know about that? (the subject is **he** and **what** is the object)

  The first set of questions has the structure of an affirmative sentence, whilst the second set has the structure of a true question, as they require the auxiliary **do / does / did**.

B

- **What** can function as both an adjective and a pronoun.
  What are you doing? (pronoun)
  What flowers do you like? (adjective)

- **Which** can also function as both an adjective and a pronoun. When it's used as a pronoun, it's usually followed by **of** + plural noun or by **of** + object pronoun (**you / them**...).
  Which of the stories in the book did you read?
  Which of you would like an ice-cream?

- The difference between **which** and **what**, when used as adjectives, is the following: **which** is used when there is a limited selection of people or things to choose from, whilst **what** is used in a general sense.
  'Which cake do you prefer?' 'The one with fruit on top.' (the choice is between a few cakes)
  'What cakes do you prefer?' 'Chocolate cakes.' (in general, not between a few in particular)

- **What** is usually accompanied by **kind** (genre / type).
  'What kind of films do you like?' 'Action films.'

- **Whose** can be used both as an adjective and a pronoun.
  Whose pen is this? (adjective) / *Whose is this pen?* (pronoun)

C

- For exclamations, we use the following expressions:

| **What** + a / an + singular noun | **What** + uncountable or plural noun | **How** + adjective |

What a fine day!   *What nice people!*
How kind of you!   *What awful weather!*

EXERCISES

Interrogative adjectives and pronouns; exclamations

UNIT 98

98.1 Read the answers and write suitable questions using *who* or *whose*.

1 <u>Whose CD-ROMs are they?</u> They're my father's CD-ROMs.
2 .... It's my brother's MP3 player.
3 .... I was talking to Michael on Skype.
4 .... I wrote about Napoleon on Wikipedia.
5 .... I used Angela's laptop.
6 .... I heard Bill Gates's lecture.
7 .... It's my mobile. You can use it if you want.
8 .... I was chatting with my Australian penpal last night.

98.2 Choose the correct alternative.

1 There are two cakes left. **What / (Which)** one do you want?
2 **What / Which** do you want to do tonight?
3 **What / Which** happened to you when you got there?
4 **What / Which** of these is your bike?
5 **What / Which** of the films did you watch last night?
6 **What / Which** kind of films do you like watching?
7 **What / Which** were the bedrooms like at the hotel?
8 **What / Which** one is your sister? The girl on the right or the one on the left?

98.3 Change the interrogative pronouns into adjectives and vice versa. Make any necessary changes to the questions.

1 What book is this? <u>What is this book?</u>
2 Whose are these CDs? ....
3 What computer is that? ....
4 Which memory stick is his? ....
5 Whose satnav is this? ....
6 Which are our cables? ....
7 Whose is this laptop? ....
8 Which earphones are yours? ....
9 What's the time? ....
10 Which is my suitcase? ....

98.4 Write exclamatory sentences using *What (a / an)...* and the information given.

1 That girl has got beautiful eyes. <u>What beautiful eyes that girl has got!</u>
2 That man has got long legs. ....
3 They're sweet puppies. ....
4 She's a wonderful cook. ....
5 Mr Smith's an excellent teacher. ....
6 The hotel is very comfortable. ....
7 This mobile phone is really small. ....
8 Those are brilliant video games. ....

UNIT 99 Interrogative adverbs

A The main interrogative adverbs are:

	to ask questions...
why	on the motive of something
when	regarding time
where	regarding location
how	on the way something happened

- These adverbs are always placed first in a question.
  How are you? When's your birthday?
  Where are my keys? Why don't you like it?

B
- **Where** can be accompanied by a preposition (**from, to...**) that is placed at the end of the sentence.
  Where do you come from?

- **Why** is used in questions and in indirect interrogatives, whilst in answers we use **because**.
  'Why are you late?' 'Because I missed the train.'
  I asked him why he hadn't come.

- **How** can be followed by the adverbs of quantity **much** or **many**. **How much** and **how many** can be used both as adjectives and pronouns.
  'How much flour do we need?' 'One kilo.'
  'How much did you pay?' 'Six euros twenty.'
  'How many letters did you get?' 'A lot!'

C
- **How** can be followed by other adverbs and adjectives, for example:

	for information on...
how fast	speed
how often	frequency
how old	age
how long	duration
how long / wide / deep	dimension
how tall / high	height (of people of things)
how big / large	size

'How fast can you go on this road?' 'Fifty miles per hour.'
'How often do you buy this magazine?' 'Every month.'
'How old is your sister?' 'She's 12 years old.'

NB: In answers and questions on dimensions, the adjective is placed after the number.
'How high is Mount Everest?' 'It's 8,846m high.' (not: It's high 8,846m) '
'How long is the river Mekong?' 'It's about 4,500 km long'

- Note that the expressions **How about...? / What about...?** followed by a noun or by a verb + **-ing** are also used to make suggestions and offers.

  How about a cup of tea?
  What about joining us?

EXERCISES

UNIT 99 — Interrogative adverbs

99.1 Complete the questions with the correct interrogative: *why, when, where* or *how*.

1 '...*Why*... did he do it?' 'Because he's not a nice person.'
2 .... are you going to stay when you're in Rome?
3 .... will they get here? It's late already.
4 .... did you travel to Italy? Plane or train?
5 .... is the person I came here to talk to?
6 .... is it so cold today? The sun's shining!
7 .... do you think you can see me? Tomorrow?
8 .... do you like your tea? With milk or lemon?

99.2 Complete the questions using *much* or *many*.

1 How ...*much*... did your new computer game cost?
2 How .... time have you got before you have to go?
3 How .... times have I told you to close down the computer?
4 How .... butter is there in the fridge?
5 How .... do you love me?
6 How .... people went to the concert?
7 How .... megabites has your memory stick got?
8 How .... memory is needed for this software?

99.3 Complete the questions using the words from the box.

| fast | often | old | deep | long | high | big | wide |

1 How ...*fast*... is your Internet connection?
2 How .... is the memory on your laptop?
3 'How .... is this computer?' 'About six years.'
4 How .... do you send e-mails to your friends?
5 How .... is the River Thames at Tower Bridge?
6 How .... is a football pitch from goal to goal?
7 How .... is Everest?
8 How .... is Loch Ness? Has anyone ever been to the bottom?

99.4 Use the words to write suggestions with *What / How about + -ing*.

1 go / to Spain on holiday
   What / How about going to Spain on holiday?
2 visit / your parents tomorrow
   ....
3 watch / a DVD tonight
   ....
4 cook / spaghetti for dinner
   ....
5 play / a computer game later
   ....
6 take / the dog for a walk
   ....
7 send / e-mail to our German friends
   ....
8 download / music on our iPod
   ....

UNIT 100 Structure of *Yes / No* questions and *Wh-* questions

There are two types of questions: *Yes / No* questions and *Wh-* questions.

A *Yes / No* questions:
- begin with an <u>auxiliary</u> (**be**, **have**, **do** in the various tenses) or with a <u>modal</u> (**can**, **could**, **shall**, **will**…) followed by the <u>subject</u> and by the other elements of the sentence (main verb, objects…).
- We usually answer them with a short answer, affirmative or negative, in which we reuse the subject pronoun and the auxiliary with which the question starts.

    '***Is** Janet* here on holiday?' 'No, she **isn't**. She lives here.'
    '***Does** Peter* go to your school?' 'Yes, **he does**.'
    '***Can** you* come with me?' 'No, **I can't**. Sorry.'
    '***Have** you* ever been to Malta?' 'Yes, **I have**. Many times.'

    In colloquial English, however, short answers aren't always used: **Yes** and **No** can be one-word answers.

B *Wh-* questions:
- begin with a pronoun, adjective or <u>interrogative</u> adverb (**who**, **what**, **where**…), which is then followed by an <u>auxiliary</u> or <u>modal</u>, the <u>subject</u> and other elements of the sentence.
- We answer by giving the information asked for, often without repeating the subject and verb.

    '<u>Where did she</u> go last Sunday?' 'She went to Bath.'
    '<u>How long have you</u> been waiting?' 'Ten minutes.'
    '<u>What gate shall I</u> go to?' 'Gate 16.'

C Interrogative sentences always have a rigid structure: the order of the words cannot be changed. The subject, even if it's very long, always maintains the same position.

What time does <u>the train to Leeds</u> leave?
Where does <u>the girl with blond hair who is in your class</u> come from?

Questions can also be formulated in a negative way. In this case, the negative form of an auxiliary or modal is used, usually in its short form (**isn't**, **wasn't**, **don't**, **doesn't**, **wouldn't**…).
Isn't it late?
Why didn't you go?

NB: Questions in which **who, what** or **which** function as subject maintain the structure of an affirmative sentence, i.e. subject + verb (see p.266A).
Who went on the school trip?
What comes next?
Which came first, Morse code or the wireless telegraph?

Even indirect interrogatives have the structure of an affirmative sentence (see p.314).
Do you know what time it is? (not: …what time is it?)
Could you tell me how I get to the bus station?
(not: … how do I get…?)

EXERCISES

Structure of *Yes / No* questions and *Wh-* questions

UNIT 100

100.1 Use the words to write *Yes / No questions*. Then write a short affirmative (+) or negative (−) answer. Pay attention to the verb tense!

1. Janet / be / at school / today / + — 'Is Janet at school today?' 'Yes, she is.'
2. the boys / play / football / now / +
3. she / feed / the dogs / this morning / −
4. you / ever / be / to Venice / −
5. can / she / swim / very well / +
6. your mother / cook lunch / tomorrow / −

100.2 Rearrange the words and write *Wh-* questions.

1. my – Where – stick – put – you – memory – new – did – ?
   Where did you put my new memory stick?
2. pictures – you – for – download – When – me – can – those – ?
3. install – long – to – it – How – program – take – this – does – ?
4. satellite – is – channels – decoder – the – the – for – Where – ?
5. you – dial-up – Why – using – connection – that – are – still – ?
6. how – Microsoft – Who – operate – knows – new – system – to – this – ?

100.3 Use the words to write negative questions. Pay attention to the verb tense!

1. you / not / want / to go / out / now / ? — *Don't you want to go out now?*
2. she / not / be / on / the trip / yesterday / ?
3. you / would / not / like / to come / with us / ?
4. you / can / not / ask / him / to help / them / ?
5. she / will / not / play / her / guitar / for me / ?
6. he / not / travel / there / by train / last week / ?

100.4 Circle the pronouns or interrogative adjectives that function as subject and underline those that function as objects. Then match the questions to the answers.

1 _d_   2 ......   3 ......   4 ......   5 ......   6 ......   7 ......   8 ......

1. Who did you go on holiday with last summer?
2. Who went to the sea with you last summer?
3. Which of the two players is your brother?
4. Who helped you fix your DVD player?
5. What happened to your old mobile? Did you lose it?
6. Which of these video games do you like best?
7. Which earphones are yours? The ones on the table?
8. What brings you to England, Manuel? You haven't been here for ages!

a Yes, I did. I must have left it on the train.
b My friend Alfred. He's a good technician.
c The one with the blue shirt.
d I went with my girlfriend.
e No, those aren't mine.
f I missed my old friends.
g My cousin and a couple of friends came with me.
h I like this one. It must be very good.

UNIT 101 Asking for confirmation: question tags

A To ask for confirmation of what has just been said, we often use question tags, that is, short questions that come at the end of a sentence. They are always separated from the main clause by a comma.

*It's nice, **isn't it**?*
*You've got a brother, **haven't you**?*
*Jane will give you a lift, **won't she**?*

As you can see in the examples, question tags reuse the auxiliary or the modal in the main clause, in the same verb tense, followed by the subject pronoun.

If the main clause doesn't contain an auxiliary or a modal, the question tag is formed using the same verb tense as the main verb.

*You know what I mean, **don't you**?*
*Peter sent you a text message, **didn't he**?*
*Your mother wasn't home last night, **was she**?*

B If the main sentence is affirmative, the **question tag** is negative and vice versa.

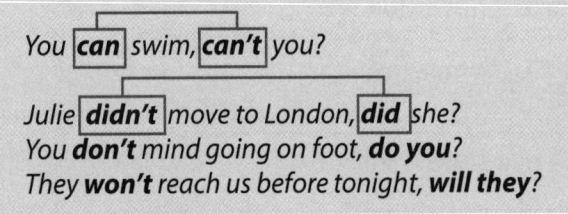

*You **can** swim, **can't** you?*
*Julie **didn't** move to London, **did** she?*
*You **don't** mind going on foot, **do you**?*
*They **won't** reach us before tonight, **will they**?*

C In colloquial English:

- the expression **right?** can be used instead of a question tag, to ask for confirmation.
  'You're John's friend, right?' 'Yes, that's right.'

- sometimes the first part of an affirmative sentence can be implied.

Lovely day isn't it?

Awful weather isn't it?

D Auxiliaries and modals can also be used in short questions to show interest or surprise. They can be accompanied by the adverb **really**.

*'I'm terribly tired.' 'Oh. **Are you** really? How come?'*
*'I've written ten pages of my essay so far.' '**Have you**? I've only written three.'*

EXERCISES

Asking for confirmation: question tags

UNIT 101

101.1 Complete the sentences with the appropriate question tag.

1 He's a nice man, *isn't he?*
2 It was cold today, ...
3 You've bought a new computer, ...
4 He'll buy me some flowers, ...
5 They'd like it, ...
6 She'd seen it before, ...
7 Sarah called you yesterday, ...
8 John taught you to use this program, ...
9 The children were having a good time, ...
10 She's been married for a couple of years, ...

101.2 Match the sentences to the appropriate question tag.

1 ..c.. 2 .... 3 .... 4 .... 5 .... 6 .... 7 .... 8 ....

1 Dick often goes there,
2 Jane sometimes plays with us,
3 The boys went last week,
4 The players try very hard,
5 You and I won easily,
6 The hotel looked nice,
7 You didn't have to wait long,
8 They don't look very pleased,

a didn't we?
b didn't they?
c doesn't he?
d doesn't she?
e did you?
f don't they?
g do they?
h didn't it?

101.3 Choose the correct alternative.

1 He's been here before, **has / (hasn't)** he?
2 It was a good match, **was / wasn't** it?
3 They hadn't told us, **had / hadn't** they?
4 You've never met him, **have / haven't** you?
5 He wouldn't leave her, **would / wouldn't** he?
6 Chelsea beat Arsenal, **did / didn't** they?
7 The browser's working today, **is / isn't** it?
8 You haven't got a new digital camera, **haven't / have** you?

101.4 Write short questions for the following affirmative sentences.

1 Of course, John's a very clever boy.   *Is he really?*
2 The service is always bad here.   ....
3 Nelson was a very brave man.   ....
4 The soldiers had no guns.   ....
5 I really don't like pancakes.   ....
6 They'd never do a thing like that.   ....
7 I really didn't want to spend the weekend at home.   ....
8 Lucy wants to become a web designer.   ....

UNIT 102 — Agreeing (So do I / Neither do I / Nor do I. / I think so.); disagreeing (Don't you? I do. / Do you? I don't. / I don't think so.)

A To agree with what has been said by the speaker, we use the adverbs **so** or **neither / nor** followed by an auxiliary verb or modal and by the subject. The verb tense is the same as that of the sentence we are agreeing with. In particular:

- to express agreement with an affirmative statement, we use expressions such as:

  So am I. / So do I. / So can I. / So did I. / So would I…

  'We're ready to go.' 'Yes, so am I.' (also: 'Me too' in colloquial English)
  'I think he's right.' 'So do I.'

- to express agreement with a negative statement, we use expressions such as:

  Neither am I. / Neither do I. / Neither can I. / Neither did I. / Neither would I…

  or Nor am I. / Nor do I. / Nor can I. / Nor did I. / Nor would I…

  'I don't think this is a good idea.' 'Neither do I.' (also: 'Me neither' in colloquial English)
  'I'm not going to dive in this sea.' 'Nor am I. It's far too rough.'

B To express disagreement or contradict what's been said, we use short affirmative or negative sentences, consisting of:

  subject + auxiliary or modal   (affirmative if the first sentence is negative and vice versa)

  'I think the Redbulls are great.' 'Do you? I don't.'
  'I was quite surprised to hear she failed her exam.' 'I wasn't. In fact, I was expecting it.'

C In sentences that express agreement or disagreement, there can also be a name or pronoun different to **I**.

  'I'm going for lunch now.' 'So are we.'
  'Sheila didn't go camping last summer.' 'Nor did Helen. But Laura did, I think.'

D NB: In English it isn't possible to agree or disagree by saying just **I, yes**. or **I, no**. The auxiliary or modal is always repeated with the subject.

  'I liked it a lot.' 'I didn't (like it a lot).'
  'I wouldn't like to work part-time.' 'I would (like to work part-time).'

E With verbs like **believe, expect, guess, hope, imagine, suppose, think, be afraid**, we usually use the following constructions as an alternative to repeating the auxiliary or modal:

- to agree: affirmative verb + **so**

  'Do you think she'll like our present?' 'I hope so!' (= I hope she will.) (also: I think so. / I expect so. / I guess so. / I suppose so.)
  'Was the test difficult?' 'I'm afraid so.' (= I'm afraid it was.)

- to express a contrary opinion: negative verb + **so** or affirmative verb + **not**

  'Are they coming?' 'I don't suppose so. / I suppose not.' (also: I don't think so. I don't expect so.)
  With **hope** and **be afraid**, we only use the construction: affirmative verb + **not**
  'Is it going to rain?' 'I hope not.'

EXERCISES

Agreeing; disagreeing

UNIT 102

102.1 Agree with these statements. Use the pronouns in brackets.

1. I love playing computer games. (I) — So do I.
2. She enjoys swimming. (he) — ....
3. We often went to Milan. (they) — ....
4. I'm going to the cinema. (she) — ....
5. I'd like a new computer. (I) — ....
6. He'll buy some rewritable CDs. (we) — ....
7. We need some DVDs. (she) — ....
8. Tricia's worked hard this week. (I) — ....

102.2 Choose the correct alternative to agree with these negative statements.

1. I don't like studying physics.
   - **(A) Neither do I.**   B So do I.   C Neither am I.
2. He doesn't want to go to school today.
   - A So does she.   B Neither does she.   C Neither is she.
3. We didn't eat any lunch yesterday.
   - A So did they.   B Nor do they.   C Nor did they.
4. The boys couldn't play football yesterday.
   - A Neither can I.   B Neither could I.   C So could I.
5. She isn't very pleased with it.
   - A Nor is he.   B So is he.   C Nor does he.
6. Mike wouldn't tell me about it.
   - A Neither does Liz.   B So would Liz.   C Neither would Liz.

102.3 Match the following expressions of disagreement (a–f) to the statements (1–6).

1 _b_ 2 ...... 3 ...... 4 ...... 5 ...... 6 ......

1. I love watching football.   a. Oh, we would!
2. She enjoys swimming.   b. Really? I don't!
3. We'd never go skiing there.   c. No, it isn't.
4. I'm going out tonight.   d. Does she? Her brother doesn't.
5. It's very warm outside.   e. Never mind, Paul can.
6. I can't drive yet.   f. Really? I'm not. It's raining.

102.4 Answer the questions using the verbs in brackets in the affirmative (+) or negative (–) form.

1. Will you go there tomorrow? (think / +) — I _think so._
2. Will they enjoy themselves? (hope / +) — I ....
3. Are they coming here later? (think / –) — We ....
4. Do you think they'll win? (expect / +) — We ....
5. You weren't right, were you? (suppose / –) — I ....
6. There's a test tomorrow, isn't there? (am afraid / +) — I ....
7. Is the boss buying a new printer for your office? (guess / +) — We ....
8. Will the dentist see you this afternoon? (am afraid / –) — I ....

275

REVIEW 21 EXERCISES Units 98–102

R21.1 Complete the questions using the prepositions from the box.

~~for~~ with from after like about to (x2)

1 Who are you waiting *for* ?
2 What are you talking .... ?
3 Who is she travelling .... ?
4 What does it look .... ?
5 Where are we going .... ?
6 Where is he coming .... ?
7 What are you listening .... ?
8 Who does the baby take .... ?

R21.2 Complete the questions using the interrogatives from the box.

~~how~~ what when which whose why where who

1 *How* do you upload this new program?
2 .... wants to buy a cheap iPod?
3 .... of these digital cameras is the best?
4 .... are you going to do with your old monitor?
5 .... don't you buy a widescreen TV?
6 .... are these headphones?
7 .... did you go to buy your new laptop?
8 .... have you got time to show me that website?

R21.3 Choose the correct alternative.

1 How **old** / **many** is your CD player?
2 How **many** / **much** Internet domains have you bought?
3 How **often** / **about** do you use your computer in the week?
4 How **high** / **large** is that file you just downloaded?
5 How **long** / **tall** was the film you watched last night?
6 How **much** / **many** did that memory card cost?
7 How **fast** / **about** coming to play *Action Attack 5*?
8 How **often** / **big** is your new hard drive?

R21.4 Match the questions to the answers.

1 *d* 2 .... 3 .... 4 .... 5 .... 6 ....

1 How long have you been waiting?
2 How about playing tennis?
3 How high is the new office building?
4 How large is Jack's new house?
5 How old is your dog?
6 How often do you play tennis?

a The same height as the Trek Tower.
b It's enormous.
c Sorry, I can't today.
d For ages!
e I play it once a week.
f About ten, I think.

REVIEW 21

R21.5 Use the words to write *Yes / No* questions. Then write short answers.

1 you / go / holiday / Monday / ?
   Are you going on holiday on Monday? (+) *Yes, I am.* .
2 she / play / handball / every / week / ?
   .... (+) ....
3 he / be / the boy / you / like / ?
   .... (−) ....
4 they / visit / the Forum / last / week / ?
   .... (+) ....
5 you / ever / be / to / Africa / ?
   .... (−) ....
6 you / go / to / the cinema / tomorrow?
   .... (+) ....
7 he / can / sit / next to / you / ?
   .... (−) ....
8 you / like / another / cup / of coffee / ?
   .... (−) ....

R21.6 Complete the sentences with the appropriate question tags.

1 She knows your brother well, ... *doesn't she* ..... ?
2 They don't like holidays abroad, ... ?
3 Mike isn't going on the class trip, ... ?
4 We played really well today, ... ?
5 Liz wouldn't do the puzzle with us, ... ?
6 They can set up a new computer, ... ?
7 You hadn't visited that website before, ... ?
8 She's already worked with this program, ... ?

R21.7 Complete the sentences to agree or diasagree.

1 'I don't like seafood.' (disagree)   'I ..... *do* ..... .'
2 'We like rock music.' (agree)   '..................... does my brother.'
3 'I don't think she is happy.' (agree)   '..................... do we.'
4 'We didn't go to the lecture.' (disagree)   'My sister ....'
5 'Will I see you at the trade fair?' (disagree) 'I'm afraid ....'
6 'Was Sue made redundant?' (disagree)   'I hope ....'
7 'We wouldn't accept such an offer.' (disagree) 'They ....'
8 'Do you think they'll be pleased?' (agree) 'I expect ....'

K Exam preparation

K.1 PET Reading Part 5

Read the text and choose the correct word(s) (A, B, C or D) for each space.

Last Saturday, I didn't know (1) ...A... to do, or (2) .... to go. My friend Peter, (3) .... I had arranged to meet in town, was ill for the (4) .... time this year, and so I was on my own. There were one or two things (5) .... I needed to buy, so I walked to the shops, (6) .... I hoped to find some of them. But the shop (7) .... I wanted to go to had moved. I asked a man (8) .... I met in the street if he knew (9) .... the shop had moved to, but he told me (10) .... he was a stranger in the area and didn't know. I walked a few (11) .... metres down the road and soon found (12) .... I was looking for.

1	**A** what	**B** who	**C** where	**D** which
2	**A** what	**B** who	**C** where	**D** which
3	**A** whose	**B** that	**C** who	**D** which
4	**A** twentyth	**B** twenth	**C** twentyeth	**D** twentieth
5	**A** what	**B** who	**C** whose	**D** which
6	**A** what	**B** who	**C** where	**D** which
7	**A** what	**B** who	**C** where	**D** which
8	**A** whom	**B** whose	**C** where	**D** which
9	**A** what	**B** who	**C** where	**D** that
10	**A** what	**B** who	**C** whose	**D** that
11	**A** hundreds	**B** hundredth	**C** hundred	**D** a hundred
12	**A** what	**B** who	**C** where	**D** which

K.2 PET Writing Part 1

Complete the second sentence so that it means the same as the first. Use no more than three words.

1. 50% of the people we interviewed preferred margarine to butter.
   One- ......half...................... of the people we interviewed preferred margarine to butter.
2. I read in the paper that only 25% of all women like football.
   So that means that .... of all women don't like the game!
3. Why don't we join them?
   How .... them?
4. This is the bike on which I rode from London to Brighton.
   This is the bike .... from London to Brighton on.
5. Birmingham is the city in which I was born.
   Birmingham is the city .... I was born.
6. Come and sit down and tell me everything about your holiday.
   Come and sit down and tell me .... about your holiday.

K.3 PET Writing Part 2

These are instructions for a school composition. Read them and carry out the task.

In about 100 words, write about the people **who** live in your block of flats or street, and **what** they do. Also write about the places **where** you go in your neighbourhood – the shops, clubs and so on – and the things **that** you do there.

....
....
....
....
....

Exam preparation

K.4 FCE Use of English Part 2

Read the dialogue below and think of the word which best fits each space. Use only one word in each space.

Lynn: Hi, Mike. I need a new mobile phone. Do you know a shop (1) ....*where*.... I can buy a cheap one?

Mike: Browns, (2) .... is on the High Street, has got some special offers on at the moment (3) .... sound very good.

Lynn: Is that the shop (4) .... you bought your laptop last month?

Mike: That's right. I was told about it by my brother, (5) .... friend Steve works there. If you go, you can ask for Steve and tell him it was me (6) .... sent you.

Lynn: Thanks, Mike. Do you know (7) .... phones they've got the offers on? I mean, the one (8) .... I've got now is still very good, but I'd like a change.

Mike: No, I don't know, but Steve, (9) .... works in the mobiles department, will know for sure. (10) .... are you going to go there? I may come with you.

K.5 FCE Use of English Part 3

Read the text below. Use the word given in capitals at the end of each line to form a word that fits in the space in the same line.

I'm really interested in (1) ..*environmental*.. issues these days, because I think we should all be (2) .... with the problems that surround us. (3) .... warming is a proven fact now, although some world leaders are in (4) .... about it. Their efforts to protect the (5) .... of their country's industries rather than the world we live in may have (6) .... consequences for us all.

ENVIRONMENT
CONCERN
GLOBE

DENY
PRODUCT

DISASTER

K.6 FCE Use of English Part 4

Complete the second sentence so that it has a similar meaning to the first sentence, using the word given. Do not change the word given. You must use between two and five words, including the word given.

1. The man I met at the party is a doctor.
   WHOM
   The man ..*whom I met*.. at the party is a doctor.

2. About 25% of the population are now unemployed.
   ONE
   About .... of the population are now unemployed.

3. It rained the day when she organised the party.
   WHICH
   It rained .... she organised the party.

4. There were a lot of people queuing outside the museum today.
   WHO
   There were a lot of people .... outside the museum today.

5. 'We didn't expect this horse to win the race.' 'Neither did we'.
   EITHER
   'We didn't expect this horse to win the race.' 'We ....'

UNIT 103 Adverbs of manner (quickly, slowly)

Adverbs of manner are used to indicate how something happens or is done.
They answer questions that begin with **How...?**
'How does he drive?' 'He drives carefully.'

A

They are formed by adding the suffix **-ly** to the adjective.

adjective:	quick	slow	careful	strict
adverb:	quickly	slowly	carefully	strictly

He looked at me sadly. (= in a sad way)
She speaks far too quickly! (= in a quick way)

B

These adverbs are generally found after a verb, but they can also precede an adjective, a past participle or another adverb, to modify or specify the meaning.

*I'm **terribly sorry**.* (adverb + adjective)
*No one was **seriously injured** in the accident.* (adverb + past participle)
*He's writing **incredibly slowly**.* (adverb + adverb)

C

Note the spelling changes that occur in the formation of adverbs:

- if the adjective ends in **-y**, the **-y** becomes **-i** before adding the suffix **-ly**.

  lucky → luckily   happy → happily

- if the adjective ends in **-ple**, **-ble** or **-tle**, endings will be **-ply**, **-bly** or **-tly**.

  simple → simply   terrible → terribly
  gentle → gently

NB: Not all words that end in **-ly** are adverbs. Some are adjectives, for example:

lonely, lovely, friendly, elderly, silly...

D

Certain adverbs of manner have the same form as the adjective, for example:

I'll have an early departure. I'll leave early tomorrow.
Bob has got a fast car. He usually drives fast.
She has long straight hair. Go straight ahead!

The adverb derived from the adjective **good** is **well**. The adverb derived from the adjective **bad** is **badly**.

He swims very well. It's badly written.

Some adverbs have two forms, with or without **-ly**, with different meanings, for example:
hard – hardly; high – highly; late – lately; near – nearly; fine – finely

He's working hard.	*He's hardly ever at work.*
How high the kite's flying!	*It's highly improbable.*
Is everything fine?	*Chop the parsley finely.*

For the comparative and superlative of adverbs (**faster than..., fastest / more quickly than..., most quickly**), see page 218.

EXERCISES

Adverbs of manner

UNIT 103

103.1 Solve the anagrams and write the adverbs.

1 lyolws _slowly_
2 ritclyst ....
3 laisey ....
4 clubilpy ....
5 dlaby ....
6 cryclerto ....
7 luqetiy ....
8 palpihy ....

103.2 Change the adjectives in the box into adverbs and write them in the correct column.

| strong   angry   technical   lazy   possible   political   lucky |
| quick   comfortable   soft   anatomical   probable |

1 smartly	2 easily	3 capably	4 socially
strongly			

103.3 Adjective or adverb? Choose the correct alternative.

1 Isn't this birthday cake decorated **beautiful / (beautifully)**?
2 Lily doesn't drive in the city. She says people drive too **quick / quickly**.
3 Just read the children a **quiet / quietly** story, then they can go to sleep.
4 Do you think the actor's name is spelt **correct / correctly**?
5 I would **happy / happily** lend you my bike, but it has a puncture.
6 Harold did a **good / well** test this morning.
7 Your essay is **well / good** written. Congratulations!
8 It's been a **hard / hardly** day. I'll go to bed early.
9 They **hardly / hard** ever go out in the evenings, because they get up early in the mornings.
10 He's a good film director, but his last movie was too **slow / slowly**.

103.4 Match the two parts of the sentences.

1 _f_   2 ....   3 ....   4 ....   5 ....   6 ....

1 I'm afraid we'll have to get up terribly
2 That famous singer walked straight
3 My maths teacher speaks incredibly
4 The computer got seriously
5 She said she was awfully
6 He was a completely

a sorry to have hurt me.
b slowly and quietly.
c changed person when he came back from Africa.
d past me, and I didn't see him.
e damaged in the fire.
f early to catch the plane.

103.5 Complete the sentences using the words from the box.

| happily   nearly   quickly   hardly   well   badly   slowly   quietly |

1 Speak _quietly_ . The children are asleep.
2 I think I did the test quite .... I should pass.
3 My parents have been .... married for 20 years.
4 I'm sixteen. Well, I'm .... sixteen. My birthday's this Friday.
5 The accident was serious, but nobody was .... hurt.
6 Don't walk so .... I can't keep up with you.
7 The music was so quiet you could .... hear it.
8 Please talk .... I can't understand you.

281

UNIT 104 Adverbs of time

A The most common adverbs and expressions of **time** are:
- **now**, **today**, **this week / month / year…**, which are usually used with the present continuous (see p.42) or with the present perfect (see p.76).
- **yesterday**, **last week / month / year…**, **three days / months… ago**, **then**, which are used with the past simple (see p.58).
- **tomorrow**, **soon**, **next week / year…**, **in two weeks / months…** which are used with the future tenses.

Adverbs of time are usually placed at the end of a sentence. However, if you want to give more emphasis on the time, they can also be placed at the beginning.
I went to Berlin last week.
Next week, I'm flying to Paris.

B Other common adverbs and expressions of **time** are:
- **just**, **already**, **yet**, **not… yet**, **lately / recently**, **ever**, **before**, which are usually used with the present perfect or the past perfect (see p.92).

Just, **already** and **ever** are placed between the auxiliary **have** and the past participle. **Yet**, **before**, **lately** and **recently** are placed at the end of the sentence.
I've just arrived from the airport.
Have you booked the flight yet?

C The most common adverbs and expressions of <u>frequency</u> are:
- **always**, **usually**, **often**, **sometimes**, **occasionally**, **seldom / rarely**, **hardly ever**, **never**, **once / twice a day**, which are usually used with the present simple (see p.32).

In affirmative and interrogative sentences, **always**, **usually**, **often**, **seldom**, **hardly ever** and **never** are placed between the subject and the verb. However, they follow the verb **to be**. In negative sentences, they are placed between the auxiliary and the main verb.
I always work on Saturday. Do you often go to the cinema?
I'm never late. She doesn't usually work hard.

Sometimes and **occasionally** are also be placed either at the beginning or at the end of a sentence, whilst **once a day** and other similar expressions are usually placed at the end.
We sometimes meet our friends after school. / Sometimes we meet… / We meet… sometimes.

EXERCISES

Adverbs of time

UNIT 104

104.1 Complete the sentences using an adverb or expression of time from the box.

~~last week~~   this month   now   yesterday   last year   next week

1 Did you go to the opening ceremony ....*last week*.... ?
2 I'm meeting Martin Scorsese .... – he's giving me an interview on Tuesday.
3 Was it an Australian actress who won the Oscar .... ?
4 We have wasted nearly two weeks on this project ....
5 Don't answer the phone, please. I can't talk to anybody ....
6 I needed that information .... , not today! It's too late now!

104.2 Rearrange the words and write sentences.

1 heard – Nobody – before – him – ever – of – has
   Nobody has ever heard of him before.
2 must – Cannes – You – if – yet – go – haven't – to – you – been
   ....
3 your – I – met – lovely – have – just – wife
   ....
4 tickets – already – unfortunately – sold – been – The – have
   ....
5 you – recently – good – any – Have – gossip – heard – ?
   ....

104.3 Write questions for these answers. Use the adverbs of frequency in brackets.

1 *Do you often go to the theatre?* .... (often)
   Yes, I often go to the theatre.
2 When .... (usually)
   I usually surf the Internet in the evening.
3 .... (always)
   Yes, we play tennis whenever the weather is fine.
4 .... (ever)
   No, he never plays the piano any more.
5 .... (occasionally)
   No, I never see her any more.

104.4 Complete the second sentence using the word in brackets without changing the meaning.

1 Little Eliza was asleep when the celebrations started and she hasn't woken up yet.
   (still) Little Eliza ....*is still asleep*.... now.
2 *The Godfather* was a popular film when it came out, and things haven't changed.
   (still) It .... today.
3 Michael Brown was given the Best Supporting Actor award for the second time.
   (again) Michael Brown .... the Best Supporting Actor award.
4 The film will soon start once the adverts have finished.
   (shortly) The film .... after the adverts have finished.
5 She won't allow herself to be photographed any more.
   (no longer) She will .... herself to be photographed.
6 Actors don't usually go to bed early.
   (rarely) Actors .... early.

283

UNIT 105 Adverbs of degree *(too, very, quite, rather...)*

Adverbs of degree, also referred to as modifiers, modify adjectives or other adverbs by making their meaning stronger or weaker. They normally precede the adjective or adverb they modify.

A The most common adverbs of degree that strengthen are: **too**, **very**, **extremely**, **really**, **absolutely / definitely**.
It's too late to go.   It was a very good trip.
I'm really surprised. He was extremely patient.

B Other adverbs of degree commonly used are: **fairly / quite / pretty**, **rather**, **not very**, **not at all**.
The lesson was fairly interesting.
I know them quite well.
I don't know them very well.

Note the difference between the use of **fairly** and **rather**: the first is used with adjectives and adverbs with a positive meaning (**fairly good, fairly well...**), implying approval from the speaker; the second is used with adjectives and adverbs with a negative meaning (**rather stupid, rather bad...**), implying disapproval. The definite article (**a / an**) precedes the adverb **fairly**, but it can be placed both before and after **rather**.
It's <u>a fairly long</u> report. (the speaker approves of long reports)
It's <u>a rather long</u> report. / It's <u>rather a long</u> report. (the speaker doesn't approve of them)

Quite can mean 'very', 'completely' or 'really' and can be used as an intensifier, especially with strong adjectives such as **amazing**, **horrible** and **perfect** or with adjectives that have a meaning of completeness, like **full**, **right**, **wrong**, **sure**, **certain** or **ready**.
You're quite right.   It's quite amazing.

C The adverb **enough**, unlike the others, is placed *after* the adjective (see p.208).
He's old enough to cook his own meals.

D It's rare to find adverbs of degree before adjectives that already have a superlative meaning, like **huge / enormous, impossible, wonderful / marvellous, awful, fantastic / great, essential, ultimate**.

Only **really**, **absolutely** or **quite** are sometimes found before these adjectives: absolutely impossible, really awful, quite essential... (not: ~~very impossible~~, ~~fairly awful~~, ~~too wonderful~~ or similar combinations).

E Some adverbs of degree can be placed before a verb to modify its meaning: **nearly / almost**, **hardly / scarcely / barely**, **just / quite / rather**, **only**. **Very much / a lot** are instead placed after the verb, to end the sentence.
She almost fainted when she heard the news.
I could only say a few words.
You can hardly breathe. The heat is stifling.
I enjoyed the concert very much.

F Note the use of the intensifying adverbs **so** and **such** in exclamatory expressions:
| **so** + adjective or adverb | **such a...** + adjective + noun |
Ryan is so cute! And he's such a smart guy, too!

EXERCISES

UNIT 105 — Adverbs of degree

105.1 Complete the sentences using the adverbs of degree in the box.

~~too~~ too extremely fairly rather not very

1. The swimming pool was .... *too* .... crowded, so I didn't go in.
2. I don't like their new CD; it's .... good. They've done better.
3. I'm afraid I ate .... too many burgers yesterday. I don't feel well.
4. Paul's .... quiet, but when you get to know him, he opens up.
5. It was a wonderful party. I'm .... grateful that you invited me.
6. The band's music was much .... loud to enjoy.

105.2 Complete the sentences by placing a suitable adjective after *quite*.

~~enchanting~~ certain happy wrong full disgusting

1. I really enjoyed the performance, it was quite .... *enchanting* ....
2. I couldn't eat that food they gave us – it was quite ....
3. It was quite .... of him to behave like that at the wedding.
4. I was quite .... to help him fix his computer – it's fine now.
5. By the time we arrived at the pub, it was already quite ....
6. I think he's coming at four o'clock, but I'm not quite ....

105.3 Rearrange the words and write sentences.

1. in – We – holiday – Sicily – really – a – last – had – nice – year
   We had a really nice holiday in Sicily last year.
2. so – barely – He – he – speak – was – could – tired
   ....
3. new – sweet – puppy – Your – so – is – !
   ....
4. think – car – enough – everyone – big – I – is – for – don't – the
   ....
5. person – a – boss – Our – such – new – nice – is – !
   ....
6. state – disgraceful – is – of – roads – The – here – absolutely – the
   ....

105.4 Complete the text with the adverbs in the box.

~~completely~~ well enough quite absolutely such

Tamie and Mark tried hard, but they soon realised it was (1) .... *completely* .... impossible to find a ticket for the Rolling Stones concert. They thought that was (2) .... bad, but next time they will remember that buying tickets (3) .... in advance is (4) .... essential with (5) .... popular groups. The stadium wasn't big (6) .... to contain all the people who wanted to see the myths of rock and roll performing live.

105.5 Match the two parts of the sentences.

1 ... *d* ...   2 ....   3 ....   4 ....   5 ....   6 ....

1. It's such a beautiful song,
2. I'm not feeling very well,
3. I could hardly talk
4. It's absolutely impossible.
5. It was quite late,

a. so we went to bed.
b. I was so upset.
c. my head hurts.
d. I love it.
e. I don't believe it.

UNIT 106 Word order in statements

Affirmative sentences usually have the subject first, followed by the verb then by the complements.

A If a sentence contains the verb **be** or other copular verbs like **look / seem** or **feel**, these verbs are followed by a noun phrase consisting of an adjective and / or a noun that functions as the predicate.

You are a good student.
He looks happy.
I feel great.

B If a sentence contains an intransitive verb, for example a verb of movement like **go** or **arrive**, the sequence of complements can be summarised with the abbreviation SVPMT:

subject + verb + place + manner + time

Phil went to London by car yesterday.

Obviously all complements aren't always present. If there is, however, a complement of place and of time, the place would come before the time. Alternatively, the complement of time can be placed at the beginning of the sentence to give it more emphasis.

My mother's coming to Bristol in a week's time.
In a week's time, my mother's coming to Bristol.

C If a sentence contains a transitive verb, the direct object is placed immediately after the verb, followed by other indirect objects that follow the sequence summarised with the abbreviation SVOMPT:

subject + verb + object + manner + place + time

I play basketball with my team in the school gym every Monday.

The order SVOMPT is followed even if all complements aren't present.

You speak English very well. (not: You speak ~~very well English~~.)
I have a quick breakfast in the school cafeteria on weekdays.

D If there is an adverb or an adverbial expression with a negative meaning at the beginning of a sentence, e.g. **never, seldom, scarcely / hardly ever, nowhere, not only, no sooner, only in this way, only when, only if, only by doing this**, the structure of the sentence is modified: the verb is placed before the subject and the auxiliary **do / does / did** is inserted if there are no other auxiliaries or modals.

Never have I seen such a beautiful landscape.
Hardly ever did he come on time.
No sooner had he got his degree than he was offered a good job.
Not only did he behave badly, but he also refused to apologise.
Only in this way can you get the problem solved.
Only if we train really hard can we hope to win the tournament.

EXERCISES
Word order in statements

UNIT 106

106.1 Rearrange the words and write sentences.

1 very – is – person – Paul – nice – a
   Paul is a very nice person.

2 cities – Rome – are – beautiful – and Florence – extremely
   ....

3 Cyprus – holiday – good place – a – for – seems – a
   ....

4 carefully – essay – writing – She – her – finished
   ....

5 after – mountains – a – very – feel – week – I – in – the – well
   ....

6 was – My – teacher – progress – my – with – pleased
   ....

The ruins at Paphos, Cyprus

106.2 Put the complements in the correct order.

1 I went	(a) by train	(b) yesterday	(c) to Paris.	c – a – b
2 Paul arrived	(a) last week	(b) by plane	(c) in Rome.	....
3 Diana travelled	(a) round France	(b) last summer	(c) by bike.	....
4 We went	(a) on foot	(b) across the Alps	(c) in 2005.	....
5 My mother visited	(a) at Easter	(b) by boat	(c) the islands.	....
6 Walter journeyed	(a) by motorbike	(b) across the USA	(c) in a month.	....

106.3 Complete the second sentence by changing the order of the words but without changing the meaning.

1 I have never seen such a wonderful painting.
   Never *have I seen* such a wonderful painting.

2 He hardly ever gets the answers correct.
   Hardly ever .... the answers correct.

3 We have seldom experienced such hot weather here.
   Seldom .... such hot weather here.

4 I left and he started playing loud music again.
   No sooner .... than he started playing loud music again.

5 The story is not only well written, but it's also beautifully illustrated.
   Not only .... well written, but it's also beautifully illustrated.

6 I haven't seen a place like it anywhere in the world.
   Nowhere in the world .... a place like it.

106.4 Rewrite these sentences by starting with *Only*.

1 I could only continue living here in this way.
   Only *in this way could I continue living here*.

2 They can win this match only if they play harder.
   Only ....

3 I can help you with your homework only after I've finished cooking.
   Only ....

4 You will only take good photos by doing it this way.
   Only ....

287

UNIT 107 Prepositions of time (1)

The prepositions **at**, **in** and **on** are most often used with times.

*The annual conference is starting **on** Monday, May 15th **at** three o'clock **in** the afternoon.*

A

The preposition **at** is used in particular with:

- timetables.
  The last bus leaves at 11.30.
  The lessons start at 8.45.

- certain times or parts of the day: **at dawn / at sunrise, at sunset, at midday / at noon, at midnight, at night, at breakfast, at lunchtime / dinnertime / teatime.**
  The view of the lake is wonderful at sunrise.
  Let's meet at lunchtime tomorrow.

- festive periods, such as **at Christmas, at Easter, at the weekend** (also: **on the weekend**).
  We sometimes go skiing at Christmas.
  What do you usually do at the weekend?

B

The preposition **in** is used with:

- other parts of the day: **in the morning, in the afternoon, in the evening.**
  I prefer studying in the evening.
- months: *The school year in Italy starts in September.*
- years: *I was born in 1975. Shakespeare died in 1616.*
- centuries: *in the 18th century, in the 21st century*

C

The preposition **on** is used:

- with dates that are expressed with the day.
  I was born on 18th November.

- with the days of the week, even when a noun referring to a part of the day follows.
  on Monday, on Friday evening, on weekdays
  I'm leaving for Manchester on Tuesday night.

- when nouns referring to parts of the day are preceded by one or more adjectives.
  On a cold winter morning…
  On a dark rainy night…

The days and parts of the day are expressed in the plural form when we want to indicate that something happens regularly on that certain day.
I usually go out on Fridays / on Friday nights.

D

Compare the expressions:
- **on** time (on that set time) / **in** time (not late)
- **at** the end of… (the month, the year…) / **in** the end (opposite of: **at** first)

EXERCISES

Prepositions of time (1)

UNIT 107

107.1 Complete the sentences with the correct preposition. Choose between *at*, *on* or *in*.
1 The film stars arrived in Cannes ...*at*... ten o'clock last night.
2 We went to a great party .... Saturday. Lots of celebrities were there.
3 The first time I went to Hollywood was .... 2008.
4 My sister was born .... 1st November .... 1999.
5 Is your birthday .... January?
6 We arrived just .... time to see the beginning of the play.
7 The singer of the group was still chatting in the hotel lounge .... three o'clock .... the morning.
8 We want to go to the Venice film festival .... the end of August.

107.2 Complete the text with the prepositions *at*, *on* and *in*.
(1) ...*At*... five o'clock (2) .... Tuesday morning, I was woken up by a terrible noise outside. I had got back from a business trip (3) .... midnight and had hoped for a proper night's sleep. (4) .... breakfast, I asked my family what was going on. My brother said that (5) .... Monday they'd started working with a drill (6) .... dawn, and that they were still drilling when he'd come back home late (7) .... the afternoon. He thought it was in one of the neighbours' houses. I went to the office and didn't think about it any more. (8) .... about eight o'clock (9) .... the evening, a neighbour called to ask if we could stop drilling, as he wanted some peace. We told him we weren't drilling at all and he said that none of the other neighbours was. Only a few days later did we discover that the developers had taken over the block of flats opposite (10) .... the beginning of the month, and contractors had been called in to do renovation work.

107.3 Match the two parts of the sentences.

1 ..*e*.. 2 .... 3 .... 4 .... 5 .... 6 ....

1 I always get up at   a February.
2 Peter never works in   b Friday evenings.
3 I like to go abroad at   c breakfast time.
4 Jane often goes out on   d the morning.
5 We always drink tea at   e seven o'clock in the morning.
6 I met him first in   f Christmas.

107.4 Choose the correct alternative.
1 We start work on the film **at** / **on** three o'clock sharp.
2 Please be **in** / **on** time for the start of the film premiere.
3 **At the end** / **In the end**, we went to see Arctic Monkeys not Keane.
4 I ran all the way and was just **in** / **on** time to see Johnny Depp.
5 We're going to Hollywood **at the end** / **in the end** of March.
6 **At first** / **At the first**, I didn't realise it was Sir Elton John.

107.5 Complete the sentences using the correct preposition and the relevant personal information.
1 I was born ...*in*... (month)
2 I was born .... (year)
3 I was born .... (clock time)
4 I was born .... (part of the day)
5 I was born .... (season)

289

UNIT 108 Prepositions of time (2)

The following prepositions of time indicate the duration of an action or of an event.

A
- **from… to / till…** and **between… and…** indicate the start and finish of an action; they are usually followed by times, days, months, year.
  Working hours are from 9 a.m. to 5 p.m.
  Mr Robson will be in Chicago between the 19th and 21st this month.

B
- **during** and **throughout** indicate a period of time and are usually followed by the nouns **day**, **night**, **week**, **month**, **year**, **morning**, **afternoon**, **evening** or by the seasons.
  I travel a lot during the summer.
  It's warm and sunny throughout the year.

C
- **for** indicates the duration of an action or event, which is expressed with a period of time, e.g. **two hours**, **three weeks**, **four months…**
  I've been working for three hours.
  I really deserve a cup of tea!

- **since** indicates the moment an action started, e.g. **seven o'clock**, **Tuesday**, **2005…**
  I've been working since two o'clock.
  I deserve a cup of tea now!

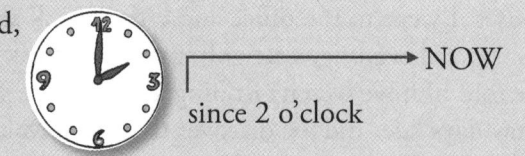

  For and **since** are usually found in sentences with the present perfect simple or continuous (see p.80), as they refer to actions that started in the past but that continue in the present.

D
- **before** and **after** are usually followed by a time, date, festivity or by a verb in the **-ing** form.
  Students should hand in their projects before the end of May.
  Visitors are not admitted after six o'clock.
  Why don't we have dinner together after playing tennis?

E
- **till / until** indicate the end of an action.
  Do you have to work till / until seven every day?

- **by** is usually followed by a precise moment in time (timetable, day, date…) in which a specific action will be concluded.
  The goods have to be delivered by 30th April.
  I have to be back home by 11 o'clock tonight.

F
- **in / within** are followed by a period of time in which a specific action will be concluded. **Within** is usually used in more formal contexts.
  John is coming back from Canada in a week / in a week's time.
  Please settle the invoice within 60 days from delivery of the goods.

EXERCISES

Prepositions of time (2)

UNIT 108

108.1 Complete the second sentence so that it has the same meaning as the first one. Use the prepositions in brackets.

1 Our office hours are from 10 a.m. to 4 p.m.
  (between) Our office is ......*open between 10 a.m and 4 p.m.*......
2 My lost wallet could be anywhere from Oxford to Cambridge.
  (between) My lost wallet could be anywhere ....
3 The magician asked me to think of a number between one and 20.
  (from) The magician said, 'Think .... '.
4 My boss said he'd be in the States from January to April.
  (between) My boss said he'd be ....
5 Lizzie worked in Africa between 1995 and 2002.
  (from) Lizzie worked ....
6 My sister has exams from today until Thursday.
  (between) My sister has exams ....

108.2 Choose the correct alternative.

1 I have lived in Leeds **(for)** / **since** three years.
2 Paul has been having piano lessons **for** / **since** six months.
3 I've liked Oasis **for** / **since** last year, when I first saw them live in Manchester.
4 We've only seen two films **for** / **since** Christmas.
5 I've been watching David Beckham play **for** / **since** years.
6 I've only been interested in blues music **for** / **since** August.
7 They've been waiting **for** / **since** a very long time.
8 The Oscars for outstanding film achievements have been awarded **for** / **since** 1929.

108.3 Complete the sentences using the prepositions in the box.

~~during~~ before by until within after

1 We only come to Venice ......*during*...... the film festival to see the stars.
2 The teacher wants me to finish that project .... the next week.
3 I'll give you .... six o'clock to bring me the report.
4 Just three days .... her marriage, she was still trying to organise the wedding reception.
5 If you've not made it in Hollywood .... the time you're 25, you'll never make it.
6 If you can stay on .... the match, I'll introduce you to Nadal and Federer.

108.4 Match the two parts of the sentences.

1 ...*d*... 2 .... 3 .... 4 .... 5 .... 6 ....

1 The actors have been rehearsing
2 We're having dinner with the director
3 The audience must be in their seats
4 Turn off your mobile phone
5 I visited the city
6 I didn't see the play

a during the Berlin film festival.
b until it came to my town.
c before the film starts.
d since three o'clock.
e after the play.
f by six o'clock.

291

UNIT 109 Prepositions indicating place and position (1)

Prepositions indicating place and position express where a person or object is. They always follow verbs of state, e.g. **be, stay, live, lie, stop, sit** and **stand**. They are frequently used to describe places using **there is / there are, there was / there were**.

A The preposition **in** is used to indicate that something or someone is:
- inside a confined area.
  They are still in the garden.
- in a street/road or in a city.
  I live in Cliff Lane in Leeds.
- in a specific geographical position.
  Milan is in the north of Italy.

Sometimes the preposition **in** can be substituted by **inside**.
There must be someone inside that old house.

Remember the expressions: **in bed, in hospital, in town, in the country(side), in the mountains, in the newspaper, in the rain, in the sun.**

B The preposition **at** is used to indicate that something or someone is:
- near a confined area, not necessarily inside (**at the cinema, at the pub, at the park…**) or in a non-confined area (**at the bus stop, at the door, at the traffic lights…**).
  There's an old pub at the end of the road.
  Turn right at the traffic lights.
- in a street / road and the street number is indicated.
  Leslie lives at 23, Milford Street.

Remember the expressions: **at work, at home, at the sea(side), at college, at university, at the top of…, at the bottom of…**

C The preposition **on** indicates that something or someone:
- is on top of another thing (leant on, in contact).
  There are two bottles of water on the table.
- extends or faces onto something else.
  Orta is a little town on a picturesque lake.

REMEMBER: **on the coast** (BUT: **by the sea**), **on the first/second… floor, on the right / left, on holiday, on a trip, on the way home, on a farm, on the radio, on TV, on Channel 5.**

D The prepositions **over / above** (suspended, without contact) and **under / below** indicate that something is above or below something else.

Remember the expressions: **above / below average, above / below zero, over / under 18.**

Under can be substituted by **underneath** and **below** by **beneath..**
There may be a nest underneath that bush.
This behaviour is beneath your dignity!

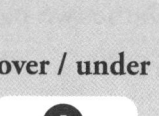

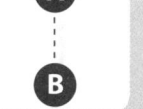

EXERCISES

Prepositions indicating place and position (1)

UNIT 109

109.1 Complete the sentences by writing the article *the* after the preposition *in* or write *0* if the article isn't necessary.

1. Pamela lives in ....*the*.... middle of London.
2. Dave lives in .... country, but I live in .... town.
3. 'Where did you read about it?' 'In .... newspaper.'
4. My mother works in .... tourist office next to the park.
5. Dad's been in .... bed all week with terrible flu.
6. You're freezing cold! Have you been out in .... snow?
7. My brother lives in .... Victoria Road.
8. We spent a lovely holiday in .... Alps.

109.2 Match the two parts of the sentences.

1 ..*d*.. 2 .... 3 .... 4 .... 5 .... 6 ....

1. My father works at
2. I don't want to go out. Let's stay at
3. It must be dangerous at
4. Meet me at
5. No, she's not here. She's at
6. They're on holiday now, at

a work until five o'clock.
b the top of that ladder.
c the seaside.
d the town library.
e home.
f the station at nine o'clock.

109.3 Complete the sentences with the prepositions in the box.

~~under~~ over above below underneath beneath

1. Come ....*under*.... my umbrella and get out of the rain!
2. The temperature fell three degrees .... zero last night.
3. Mr Johnson lives in the flat .... mine.
4. Don't talk like that! It's .... you!
5. The police helicopter hovered .... the scene of the crash.
6. I found my passport. It was .... some papers on my desk.

109.4 Complete the sentences with the correct preposition.

1. My parents were ....*on*.... holiday for a month last year.
2. My son has been .... college for six months now.
3. They live in the third house .... the right.
4. There weren't many people .... the hotel lounge last night.
5. Is there anything good to watch .... television tonight?
6. They haven't come back yet. They're still .... work.
7. Our school is going .... a trip to Lake Garda next week.
8. The programme you want to watch is .... BBC2.
9. Did you spend the weekend .... the country?
10. Danny worked .... a farm before going to university.
11. We live .... a nice little town .... the seaside.
12. Mrs Ferns lives .... the town centre .... 21, Farrell Road.

293

UNIT 110 Prepositions indicating place and position (2)

Other prepositions of place and position are:

A
- **near (to)** – indicates general closeness.
  There's a little lake near the village.
  We live near Nottingham.

- **close to** – also used in an emotional way.
  The hotel is close to the city centre.
  John and Mary are quite close to each other.

- **next to**, **beside** – indicates being connected.
  The bank is beside the post office.
  Jack always sits next to Vicky in the classroom.

- **from** – indicates distance.
  The school is only half a mile from my house.

B
- **behind** – also used in a figurative sense meaning support.
  I've been successful in my job because my wife has always been behind me.

- **in front of** – opposite to **behind**.
  Tom is the boy sitting in front of Sally.
  There's a bus stop in front of the hotel.

- **opposite** – indicates that two things or people are facing each other.
  Tom is sitting opposite Sally in the school cafeteria.
  The baker's shop is opposite the pub.

C
- **between** – is used to indicate that something / someone is in the middle of two other things.
  The bookcase is between the door and the window.

  In geographical languages, **between** in also used when there are more than two things.
  Switzerland lies between Germany, France, Austria, Liechtenstein and Italy.

- **among** – indicates a position surrounded by various things (three or more).
  There's a fishermen's hut among those trees.

- **around / round**
  There are Roman walls around the old town.

- **along**
  There are lots of nice little shops along the main street.

D
Remember also the expressions:
in / on the corner   at the corner of ... (two roads)
Write your name in the top left-hand corner.
Let's meet at the corner of Kearny and Grant Street.

at the front   at /on the back
There's a garden at the back of the house.

BUT: **in the back / in the front (of the car / bus)**
She was sitting in the front of the car.

EXERCISES

Prepositions indicating place and position (2)

UNIT 110

110.1 Read the descriptions and complete the sentences with the correct preposition.

1 The boy is standing ......*next to*...... the girl.

2 The bookshop is .... the bank .... the café.

3 I'm standing in a queue at the post office .... a tall man. The tall man is .... me.

4 The greengrocer's is .... the baker's.

5 There are beautiful trees .... the river.

6 The children scattered .... the market stalls.

110.2 Complete the sentences with the correct preposition: *round, between, among, from, around* or *along*.

1 It was cold that evening, so Mandy wore a scarf ......*round*...... her neck.
2 It was dark, so Don decided to walk .... the road, not go across the field.
3 The equator lies .... the Tropics of Cancer and Capricorn.
4 The land was private, so we had to go .... the outside of it.
5 We auditioned lots of sax players, but Coltrane was the best .... them.
6 The supermarket is only five minutes .... my house.

110.3 Choose the correct alternative.

1 The boy stood **(in the corner)** / **on the corner** of the classroom.
2 There's a newsagent's shop **in the corner** / **on the corner** of the street.
3 I met my friend **on the corner** / **at the corner** of Hill Street and Wall Road.
4 There's a swimming pool **in the back** / **at the back** of the house.
5 They were sitting **in the front** / **at the front** of the car.
6 'Where's my jacket?' 'It's hanging **in the back** / **on the back** of the chair.'

110.4 Match the two parts of the sentences.

1 ...*e*... 2 .... 3 .... 4 .... 5 .... 6 ....

1 Michael is very close to
2 The post office stands beside
3 Luton isn't very far from
4 Janet was standing among
5 I put my suitcase in the back of
6 There was a fight, so I got between

a her school friends.
b London.
c the two angry boys.
d the car.
e his mother.
f Barclay's Bank.

295

UNIT 111 Prepositions indicating movement (1)

Prepositions of movement express a shift from or to something.
They always follow verbs of movement, e.g. **go**, **come**, **get**, **return**, **drive**, **take**, **be sent**.

A
- **to** is used to indicate movement towards something.
  We're going to Edinburgh by train tomorrow.
  I met Susan on my way to school.

  The preposition **to** is never used with the word **home**.
  Let's go home. (the speaker's house)
  BUT: *We're going to Sam's house for dinner.*

  NB: Don't mix up the preposition **to** (of movement) with **in / at** (of place and position).
  They went back to the USA last week. (not: in the USA)
  They are in the USA now.

  Remember the expressions: **go to work / to school / to hospital**, **go to prison / jail**, **go to bed**, **welcome to…**, **a journey / trip to…**, **Have you ever been to…?**

B
- **into** indicates movement towards the inner part of a closed place.
  They went into the shop.

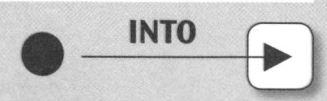

  Note the use of **into** with the verbs **translate** and **change** that imply the transformation of something.
  I translated this book from English into Italian.
  He wants to change euros into / to dollars.

- **onto** (also written **on to**) indicates movement on something.
  The cat climbed onto the roof.

C
- **from** indicates movement from something and origin.
  I got a letter from my Australian penfriend.
  The new student comes from Spain.

- **away from** indicates breakaway.
  Why don't we go away from here? It's too crowded.

- **out of** indicates movement from a closed place towards the outside.
  The rock star is just coming out of the hotel.

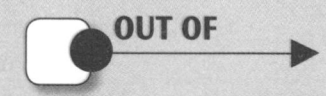

- **off** indicates movement, often quick and sudden, from something.
  The boy fell off the tree / off his bike.

- **beyond** is also used in a figurative way.
  Don't go beyond that point!

D Look at the prepositions used to talk about getting on and off means of transport.
get into / get out of a car, a taxi, a van
get on / onto / get off a train, a bus, a boat, a plane, a motorbike

EXERCISES

Prepositions indicating movement (1)

UNIT 111

111.1 Complete the sentences by writing the correct form of the verbs in the box before the preposition *to*.

~~go~~   come   get   return   drive   be sent   take

1 Would you like to ......*go*...... **to** the park this afternoon?
2 Can you .... me **to** school in your car, Dad?
3 When David .... **to** the town where he'd been born, it had all changed.
4 When my father was young, he .... **to** Africa for a year by his firm.
5 It's very hard to .... **to** the top of the mountain.
6 Patsy said she couldn't .... **to** our house tonight.
7 If you .... **to** the centre of town, you'll find it difficult to park.

111.2 Tick (✔) the sentences in which it is correct to use *to* and correct those with mistakes in them.

1 ....✔.... I'm just on my way **to** the shops.

2 .... Daddy's coming **to** home tomorrow.
   Daddy's coming home tomorrow.

3 .... It's time for you to go **to** bed.

4 .... Welcome **to** Hollywood!

5 .... He's staying **to** the Astoria Hotel.

6 .... My father's ill **to** hospital.

7 .... Tim fell **to** his motorbike.

111.3 *Into* or *onto*? Choose the correct alternative.

1 I put my pens and books (**into**) / **onto** my school bag.
2 It was such a nice day, I decided to walk **into** / **onto** town.
3 We were scared even before we went **into** / **onto** the roller coaster.
4 We got **into** / **onto** the M4 motorway just near Swindon.
5 Get **into** / **onto** the car quickly – it's starting to rain.
6 Linda's translating some poems **into** / **onto** English.
7 I was putting some books away, when they fell **into** / **onto** my head.

111.4 Complete the sentences with the correct preposition.

1 I received a present ....*from*......... my aunt in London.
2 I'd like to get away .... the city for a week.
3 When we came out .... the restaurant, it was snowing.
4 I've asked you three times to get .... that table!
5 You must get .... the intercity train in Mestre.
6 He got .... his bicycle and rode away down the street.
7 We saw masked men getting .... a white van and driving away.

297

UNIT 112 Prepositions indicating movement (2)

Other prepositions of movement are:

A
- **across** (width) indicates movement from one side of a surface to the other.
  Go across the bridge / the road and turn right.

  It can also be used with verbs of position.
  There's a hairdresser's across the road.

- **through** (depth) indicates movement from one side to the other by passing through the inner part of something. Note the expressions:
  Drive carefully through the tunnel.
  We can see the lake through the kitchen window.

B
- **along**
  Let's go for a bike ride along the river.

- **as far as**, **up to** indicates the end of a path.
  Go as far as / up to the station and park there.

- **towards / toward** (Am.) indicates direction.
  Who's the man walking towards us?

C
- **past**
  Walk past the church; the museum is on the right.

  The prepositions **past** and **to** are also used to express the time: **past** to indicate how many minutes have exceeded the hour, up until **half past…**; **to** to indicate how many minutes are left until the next hour.
  'What time is it?' 'It's twenty past nine.'
  'What's the time, please?' 'It's a quarter to three.'

D
- **up / down** indicate movement upwards and downwards.
  They climbed up the hill.
  The cat ran down the tree.

  Remember the prepositions that are used with verbs that indicate 'arrive':
  get to…
  arrive at… (station, airport, my house…)
  arrive in… (London, Britain, the USA…)
  reach + direct object, therefore no preposition

  She arrived at / got to my house later than expected.
  They arrived in New York yesterday morning.
  We reached our destination at dawn.

  Remember also: **leave a place / leave for a place**

  They left my house in the morning. (not: left from…)
  They left for Germany three days ago.

  Many prepositions of place are used as adverbs or adverbial particles to create phrasal verbs (see p.348).

  Get up. Sit down. Come along. Get off. Get out.
  Let's go in! (But: *Let's go into the shop. / Let's enter the shop.*)

EXERCISES

Prepositions indicating movement (2)

UNIT 112

112.1 Complete the sentences with the prepositions in the box.

| as far as | across | along | past | through | towards |

1. Go ...as far as... the supermarket on the corner, then turn right.
2. Lots of people walk their dogs .... the river bank.
3. I was really frightened when those large dogs ran .... me.
4. Young children shouldn't be allowed to go .... the road by themselves.
5. If you walk .... the city gates, you'll find the museum on your left.
6. I just walked .... the supermarket, but forgot to buy some food for tonight.

112.2 Correct the prepositions in these sentences.

1. It only takes a few minutes to drive **across** the tunnel.   ...through...
2. When we arrived **in** the station, there was nobody there.   ....
3. I didn't know Madonna had already left **to** the Bahamas.   ....
4. Is it six o'clock yet? No, it's only half **to** five now.   ....
5. When I finally got **for** the city centre, the shops had closed.   ....
6. Your train will arrive **at** Berlin later than we thought.   ....

112.3 Match the two parts of the sentences.

1 ..b.. 2 .... 3 .... 4 .... 5 .... 6 ....

1. Our cat keeps climbing up the tree,
2. It was still dark
3. It's too cloudy up here now
4. Isn't it a bit early
5. A dangerous-looking man
6. You don't need to go across

a. is walking towards the President.
b. but then it can't come down.
c. when I left the house at dawn.
d. the bridge to take good photos.
e. to see much through the window.
f. to leave for the party?

112.4 Choose the correct alternative.

1. She was the first woman to swim **across** / **along** the English Channel.
2. The plane arrived **at** / **in** Heathrow Airport two hours late.
3. When Judy arrived **at** / **in** Italy, she was very happy.
4. When we got **in** / **to** the hotel, we were very tired.
5. Mark left **to** / **for** Scotland last Monday.
6. Go **up** / **up to** the corner, then turn right.

112.5 Sally has written to you to explain how to get to her house. Look at the map and complete the directions with the missing words.

Get (1) ..off.. the bus (2) .... the bus stop next to the pub. Walk (3) .... Oak Street (4) .... the traffic lights. You'll see a supermarket (5) .... the right and a park (6) .... the left.
(7) .... the traffic lights, turn left. Walk (8) .... a bank. My house is (9) .... the next block, (10) .... the corner.

UNIT 113 Prepositions *to* and *for*; verbs with double object

A
- **to**, besides indicating movement, is used to answer the questions 'to whom?' or 'to what?'.

  Pass your book to Mandy, not to Bill.
  I wasn't invited to his party.

- **for** indicates purpose and cause.

  I bought a present for my daughter.
  She'd do anything for him.

B There are certain verbs that can be followed by two objects, one indirect and one direct. The indirect object usually refers to a person. There are two possible structures for verbs that take two objects.

| verbo + object + **to / for** + person | verb + person (without the preposition **to / for**) + object |

Give this present to Peter. → *Give Peter this present.*
I'll make a cake for Ann. → *I'll make Ann a cake.*

The second structure, also referred to as a double object, is the most common, especially when the indirect object is expressed with a pronoun.

Can you pass me a glass of water, please?

The first structure is preferable when the direct object is a pronoun, or when both the objects are pronouns.

I haven't got my dictionary because I lent it to my brother. (not: I lent my brother it.)
Did you lend it to him?

C The most common verbs that can have a double object are:
give, **offer**, **pass**, **take** (away from the speaker), **bring** (close to the speaker), **lend**, **show**, **send**, **teach**, **tell**, **ask**, **buy** (something for…), **make** (something for…), **read** (something for…), **sing** (something for…), **write** (something for…)

Remember to send Grandma a Christmas card.
My parents have bought me a lovely T-shirt.

In the passive form these verbs usually use a personal construction, i.e. the person becomes the subject of the sentence.

They offered me a lift in their car. (active) → *I was offered a lift…* (passive) (see. p.172)

D With the following verbs, the indirect object is always preceded by **to**:
explain, **dictate**, **introduce**, **say**, **speak / talk**, **describe**, **deliver**, **report**, **suggest**.

These verbs therefore don't take the double object structure, nor, consequently, the personal passive structure.

The teacher explained the rule to the students. (not: The teacher explained the students the rule)
The rule was explained to the students. (not: The students were explained the rule.)

EXERCISES

Prepositions *to* and *for*; Verbs with double object

UNIT 113

113.1 Complete the sentences with *to* or *for*.
1. I gave up my seat ...*to*... an old lady on the bus.
2. Peter sent a birthday card .... Janey last week.
3. Please give this letter .... your parents when you get home.
4. I've made a special dinner .... Mark and Liz. I hope they come on time.
5. I've got a surprise .... you when we meet next time.
6. I tried to explain the problem .... my father.

113.2 Rewrite the sentences with a double object without changing the meaning.
1. Can you give this book to Peter, please?
   Can you give Peter this book, please?
2. Can you pass this sandwich to my wife, please?
   ....
3. My mother made a new dress for Linda.
   ....
4. Dad bought a scooter for Mark.
   ....
5. Susie's eyes are bad, so will you read this letter to her?
   ....
6. My sister's new boyfriend says she's going to teach English to him.
   ....

113.3 Rearrange the words and write the sentences.
1. the – They – me – room – offered – for – a
   They offered me a room for the night.
2. them – She – to – reported – the — police
   ....
3. my – I – her – school – lent – books
   ....
4. collection – us – showed – stamp – He – his
   ....
5. song – We – a – them – traditional – sang –
   ....
6. Christmas – bought – for – They – nice – me – presents – some
   ....

113.4 Change these sentences from active to passive. Don't use the agent.
1. The postman delivered the parcel to me yesterday morning.
   The parcel *was delivered to me yesterday morning.*
2. My sister introduced me to the actor at a party.
   I ....
3. The teacher dictated the passage to the students.
   The passage ....
4. Paul described his holiday to me in great detail.
   Paul's holiday ....
5. They reported the incident to her early next morning.
   The incident ....
6. They told me the story when I went to see them.
   I ....

UNIT 114 Other prepositions

A These are some other common prepositions.
- **by** is used for means of transport.
  by car, by train, by bus, by underground, by boat, by plane, by bicycle, by motorbike.
  BUT: **on foot, on horseback.**
  I usually go to work by bus. My colleague goes by train.

  However, when these means of transport are preceded by articles, possessive adjectives or demonstratives, the prepositions **in** and **on** are used instead: **on my bike**, **on his motorbike**, **in the car.**
  I usually go to school in my mother's car.

- **by** introduces the agent with verbs in the passive form (see p.164).
  This short story was written by my father.

- **with** expresses association, company or means used.
  I'm going to the theatre with my wife tonight.
  This form must be filled in with a black pen.

  Note the difference between these two sentences:
  The dog was hit by a stone. (accidental)
  The dog was hit with a stone. (on purpose)

- **without**
  Bill is going on holiday without his parents for the first time this summer.

- **of**
  The pages of this old book are yellowish and torn.

  The preposition **of** is also used to:
  – specify the material of which something is made.
  This jumper is made of wool.

  – indicate a cause.
  The old woman died of a heart attack.

  To talk about possession or family relations, we usually use the possessive case (see p.202) and not the preposition **of**.
  John's brother (not: the brother of John)   *Jim's house* (not: the house of Jim)

- **like** indicates similarity.
  I have a camera like yours.

- **about** indicates the topic.
  The story is about a boy who gets lost in the jungle.

- **except / but** indicate exclusion.
  Everyone but / except my sister went to the concert.

B REMEMBER: When a preposition precedes a verb, the verb is always in the **-ing** form (see p.124).
Thanks for behaving so well.
He left the room without saying goodbye.
I'm not used to having dinner so late in the evening.

NB: Don't mix up **I'm used to / I'm getting used to doing something** with **I used to do something** (see p.62). In the first case, **to** is a preposition; in the second, it's part of the infinitive form of the verb.

EXERCISES

UNIT 114 — Other prepositions

114.1 Complete the sentences with *by*, *on* or *in*.

1 My father always goes to work ....**by**.... bus.
2 We decided to tour France .... bicycle last summer.
3 John and I usually go to school .... foot.
4 I met Sandra yesterday .... the train to London.
5 I can't drive you there because my parents went out .... the car.
6 My father's boss went round the world .... yacht.
7 I had an accident when I was out .... my motorbike last weekend.
8 We sailed along the Adriatic Coast .... my friends' boat in July.

114.2 Complete the sentences with *by*, *of*, *with* or *without*.

1 This picture was painted ....**by**.... Vincent Van Gogh.
2 It's a painting .... the artist's room at Arles.
3 If you look closely, you will see that he painted it .... any shadows.
4 For a time, Van Gogh worked .... Paul Gauguin.
5 Van Gogh had only sold one painting .... the time he killed himself.
6 He had problems .... his mind, and spent time in an asylum.
7 He is now thought .... as being one of the world's greatest artists.
8 His works are sold .... the most important auctioneers in the world.

114.3 Match the two parts of the sentences.

1 ..**e**.. 2 .... 3 .... 4 .... 5 .... 6 ....

1 That chair is made   a of pneumonia.
2 My grandfather died   b of this old dress have faded.
3 The colours   c except Steve and Anne.
4 My new bike is just   d about love in wartime.
5 I think the new film is   e of oak wood.
6 We all went to the party   f like Peter's.

114.4 Complete the second sentence using the preposition in brackets and the *-ing* form, without changing the meaning.

1 We thanked them when they sang so nicely.
   (for) We thanked them *for singing so nicely* .

2 I was angry when he took my money and didn't ask.
   (without) I was angry when he took my money ....

3 I was very pleased when I won the first prize.
   (about) I was very pleased ....

4 I complained to him when he made so much noise.
   (for) I complained to him ....

5 Two men were charged after the painting was stolen.
   (with) Two men were charged ....

6 He broke his arm when he fell off a ladder.
   (by) He broke his arm ....

7 I never get up so early.
   (to) I'm not used ....

303

REVIEW 22

EXERCISES Units 103–114

R22.1 Complete with the missing adjectives or adverbs.

Adjectives	Adverbs		Adjectives	Adverbs
1 nice	nicely	7	....	easily
2 tidy	....	8	bad	....
3	fast	9	aggressive	....
4	helpfully	10	....	hard
5 terrible	....	11	beautiful	....
6 good	....	12	....	luckily

R22.2 Rewrite the sentences by inserting the adverb in brackets in the correct place.

1 Have you been to Ireland? (ever)
   Have you ever been to Ireland?

2 My mother has come back from the USA. (recently)

3 Have you finished your homework? (yet)

4 Paul has been to Greece. (never)

5 My parents hadn't been to a rock concert. (before)

6 I have seen Robbie Williams in the street. (just)

7 I'm not hungry, thanks – I've eaten. (already)

8 I haven't been skiing. (lately)

9 We don't eat out at the weekend. (usually)

R22.3 Match the two parts of the sentences.

1 _b_   2 ......   3 ......   4 ......   5 ......   6 ......

1 Pamela looks extremely   a terrible!
2 I almost   b happy.
3 The weather looks pretty   c a good footballer!
4 The new film was absolutely   d fell over when I saw her!
5 Mike is such   e a waste of time.
6 It would be rather   f good for walking today.

R22.4 Choose the correct alternative.

1 We're going to stay **(in)/ on / by** a little house in the country.
2 They'll spend a week **in / at /on** the seaside.
3 They decided to eat their picnic **in / at / by** the river.
4 Montreux is a nice place to stay – it's **in / at / on** Lake Geneva.
5 The cinema is only ten minutes **to / from / near** the school.
6 The new store is **into / in / between** the bank and the post office.
7 We went for a nice walk **around / along /among** the canal.
8 There's a big garden **behind / in / under** the house.

304

REVIEW 22

R22.5 Complete the sentences with the correct prepositions.
1. In the holidays, I sometimes get up ..*at*.. midday.
2. I don't usually go out .... the evening on school days.
3. My sister's birthday is .... 1st May.
4. My dad gets up early .... weekdays.
5. The Great Fire of London happened .... 1666.
6. I like to listen to my CDs .... night.
7. Patrick's going back to Ireland .... Friday.
8. I was very annoyed when my train wasn't .... time!
9. Sarah's going to Rome .... the end of the month.
10. I want to get there .... time to hear Donald's speech.

R22.6 Complete the sentences using *since* or *for*.
1. I've lived here ..*since*.. 1998.
2. I haven't seen him .... his last birthday.
3. I stayed in New York .... three weeks.
4. Dave hasn't visited us .... a long time.
5. I've been waiting for her e-mail .... Tuesday.
6. There hasn't been a bus .... 40 minutes.
7. Can you just keep my seat .... a moment, please?
8. He hasn't been the same .... his operation.

R22.7 Complete the text with the correct word(s) (A, B or C).

I sell ice-cream (1) ..*near*.. the park. Every evening, (2) .... six and seven, I see the same man walking his dog. He goes (3) .... the entrance to the park, but he never goes in. He turns right (4) .... the gate, crosses the road and walks (5) .... the canal for about 500 metres. Then he turns round and comes back the same way. He walks (6) .... exactly an hour. He's done this for years.
Last night, however, he wasn't alone. He had a young woman (7) .... him, as well as the dog, of course! They were talking about a trip. He said he wanted to go somewhere (8) .... boat. The woman was agreeing with him, but she wouldn't go (9) .... the dog. Before going home, they bought two ice-creams and sat (10) .... the park bench to eat them. I'd never seen him with anyone before and I was surprised. It's nearly six o'clock now and I'm anxious to see if they come back. I've even made them a special ice-cream.

1	**A** near	**B** across	**C** before
2	**A** at	**B** between	**C** for
3	**A** as far as	**B** within	**C** until
4	**A** since	**B** about	**C** in front of
5	**A** along	**B** on	**C** in
6	**A** since	**B** for	**C** between
7	**A** at	**B** for	**C** with
8	**A** by	**B** on	**C** with
9	**A** of	**B** without	**C** across
10	**A** at	**B** to	**C** on

L Exam preparation

L.1 PET Reading Part 5

Read the text and choose the correct word (A, B, C or D) for each space.

(1) ....*A*.... summer, my friends and I like to go (2) .... the mountains (3) .... a week. We have been doing this (4) .... we left school, and we have a great time together. We sleep (5) .... four small tents (6) .... a field that belongs to a sheep farmer. (7) .... the holiday, we plan what we are going to do. We always get up early (8) .... the morning and start the long walk (9) .... one of the mountains. (10) .... midday, we stop for a picnic somewhere nice, and (11) .... two and three o'clock, we are usually (12) .... the top of the mountain.

1	**A** In	**B** At	**C** For	**D** Through
2	**A** in	**B** at	**C** to	**D** up
3	**A** in	**B** at	**C** for	**D** since
4	**A** from	**B** after	**C** for	**D** since
5	**A** in	**B** at	**C** under	**D** below
6	**A** in	**B** at	**C** by	**D** into
7	**A** In	**B** Before	**C** After	**D** Through
8	**A** in	**B** at	**C** on	**D** by
9	**A** at	**B** by	**C** down	**D** up
10	**A** In	**B** On	**C** At	**D** From
11	**A** into	**B** between	**C** through	**D** for
12	**A** in	**B** at	**C** by	**D** from

L.2 PET Writing Part 1

Complete the second sentence so that it means the same as the first. Use no more than three words.

1. The office is open from ten o'clock to four o'clock.
   The office is open *between ten o'clock* and four o'clock.

2. I no longer live in Victoria Road.
   I don't live in Victoria Road ....

3. That film we saw was so nice!
   That was .... nice film we saw!

4. I have never seen such lovely drawings.
   Never .... such lovely drawings.

5. Only by hard work will you succeed in the business world.
   Only if .... will you succeed in the business world.

6. Take your grandmother these cakes.
   Take these .... grandmother.

L.3 PET Writing Part 3

This is part of an e-mail from your Australian penfriend, Michael. He is asking you about your recent summer holiday with your friends. Answer his questions and tell him what you did. (about 100 words)

So, where did you go for your summer holiday? Where did you stay, and what did you do there? What was the weather like? Did you visit any interesting sights? Write and tell me about it!	....

Exam preparation

L.4 FCE Use of English Part 2

Read the dialogue below and think of the word which best fits each space. Use only one word in each space.

Andy: So, what do you (1) _usually_ do on Saturdays?
Sally: Well, I (2) .... get up late – never before ten o'clock!
Andy: That's a good start! When do you go to bed?
Sally: That depends, but it's (3) .... before midnight.
Andy: Wow! I have to be home (4) .... midnight or my parents get angry (5) .... me.
Sally: And then (6) .... the day, I do different things. I meet my friends (7) .... town and we go (8) .... the cinema or a café.
Andy: How do you travel (9) .... town? Have you got a car?
Sally: No, we use public transport – I go everywhere (10) .... bus.

L.5 FCE Use of English Part 3

Read the text below. Use the word given in capitals at the end of each line to form a word that fits in the space in the same line.

In winter, I (1) _occasionally_ visit some distant relatives of   **OCCASION**
mine who are in the (2) .... business. That is,   **RESTORE**
they buy old furniture and make it look (3) ....   **ABSOLUTE**
beautiful – like new! It is quite a (4) .... job,   **LABOUR**
and my uncle works long hours (5) .... the   **POLISH**
wood until it shines. Then they sell the things for a good
price.

L.6 FCE Use of English Part 4

Complete the second sentence so that it has a similar meaning to the first one, using the word given. Do not change the word given. You must use between two and five words, including the word given.

1 I was given some lovely books for my birthday.
   ME
   They .... _gave me_ .... some lovely books for my birthday.

2 The doctor told the young mothers about child care.
   WERE
   The young mothers .... child care by the doctor.

3 In order to survive, Sam begs in the streets.
   BY
   Sam survives .... in the streets.

4 If you don't walk quickly, you'll be late.
   ONLY
   .... quickly will you be on time.

5 He finished his dinner, then left immediately.
   NO
   .... his dinner than he left.

6 That exam was so easy that I'm sure I passed.
   AN
   That was .... that I'm sure I passed.

UNIT 115 Verbs *say* and *tell*

A **Say** (past simple and past participle **said**) is used to:
- indicate who speaks the words quoted between inverted commas in **direct speech**
  'There's going to be a parents' meeting next Monday', the principal said.

  REMEMBER: **Say** is followed by the preposition **to** when the person to whom the thing is said is expressed.
  'You're right', he said to me.

- introduce **reported speech**, when the person to whom the thing is said is not expressed. Between a main clause containing the verb **say** and a secondary clause, we can use the conjunction **that**.
  The weather forecast says (that) it will be sunny tomorrow.
  Mr Brown said (that) he had moved to his new office the week before.

The verb **say** is used in the following expressions: **say a word, say yes, say no, say thank you, say please, say hello / goodbye, say something.**
Say thank you to everybody before you leave.
Don't say a word. Someone may be listening.

B **Tell** (past simple and past participle **told**) is used to:
- introduce reported speech when the person to whom the thing is said is expressed. In this case, the person is a direct object, therefore it is not preceded by a preposition (**He told me…**, **I told John…**).

  A main clause containing the verb **tell** can be followed by:
  – a secondary clause introduced by the conjunction **that**, which is often just implied.
    They told me (that) they were looking for a new instructor at the gym near my house.
  – A verb in the infinitive (**to…** / **not to…**, see pp.126 and 310)
    She told me to wait for a while.
    I told everybody not to come late.

When both the person to whom the thing is said and a direct object are present, the **double object** structure is used: person + object. (see p.300).
I'm going to tell him the truth.

The verb **tell** also has a personal passive form. (see p.172).
I was told to bring the receipt.

The verb **tell** is used in the following expressions: **tell a lie / lies, tell the truth, tell a story, tell the time, tell someone's fortune, tell the difference, tell someone about something.**
Don't tell me a lie. I can tell the difference between a liar and someone who's telling the truth.
Tell me about your trip.

EXERCISES

Verbs *say* **and** *tell*

UNIT 115

115.1 Choose the correct alternative.
1. I **said / told** her not to go snowboarding – it's too dangerous!
2. He never **says / tells** me anything about his mountain climbing.
3. Monica **said / told** that she really enjoys free climbing.
4. David **says / tells** that there's a danger of avalanches now.
5. Don't forget to **say / tell** them to take their ice picks.
6. The weather forecast **said / told** there would be heavy snow.
7. 'Don't ski off piste,' he **said / told** me.
8. He didn't **say / tell** how many people had died on that mountain.

115.2 Use the words to write sentences with the correct form of *say* or *tell*.
1. I / not know / what / say
   I don't know what to say.
2. He / not say / anything / me / yesterday
   ....
3. They / just / tell / me / about / concert
   ....
4. Not tell / anyone / our plans / for / trip
   ....
5. Remember / tell / her / to wear / comfortable shoes
   ....
6. I wonder / what / she / say / us / at the meeting / tomorrow
   ....

115.3 Place the words from the box into the correct column.

| a word | the time | goodbye | yes | the difference | me about… | a prayer |
| thank you | a lie | a story | something wrong | you how to… | | |

say	*tell*
a word	

115.4 Complete the sentences with the correct form of *say* or *tell*.
1. My father always ....*says*............ please and thank you.
2. Mike .... me that we would meet at six o'clock.
3. 'Don't forget about it,' he .... to them.
4. 'Take your umbrella,' .... her mother.
5. Can you please .... me what time the bus leaves?
6. When you are in court, you must .... the truth.
7. Can you .... the difference between a bee and a wasp?
8. Where's Sheila? I want to .... hello to her.
9. I don't know why, but they left without even .... goodbye.
10. I don't want anybody to .... me my fortune.

UNIT 116 Reported speech (1)

A Reporting orders

In direct speech, advice, orders and bans are expressed with the imperative. However, in reported speech, they are expressed with a verb in the infinitive form.

to / not to + base form

'Stay in bed for a couple of days', the doctor said to Jim. → *The doctor told Jim to stay in bed for a couple of days.*

The teacher said to the children: 'Don't run in the corridors.' → *The teacher told the children not to run in the corridors.*

B

Orders and advice can be introduced by the verb **tell** or by other verbs.
All these verbs can be followed by the infinitive or by a secondary clause, with or without the use of the conjunction **that**.

'Don't drive in this storm.' → *She warned me not to drive in a storm like that.*

'Remember to lock the windows before leaving.' → *He reminded me (that) I should lock the windows before leaving.*

C Reporting statements

The transformation from direct speech to reported speech involves a few changes that depend, above all, on the tense of the verb **say**.

- When the reported speech is introduced by the present form of the verb **say**, the changes concern only personal pronouns and possessive adjectives and *not* the tense of the verb, which remains unvaried compared to the direct speech.

  Laura always says to me: 'I love the way you dress. Your clothes are all so trendy!' → *Laura's always telling me that she loves the way I dress and that my clothes are all so trendy.*

- When the reported speech is introduced by the verb **say** in its past form, but it refers to an unchanged situation still true in the present or to something that has been said recently, the verb and the expressions of time don't change compared to the direct speech.

  The teacher said: 'The speed of a body is the distance covered over a period of time.' → *The teacher explained to us that the speed of a body is the distance covered over a period of time.* (scientific fact)

  'This monument must be at least 200 years old,' Joe said. → *Joe said that monument must be at least 200 years old.* (unchanged situation still true in the present)

  Mr Smith's son calling home from Ibiza: 'I'm having a great time here, Dad!' → *Mr Smith to his wife: 'Dave called this morning. He said he's having a great time in Ibiza.'* (the sentence is said on the same day and the situation hasn't changed)

D

Statements in reported speech can be introduced by the verb **tell** or by other verbs: **add**, **answer / reply**, **claim**, **explain**, **remark**, **recommend**, **state** (formal use).

The suspect claimed that he had been at home all day on 5th November and added that he hadn't been very well that day.

EXERCISES

Reported speech (1) — UNIT 116

116.1 Match the two parts of the sentences.

1 ..e.... 2 .... 3 .... 4 .... 5 .... 6 ....

1 The soldiers said
2 The policeman told
3 The doctor advised
4 The criminal claimed
5 My mother warned
6 The teacher ordered

a him to go to the headmaster.
b us not to stay out late.
c he had stolen nothing.
d me to get out of my car.
e that the war was nearly over.
f the patient to stop smoking.

116.2 Report these orders in reported speech, using the words in brackets.

1 'Don't go out in the cold, John,' said Mother. (tell)
 Mother told John not to go out in the cold.

2 'It's dangerous for you not to use sun cream in this heat,' said Mike. (warn)

3 'Leave your camera behind if you go to those streets, Dave,' said Lucy. (advise)

4 'You shouldn't swim when the red flag is out, boys,' said Dick. (remind)

5 'Stop making that noise, class!' said the teacher. (tell)

6 'Get out of here and never come back, Johnson!' shouted Smith. (order)

116.3 Complete the sentences in reported speech, making the necessary changes where needed.

1 Mary often says to him: 'I don't like you smoking.'
 Mary often says to him that she *doesn't like him* smoking.

2 I sometimes say to her: 'Your hair looks pretty.'
 I sometimes say to her that .... hair .... pretty.

3 The professor said: 'Elephants are herbivores, just like cows.'
 The professor said that elephants .... herbivores, just like cows.

4 The scientist exclaimed: 'It can't be true!'
 The scientist exclaimed that it .... be true.

5 My father said: 'We all die in the end.'
 My father told me that we all .... in the end.

6 Susan always tells Tim: 'I want to change the way we live.'
 Susan always tells Tim that .... to change the way .... live.

7 'My parents own a launderette,' Joe said.
 Joe said that .... parents .... a launderette.

116.4 Complete the sentences with the correct form of the verbs in the box.

| add | answer | claim | explain | recommend | state |

1 Jane told me the news and then *added* that she felt very happy about it.
2 Micky .... that it was very difficult to do it that way.
3 The Mayor .... that the Council had no intention of doing it.
4 The doctor .... that I stopped eating cheese and drinking milk.
5 The boys .... that they hadn't been near the house at that time.
6 She .... that she didn't like questions like that, and refused to reply.

UNIT 117 Reported speech (2)

Reporting statements in the past
When reported speech is introduced in the past, there are usually a few changes involved regarding verb tenses. Look at the table below: in the reported speech, someone, some time after the event, is telling a third person about a phone conversation she had with a friend who at the time was studying in London.

direct speech	reported speech
present simple Brenda said: 'I walk to school every day. I live near the school.'	**past simple** Brenda told me she walked to school every day because she lived near the school.
present continuous 'I'm going to a party tomorrow.'	**past continuous** She said she was going to a party the following day.
past simple / present perfect / past perfect 'We went to Oxford yesterday.' 'I haven't been to Hyde Park yet.' 'I hadn't been here a week when I met an old friend.'	**past perfect** She said they had been (also: they went) to Oxford the day before. She told me she hadn't been to Hyde Park yet. She said she hadn't been there a week when she met an old friend.
am / is / are going to 'I'm going to visit the new Tate Gallery next week.'	**was / were going to** She said she was going to visit the new Tate Gallery the following week.
will / would 'My teacher will be 30 tomorrow.' 'I would attend a drama course next month if I could find the time.'	**would** She said her teacher would be 30 the following day. (future in the past see p. 318) She said she would attend a drama course the following month if she could find the time.
would have 'I would have liked to have you all here with me at Christmas.'	**would have** She said she would have liked to have us all there with her at Christmas.

In the transformation from direct speech to reported speech, the following things change:

personal pronouns	possessive adjectives and pronouns	adverbs and expressions of time	
I → he / she	my → his / her	now	→ then
you → I, we	your → my, our	today	→ that day
we → they	our → their	tonight	→ that night / that evening
me → him / her	mine → his / hers	yesterday	→ the day before, the previous day
you → me, us	yours → mine, ours	tomorrow	→ the following / next day, the day after
us → them	ours → theirs	last Sunday	→ the previous Sunday
		next week	→ the following week

demonstratives this → that; these → those   **adverbs of place and position:** here → there

EXERCISES

Reported speech (2)

UNIT 117

117.1 Complete the second sentence with the correct personal pronoun.

1. Diane: 'I will go there tomorrow.'
   Diane said that ......*she*...... would go there the next day.
2. Teacher: 'You will be on holiday tomorrow, children.'
   The teacher told the children that .... would be on holiday the day after.
3. Roger: 'Paul and I can't come to the party.'
   Roger said that Paul and .... couldn't go to the party.
4. Andy: 'Teacher, we haven't finished yet.'
   Andy told the teacher that .... hadn't finished yet.
5. Bill: 'Thanks, Rob. You are a great help!'
   Bill thanked me and told me that .... was a great help.
6. Ruth: 'John, you aren't trying hard enough.'
   Ruth told John that .... wasn't trying hard enough.

117.2 Change the demonstratives and the expressions of time to adapt them to the reported speech.

1. Alan: 'I visited them today.'
   Alan said that he had visited them ....*that day*.... .
2. Peter: 'I'm going there next month.'
   Peter said that he was going there ....
3. Alison: 'I'm going to give him this book.'
   Alison said that she was going to give him .... book.
4. Larry: 'I watched a great film last night.'
   Larry said that he had watched a great film ....
5. Danny: 'I'll see you tomorrow.'
   Danny said that he would see me ....
6. Lucy: 'I'll be wearing these clothes to the dance.'
   Lucy said that she would be wearing .... clothes to the dance.

117.3 Change these statements into reported speech introduced by *said*.

1. Mike said: 'I like sky diving. It isn't dangerous.'
   Mike said that he liked sky diving and that it wasn't dangerous.
2. Suzie said: 'I'm going out on my scooter now.'
   ....
3. Bill said: 'I fell off my BMX bike eight times yesterday.'
   ....
4. Christine said: 'I really enjoyed water skiing last summer.'
   ....
5. Dave said: 'I hadn't heard this CD before you played it.'
   ....
6. Mark said: 'We're going to go paragliding tomorrow.'
   ....
7. Johnny said: 'I'll go and help them.'
   ....
8. Louisa said: 'I would love to fly in a micro-light.'
   ....
9. Pauline said: 'I would have enjoyed climbing Everest.'
   ....

UNIT 118 Reported speech (3)

Reporting questions

A Reported interrogative clauses have the same structure as affirmative sentences: the subject precedes the verb and the auxiliaries **do**, **does**, **did** (which are typical of direct questions) are not used.

He asked me what <u>the weather was</u> like in Australia in winter.
She asked me if <u>I had liked / liked</u> the present.

B Reported interrogatives are introduced by the verbs: **ask**, **inquire** (formal use), **want to know**, **wonder** or by questions such as: **Do you know…?**, **Can / Could you tell me…?**

I wonder how long it takes to get to the falls.
Could you tell me how I get to the station, please?

C **Wh-** questions are introduced by the same interrogative pronoun, adjective or adverb in both direct speech and reported speech (**what**, **where**, **who**, **how much…** see p.266). **Yes / No** questions are introduced by the conjunctions **if** or **whether**. The verb tenses undergo the same variations as already seen for statements on page 312.

The policeman asked the man: '<u>What</u> were you doing yesterday around 5 p.m.?' →
The policeman asked the man <u>what</u> he was doing / had been doing the day before around 5 p.m.
The teacher asked me: 'Have you finished your project?' → The teacher asked me if / whether I had finished my project.

D Requests for advice or directions can be made with an infinitive or with the appropriate tense of a modal verb, usually that which is found in the direct speech.

'Excuse me, sir. Where <u>can</u> I buy a map of the town?' → A tourist asked me where <u>to buy</u> / he <u>could</u> buy a map of the town.
Sally: 'Where <u>shall</u> we meet, Jane?' → Sally asked Jane where <u>to meet</u> / where they <u>should</u> meet.

E When we make suggestions or requests (**How about…?**, **What about…?**, **Why don't we / you…?**, **Let's…**), we usually use **suggest** as an introductory verb, with the following structures:

- when someone suggests that others do something, without being personally involved:

  suggest (to someone) that + subject + **should / could** + the base form of verb

  or, more simply

  suggest (to someone) that + subject + **present simple** or **past simple** of verb

  He said to his guests: 'Why don't you go to the theatre tonight?' → He suggested to his guests that they should / could go to the theatre that evening. (also: … that they went to the theatre…)
  'How about staying here for the finals?' → I suggest that you stay here for the finals.

- when the person suggesting something is personally involved in the request, we can also use:

  suggest + the verb in the **-ing** form

  He said: 'Why don't we go to the theatre tonight?' → He suggested going to the theatre that night. (all of them, including him)

- the verb **recommend** also uses the same structures as **suggest**.
  He recommended that we <u>should bring</u> / <u>brought</u> warm clothes.

EXERCISES

Reported speech (3)

UNIT 118

118.1 Change the following *Yes / No* questions into reported interrogatives.
1 'Did you enjoy the concert, John?' she asked. <u>She asked John if he enjoyed the concert.</u>
2 'Do you often go skiing, Elena?' asked Julia. ....
3 'Have you ever been to Siena, Mick?' asked Rob. ....
4 'Are you enjoying yourselves, children?' asked Jo. ....
5 'Does Muriel eat meat?' asked Angela. ....
6 'Is Donald happy in his new job?' asked George. ....

118.2 Change the following *Wh-* questions into reported interrogatives using the verbs in brackets in the past simple.
1 Mary: 'When is Jane coming tomorrow?' (ask)
<u>Mary asked when Jane was coming the next day.</u>
2 Sammy: 'How are we going to travel to Spain?' (want to know)
....
3 Alex: 'Where will you go for your holidays?' (inquire)
....
4 Joyce: 'Why did you phone him last night?' (ask)
....
5 Brian: 'Who has read this novel?' (wonder)
....
6 Laura: 'What is the time?' (want to know)
....

118.3 Match the two parts of the sentences.
1 <u>b</u>   2 ......   3 ......   4 ......   5 ......   6 ......

1 The doctor wanted to know   a whether I had finished my project.
2 The policeman asked   b if I had taken the pills.
3 The teacher inquired   c how long my cat had been ill.
4 My mother wondered   d where he could buy a bus ticket.
5 The vet asked   e how I had got home the night before.
6 The tourist asked me   f if anyone had seen the accident.

118.4 Report the suggestions or requests. Use *suggest* or *recommend*.
1 'Why don't we go scuba diving next weekend?' said Martin.
<u>Martin suggested going / that we went scuba diving the following weekend.</u>
2 'What about eating at the new Turkish restaurant tomorrow?' said Liz.
....
3 'You should tour the Greek islands next summer,' said Luke.
....
4 'How about organising a party to raise money for the WWF?' said June.
....
5 'You'd better stay in and rest, Paul,' said Martha.
....
6 'Let's not do anything energetic next week,' said Lois.
....

REVIEW 23 EXERCISES Units 115–118

R23.1 Complete the sentences with the correct form of *say* or *tell*.
1 My mind went blank and I ......*said*...... something really stupid.
2 Who .... you that she got engaged?
3 Didn't anybody .... you what happened to me?
4 He .... that he worked in a bank in New York.
5 Michael is .... to be very unkind to his dog.
6 Will you .... me all about it when we get home?
7 Hasn't he ever .... you about his years as a sailor?
8 I'm sorry, but I can't remember who .... it.

R23.2 Change the reported speech into direct speech.
1 Mary told him that she would be angry if he was late again.
 'I'll be angry if you're late again,' said Mary.
2 Doctor Smith said that he was sending her to a specialist.
 ....
3 The policeman warned Ben not to drive too fast there again.
 ....
4 The teacher said I hadn't done my homework properly.
 ....
5 The manager told the players that they were all lazy.
 ....
6 Janice reminded me to buy a birthday card for Anne.
 ....

R23.3 Tick (✔) the correct sentences and correct the ones with mistakes in them.
1 ✔ Mary told Lucy to go there.
2 ☐ Patsy said me all about it. *Patsy told me all about it.*
3 ☐ Andrew ordered him to get out. ....
4 ☐ Dilys told to him the news. ....
5 ☐ She said she hadn't heard of him. ....
6 ☐ I said them everything I knew. ....
7 ☐ Paul told terrible lies as a boy. ....
8 ☐ Lucy said to them the results. ....

R23.4 Complete the sentences in reported speech with the correct pronouns.
1 'What time are you leaving?' asked Sandy.
 Sandy asked me what time ......*I*...... was leaving.
2 'When are you two coming home?' asked Lulu.
 Lulu asked us when .... were coming home.
3 'Why are you taking a scuba-diving course, Gavin?' asked Liz.
 Liz asked .... why he was taking a scuba-diving course.
4 'When did we visit the art gallery?' asked Alan.
 Alan asked when .... had visited the art gallery.
5 'Do you like sausages for breakfast?' asked the landlady.
 The landlady asked me if .... liked sausages for breakfast.
6 'Where are you all going, boys?' asked the farmer.
 The farmer asked .... where they were going.

REVIEW 23

R23.5 Change the *Wh-* questions into reported interrogatives. Use the correct verb tense.

1 'Where is my wedding ring?' asked Karen.
   Karen asked where her wedding ring was.

2 'When did it happen?' asked Louis.

3 'Why are you standing here?' asked the manager.

4 'Who will they work with next week?' asked Lynn.

5 'How did you manage to do this?' asked the doctor.

6 'How much do oranges cost?' asked the customer.

R23.6 Complete the sentences in reported speech, without changing the meaning.

1 Arthur said to me: 'I can't come tonight.'
   Arthur *told me that he couldn't come that night*.

2 Rachel asked me: 'Do you want any more tea?'
   Rachel asked if ....

3 Tony said: 'I've had some trouble with my bike.'
   Tony said he ....

4 Damien asked her: 'Are you all right?'
   Damien wanted to know if ....

5 The bank manager asked me: 'Why don't you open a savings account?'
   The bank manager wondered why ....

6 The policeman said to Don: 'Get out of your car!'
   The policeman told Don ....

R23.7 You meet up with Jane who talks to you about your friend Sally.

Jane: You know what? Sally has taken up scuba diving.
You: Sally? Is she such a good swimmer?
Jane: No, she isn't. But she's got a new boyfriend who is very sporty. He does paragliding, rafting and canyoning. And scuba diving, of course.
You: Now I see why she has picked scuba diving. She probably thinks it's the least dangerous of all. And has she done that for long?
Jane: About a month. She quite likes it now that she has become more confident.

When you go home you tell your sister about the conversation you had with Jane. Start like this:

I met Jane this morning. She told me that Sally *had taken up scuba diving* . I asked her if she .... and she answered that ....

UNIT 119 Conditional verb forms; future in the past

A The present conditional is formed using: **would ('d) + the base form of the verb**
I would go. I would not / wouldn't go. Would you go?

This structure is used:
- in the main clause of a second conditional sentence (see p.322)
  I would go and live in a big city if I could find a job there.
- in dependent clauses and in reported speech (see p.312) after a verb in the past tense.
  (**He promised…, I knew…, I hoped…, He said…**). This structure is called 'future in the past', as it refers to previous actions compared to the tense in the main clause. Compare:

will… (future)	*would…* (future in the past)
I know that he will come.	I knew that he would come.
I'm sure it will be a lovely day.	I was sure it would be a lovely day.
I hope it won't rain.	I hoped it wouldn't rain.
Tim: 'I will pay for you, too.'	Tim said he would pay for me, too.

B The past conditional is formed using: **would have + past participle**
I wouldn't have done anything different from what you did.

It is used particularly in the main clause of a third conditional sentence (see p.324).
He would have been happier if he had followed his dream.

The past conditional of **would like** can be formed in two ways: **would have liked** followed by the present infinitive or **would like** followed by the past infinitive.
I would have liked to see him. / I would like to have seen him.

C The equivalent present conditional structure for modal verbs is:

could + base form	Are you busy? You **could help** me setting the table.
may / might + base form	They **might be** too tired to eat after their journey.
should + base form	She **should be** here soon.

The structure equivalent to the past conditional is:

could have + past participle	I **couldn't have** done better than this.
may / might have + past participle	You **might have told** me that the library was closed. (denotes a certain reproach for something that wasn't done)
should have + past participle	You **should have had** more patience! (advice given after the event)

EXERCISES

UNIT 119
Conditional verb forms; future in the past

119.1 Fill in the gaps with the present conditional of the verbs in brackets.
1 Why don't you go to the gym twice a week? You *would be* (be) fitter.
2 If you ate fruit and vegetables on a regular basis, you .... (feel) healthier.
3 'What if we didn't invite George to the party?' 'He .... (find out) anyway and he .... (be) annoyed with you.'
4 Imagine you won the lottery. What .... (you / do)?
5 'Nicole might give you a lift to the station.' 'Oh, that .... (be) nice.'
6 Look at that strange modern house. .... (you / buy) it?
7 I .... (not take) the kids to see that exhibition. They .... (get) bored.
8 'Suppose they didn't give you that job.' 'Oh, well. I .... (not mind). I still like my present job.'

119.2 Report what the people said. In the main clause, use the past simple of the underlined verb.
1 Mary: 'I'm sure Mum will like the blue hat.'
Mary was sure her mum would like the blue hat.
2 Peter: 'I believe it will rain in the afternoon.'
....
3 Anne: 'I think Paul won't get here in time to help.'
....
4 Dick: 'I know my friends will be waiting for me at the airport.'
....
5 Ellie: 'I promise I'll finish my project by tomorrow.'
....
6 Bill: 'I hope John will remember to bring his guitar.'
....

119.3 Complete the sentences using the modal verbs from the box. In some sentences, multiple solutions may be possible.

| could   couldn't   should   ~~shouldn't~~   should   might   would   wouldn't |

1 You *shouldn't* insist. I said no and I mean it.
2 .... you repeat that, please? I didn't understand.
3 'Who's knocking at the door?' 'It .... be Mark. He said he .... come today.'
4 Get dressed. Our guests .... arrive in a few minutes.
5 I think you .... ask for a discount.
6 '................. you call her?' 'No, she's so angry with me that she .... answer.'

119.4 Change these sentences from the present conditional to the past conditional.
1 I'd like to try.   *I would have liked to try. / I would like to have tried.*
2 I wouldn't go by car. I would go by train.
3 A low-cost flight would cost about the same as the train.
4 Would you really spend all this money on clothes?
5 They should be more careful.
6 He couldn't come earlier.
7 They might not be listening.
8 They could play much better.

UNIT 120 — *If* clauses – type zero and type one

A To express a consequence depending on a condition, we use the conditional, which consists of an **if** clause introduced by the conjunction **if** and by a main clause. The **if** clause can precede or follow the main clause.

When the **if** clause comes first, a comma is often placed between the two clauses.

if clause (condition)	main clause (consequence)
If you book your holiday in advance,	you get a discount.

Depending on the level of probability (certain, probable, possible or purely theoretical conditions), different tenses are used in the two parts of the conditional. There are four types of conditional: **type zero**, **one**, **two** or **three**, which are explained below and in the following two units.

B **Type zero**

In the **if** clause of the zero conditional, we describe a consequence that takes place regularly and with certainty. In this case we use the present simple in both the main clause and the **if** clause.

if clause: *if* + present simple	main clause: present simple
If I drink coffee in the evening,	I can't go to sleep.

The zero conditional is used to:

- express general truths, scientific and mathematical laws, technical procedures, instructions.
  The days get longer if you travel north.
  If you press this key, the display lights up.

- give advice. In this case, the present form of an imperative or modal (**can** or **may**) is used in the main clause.
  Go / You can go to bed if you feel tired.

C **Type one**

In the first conditional, we describe a real possibility, i.e. we talk about facts that, given certain conditions, probably or possibly will take place in the future.
In this case, the verb tenses used are usually:

if clause: *if* + present simple	main clause: *will / 'll / won't* + base form
If it doesn't rain,	we'll have a barbecue in the garden tomorrow.

NB: In the ***if* clause** it is possible to use either the present simple or the present continuous.
If you come to my house, I'll show you my paintings. (not: ~~If you'll come~~…)
If you're staying overnight, I'll try and find you a room.

In the main clause, the use of **will** indicates a certain consequence. To indicate that something is possible, we use the modal **can**, whilst for an uncertain consequence we use the modal **may**.
If you spend too much time in the sun, you may get sunburnt. (it isn't certain)

In the zero and first conditional, **If** is often substituted by **When** (see p.326).

EXERCISES

If clauses – type zero and type one

UNIT 120

120.1 Use the suggestions and the zero conditional to provide instructions for the functioning of a satellite navigation system.

1. need to determine a location / while driving / can use / satellite navigation system
   If you need to determine a location while driving, you can use a satellite navigation system.
2. want to install / satnav in car / just need / a bracket / to fix device to windscreen
3. have cigarette lighter / on dashboard / can use it / as power source
4. type in destination postcode / the satnav system / give you the best route
5. install special software / can find out / the road conditions, traffic information and speed limits

120.2 Match the two parts of the sentences. They are all in the zero conditional.

1 _b_   2 ....   3 ....   4 ....   5 ....   6 ....

1. Have a good rest
2. Buy new skis
3. Meet me at ten on the beach
4. Go bungee jumping
5. Don't eat so many cakes
6. Get the proper ropes and harnesses

a. if you want to feel an adrenaline rush.
b. if you feel exhausted after mountain biking.
c. if you think you're getting too fat for any sport.
d. if your old ones are worn out.
e. if you want to go rock climbing.
f. if you want to go surfing with me.

120.3 Use the words given and the verbs in brackets to write sentences in the first conditional.

1. (you / like) Italian painting (you / love) this exhibition.
   If you like Italian painting, you'll love this exhibition.
2. (you / want) to meet Michael (you / have to) come back tomorrow.
3. (he / hope) to pass the exam (he / need to) study much harder.
4. (they / work) this hard (they / finish) the job very quickly.
5. (she / not drive) more slowly (she / have) an accident.
6. (we / not use) a computer (it / take) too long.

120.4 Use the present continuous of the verbs in brackets and the modals given to write sentences in the first conditional.

1. (you go / may) off-piste skiing / have problems
   If you're going off-piste skiing, you may have problems.
2. (he try / should) pot-holing / go with an expert
3. (they think / can) of going paragliding / buy my old equipment
4. (you travel / might) through the Amazon / need a guide
5. (she skate / must) on the lake / check the ice

321

UNIT 121 *If* clauses – type two

A When we assume a condition to be improbable or imaginary and that we don't expect to happen but is however theoretically possible, we use the second conditional.
If I won a million dollars on the lottery, I would stop working and I would go and live in the Caribbean. (it is highly unlikely but is however possible)

The second conditional is also used when we propose a different situation to the present reality.
If you worked harder, your grades would be much better. (situation that is different to the present reality: at the moment you aren't working hard enough)

B The structure of the second conditional is:

if clause: *If* + past simple	main clause: *would* / *'d* / *wouldn't* + base form
If I <u>had</u> my own car,	I <u>would drive</u> to work.

- As you can see above, the tense used in the **if** clause is the past simple (**If I had… / If he didn't know…**).
- An **if** clause in the second conditional can also follow a main clause.
  You <u>wouldn't have</u> to hurry if you <u>got up</u> a bit earlier.
- Note how the second conditional is structured in the interrogative form.
  If you won some big money, <u>would you spend</u> it all or <u>would you save</u> part of it?
- When the verb **be** is present in an **if** clause, **were** is used for all persons. In colloquial English, **was** is also used for the first and third person singular: **If I / he / she / it were… / was…**
  He would make a very good career if he was / were a little more ambitious.
- The expression **If I were you / him / her…** is used to give advice and warnings.
  If I were you, I'd talk to her.

C In main clauses, as an alternative to **would**, other modals can be found such as: **could** to express ability and possibility, **might** to express uncertainty and **should** to express a piece of advice.
If you played a musical instrument, you <u>could join</u> the local band.
If she tried Japanese food, she <u>might find</u> that she likes it.

D The modals **would**, **should** or **could** are often found in **if** clauses, too (see p.363).
- **Would** is used in **if** clauses to express a request in a polite and formal way, or even to express willingness to do something (**If you would like…** – see p.158).
  If you would kindly tell the manager, I would really be grateful.
- The use of **should** (or **were to**) in **if** clauses renders the hypothesis more improbable.
  If it were to / should hail, the harvest would be lost.
- The use of **could** in **if** clauses indicates ability and possibility.
  If you could dance, you would have a lot more fun.

For the use of **I would rather…**, see page 158.

EXERCISES

If clauses – type two

UNIT 121

121.1 Identify the type of conditional. Write 0, 1 or 2.
1. [1] If he's competing in the next race, I'll go and see him.
2. [ ] If you go to Pamplona in July, you'll see people running with bulls in the streets.
3. [ ] If he did mountain biking, he would keep in good shape.
4. [ ] If you're looking to get started in surf, our website contains useful links to surf schools.
5. [ ] If you want to avoid getting injured while climbing, you need skill, strength and determination.
6. [ ] If I were you, I wouldn't take up rugby.
7. [ ] Will you believe me if I tell you that cheerleading is one of the most dangerous sports for women?
8. [ ] If you want to do inline skating, you'll have to wear proper safety equipment.

121.2 Write sentences in the second conditional.
1. If Paul (do) more exercise, he (be) healthier.
   If Paul did more exercise, he'd be healthier.
2. If Lucy (go) to Rome, John (follow) her there.
3. If the Johnsons (not invite) me to their Christmas party, I (be) happier.
4. If I (know) how to play American football, I (explain) it to you.
5. If you (read) Harry Potter, I'm sure you (enjoy) it.
6. If we (cycle) to Dover, we (feel) exhausted by the end of the day.
7. If I (be) younger, I (go) on a backpacking tour around Europe.
8. I (not be) surprised if he (arrive) now. He's always late.

121.3 Complete the sentences with the words in the box.

~~would~~ should could were might shouldn't would like

1. If you ...*would*... ask Mr Jones to join us, I'd be extremely pleased.
2. If he tried harder with his maths, he .... find that he could do it!
3. If I .... trust you to be quiet, I'd take you with me.
4. If you .... to come with us, we'd be happy to take you.
5. If he .... look down, I'm sure he'd fall off that tree.
6. If I .... him, I'd sell that motorbike immediately.
7. If you wanted to get slimmer, you .... eat like that!

121.4 Circle the correct alternative.
1. What **(would)** / **will** you do if Paul left you?
2. What would he say if Sandra **would found** / **found** out?
3. Where **would she go** / **did she go** if she ran away from home?
4. How would they survive, if their plane **crashed** / **crashes**?
5. When would you arrive if you **will leave** / **left** home now?
6. Who would you bring if I **will invite** / **invited** you to the party?

UNIT 122 — *If* clauses – type three

A When we propose an <u>impossible condition</u>, because it refers to the past and is therefore no longer possible, we use the third conditional.
If you had asked me, I would have helped you.

B The structure of the third conditional is:

if clause: If + past perfect (**had / 'd / hadn't** + past participle)	**main clause: would / 'd / wouldn't have** + past participle
If you <u>had come</u> to the concert with us,	*you <u>would</u> certainly <u>have enjoyed</u> it.*

If they <u>had taken</u> a taxi, they <u>would have got</u> to the airport in time and <u>wouldn't have missed</u> the plane. I'<u>d have told</u> him if he <u>hadn't</u> already <u>heard</u> the news.

- As you can see above, the tense used in the **if** clause is the past perfect (**If I had been… / If he hadn't seen…**).

- Watch out for the short form **'d**: it can be either **had** or **would**.
If I'd been you, I'd have waited for her.
(I'd been = I **had** been; I'd have waited = I **would** have waited)

- In main clauses, as in the second conditional, **would** + base form can be used instead of **would have** + past participle. This happens when the result of the action refers to the present and not to the past.
*If I had followed your advice, <u>I wouldn't be</u> broke **now**.*

C Other modals, for example **might**, **could** or **should**, can also be found in the third conditional.
You <u>might have succeeded</u> if you had tried hard enough.
If I had taken my racket with me, I <u>could have played</u> tennis with you.

Look at the summary of the different types of conditional in the table below.

	if clause	main clause	explanation
type 0	*If you <u>study</u> hard,*	*you <u>get</u> good results.*	consequence that is always true in general
type 1	*If you <u>study</u> hard,*	*you <u>will get</u> good results.* also: *you <u>may get</u> good results.*	certain result in your particular case
type 2	*If you <u>studied</u> hard,*	*you <u>would get</u> good results.* also: *you <u>could get</u> / you <u>might get</u> good results.*	possible consequence, given a condition different from the present reality of facts
type 3	*If you <u>had studied</u> hard,*	*you <u>would have got</u> good results.* also: *you <u>could have got</u> / <u>might have got</u> good results.*	impossible condition because referred to the past

EXERCISES

If clauses – type three

UNIT 122

122.1 Match the two parts of the sentences and decide whether it's zero, first, second or third conditional.

1 _b_ [1] 2 .... □ 3 .... □ 4 .... □ 5 .... □ 6 .... □ 7 .... □ 8 .... □

1 If he doesn't know,   a you wouldn't believe me.
2 If they had said nothing,   b I'll tell him.
3 If she broke up with me,   c he'll get there on time.
4 If he hurries up,   d she might have liked him.
5 If the wind blows,   e she'll win the match.
6 If he had smiled more,   f she wouldn't have known about it.
7 If she plays like that,   g all the leaves fall off.
8 If I told you,   h I'd forget about her.

122.2 Write sentences with the correct form of the verbs in brackets to form third conditional sentences.

1 If you (invite) me to go mountaineering, I (come) with you.
   If you had invited me to go mountaineering, I would have come with you.

2 If she (know) about the new snowfall, she (not go) snowboarding.
   ....

3 If she (not be) on her snowboard, she (not have) the accident.
   ....

4 If they (not enjoy) extreme sports, they (stay) at home.
   ....

5 If Lewis Hamilton (not drive) so well, he (not become) world champion.
   ....

6 If Sally (listen) to her boyfriend, she (take up) scuba diving.
   ....

122.3 Use the words to write questions and answers in the third conditional.

1 you / go / skiing / ?   *Would you have gone skiing?*
  yes / if / not / snowing   *Yes, if it hadn't been snowing.*
2 he / pass / exam / ?   ....
  yes / if / work / harder   ....
3 they / enjoy / show / ?   ....
  yes / if / be / shorter   ....
4 she / win / the competition / ?   ....
  yes / if / not / fall over   ....
5 you / eat / all that food / ?   ....
  yes / if / not / already / have / dinner ....
6 he / work / in Argentina / ?   ....
  yes / if / not / accept / job / in Spain..

325

UNIT 123 — Conditional clauses introduced by *when, unless...* / *I wish... / If only...*

A The conditional can be introduced by conjunctions other than **if**. A dependent clause, for example, can begin with:

- **when**, to talk about conditions that are certain to happen.
  When we finish our exams, we'll go on a trip to the seaside. (it is certain that we will finish them)

- **unless**, to propose a negative condition, equivalent to **if... not.**
  They won't show you your exam papers, <u>unless you ask</u> to see them. (also: ...if you don't ask...)

  Note that **unless** is followed by a verb in the affirmative form.

- **provided (that)**, to highlight the idea of restriction or limitation. It's often used when referring to permissions.
  You can have a sleepover at your friend's, provided his parents are at home.

- **but for**
  But for your help, we would never make it. (also: If it weren't for your help...)

- **in case / just in case**
  'Take your umbrella in case it rains.' (also: In case it should/might rain...)

B To express wishes or dreams that are hard to fulfil, other than the forms **I would really like / love to**, the verb **wish** can be used with the following structures:

- wishes referring to present situations.
  wish + past simple / past continuous or **wish + could** + base form of verb
  I wish I were / was a maths genius.
  I wish my son could play the violin.
  We wish it wasn't raining. (but it is raining).

  wish + would + base form of verb is used only if we want *someone else* to do something different.
  I wish you would listen to me.
  His parents wish he would stop smoking.

- regrets, wishes referring to past situations now unchangeable.
  wish + past perfect
  He wishes he had never met her.
  I wish I hadn't bought this computer. It's causing me a lot of trouble.

C The conjunction **if only** is used the following constructions:

- to express desire, but also disappointment or regret for a present fact.
  if only + past simple or **would / could** + base form of verb
  If only I could have a glass of water!
  If only she didn't / wouldn't cry.

- to express regrets regarding a past situation.
  if only + past perfect
  If only I hadn't said those words. (also: I wish I hadn't said those words.)

EXERCISES

Conditional clauses introduced by *when, unless ... I wish ... / If only...*

UNIT 123

123.1 Complete the sentences with the words from the box.

~~when~~ when unless provided that but for in case

1 We'll go out for dinner ......*when*...... I've finished this work.
2 .... the money he lent me, we'd never have bought our house.
3 Take this £20 note .... the T-shirt costs more than you expect.
4 You can't get into the museum .... you show your tickets.
5 Everybody can come to the party .... they bring some food.
6 .... it stops raining, we'll go out for a walk in the park.

123.2 Use the suggestions to express desires / wishes.

1 Bruce / go trekking in Nepal — *Bruce wishes he could go trekking in Nepal.*
2 They / win the World Cup
3 I / be 10cm taller
4 Barbara / John / come back from the USA soon
5 We / our neighbours / be so noisy
6 She / act with Johnny Depp
7 I / have a brand new motorbike

123.3 Express disappointment or regret by using the words in brackets.

1 Peter spent all his money. (if only)
   If only Peter hadn't spent all his money!
2 Mike lost his job in a bank. (if only)

3 Sue went on holiday without me. (I wish)

4 Dave lost his wallet at the market. (if only)

5 John has run off with my best friend. (if only)

6 I wasn't very lucky. (I wish)

123.4 Tick (✔) the correct sentences and correct the sentences with mistakes in them.

1 ✔ If only I hadn't been rude to Paul yesterday!

2 ☐ I wish I remember that girl's name.
   I wish I remembered that girl's name.

3 ☐ You can't get into that club unless you're over 21.

4 ☐ Don't forget your sun cream, in just case it gets hot.

5 ☐ The team would have lost but Dave's brilliant goal.

6 ☐ He can come with us provided he's quiet.

327

REVIEW 24
EXERCISES Units 119–123

R24.1 Match the two parts of the conditional sentences.

1 .b. 2 ...... 3 ...... 4 ...... 5 ...... 6 ......

1 If he says he can't wait for me,
2 If Jane wants to go on the expedition,
3 If I wanted a new jacket,
4 If they hadn't warned us of the danger,
5 If she buys the tickets,
6 If you'd thought it was an insult,

a I would go to the new clothes store in the high street.
b I'll get a lift from somebody else.
c I'm sure you wouldn't have said that.
d we'll go to the concert with her.
e we would have fallen down the ravine.
f she'll have to buy the proper equipment.

R24.2 Complete the sentences with the correct tense of the verbs in brackets

1 If he worked harder, he ......would be...... (be) more successful.
2 If she doesn't like hang gliding, she .... (not have) to do it.
3 If you hadn't used all the coffee, we .... (have) some left now.
4 If we ask him, I'm sure he .... (lend) us his camper van.
5 If they tried kayaking once, I'm sure they .... (enjoy) it.
6 If we'd left earlier, we .... (not be) back so late.

R24.3 Use the words to write questions in the conditional form indicated.

1 Type 1: what / you / do / if / he / come / ?
   What will you do if he comes?
2 Type 2: what / he / think / if / you / do / that / ?
   ....
3 Type 0: what / she / say / if / he / go / out at night / ?
   ....
4 Type 3: where / you / go / if / you / have / the money / ?
   ....
5 Type 1: how / they / meet / if / she / move / to Milan / ?
   ....
6 Type 2: how much / you / have to pay / if / you / rent / this flat / ?
   ....
7 Type 0: who / try / hard / if / they / not have / a good reason / ?
   ....
8 Type 3: why / he / invite / her / out / if / he / not like her / ?
   ....

R24.4 Write what the short form *'d* corresponds to (*had* or *would*).

1 If they'd (..*had*..) told us they were going to the match, we'd (..*would*..) have gone with them.
2 If they'd (..........) behaved better, they'd (..........) have been allowed to go on the school trip.
3 We'd (..........) have joined the group if we'd (..........) known they were going to work on ancient Greece.
4 She'd (..........) have enrolled in our school if she'd (..........) moved to the town centre.

REVIEW 24

R24.5 Use the words to write sentences in the conditional form indicated.

1 Type 2: if / you / really love / me / you / not say / that
   If you really loved me you wouldn't say that.
2 Type 1: if / he / behave / like that / we / get into trouble
   ....
3 Type 3: if / he / not drop / the ball / he / score
   ....
4 Type 1: if / you / not stop / doing that / I / get very angry
   ....
5 Type 0: if / she / want / a new hairstyle / she / go / to the hairdresser's
   ....
6 Type 2: if / he / arrive / earlier / we / leave / on time.
   ....

R24.6 Complete the sentences with the verbs from the box.

~~would~~ might have should have may would have could

1 He said that they ....*would*............ meet me at ten o'clock.
2 It .... been nice if he'd stayed here longer.
3 If you'd asked me, I .... have told you he's out.
4 You .... chosen a different present if you thought she wouldn't like this one.
5 I .... known you would do something stupid!
6 If you ask me very nicely, I .... go to the dance with you.

R24.7 Offer advice for each situation. Use *If I were*... and the suggestions in brackets.

1 Paul told me he has a stomachache. (go to the doctor's)
   If I were him, I'd go to the doctor's.
2 Jane said that she's going to stay in the office until 8 p.m. (not work such long hours)
   ....
3 The Smiths said their car keeps breaking down. (take it to the mechanic)
   ....
4 My wife and I are very short of money. (ask the bank for a loan)
   ....
5 It looks like rain and the kids are going on a hike. (their mother / not let them go)
   ....
6 My boss, John, is getting very stressed out at work. (take a break)
   ....

M Exam preparation

M.1 PET Reading Part 5

Read the text and choose the correct word(s) (A, B, C or D) for each space.

If I wanted to have a good holiday, (1) *A* go to Italy. You can find everything (2) .... want if you go there. If you wanted, you (3) .... go to the seaside or the mountains. But if I (4) .... you, I would take a sightseeing tour. If you visit Florence, for example, you (5) .... see masterpieces by Botticelli and Michelangelo's *David*. On the other hand, if (6) .... stay in Rome, there are Caravaggio's paintings and Bernini's sculptures to admire. If you'd come with me last year, you (7) .... the hilltop town of Siena. You really (8) .... there! It was magnificent! The colour of the stone is warm, the views extensive, the buildings impressive! I could have stayed there a month if I (9) .... enough money. And I haven't even mentioned the food yet! If I (10) .... talking about that, I would never finish! So I think it's a good idea if you (11) .... your holiday now, then you can see for yourself.

1. **A** I'd (circled) **B** I **C** I've **D** I'll
2. **A** they're **B** you've **C** you **D** they
3. **A** should **B** could **C** would **D** can
4. **A** be **B** am **C** was **D** were
5. **A** are **B** would **C** will **D** were
6. **A** you **B** you'll **C** you've **D** you'd
7. **A** would see **B** would have seen **C** will see **D** have seen
8. **A** would be **B** should be **C** should **D** should have been
9. **A** had **B** had had **C** have **D** have had
10. **A** started **B** have started **C** would start **D** will start
11. **A** booking **B** books **C** book **D** would book

M.2 PET Writing Part 1

Complete the second sentence so that it means the same as the first. Use no more than three words.

1. If Tom didn't get up so late, he'd manage to catch his bus.
   If Tom ...*got up*... earlier, he'd manage to catch his bus.
2. If Liz didn't drive so fast, she wouldn't have so many accidents.
   If Liz .... more slowly, she wouldn't have so many accidents.
3. I wish I hadn't been so rude to the teacher!
   If .... I hadn't been so rude to the teacher!
4. I wish you understood what I'm saying.
   I wish you .... understand what I'm saying.
5. Mike: 'I will always love you.'
   Mike said .... always love me.
6. Unless you had helped me, I would never have done it.
   But for .... , I would never have done it.

M.3 PET Writing Part 3

This is part of a conversation you heard between two friends. Write an e-mail to another friend reporting what you heard. (about 45 words)

Paul: But you have to give Mary some of the money we found.
John: I'm not going to. She'll show it to everyone, and we'll be in trouble.
Paul: I'm sure she won't say anything to anyone.

Paul told John that... ....

Exam preparation

M.4 FCE Use of English Part 2

Read the text below and think of a word which best fits each space. Use only one word in each space.

Mandy: What (1) ...*would*... you do if you (2) .... the lottery on Saturday, Denise?

Denise: Well, first of all, I would (3) .... all the money in the bank and think about what I (4) .... to spend it on.

Mandy: Really? I wish I (5) .... as sensible! I'm sure I'd (6) .... it all in the first week!

Denise: If you won millions of pounds, you (7) .... possibly spend it that quickly, could you?

Mandy: I suppose you're right. But even so, I (8) .... want to use some of it immediately – even for a few silly things like clothes and books.

Denise: I'd want to think for a long time if I (9) .... resist the temptation… and then afterwards I would really (10) .... spending every penny.

M.5 FCE Use of English Part 3

Read the text below. Use the word given in capitals at the end of each line to form a word that fits in the space in the same line.

Last week, I walked past an old-fashioned (1) ...*bakery*... in a small	**BAKE**
village which I was passing through. The window was full of	
the most (2) .... cakes you have ever seen. I would	**TANTALISE**
love to have tasted them all, but I made a small (3)	**SELECT**
in my mind. Imagine my (4) .... when I pushed the door	**DISAPPOINT**
and found it was shut. Then I noticed that it was the shop's half-day	
closing that day, so, with my mouth (5) ...., I got back	**WATER**
to the (6) .... lot, got into the car and headed for home.	**PARK**

M.6 FCE Use of English Part 4

Complete the second sentence so that it has a similar meaning to the first sentence, using the word given. Do not change the word given. You must use between two and five words, including the word given.

1. 'It has just started raining,' said Michael.
   THAT
   Michael ...*said that it had*... just started raining.

2. Paula to me: 'Do you want to go for a walk?'
   IF
   Paula .... to go for a walk.

3. He won't help you if you don't ask him nicely.
   UNLESS
   He won't help you .... him nicely.

4. Take these sandwiches just in case you get hungry.
   SHOULD
   Take these sandwiches in case ....

5. Lucy to me: 'Don't walk through that part of town.'
   WARNED
   Lucy .... walk through that part of town.

UNIT 124 Connectors and linkers (1): coordinating, concessive

To join elements within a sentence or sentences within a text, we use conjunctions, prepositions, adverbs or adverbial expressions called **'connectors'** or **'linkers'**. The main function of a connector is to give cohesion to a text, by indicating a logical and chronological order. The following list shows the most common connectors.

A

- **and / both… and…** join two or more elements of a sentence. **And** is also used at the end of a list, after other terms separated by commas.

    I play the piano <u>and</u> I sing in the choir.
    My mother can <u>both</u> speak <u>and</u> write in Arabic.
    In my room, there's a bed, a wardrobe, a desk <u>and</u> a chair.

B

- **or / either… or…** propose an alternative.

    You can have a cake <u>or</u> a sandwich.
    <u>Either</u> you do it now <u>or</u> you'll never do it.

- **neither… nor** excludes both elements.

    <u>Neither</u> Helen <u>nor</u> Simon can go.

For the use of **both**, **either** and **neither**, see page 240.

C

- **but** contradicts two sentences or two elements of a sentence.

    I like her hat <u>but</u> it doesn't go with her dress.
    I had no choice <u>but</u> to accept their offer.

- **on the other hand…** balances two different ideas. It can be preceded by **on the one hand…**

    I would like to get a degree, but <u>on the other hand</u>, I don't feel like studying for so many years.

- **however / though** (informal use) are adverbs. **Though** is placed at the end of a sentence. **However** can be placed either at the beginning or end of a sentence.

    He looks like a tough guy. He's quite shy, <u>though</u>.
    The film was good. A bit too long, <u>however</u>.
    His story is true. <u>However</u>, I wouldn't trust him.

D

- **although / though** introduce a clause that makes the statement in the main clause seem surprising or unexpected.

    <u>Although / Though</u> he's a very young writer, he's already won an important award.

- **even though** refers to a real fact, as opposed to **even if** that is used to make a hypothesis.

    I went to the beach <u>even though</u> it was raining.
    We'll go to the beach, <u>even if</u> it rains.

- **despite / in spite of** (+ noun or verb in **-ing** form, often preceded by a possessive adjective).

    I'm going to buy that house <u>in spite of its price</u>.
    I couldn't eat any of that food <u>despite (my) being</u> very hungry.
    (also: …even though I was very hungry.)

- **however** (+ adjective or adverb).

    <u>However hard</u> you may try, the boss will never be satisfied with your work.

EXERCISES

Connectors and linkers (1): coordinating, concessive

UNIT 124

124.1 Join the two sentences using *both... and...*

1 I eat meat. I eat fish. — I eat both meat and fish.
2 She cooked on Saturday. She cooked on Sunday. _____.
3 We drank white wine. We drank red wine. _____.
4 He had lunch at home. He had dinner at home. _____.
5 She wants a starter. She wants a main course. _____.
6 Paul's eaten enough. Jane's eaten enough. _____.

124.2 Complete the sentences using *either... or* (+) or *neither... nor* (–).

1 (German / Dutch) (+)   The beer I drank was *either German or Dutch*.
2 (a Jonathan / a Cox) (+)   The apple I ate was _____.
3 (polite / fast) (–)   The service in the restaurant was _____.
4 (cheap / good) (–)   The oranges I bought were _____.
5 (a carrot / tomato soup) (+) You can have _____.
6 (long / interesting) (–)   The new menu was _____.

124.3 Complete the sentences with the words from the box.

| ~~but~~   on the other hand (x2)   however (x2)   though |

1 I liked most of the food, *but* I was disappointed with the dessert.
2 It's a beautiful morning, _____ they say it'll rain after lunch.
3 I'd love to go on a cruise, but _____ it's so expensive.
4 Paul took the last copy of the CD, _____ he knew that I wanted it.
5 This is a difficult task. _____, I'd like to undertake it.
6 On the one hand, it's a big flat, but _____, it's too far away.

124.4 Match the two parts of the sentences.

1 _c_ 2 ____ 3 ____ 4 ____ 5 ____ 6 ____

1 He's a very rude boy,   a however much you study.
2 I got lost in the city,   b though it seems like a good idea.
3 I arrived at work on time,   c although he's from a good family.
4 You'll never understand Latin,   d even though I had a map.
5 It will never work in practice,   e despite her greying hair.
6 She still looks very young,   f in spite of the transport strike.

124.5 Complete the paragraph with the appropriate connectors.

I always have breakfast in the morning. On weekdays, I have milk ⁽¹⁾ *and* cereal, toast ⁽²⁾ _____ jam, ⁽³⁾ _____ I drink a cup of tea. You may say it's a big breakfast, ⁽⁴⁾ _____ you should see what I eat on Saturdays ⁽⁵⁾ _____ Sundays. I always have either bacon ⁽⁶⁾ _____ sausages and eggs. I drink ⁽⁷⁾ _____ fruit juice and tea and I eat some fruit as well. I hardly ever have lunch, ⁽⁸⁾ _____ .

UNIT 125 — Connectors and linkers (2): reason, result and purpose

- **because** explains the motive, the cause.
  He didn't go out <u>because</u> he was very busy.

- **as / since** (conjunctions that explain the circumstances or reasons for an action).
  <u>As</u> he couldn't find a job, he enrolled on a web-design course.
  <u>Since</u> we had spent all our money, we couldn't even buy a little souvenir.

- **so** explains what the result is, the consequence.
  We woke up late, <u>so</u> we missed our bus.

  Compare with the causal phrase: *We missed the bus because we woke up late.*

- **therefore**, **as a result / consequently**, **for this reason** are more formal ways to express a result.
  He's broken his leg, <u>therefore</u> he won't be able to play in the next match.
  The bus drivers are on strike today. <u>As a result,</u> the traffic in the city has doubled.

- **so...** + adjective / adverb + **that**
  The pudding was <u>so nice that</u> everyone asked for a second helping.

- **so as to... / not to...**
  Speak softly <u>so as not to</u> disturb them.

- **such a** + adjective + noun + **that...**
  The teacher spoke for <u>such a long time that</u> no one was listening in the end.

For the use of **such**, see page 284.

- **to / in order to** (+ base form of verb) expresses the purpose or the aim of an action.
  In order to... has a more formal use.
  He's qualifying <u>to</u> become an accountant. (not: ...<s>for become an accountant.</s>)
  He has taken a course in business administration <u>in order to</u> gain career advancement.

- **so that** introduces a clause that usually contains a modal: **will / would**, **can / could** or **may / might**.
  <u>So that</u> we can / may win, we'll have to train really hard.

I'll use a microphone <u>so that</u> everybody can hear.

EXERCISES

Connectors and linkers (2): reason, result and purpose

UNIT 125

125.1 Choose the correct alternative.

1 We couldn't visit the museum **because** / **since** it had closed at four o'clock.
2 Mick didn't come with us **since** / **because** he had a bad cold.
3 **In order that** / **Since** the weather is so awful, I think we'll stay at home.
4 **So** / **As** you're obviously not interested, I'll go by myself.
5 She went to bed a nine o'clock **because** / **since** she was so tired.
6 **Since** / **Therefore** you're so clever, you can do it!

125.2 Complete the sentences using the words from the box.

| so | so as to | so | so as not to | so tasty that | such a good | so often that |

1 He ate too much at the party, ...**so**............ he felt sick in the night.
2 She cooks chicken .... I'm fed up with eating it!
3 Mother always gets up early .... get the breakfast ready for us.
4 The food is .... we go to The Three Bells once a week.
5 He washed up after dinner .... leave a mess for the morning.
6 They were out of flour and sugar, ... I went to the supermarket for them.
7 He's .... chef that a lot of restaurants want to employ him.

125.3 Match the sentences (1–7) to the consequences (a–g). Then join them with the connector indicated.

1 ...**c**... 2 .... 3 .... 4 .... 5 .... 6 .... 7 ....

1 *He lost his wallet so he went to the police.*
2 ....
3 ....
4 ....
5 ....
6 ....
7 ....

1 He lost his wallet.
2 He went out in the rain.
3 He forgot to feed his goldfish.
4 It's a very important matter.
5 It's a secret.
6 He was feeling bored.
7 He has been lifting heavy weights.

a I don't want any questions. (and therefore)
b He switched on the radio. (so)
c He went to the police. (so)
d We mustn't say anything to anyone. (and for this reason)
e He's got a backache. (and as a result)
f It died. (and consequently)
g He caught a bad cold. (and as a result)

125.4 Complete the sentences using *so that, to* or *in order to*.

1 He's starting a course ....**to**............ improve his driving skills.
2 She's taking the tablets .... lose weight.
3 He bought all the ingredients .... he could make a pizza.
4 They're moving .... they can be closer to their son.
5 I went to the bank .... meet the manager.
6 The taller boys sat at the back .... everybody could see.
7 He washed the car .... get some pocket money.
8 The children switched on the TV .... watch their favourite cartoon.

335

UNIT 126 — Connectors and linkers (3): time linkers and sequencers

A
- **when** indicates the moment in which something took place. The verb that follows is never in the future tense with **will**. This is the same for all time conjunctions.
  When you have finished this exercise, do the next one. (not: When ~~you will have finished~~...)
  When I was on holiday, I used to get up late.

- **whenever**
  Come whenever you like.

- **while** indicates the simultaneity of two actions. It is usually found with the present continuous or past continuous.
  While I was skiing last Sunday, I fell and hurt my leg.

- **as long as** indicates the duration of an action.
  I will love you as long as I live. (not: ...as long as ~~I will live~~.)

- **until** indicates the limits of an action.
  I waited until they were all gone.

- **as soon as...** indicates the immediacy of an action. It is followed by a verb in the present simple, the present perfect or the past perfect.
  I'll tell him about the prize he has won as soon as I see him. (not: ...as soon as ~~I will see him~~.)

- **before** indicates that an action precedes another action. It is followed by a verb in the **-ing** form or by: subject + verb in the present or past simple.
  Before going / Before he goes to school, he delivers the newspapers in his neighbourhood.

- **after** (+ verb in **–ing** form or subject + verb in the present or past simple) indicates that an action follows another action.
  After delivering / After he has delivered the newspapers, he goes to school.

B Another particular category of time connectors is that of sequencers, which are used to indicate the chronological succession of a series of events, in particular when:

- telling a story: **(at) first, then, after that, next, later, finally / eventually / in the end, at last**.

- presenting a series of discussions, for example in a written report: **firstly, , secondly, in addition, another point is, finally / lastly / in conclusion, last but not least**.

- giving instructions.
  *Here's some advice for you to follow when doing grammar exercises. **First**, put everything you need on your desk: your book, a pencil and an eraser. **Then** read the instructions of the activity carefully. **After that**, read the whole exercise and the grammar rules and start writing the answers. **Finally**, check your answers with the answer key or with your teacher.*

EXERCISES

Connectors and linkers (3): time linkers and sequencers

UNIT 126

126.1 Complete the sentences with the words from the box.

| ~~when~~   whenever   while   as long as   until   as soon as |

1 I like to spend a lot of time on the beach ....*when*........ I'm on holiday.
2 I can only stay here .... four o'clock today.
3 I can't swim under water for .... Mike can.
4 She cleaned the bathroom .... I cooked the lunch.
5 .... I go to London, it always seems to rain!
6 Come back home .... the disco has finished.

126.2 Choose the correct alternative.

1 **Before** / After you leave home, remember to lock all the doors.
2 You're always late! You must get to school **before / after** the lessons start.
3 Can you help me clear up **before / after** the party has finished, please?
4 **Before / After** the baby had gone to sleep, I started doing some housework.
5 **Before / After** we heard the good news, we were very happy.
6 We got there too early – long **before / after** everyone else did.

126.3 Complete the sentences with the words from the box.

| ~~first~~   finally   after that   then   until   next |

Do you want to make proper custard? Just follow these instructions.
(1) ....*First*............, bring 1 pint of milk and 2 fl.oz. of cream to simmering point.
(2) .... whisk 4 yolks with 1oz. of sugar and two spoonfuls of cornflour.
(3) ...., pour the hot milk and cream onto the eggs and sugar, whisking all the time. (4) .... return to the pan and add ½ a teaspoon of vanilla extract. Keep stirring with a wooden spatula (5) ....
thickened. (6) .... pour the custard into a jug and serve at once.

126.4 Rearrange the words and write sentences.

1 come – happy – see – I'm – when – home – him – very – always – I
I'm always very happy when I see him come home.
2 Wash – eating – dinner – hands – your – before
....
3 lesson – ran – We – the – over – outside – as soon as – was
....
4 excited – a – She – party – gets – whenever – birthday – very – there's
....
5 after – He – school – got – wonderful – leaving – job – a
....
6 You'll – finished – until – I've – wait – just – to – have
....

UNIT 127 Other connectors and linkers (4)

A
- **moreover / furthermore** (formal use, above all in written language) / **what's more** (more informal) intensify a discussion by adding further information or ideas.
  He was sentenced to six months. Moreover, he had to pay a big fine.
  The house is large and comfortable and, what's more, it has a nice garden.

- **also / besides (that) / in addition to that besides / in addition to** + verb in **-ing** form.
  I don't want to spend so much on a dress; besides it's not even the colour I prefer.
  You shouldn't eat so much and, in addition to that, you should take more exercise. (also: and you should also take)
  Besides being clever, he's also generous.

B **Comparative function**
- **as… as…**, followed by adjectives or adverbs, expresses a similarity (see p.214)
  It wasn't as easy as I thought it would be.
  You can't jump as high as I can!

- **as… / like…** (colloquial use), followed by subject + verb.
  When in Rome, do as the Romans do.
  Do as you like, I don't mind.
  We danced like we'd never danced before.

- **than…**, followed by adjectives or adverbs, expresses a comparison (see p.212)
  The place is better than we expected.
  When the verb in the comparative clause is the same as the verb in the main clause, it is often not expressed.
  It is much colder today than (it was) yesterday.
  I can run faster than you (can).

C **Conditional function**
- **if**, **in case**, **provided / providing**, **unless** (see p.320)
  I'll drive, provided you tell me the way.

- **as if / as though…**
  He turned pale, as if he had been frightened.

D **Explanatory function**
- **that** is the most used conjunction, for example in reported speech after the verbs **say** and **tell** (see pp.308–310), after the verbs **hope**, **promise**, **know** and many others. This conjunction, however, is very often implied.
  He said (that) he hadn't heard about the accident.
  I know (that) she's a Tottenham fan.

- **that is (to say)**, abbreviated as **i.e.** in written language, is used to clarify the meaning of something.
  Admittance is free for senior citizens, that is to say people over 65.

EXERCISES

Other connectors and linkers (4)

UNIT 127

127.1 Choose the correct alternative.

1 He's always eating. ......**B**......, he eats unhealthy food!
 A Unless **(B)** What's more **C** Also

2 That restaurant is very expensive and ...., the service is very slow.
 A in addition to that **B** although **C** that

3 .... being very nice fruit, kiwis are also rich in vitamins.
 A Moreover **B** Besides that **C** Besides

4 He talks a lot of rubbish about cooking. ...., people listen to him!
 A Furthermore **B** As though **C** Providing

5 They are excellent vegetables and, ..., they're organic.
 A than **B** moreover **C** that is to say

6 We can come with you, ... we come back before dinner.
 A besides **B** that **C** provided

7 They looked .... they were going away for ever.
 A as if **B** besides **C** in case

8 The food in this restaurant is .... at the Ritz, but the service is better.
 A as if **B** as though **C** as good as

127.2 Rearrange the words and write sentences.

1 like – move – do – you – you – as – can – When – out
 When you move out, you can do as you like.

2 as – as – be – She's – to – fit – not – used – she
 ....

3 book – than – This – more – expected – is – I – interesting – much
 ....

4 played – before – played – as – they'd – They – never
 ....

5 much – mine – painting – than – Your – better – is
 ....

127.3 Match the two parts of the sentences.

1 ..c.. 2 .... 3 .... 4 .... 5 .... 6 ....

1 I won't help you   a unless it's really urgent.
2 He held on to the rail   b as if someone were following him.
3 You can go to the ball,   c if you don't ask me nicely.
4 I won't call you   d in case the bus started suddenly.
5 He walked very quickly,   e as though inspired by the gods.
6 They played beautifully,   f provided you're home by midnight.

127.4 Indicate (∧) where *that* can be placed in the following sentences.

1 Paul said ∧ he was leaving the next day.
2 Linda told me she doesn't like Steve.
3 I don't think it matters very much.
4 Pat's mother hopes she will go to college.
5 Will you promise you won't tell anyone?
6 Danny was sure nobody had seen him.

UNIT 128 Word formation (1): Prefixes

A prefix is a group of letters that, when placed at the beginning of a word, changes its meaning and forms a new word. The following list shows the most common prefixes with examples.

Negative prefixes that form words of the opposite meaning
- **dis-**   **dis**honest, **dis**advantage, **dis**agree, **dis**appear
- **il-**   **il**legal, **il**liberal, **il**licit, **il**literate
- **im-**   **im**possible, **im**perfect, **im**modest, **im**patient
- **in-**   **in**accessible, **in**correct, **in**adequate, **in**calculable
- **ir-**   **ir**responsible, **ir**regular, **ir**rational, **ir**relevant
- **un-**   **un**happy, **un**friendly, **un**fair, **un**believable

Prefix that indicates repetition
- **re-**   **re**arm, **re**birth, **re**build, **re**write

Prefix that indicates cooperation
- **co-**   **co**operation, **co**-exist, **col**laborate, **co**ordinate

Prefix that indicates reduction, deprivation
- **de-**   **de**forestation, **de**frost, **de**hydrate, **de**regulate

Prefixes that indicate that something is badly done or incorrect
- **ill-**   **ill**-bred, **ill**-judged, **ill**-informed, **ill**-treated
- **mis-**   **mis**understanding, **mis**behaviour, **mis**trust, **mis**fortune

Prefix that indicates that something is in excess
- **over-**   **over**population, **over**weight, **over**sleep, **over**estimate, work **over**time

Prefix that indicates that something is lacking, isn't sufficient
- **under-**   **under**weight, **under**nourished, **under**cooked, **under**estimate

Prefix that indicates prediction, anticipation
- **fore-**   **fore**tell, **fore**see, **fore**cast, **fore**thought

Prefixes that indicate quantity
- **mono-**   **mono**lingual, **mono**chrome, **mono**rail, **mono**theistic
- **bi-**   **bi**lingual, **bi**monthly, **bi**centenary, **bi**cameral
- **tri-**   **tri**lingual, **tri**angle, **tri**pod, **tri**mester
- **poly-**   **poly**theistic, **poly**syllabic, **poly**phony, **poly**ethylene
- **multi-**   **multi**-millionaire, **multi**-storey car park, **multi**purpose, **multi**national

EXERCISES

Word formation (1): Prefixes

UNIT 128

128.1 Complete the words using the negative prefixes in the box.

| ~~dis-~~ in- im- un- ir- il- |

1 I'm sorry, but I completely ..*dis*..agree with what you said.
2 None of them can read or write. They're all ....literate.
3 That is totally ....relevant to what we're talking about.
4 The supplies they have sent are ....adequate for our needs.
5 It was ....believable how aggressive he became!
6 I got very ....patient with the children by the end of the day.

128.2 Choose the correct alternative.

1 He has become obese. He **overeats** / **undereats** at every meal.
2 I can't eat this meat – it's raw! You **overcooked** / **undercooked** it again.
3 It's too hot in here. Why do they always **overheat** / **underheat** the room?
4 He's not very good. I **overestimated** / **underestimated** his ability.
5 She's failed again! Why does she **overachieve** / **underachieve** in exams?
6 Fifty pounds? It's far too much! They've **overcharged** / **undercharged** you!

128.3 Match the words to the definitions.

1 ..*e*.. 2 .... 3 .... 4 .... 5 .... 6 ....

1 monolingual   a It's a shape with four sides.
2 multipurpose   b It's got two wheels.
3 bicycle   c A person who can speak a lot of languages
4 polyglot   d A camera stand with three legs
5 tripod   e It's only written in one language.
6 quadrilateral   f It can be used in many ways.

128.4 Add prefixes to the words in the box and complete the sentences.

| operate   forestation   ~~building~~   mix   exist   fortunes |

1 They are ..*rebuilding*.............. the old house at the end of our street.
2 Two opposite economic policies cannot .... in our organisation.
3 The .... of the Amazon is one of the world's major problems.
4 He suffered a number of .... after his wife died.
5 The DJ wants to .... that old Beatles record for his next show.
6 The police asked us to .... with them in their enquiries.

128.5 Complete the words with a suitable prefix.

1 We can't ..*fore*see the results of a merger between the two companies.
2 You can use the microwave to .... frost bread.
3 Jude's mum is Spanish and her dad English. She's .... lingual.
4 I was late for work today because I .... slept.
5 My brother and I had an argument because of a .... understanding.
6 Clare earnt a lot this month – she worked four hours .... time.
7 The thief .... appeared before we could see who it was.
8 Ted needs to diet – he's .... weight.

UNIT 129

Word formation (2): Suffixes

A suffix is a group of letters that, when placed at the end of a word, changes its meaning and forms a new word. This often involves a change in grammatical function, for example from noun to adjective: **beauty → beautiful**. The following list shows the most common suffixes:

Abstract nouns

-ness	happi**ness**, dark**ness**, ill**ness**, sweet**ness**
-ship	friend**ship**, relation**ship**, partner**ship**
-hood	child**hood**, brother**hood**, mother**hood**
-ment	develop**ment**, disappoint**ment**, involve**ment**
-ance / -ence	perform**ance**, independ**ence**, prefer**ence**
-y / -ity / -iety	jealous**y**, urgenc**y**, immun**ity**, var**iety**
-ation / -tion	educ**ation**, explan**ation**, connec**tion**
-dom	king**dom**, martyr**dom**, bore**dom**

Nouns that indicate professions or functions of objects

-er / -or	employ**er**, act**or**, cook**er**, calculat**or**
-ee	employ**ee**, interview**ee**, train**ee**
-ist	art**ist**, novel**ist**, scient**ist**
-ian	histor**ian**, politic**ian**, electric**ian**
-ant / -ent	serv**ant**, assist**ant**, superintend**ent**

Adjectives that indicate a quality or a characteristic

-able / -ible	reason**able**, reli**able**, respons**ible**, convert**ible**, (im)poss**ible**
-ive	attract**ive**, creat**ive**, explos**ive**
-ous	spaci**ous**, danger**ous**, ambiti**ous**

Adjectives that indicate a nationality

-an	Itali**an**, Americ**an**, Indi**an**, Austri**an**
-ish	Engl**ish**, Span**ish**, Swed**ish**, Finn**ish**
-ese	Chin**ese**, Portugu**ese**, Japan**ese**

Adjective that indicates a quality

-y	nois**y**, angr**y**, prett**y**, tin**y**, health**y**

Adjective with a reductive meaning and often a negative connotation

-ish	child**ish**, grey**ish**, yellow**ish**, boy**ish**

Adjectives that indicate the presence or lack of something

-ful	hope**ful**, power**ful**, use**ful**, care**ful**
-less	hope**less**, meaning**less**, use**less**

Adjectives of scientific, technical or cultural language

-al	cultur**al**, nation**al**, natur**al**
-ar	circul**ar**, nucle**ar**, molecul**ar**
-ic / -ical	atom**ic**, romant**ic**, panoram**ic**, histor**ical**

Verbs that indicate 'to make', 'to become'

-ize, -ise	modern**ize**, commercial**ize**, legal**ise**
-ify	pur**ify**, just**ify**, clar**ify**, test**ify**
-en	thick**en**, short**en**, soft**en**

Adverb, above all of manner

-ly	easi**ly**, main**ly**, careful**ly** (see p.280)

EXERCISES

Word formation (2): Suffixes — UNIT 129

129.1 Complete the abstract nouns using the suffixes in the box.

| -ness | -ship | -hood | -ment | -ance | -ation |

1 He had a serious ill...**ness**... when he was a child.
2 He always had a good explan................ for everything he did.
3 He was always ready to help when the family was facing hard................ .
4 The doctors all say that mother................ is important for young women.
5 His involve................ in the project has been very disappointing.
6 There's going to be a perform................ in the school hall on Saturday afternoon.

129.2 Write the nationalities.

1 Italy — _Italian_
2 Sweden — ....
3 Austria — ....
4 Portugal — ....
5 Bolivia — ....
6 Poland — ....
7 Japan — ....
8 Scotland — ....
9 Ireland — ....
10 England — ....
11 Hungary — ....
12 Chile — ....
13 Canada — ....
14 Denmark — ....
15 China — ....

129.3 Complete the adjectives and the verbs with a suitable suffix.

1 He was always a care**ful** man who did everything correctly.
2 The report was completely use................ . Nobody ever read it.
3 We watched all of the new histor................ series on TV.
4 The town council has decided to modern................ the building next year.
5 I hope he will be able to testi................ in the court case.
6 You need to short................ the visiting hours at the hospital.

129.4 Complete the sentences using the words in the box.

| Japanese | pleasant | careful | childhood | fashionable | careless | romantic | sentimental | tiny |

1 Simon is a _careless_ child. He keeps losing things, and his notebooks are a real mess.
2 You can trust Peter. He's always very .... when he has to look after his younger brother.
3 When I think of my ...., lots of .... memories come to my mind. It was the best period of my life.
4 I don't like that movie. It's too .... and ....
5 Their room was so ...., they could hardly walk around the bed.
6 .... restaurants are very .... these days.

129.5 Complete the second sentence so that it has the same meaning as the first one. Use words with a suffix.

1 This makes no sense. It is _senseless_ .
2 He has a lot of power. He's very ....
3 This telephone is without any cords. It's a ....
4 He plays very well. He's a very good ....
5 There's a lot of noise here. It's a .... place.
6 Beer has got alcohol in it. It's an .... drink.
7 These shoes are in fashion. They are .... shoes.

UNIT 130 Prepositional verbs

The verbs listed below are usually followed by prepositions. They therefore take indirect objects. In some cases, another verb (in the **-ing** form) can follow the preposition.

- agree **with** sb **on** sth / **on** doing sth
  I agree with you on reorganising the office.

- apologise **to** sb **for** sth / **for** doing sth
  I apologised to the teacher for my delay / for being late.

- apply **to** sb **for** sth
  She applied to the job centre for a new job.

- approve / disapprove **of** sth
  I don't approve of your decisions.

- ask sb **about** sth
  He asked me about my exam.

- ask **for** sth
  Ask her for £10.

- believe **in** sb / sth
  I believe in friendship.

- belong **to** sb
  The old cottage belongs to Mrs Dell.

- borrow sth **from** sb
  He borrowed a lot of money from his sister.

- call **at** sb's / a place
  Call at my house for a cup of tea tomorrow.

- care **about** sb / sth
  Everybody should care about the environment.

- charge sb **for** sth
  The hotel charged me £10 for the car park.

- complain **to** sb **about** sth
  She complained to the manager about her room.

- congratulate sb **on** sth
  I congratulated Jim on his success.

- deal **in** sth
  He deals in furniture.

- deal **with** sb / sth
  Which firm are you dealing with?
  This novel deals with the diamond wars.

- depend **on** sb / sth
  It all depends on you.

- dream **about** / **of** sb / sth
  I dreamt of you last night.

- fill **with** sth
  Fill the bottle with water.

- hear **from** sb
  I haven't heard from you for a long time.

- keep **to** sth
  You should keep to the rules when playing cards.

- laugh **at** sb / sth
  Are you laughing at me or at my joke?

- leave **for** a place
  I'm leaving for Pisa tomorrow.

- listen **to** sb / sth
  Please listen to me!

- look **after** sb / sth
  The babysitter is looking after the children tonight.

- look **at** sb / sth
  Look at that star!

- look **for** sb / sth
  She's looking for her keys.

- look **into** sth
  The police promised to look into the matter.

- pay **for** sth
  Let me pay for the meal.

- succeed **in** sth / **in** doing sth
  He has succeeded in publishing his novel.

- thank sb **for** sth
  You must thank Sarah for her hospitality.

- think **of** / **about** sb / sth
  I'm always thinking of you.

- Wait **for** sb / sth
  Lots of people are waiting for the cable car.

344

EXERCISES

Prepositional verbs

UNIT 130

130.1 Complete the sentences with the correct form of the verbs in the box.

| ~~ask~~ apply agree apologise thank approve dream ask |

1 I ......*asked*...... the teacher about the arrangements for the exam.
2 I hope you .... of the new furniture in the office.
3 I would like to .... to you for what I said yesterday.
4 We would call you for an interview if you .... for this position.
5 I .... for a pay rise when I see the boss tomorrow.
6 I didn't .... with Michael about the causes of the problem.
7 I .... about being lost in the Tube when the alarm woke me up.
8 Did you .... Auntie Sarah for the beautiful present?

130.2 Choose the correct alternative.

1 I think we all agree **in** / **on** the importance of organic food.
2 Do you belong **to** / **of** any dining clubs or associations?
3 I borrowed these recipe books **from** / **out of** my father last week.
4 I'm going to call **to** / **at** the Indian takeaway on the way home.
5 I don't think Ron cares **of** / **about** anything except eating.
6 They charged me a lot of money **for** / **from** this tin of caviar.
7 Everybody working in this restaurant must keep **at** / **to** the safety rules.
8 They finally succeeded **at** / **in** fulfilling their dream: a meal at the Savoy Hotel.

130.3 Match the two parts of the sentences.

1 ...*d*... 2 .... 3 .... 4 .... 5 .... 6 ....

1 We complained   a in international cheeses.
2 I congratulated him   b preparing local dishes.
3 Amanda's firm deals   c from the Wine Society yet.
4 I haven't heard   d about the quality of the food.
5 They should keep to   e at her – she's never roasted duck before.
6 You mustn't laugh   f on cooking such a good dinner.

130.4 Which prepositional verbs formed with *look* can substitute the verbs in bold in the following sentences?

| ~~look round~~ look at look for look after look into look up |

1 We're going to **visit** an old castle this afternoon.   ......*look round*......
2 We have to **care for** next door's dog while they're away.   ....
3 I must **find** the meaning of *serendipity* in the dictionary. ....
4 The local police said they **are investigating** the problem.   ....
5 We **examined** the paintings for a long time.   ....
6 We **searched for** her lost ring everywhere.   ....

130.5 Complete the paragraphs using the appropriate form of the verbs on the previous page. The prepositions have already been inserted.

1 We (1) ......*complained*...... to the restaurant manager because they (2) .... us for a bottle of champagne we hadn't drunk. They also wanted us (3) .... for parking our car in their courtyard!

2 If he's (4) .... of becoming a great chef, he should be ready to (5) .... for a city like Paris, where he could (6) .... for a job in a renowned restaurant.

UNIT 131 Adjectives followed by prepositions

The adjectives below are usually followed by prepositions. In some cases, another verb (in the **-ing** form) can follow the preposition.

- afraid **of** sb / sth
  He's terribly afraid of spiders.
- angry **about** sth
  He was angry about the train delay.
- angry **with** sb **for** sth
  Mum was angry with Matthew for getting another bad mark.
- ashamed **of** sb / sth
  I'm ashamed of your behaviour.
- bored **with** sth
  The boys were bored with the long play.
- born **of** sb
  He was born of Italian parents.
- busy **with** sb / sth
  The manager is busy with the budget.
- critical **of** sb / sth
  Professor Hall was critical of his students.
- crowded **with** sb
  The square was crowded with hundreds of people.
- different **from** sb / sth
  This town is very different from the place where I live.
- disappointed **with** sb / sth
  I was really disappointed with the exam results.
- engaged **in** sth
  He's engaged in a profitable business.
- engaged **to** sb
  Paul is engaged to Louise.
- fed up **with** sth
  I'm fed up with listening to this story!
- fond **of** sb / sth
  She's very fond of me.
  He's fond of model making.

- frightened **of** sb / sth
  He is frightened of thunder.
- good **at** sth
  I'm quite good at maths.
- hopeless **at** sth
  I'm hopeless at skiing, I'll never learn.
- important **to** sb
  Her family is more important to her than her career.
- interested **in** sth
  We're interested in the flat on the top floor.
- keen **on** sth
  My husband is keen on science-fiction films.
- married **to** sb
  Is Brad still married to Angie?
- nervous **about** sth
  Are you nervous about your driving test?
- popular **with** sb
  Jack is very popular with his colleagues.
- satisfied / dissatisfied **with** sth
  We're really satisfied with this hotel.
- sorry **about** sb / sth
  I'm sorry about Peter. He didn't deserve being sacked.
- surprised **at** sth
  He was much surprised at the news he heard.
- tired **of** sth
  I'm tired of my job.
- worried **about** sb / sth
  I'm worried about the kids. Where are they?

EXERCISES

Adjectives followed by prepositions

UNIT 131

131.1 Complete the sentences with the correct form of the verb *be* and with the adjectives in the box.

| afraid | angry | ashamed | bored | disappointed | born | busy |

1. When he was a boy, he ......*was afraid*...... of the dark.
2. I .... with these physics lesson – they're so theoretical!
3. I .... of myself when I saw the poor results I got in the test.
4. Diego .... of Spanish and French parents.
5. I'm afraid he can't see you now. He .... with another client.
6. The coach .... with the 1–1 draw, even though the team had played really well.
7. The students .... about the changes to their timetable.

131.2 Match the two parts of the sentences.

1 ..*e*.. 2 .... 3 .... 4 .... 5 .... 6 ....

1. Paul was angry
2. The students are very critical
3. The bus was so crowded
4. Janice is very different
5. The students were engaged
6. I'm very good

a. at drawing people's portraits.
b. in a difficult experiment.
c. from her elder sister.
d. of the organisation of their classes.
e. with his mother for ruining his jeans.
f. with people I could hardly get on.

131.3 Choose the correct alternative.

1. I was very disappointed **(with)** / **of** the food we got in that restaurant.
2. Did you know that Gill got engaged **with** / **to** Simon?
3. You can tell Dave is very fond **of** / **with** good food and drink.
4. I'm afraid I'm absolutely hopeless **for** / **at** baking cakes.
5. She's very interested **in** / **from** Japanese cuisine.
6. She's rather nervous **on** / **about** cooking for so many people.
7. Hamburgers and chips are very popular **with** / **for** teenagers.
8. My sister is hopeless **with** / **at** cooking, but her husband is quite good **at** / **in** it.

131.4 Rearrange the words and write sentences.

1. 20 – been – him – married – years – to – Jane's – for
   Jane's been married to him for 20 years.

2. keen – racing – John – on – seems – motor – be – to – very
   ....

3. to – very – three – my – dogs – mother – important – The – are
   ....

4. with – The – nowadays – circus – children – popular – isn't – very
   ....

5. of – been – spiders – has – frightened – Lucy – always
   ....

6. sorry – Duncan – mistake – his – was – about
   ....

7. Clare – tomorrow's – is – about – exam – worried
   ....

8. was – critical – government's – housing – the – everyone – of – policy
   ....

UNIT 132 Phrasal verbs (1)

Phrasal verbs are very common in spoken English. They consist of a verb and one or more adverbial particles or prepositions that modify the meaning of the verb.

In some cases, we can work out the meaning of a phrasal verb by knowing the meaning of its parts. However, in many other cases, the verb adopts a meaning that isn't obvious to someone whose mother tongue isn't English.

Phrasal verbs consisting of a verb + adverbial particle can be:
- intransitive, when they aren't followed by a direct object.
  Why don't you sit down? Stand up, please.

- transitive, when they are followed by a direct object.
  - If the direct object is a noun, the noun can be placed either before or after the adverbial particle.
    Switch on the light. / Switch the light on.
    Cut out the pictures. / Cut the pictures out.
  - If the direct object is a pronoun, the pronoun always precedes the adverbial particle.
    Switch it on. (not: *Switch on it.*) *Cut them out.*

Phrasal verbs consisting of verb + adverbial particle + preposition are followed by an indirect object: *I can't put up with his smoking.*

The table below shows a few of the most common phrasal verbs, in alphabetical order.

be	off	I'm off now.
	on	What's on at the cinema?
	over	The lesson is over.
	up to	What are you up to?
break	down	His car broke down on the way to work. She broke down when she heard the bad news.
	out	The Great Fire of London broke out in a baker's shop.
	up	Mandy and Bob have broken up.
bring	about	What has brought about this misunderstanding?
	back	Bring the newspaper back!
	round	We managed to bring the principal round to our point of view. This medicine should bring her round.
	up	One of my cousins has brought up eight children. We decided to bring up the matter at the next meeting.
call	in	Helen called in to see me the other day.
	off	The match was called off.
catch	up with	You were absent for some time, so you have to catch up with the work we've been doing.
carry	on	Carry on like that, and you'll pass your exam.
	out	Why didn't you carry out the experiment?

EXERCISES

Phrasal verbs (1)

UNIT **132**

132.1 Complete the second sentence with a verb from the box so that it has a similar meaning to the first one.

| be off be on be on be over be up to (x2) |

1 What's showing at the theatre next week?
   What 's on .... at the theatre next week?
2 What did you do at the seaside last Saturday?
   What .... at the seaside last Saturday?
3 I think John's going to leave in a moment.
   I think John .... in a moment.
4 You fell asleep! The film finished an hour ago!
   You fell asleep! The film .... for an hour!
5 The man behaved in a suspicious way. He was certainly doing something illegal.
   The man behaved in a suspicious way. He .... certainly .... something illegal.
6 They are showing a good documentary film this afternoon.
   A good documentary film .... this afternoon.

132.2 Choose the correct alternative.

1 Do you know what has brought **about** / **along** his depression?
2 Bring **on** / **back** free bus passes for students!
3 She's fainted, but these smelling salts will bring her **up** / **round**.
4 We brought **up** / **in** the issue of payment with our boss.
5 When he heard about the accident, he broke **up** / **down** in tears.
6 It was some time after the fire broke **in** / **out** that the fire engine arrived.
7 I was saddened when I heard that Andy and Liz had broken **up** / **down**.
8 Both my parents were brought **up** / **about** in the country.

132.3 Complete the sentences using the verbs in the box.

| call call catch carry (x2) |

1 I'm going to .... call ...... in at my mother's on the way home.
2 He ran so fast that I couldn't .... up with him.
3 The soldiers didn't .... out the mission as they could have done.
4 On the day before her big party, Sally decided to .... it off.
5 I had to take a rest – I was just too tired to .... on.

132.4 Complete the sentences with the correct prepositions.

1 Ben's acting strangely. I wonder what he's .. up to .. ?
2 Mandy was brought .... by her grandparents.
3 Why don't you call .... and see us tomorrow?
4 The 1st World war broke .... in 1914.
5 Joe just carried .... talking even when Grandpa went to sleep!
6 I missed a class so I have to catch .... next week.

349

UNIT 132 Phrasal verbs (2)

come	back	Come back home by six o'clock.
	in	Why don't you come in?
	up up with	Something strange came up in my office yesterday. Did you come up with any good ideas?
cut	down	You should cut down your personal expenses.
	off	Electricity was suddenly cut off last night.
	out	David is cutting out pictures from a newspaper.
do	away with	In 1865, slavery was done away with all over the USA.
	without	She couldn't do without her morning coffee.
drop	in at (place) in on (person)	Drop in at our house / on us when you next come to London.
	out of	One of the runners twisted his foot and had to drop out of the race.
fill	in	Fill in this form, please.
get	across	Did you get your message across?
	away away with	The robbers got away as soon as the police arrived. They cheated during the test, but didn't get away with it.
	back	When did you get back?
	by by with	It's hard to get by. We get by with just one PC.
	on with	How are you getting on with your French? I get on very well with my brother.
	up	What time did you get up?
give	in	The game was too difficult, so I gave in.
	out	Who can help me give the photocopies out?
	up	I gave up smoking 13 years ago.
go	down with	A few boys went down with flu last month.
	off	The lights went off. Luckily, the bomb didn't go off. The fridge was out, of order and most of the food went off.
	out	When the fire went out, the room got terribly cold.

EXERCISES

Phrasal verbs (2)

UNIT 132

132.5 Add a particle after the verb so that the second sentences has a similar meaning to the first one.

1 They said they'd return next year.
  They said they'd come ..*back*.. here next year.
2 Darling, I'll be late home tonight. Something's happened at work.
  Darling, I'll be late home tonight. Something's come .... at work.
3 When I asked if we could enter, they said we could.
  When I asked if we could come .... , they said we could.
4 I couldn't think of anywhere to go for the weekend.
  I couldn't come .... with anywhere to go for the weekend.
5 The line went dead last night while I was making a phone call.
  I was cut .... in the middle of a phone call last night.
6 If you can't stop smoking, at least try to smoke less.
  If you can't give it .... at least try to cut .... on your smoking.

132.6 Complete the sentences using the verbs *do*, *drop* or *fill*.

1 I'm going to ......*drop*.......... in on my aunt and uncle when I'm in Devon.
2 They'll have to .... away with the trees when they build the new road.
3 When we got to the customs office, they made us .... in a form.
4 It was rather inconvenient to have them .... in on us at such short notice.
5 The manager is so busy. He can't .... without an assistant.
6 Tamara promised her parents she wouldn't .... out of school.

132.7 Choose the correct alternative.

1 I have been trying to get my meaning **in /(across)** all morning!
2 What time did you manage to get **over / away** from work last night?
3 Annie got **back / out** from the party very late last night.
4 We've so little money these days, I don't know how we'll get **over / by**.
5 Eddy's OK, but we don't really get **on / off** very well.
6 What time do you usually get **up / down** on Sunday morning?
7 They nearly got **away with / out of** stealing all our money.

132.8 Without changing the meaning, substitute the words in bold with *give* + particle.

1 I **admitted defeat** when I realised how strong he was.
  I ....*gave in*....... when I realised how strong my opponent was.
2 When did you **stop** eating chocolate?
  When did you .... eating chocolate?
3 Could you **distribute** the food to the children, please?
  Could you .... the food to the children, please?
4 He **agreed to stop guessing** because the quiz was too difficult.
  He .... because the quiz was too difficult.

132.9 Complete the sentences with the correct particle after the verb *go*.

1 The TV programmes usually go ......*off*......... at midnight on this channel.
2 The bomb went .... in the hotel across the street.
3 It's so windy that the matches go .... when you light them.
4 After his trip to Africa, Paul went .... with a nasty tropical disease.
5 Fish will go .... very quickly in this heat.

351

UNIT 132 Phrasal verbs (3)

hand	in	Hand in your projects by next week.
keep	up with on off	I can't keep up with you. You're walking too fast. Keep on with your great work. Smoke keeps mosquitoes off.
look	forward to	We're looking forward to meeting you.
	up	When you don't know a word, look it up in a dictionary.
make	out	There are two people at the door, but I can't make out who they are. They were making out in the back seat of the car.
	up	He made up an unbelievable story. Make up a nice parcel and send the present by post.
pick	up	Pick up that piece of paper. Can you pick me up at the station, please?
put	off	The meeting has been put off.
	on	Put your jumper on. It's cold.
	out	The firefighters put out the fire quickly.
	up up with	I could put you up for a couple of nights. I just can't put up with your smoking in the car.
run	out of	We've run out of milk. Can you go and buy some?
set	off	We set off early in the morning so as to avoid the traffic.
take	off	The plane is due to take off in half an hour. He took his hat off.
	up	The kids have taken up tennis this year.
turn	on	Turn on the lights, please.
	off	Turn off the tap.
	up	Turn up the heating.
	down	Turn down the TV. It's too loud.

EXERCISES

Phrasal verbs (3)

UNIT 132

132.10 Match the following verbs followed by *off* to their definitions.

1 ..e.. 2 .... 3 .... 4 .... 5 ....

1 put off   a to begin a journey
2 set off   b to go up into the air in a plane
3 take off   c to close something such as a tap, or to flick a switch
4 turn off   d to stay away from
5 keep off   e to postpone an action until later

132.11 Choose the correct particle after *make*.

1 I looked at the map, but I still couldn't make **up / (out)** where we were.
2 He hadn't done his homework, so he made **up / out** a reason why.
3 Jane and Steve started making **up / out** on the sofa at Lucy's party.
4 Have you made **out / up** a list of all the people you are going to invite?

132.12 Complete the sentences using the particles in the box.

| up   out   ~~up with~~   up with   out of   down   in |

1 He's so rude! I really can't put ..up with.. his manners!
2 My father's coming to pick me .... after the party.
3 We put .... the pan fire by covering it with a towel.
4 He ran .... petrol a long way from a petrol station.
5 Could you turn the radio ...., please? It's too loud!
6 We have to hand .... our homework at nine o'clock tomorrow.
7 He's got so many new computer add-ons, I can't keep .... them.

132.13 Complete each sentence with the correct form of one of the verbs on the previous page.

1 You have to .....hand in..... your tests at 10.30.
2 'Do you know Mr Jackson's phone number?' 'No, but I can .... it .... in the telephone directory.'
3 Can you .... who those people on that balcony are?
4 John, remember to .... the children from school at four.
5 The international conference was .... because riots had broken out in the country.
6 'What time is your plane ....?' 'At 3.30, if there are no delays.'
7 It's very hot in here. Can't you .... the heating and set it to a more pleasant temperature?
8 Don't even try to .... an excuse. You forgot our appointment. That's the real truth.

132.14 Complete the sentences with the correct prepositions.

1 Keep ..off.. the grass!
2 Can you turn .... the volume? I can't hear.
3 It's warm in here. Why don't you take your jacket ....?
4 My plane took .... two hours late!
5 Who made this story ....? It's totally untrue.
6 I'm really looking forward .... my trip to Japan.

REVIEW 25 EXERCISES Units 124–132

R25.1 Complete the sentences using the connectors in the box.

| ~~and~~ both either neither although despite |

1 My father ...*and*... mother went to a French restaurant last night.
2 The waiter said they could eat .... inside or on the terrace.
3 .... it was a warm evening, my mother preferred to sit inside.
4 They had .... frog legs nor snails on the menu.
5 .... my mother and my father ordered French onion soup.
6 .... waiting for a long time, the food was still badly served.

R25.2 Choose the correct alternative.

1 She didn't eat at the restaurant **because** / **although** she was short of money.
2 He had a car crash last week **because** / **so** he won't be able to drive us there.
3 He is related to the President **because** / **therefore** he cannot stand for office.
4 Sue set her alarm clock **consequently** / **so as not** to be late for the meeting.
5 He is moving to New York **because** / **in order to** start a new branch.
6 They will get there early **so that** / **although** they can start on time.

R25.3 Complete the sentences using the connectors in the box.

| as soon as before ~~whenever~~ after until as long as |

1 I always feel very happy ......*whenever*...... I see you.
2 I didn't visit them .... the day after Christmas.
3 .... paying the bill, he quickly left the restaurant.
4 I will continue to work here .... you want me to.
5 Don't leave the office .... finding that file.
6 Telephone me .... you hear any news.

R25.4 Choose the correct alternative.

There are some ways of behaving I can't (1) **put up with** / **support**, however (2) **trivial** / **coarse** they may be. One of the most (3) **fastidious** / **annoying** to me is when people shout and make a lot of (4) **rumour** / **noise** in the streets or in restaurants. But I also can't (5) **stand** / **support** people who chew gum with their mouth open or yawn loudly. (6) **Ultimately** / **Finally**, I can't (7) **support** / **bear** anyone from my family walking on the wet (8) **pavement** / **floor** that I have just washed!

R25.5 Complete the sentences using the words in the box.

| ~~moreover~~ besides like than provided unless |

1 He's a very honest man, and ......*moreover*......, he's very generous.
2 Don't sign a contract .... you are absolutely sure it is valid.
3 .... fishing, I also enjoy playing tennis.
4 In the Olympic final, he ran .... he had never run before!
5 The new trainee has proved to be much more skilful .... we thought.
6 You can go where you want, ... you tell me where you're going.

R25.6 Choose the correct alternative.

1. He's an extremely **unhonest / dishonest** person.
2. So far, all the plans I've seen have been **unperfect / imperfect**.
3. What he said was completely **unbelievable / disbelievable**.
4. His behaviour is increasingly **unrational / irrational**.
5. There are a number of **illiterate / disliterate** people who can't even spell their names.
6. All the results of this study seem to be **uncorrect / incorrect**.

R25.7 Add the suffixes in the box to the words given to form abstract nouns. If necessary, make spelling changes.

| -ness | -ship | -hood | -ment | -ation | -ance | -ility |

1. sweet — *sweetness*
2. educate
3. enjoy
4. hard
5. perform
6. sister
7. establish
8. liberate
9. possible
10. kind
11. endure
12. friend
13. credible
14. leader

R25.8 Rearrange the words and write sentences.

1. forward – party – We – Christmas – to – look – our – always
   We always look forward to our Christmas party.
2. Internet – train – looked – the – the – on – up – She – times
3. up – nights – week – Could – for – next – two – you –me – put – ?
4. golf – Alison – retired – took – last – when – up – year – she
5. radio – kitchen – the – when – usually – I'm – I – on – in – turn – the
6. out – We – petrol – twice – week – ran – last – of
7. up – It's – smoking – good – give – a – to – idea
8. morning - can't – without – coffee – do – I – the – in

N   Exam preparation

N.1   PET Reading Part 5

Read the text and choose the correct word(s) (A, B, C or D) for each space.

Last night, my brother (1) ..A.... sister went out to a fancy, dress party. (2) .... my brother nor my sister knew what to wear, (3) .... I made a few helpful suggestions and so they (4) .... went dressed as vampires. (5) ...., when they got to the party, they found that everybody else had had the same idea! This was probably (6) .... they had all seen the same film as me the night before. It didn't matter, (7) ...., because it was the night before Halloween, (8) .... people usually wear scary costumes. (9) ...., there was spooky music and a party game in which people had to solve a murder mystery. (10) .... prizes were given out for guessing the solution, they all watched a horror video.

1 **A** and	**B** both	**C** either	**D** neither
2 **A** Either	**B** Or	**C** Neither	**D** And
3 **A** or	**B** either	**C** nor	**D** but
4 **A** both	**B** and	**C** either	**D** or
5 **A** Despite	**B** Though	**C** However	**D** Even though
6 **A** so	**B** such a	**C** therefore	**D** because
7 **A** though	**B** as soon as	**C** so	**D** but
8 **A** when	**B** while	**C** because	**D** unless
9 **A** Moreover	**B** Whenever	**C** Though	**D** While
10 **A** When	**B** After	**C** Provided	**D** Before

N.2   PET Writing Part 2

Complete the second sentence so that it means the same as the first. Use no more than three words.

1. He left school immediately after the bell had rung.
   He left school ......*as soon as*...... the bell had rung.
2. She ate dinner, then she went out.
   Before ...., she ate dinner.
3. He's very tall; moreover, he's very well-built.
   Besides .... very tall, he's also very well-built.
4. I can run much faster than he can.
   He can't .... as I can.
5. Speak quietly in order not to disturb your father.
   Speak quietly so .... disturb your father.
6. We went there in order to buy some new shoes.
   We went there because .... buy some new shoes.

N.3   PET Writing Part 3

Write the instructions to a friend about how to make a sandwich. Organise your writing using sequencers. (about 100 words)

First of all, ...
....
....
....

Exam preparation

N

N.4 FCE Use of English Part 2

Read the text below and think of the word or short form which best fits each space. Use only one in each space.

A ⁽¹⁾ _lot_ of students in Europe spend some time picking fruit ⁽²⁾ .... farms in the summer. ⁽³⁾ .... being a healthy open-air activity, this is ⁽⁴⁾ .... an excuse to go ⁽⁵⁾ .... from their families for a while and have a holiday with other young people. ⁽⁶⁾ .... they spend all the time in a big group, they also have to learn to put ⁽⁷⁾ .... with one another and become more tolerant. Most of them won't complain about trivial things, such ⁽⁸⁾ .... queuing up for a shower or sleeping in rather uncomfortable bunk beds. However, a few can't do ⁽⁹⁾ .... their comforts and leave the farm ⁽¹⁰⁾ .... a few days. ⁽¹¹⁾ .... fruit picking being hard work, about half of the students decide to go back to the same farm the following year, ⁽¹²⁾ .... means they've really enjoyed the experience.

N.5 FCE Use of English Part 3

Read the text below. Use the word given in capitals at the end of each line to form a word that fits the space in the same line.

It is quite normal that there are ⁽¹⁾ _disagreements_ in families   **AGREE**
and that there are regular ⁽²⁾ .... , because   **UNDERSTAND**
everyone has their own ideas about what should happen when
and how. In fact, it's almost ⁽³⁾ .... that most   **BELIEVE**
families actually manage to live together relatively happily. It is
normal for teenagers to fight for their ⁽⁴⁾ ....   **DEPEND**
and for parents to feel very ⁽⁵⁾ .... towards   **PROTECT**
them. Each family deals with the situation in a ⁽⁶⁾ .... way. **DIFFER**

N.6 FCE Use of English Part 4

Complete the second sentence so that it has a similar meaning to the first sentence, using the word given. Do not change the word given. You must use between two and five words, including the word given.

1. You can go home once you have finished.
   AS
   You can go home .... _as soon as_ .... you have finished

2. Despite working hard all day, he played tennis in the evening.
   IN
   .... working hard all day, he played tennis in the evening.

3. He felt ill, and consequently was rushed to hospital.
   AS
   He felt ill and .... was rushed to hospital.

4. The ice-cream was wonderful; everyone wanted more.
   SO
   The ice-cream was .... everyone wanted more.

5. He travelled round the world, then he settled down.
   BEFORE
   .... , he travelled round the world.

6. You watch too much TV; also you don't read enough.
   IN
   .... enough, you also watch too much TV.

APPENDIX British and American English – main grammatical differences

There are various differences between British English and American English: differences in vocabulary, pronunciation and spelling, which are pointed out in dictionaries, and a few grammatical differences. The following list shows some of the most significant differences.

- In American English, the past simple is used more than in British English. For example, it is used instead of the present perfect when there isn't a specific time reference and with the adverbs **just**, **already**, **yet**, **ever** and **never**.

Br*	Am*
'Have you seen Jane?' 'Yes, I've seen her.'	'Did you see Jane?' 'Yes, I saw her.'
Has he arrived yet?	Did he arrive yet?
I've never tried Thai food.	I never tried Thai food.

- The form **have got / haven't got** isn't used very often in American English.

Br	Am
Have you got a pen?	Do you have a pen?
I haven't got many friends here.	I don't have many friends here.

- **Question tags** aren't used as often in American English as they are in British English.

Br	Am
You're 16, aren't you?	You're 16, right?
Don't be late, will you?	Don't be late, OK?

- The verb **need**, often used in British English as a semi-modal, is always used as an ordinary verb in American English.

Br	Am
You needn't wait for me.	You don't need to wait for me.

- In American English, it's more common to use the modal **should**, rather than **shall**.

Br	Am
What shall we do tonight?	What should we do tonight?
Shall I go now?	Should I go now?

- Collective nouns such as **family**, **team** and **government**, which in British English can be singular or plural, are always singular in American.

Br	Am
John's family is / are leaving tomorrow.	John's family is leaving tomorrow.

- The past participle of **get** is **got** in British English and **gotten** in American.

Br	Am
Your Spanish has got much better.	Your Spanish has gotten much better.

- In American English, the verb **take** is used instead of **have** in expressions such as **take a bath / a shower / a break...**

Br	Am
I have a shower every morning.	I take a shower every morning.

- Americans use the forms **go get**, **go see...**, whilst English people say **go and get**, **go and see...**

Br	Am
Go and get the newspaper, please.	Go get the newspaper, please.

- In colloquial American, some adverbs ending in **-ly** lose the suffix when they precede an adjective.

Br	Am
She's really crazy.	She's real crazy.

- In American English, the verb **help** isn't followed by **to**.

Br	Am
Can you help me to do my homework?	Can you help me do my homework?

* **Br** = British English   * **Am** = American English

International Phonetic Alphabet (IPA)

APPENDIX

The following table lists the symbols that represent the sounds of British English.

Vowels			
ɪ	sit, cricket, biscuit, this	ɔː	floor, more, thought
iː	see, mean	ʊ	foot, put
e	pen, spread, edge, said	uː	moon, suit, through
æ	sad, add, adapt	ʌ	bus, touch, tough, blood, upset
ɑː	father, car, glass, calm	ɜː	girl, burn, work
ɒ	stop, golf, rock, continent	ə	adopt, number, actor, actress, bishop

Diphthongs							
eɪ	take, rain, day	aɪ	fly, kite, right	ɔɪ	boy, boil	eə	hair, where
əʊ	fold, show, though	aʊ	now, mouse, shower	ɪə	near, here	ʊə	sure, poor

Consonants							
b	bad, tub	dʒ	jam, fridge	ŋ	song	ʒ	vision, measure
k	cat, kit, act	h	house	p	post, up	t	tree, suit
tʃ	chair, crunch	j	you	r	run, barrier	θ	thin, bath
d	do, did	l	last, all	s	sit, rice, cross	ð	this, with
f	fast, rough	m	must, room	z	zoo, rose, days	v	van, starve
g	get, pig	n	no, ten	ʃ	sharp, cash	w	well

Accenti – Accents
If the word has more than one syllable, the syllable on which the stress falls is preceded by an accent, for example: /ɪnˈtelɪdʒənt/, /nəˈsesəti/, /fəˈget/, /ˈhʌŋgri/, /ˈmɑːvələs/.

1 Read the phonetic transcription and write the words.

1 /θɪŋ/ .... 5 /faɪnd/ .... 9 /ˈfaɪə/ ....
2 /θɪn/ .... 6 /faɪn/ .... 10 /fɪə/ ....
3 /siːn/ .... 7 /pɒt/ .... 11 /buːt/ ....
4 /sɪns/ .... 8 /pɔːt/ .... 12 /bʌt/ ....

2 Read the phonetic transcription and write the sentences.

1 /wi ɑː ɪn ðə gɑːdn/

2 /duː ju ʌndəˈstænd ?/

3 /aɪ lʌv ˈtʃɒkələt/

4 /juː kən juːz maɪ ˈdɪkʃənəri/

5 /weə ɪz ðə dʒæm dʒɑː ?/

6 /ðeɪ wɒtʃt ˈtelɪvɪʒn fə tuː ˈaʊəz/

7 /ʃiː ˈwʊdnt laɪk tə kʌm tə ðə biːtʃ/

8 /juːv gɒt ə naɪs ˈbreɪslət/

9 /hiː ræn tə kætʃ ðə bʌs/

10 /ɪt wəz kəʊld, dɑːk ənd ˈraɪnɪŋ/

11 /aɪm ʃʊə ðeɪ ɑː ˈɪŋglɪʃ/

12 /θæŋks, ðiːz θɪŋs bɪˈlɒŋ tə miː

3 Write the phonetic symbol for the first sound of the following words.

1 knife .... 2 philosophy .... 3 ice .... 4 pseudonym .... 5 thirsty .... 6 these ....

4 Write the phonetic symbol for the last sound of the following words.

1 lamb .... 2 catch .... 3 tooth .... 4 judge .... 5 rush .... 6 path ....

APPENDIX: Punctuation marks

. **full stop / period** (Am)
at the end of a sentence. *He arrived yesterday.*

, **comma**
– separates the different elements of a list. *He had ham, salad, apple pie and a cup of tea.*
– separates clauses, comments. *My father, who works in Bristol, comes home at the weekend.*
– after expressions or introductory sentences. *When it stops raining, I'll go out to play.*
– with direct speech. *'Come and see me', said Pete, 'I'll show you my new flat.'*

: **colon**
introduces an explanation, a list, a quotation.
For the trip, you need: an anorak, walking boots, a rucksack and a cap.
Martin Luther King started his famous speech with the words: 'I have a dream…'

; **semicolon**
– is placed between two main clauses that are related in meaning.
  I don't like eating in restaurants; I prefer cooking my own meals.
– separates elements of a list if these elements are long and complex.
  The characters in the play include Dennis, a London teenager; Debbie, his girlfriend; Mr Johnson, Debbie's stepfather; and Ms Ross, Dennis's mother.

? **question mark**
at the end of a direct question. *How long will you be away?*

! **exclamation mark**
to give particular emphasis. *What a lovely day!*

… **dots / ellipsis**
to show that a sentence, quotation, etc. is incomplete. *Let me see… I think I'll have roast beef.*

– **dash (en rule)**
defines a non-essential clause or adds information.
Spend a weekend in San Francisco – the liveliest city of the Bay Area!

/ **slash / stroke**
to provide an alternative. *Part-time / Full-time jobs as waiters / waitresses. Apply inside.*

- **hyphen**
– in compound nouns and adjectives. *My mother-in-law is a bit absent-minded.*
– after prefixes, when the word starts with the same vowel. *The animals all co-operated with no problem.*
– to split a word when we start a new paragraph.

( ) **brackets / parentheses**
define a clause, especially when cross-references are used.
Study the verb forms (see p.43).

" " **inverted commas / quotation marks**
' ' (double or simple) mark a quotation or direct speech.
'A witty portrait of literary life in New York' (Sunday Telegraph)

' **apostrophe**
in short forms and the possessive case. *That isn't James's car.*

A **capital letter**
in English, the following are always written with a capital letter:
– proper nouns. *Paul Smith, my dog Rex, the Statue of Liberty, Mount Etna, Lake Erie*
– titles and professions. *Mr Bell, Ms Derrick, Professor Dawson, Queen Elizabeth II*
– the days of the week, the months and festivities. *Sunday, August, Easter*
– adjectives and nouns indicating nationality and languages. *Brazilians speak Portuguese.*
– nouns indicating family members when they are used alongside proper nouns.
  Are you ready, Mum? Uncle Jim is waiting for us.
– titles of books, films, newspapers… *'The Good Life' by Jay McInerney is a moving novel.*

a **small letter**

Modals and other verbs related to communicative functions

APPENDIX

obligation or necessity	lack of necessity	prohibition
We must study hard. We have to study hard. We've got to study hard. We need to study hard. We had to study hard last year. We'll have to study hard next year.	We don't have to study hard. We don't need to study hard. We needn't study hard. We didn't have to study hard last year. We won't have to study hard next year.	You mustn't talk in the library. You can't talk in the library. Don't talk in the library. No talking in the library.
advice	**assumptions**	**requests for instructions**
You should study hard. You ought to study hard. You had better study hard. You shouldn't worry about the exam.	It must be late. It can't be late. It should be easy. It ought to be easy.	What shall I do? What should I do? What can we do? Shall we turn right or left?
offers of help	**ability**	**possibility**
Shall I help you? Can I help you? Could I help you? I'd like to help you. Do you want me to help you? Let me help you! I'll help you!	I can ski. I could ski when I was young. I can't ride a horse. I couldn't ride a horse last year. I wasn't able to break his record. I'm afraid I won't be able to break his record.	I can go out tonight. (there's no problem) I may go out tonight. (it's possible) I might go out tonight. (I'm not sure) I'm likely to go out tonight. (it's probable) The odds are that I'm going out tonight. (colloquial)
permission	**requests (to have)**	**requests (to make others do)**
Can I go now? Could I go now? May I go now? You can go now. You may go now. I wasn't allowed to go. They didn't let me go. I'm sure I will be allowed to go. I'm sure they will let me go.	Can I have a coke, please? Could I have a coke, please? I'd like (to have) a coke. I want a coke.	Will you come here, please? Can you come here? Could you come here? Do you mind coming here? Would you mind coming here? I'd like you to come here. I want you to come here right now!
offers	**suggestions**	**wishes and preferences**
Will you have a coke? Would you have a coke? Would you like a coke? Do you want a coke? How / What about a coke? Have a coke!	Shall we go to the park? Should we go to the park? Let's go to the park. How / What about going to the park? Why don't we go to the park?	I want to go home. I'd like to go home. I wish I could go home. If only I could go home. I'd prefer to go home. I'd rather go home (than stay here).

Appendix: Modal verbs – tenses

can, could, be able to

present simple	past simple	future
can / can't am / is / are able to 'm not / isn't / aren't able to	could / couldn't was / were able to wasn't / weren't able to	will be able to won't be able to
present perfect have / has been able to haven't / hasn't been able to	**past perfect** had been able to hadn't been able to	**future perfect** will have been able to won't have been able to
conditional could / couldn't would / wouldn't be able to	**past conditional** could have / couldn't have would have / wouldn't have been able to	

may, might, be allowed to

present simple	past simple	future
may / may not am / is / are allowed to 'm not / isn't / aren't allowed to	was / were allowed to wasn't / weren't allowed to	will be allowed to won't be allowed to
present perfect have / has been allowed to haven't / hasn't been allowed to	**past perfect** had been allowed to hadn't been allowed to	**future perfect** will have been allowed to won't have been allowed to
conditional might / might not would / wouldn't be allowed to	**past conditional** might have / might not have would have been / wouldn't have been allowed to	

must, have (got) to, need, be compelled to, be obliged to, should

present simple	past simple	future
must / mustn't need / needn't don't / doesn't need to have / has (got) to haven't / hasn't got to don't / doesn't have to	had to didn't have to didn't need to was / were compelled / obliged to wasn't / weren't compelled / obliged to	will have to won't have to will be compelled / obliged to won't be compelled / obliged to
present perfect have / has been compelled to have / has been obliged to haven't / hasn't been compelled to haven't / hasn't been obliged to	**past perfect** had been compelled to had been obliged to hadn't been compelled to hadn't been obliged to	**future perfect** will have had to won't have had to will have been compelled / obliged to won't have been compelled / obliged to
conditional should / shouldn't would have to wouldn't have to	**past conditional** should have / shouldn't have would have had to wouldn't have had to	

Use of modal verbs in *if* clauses

APPENDIX

If clauses – Type 2

Dependent clause	Main clause
If I could… If I were able to…	I could… I would be able to… I might… (maybe)…
If I wanted to… If you would…	I would like to…
If I were to… (eventuality) If I should… (eventuality) If I had to… (obligation)	I should… (personal obligation) I ought to… (personal obligation) I would have to… (obligation deriving from external circumstances or people)

If I could find a better-paid job, I would be able to pay off my mortgage earlier.

If I should win the race, I should thank the coach for his help.

If I had to work at the weekend, I would have to ask someone to come and look after the kids.

If you wanted to start a new business, we might be able to give you some financial backing.

If he were to arrive earlier, could you please meet him at the airport?

If clauses – Type 3

Dependent clause	Main clause
If I could have… If I had been able to…	I could have… I would have been able to… I might have… (maybe)…
If I had wanted to…	I would have liked to… (also: I'd like to have + past participle)
If I should have… If I had had to…	I should have… I ought to have… I would have had to…

If I had had to pay a higher rent, I would have had to find a smaller flat.

If I had been able to ski, I would have liked to spend a holiday in the Swiss Alps.

If I had had to wait for you a bit longer in the street, I might have got frozen!

If I had really wanted to reach the top, I could easily have done so.

APPENDIX Comparing quantities

a lot of with countable plural nouns and uncountable nouns in affirmative sentences	**a lot of** Annie got a lot of presents / money. We had a lot of guests last summer.	**more** Simon got more presents / money than her. We had more guests than usual.	**the most** Jessica got the most presents / money of all. Last year, we had the most guests ever. (of always).
many with countable plural nouns in negative and interrogative sentences	**many** I didn't have many friends then. Did you have many problems at the customs?	**more** I don't have more friends than you. Did you have more problems than last year?	**the most** Which student had the most friends of all? When did you have the most problems?
much with uncountable nouns in negative and interrogative sentences	**much** Pete didn't have much time to train. Did they have much money?	**more** Sam didn't have more time than Pete. Did they have more money than you?	**the most** Which player had the most time of all? Who had the most money?
few / a few with plural countable nouns	**few / a few** There were few seats available. There are only a few biscuits left.	**fewer** There will be fewer seats tomorrow night. And there are even fewer sandwiches.	**the fewest** This stadium has got the fewest seats of all. Who ate the fewest sandwiches? (out of everyone)
little with uncountable nouns	**little** Arlene has little patience with the children. We'll have little time to go shopping.	**less** I have got less patience than Arlene. You should spend less time watching TV.	**the least** Charlie has got the least patience of all. This is the least of my worries. (out of all them).

Conjugation of a regular verb: *check*

APPENDIX

| base form **check** | infinitive **to check** | past participle **checked** | gerund **checking** |

ACTIVE FORM

present simple
I / You / We / They check
He / She / It checks

present continuous
I am checking
You / We / They are checking
He / She / It is checking

past simple
I / You / He / She / It / We / They checked

past continuous
I / He / She / It was checking
You / We / They were checking

present perfect simple
I / You / We / They have checked
He / She / It has checked

present perfect continuous
I / You / We / They have been checking
He / She / It has been checking

past perfect simple
I / You / He / She / It / We / They had checked

past perfect continuous
I / You / He / She / It / We / They had been checking

future simple
I / You / He / She / It / We / They will check

future continuous
I / You / He / She / It / We / They will be checking

future perfect simple
I/You/He/She/It/We/They will have checked

future perfect continuous
I/You/He/She/It/We/They will have been checking

***going to* future**
I'm going to check
You're / We're / They're going to check
He's / She's / It's going to check

***going to* past**
I / He / She / It was going to check
You / We / They were going to check

present conditional
I / You / He / She / It / We / They
would check

past conditional
I / You / He/ She / It / We / They
would have checked

PASSIVE FORM

present simple
I am checked
You / We / They are checked
He / She / It is checked

present continuous
I am being checked
You / We / They are being checked
He / She / It is being checked

past simple
I / He / She / It was checked
You / We / They were checked

past continuous
I / He / She / It was being checked
You / We / They were being checked

present perfect
I / You / We / They have been checked
He / She / It has been checked

past perfect
I / You / He / She / It / We / They had been checked

future
I/You/He/She/It/We/They will be checked

future perfect
I/You/He/She/It/We/They will have been checked

***going to* future**
I'm going to be checked
You're / We're / They're going to be checked
He's / She's / It's going to be checked

***going to* past**
I / He / She / It was going to be checked
You / We / They were going to be checked

present conditional
I / You / He/ She / It / We / They
would be checked

past conditional
I / You / He/ She / It / We / They
would have been checked

APPENDIX: Main irregular verbs

infinitive	past simple	past participle
be	was, were	been
beat	beat	beaten
become	became	become
begin	began	begun
bend	bent	bent
bet	bet	bet
bind	bound	bound
bite	bit	bitten
blow	blew	blown
break	broke	broken
bring	brought	brought
broadcast	broadcast	broadcast
build	built	built
burn	burnt	burnt
burst	burst	burst
buy	bought	bought
catch	caught	caught
choose	chose	chosen
come	came	come
cost	cost	cost
cut	cut	cut
deal	dealt	dealt
dig	dug	dug
do	did	done
draw	drew	drawn
dream	dreamt / dreamed	dreamt / dreamed
drink	drank	drunk
drive	drove	driven
eat	ate	eaten
fall	fell	fallen
feed	fed	fed
feel	felt	felt
fight	fought	fought
find	found	found
fly	flew	flown
forecast	forecast	forecast
foresee	foresaw	foreseen
forget	forgot	forgotten
freeze	froze	frozen
get	got	got
give	gave	given
go	went	gone
grow	grew	grown
hang	hung, hanged	hung, hanged
have	had	had
hear	heard	heard
hide	hid	hidden
hit	hit	hit
hold	held	held
hurt	hurt	hurt
keep	kept	kept
kneel	knelt	knelt

APPENDIX

infinitive	past simple	past participle
know	knew	known
lay	laid	laid
lead	led	led
learn	learnt / learned	learnt / learned
leave	left	left
lend	lent	lent
let	let	let
lie	lay	lain
light	lit	lit
lose	lost	lost
make	made	made
mean	meant	meant
meet	met	met
pay	paid	paid
put	put	put
quit	quit	quit
read /ri:d/	read /red/	read /red/
ride	rode	ridden
ring	rang	rung
rise	rose	risen
run	ran	run
say	said	said
see	saw	seen
seek	sought	sought
sell	sold	sold
send	sent	sent
set (up)	set	set
shake	shook	shaken
shine	shone	shone
shoot	shot	shot
show	showed	shown
shrink	shrank	shrunk
shut	shut	shut
sing	sang	sung
sit	sat	sat
sleep	slept	slept
smell	smelt / smelled	smelt / smelled
speak	spoke	spoken
spend	spent	spent
stand	stood	stood
steal	stole	stolen
swim	swam	swum
take	took	taken
teach	taught	taught
tell	told	told
think	thought	thought
throw	threw	thrown
understand	understood	understood
wear	wore	worn
win	won	won
write	wrote	written

Index

a/an 182, 196
about 302
(be) about to 100D
above 292D
across 298A
adjectives
– followed by a preposition 348
– nouns used as adjectives 210B
– qualifying 208
– used as nouns 200C
– with *-ed* or *-ing* endings 210A
– see also comparative, superlative
adverbs
– interrogative 268
– of degree 208D, 284
– of frequency 32, 58E, 282C
– of manner 280
– of time 282
– relative 262
– word order 286D
– see also comparative, superlative
after 92C, 130E, 290D, 336A
after that 336B
agreeing 274
all (of) 240D, 244B, 244D
all that 262 D
allow sb to do sth 174A
(be) allowed to 138 G
along 294C, 298B
already 76
also 338A
although 332D
among 294C
and 332A
any 196, 198, 242
– compounds *anybody, anyone, anything, anywhere* 246, 248
any of 248B
around / round 294C
articles
– definite article *the* 184, 186, 188, 196
– indefinite article *a/ an* 182, 196
– no article 188
as 66B, 334, 338B
(not) as… as 214, 218C, 338B
as a result 334
as far as 298B,
as if 338C
as long as 336A
as soon as 92C, 110D, 336A
as though 338C

as well 140B
at
– place 292B
– time 288A
at first 336B
at last 336B
away from 296C

be
– future 102E
– used in the passive form 164, 166, 168
– past simple 52
– present simple 12, 14
– *were* in conditional sentences 322
be able to 138G
be used to
– followed by the *-ing* form 130C
– vs *used to* 130C, 302B
because 334
before 92C, 130E, 290D, 336A
behind 294B
below 292D
beneath 292D
beside 294A
besides 338A
between
– place 294C
– time 290A
(a) bit 212C
both (of) 240
both… and 240E, 332A
(be) bound to 154D
British and American English 358
but
– connector 332C
– preposition 302
but for 326A
by
– as 'agent' 302
– means of transport 302
– time 290E
– with a reflexive pronoun 232F

can/could
– general characteristics 136
– usage 138, 371
close to 294A
collective nouns see nouns
comparative of adjectives 212, 214
– irregular forms 220

Index

– with *much, far, a lot, a bit, a little, slightly* 212C
comparative of adverbs 218
(be) compelled to 148D
compound nouns see nouns
compounds with *-ever* 248
compounds of *some, any, no* 246, 248
conditional verb form
– type zero 320B
– type one 320C
– type two 322
– type three 324
– mixed 324B
– introduced by *when, unless/I wish/If only* 326
– with modals 318, 372, 373
connectors and linkers
– coordinating 332
– concessive 332
– reason, result and purpose 334
– time linkers and sequencers 336
– other connectors 338
consequently 334
could
– past of *can* 136, 138, 371
– present conditional 318
– in type two conditional sentences 322C, D, 373
could have
– past conditional 318
– in type three conditional sentences 324C, 373
countable nouns see nouns

dates 256C
definite article see articles
despite 332D
demonstrative adjectives and pronouns 234
distributive adjectives and pronouns 238, 240
did 56
disagreeing 274
do/does 30
double genitive 202D
double object
– with the passive form 172
– verbs with two objects 300
down 298D
due to 154C
during 290B

each (of) 238, 240D
each other 238
either (of) 240
either… or 240E, 332B

else 248D
enough 122B, 208D, 244C, 284C
exclamations 266
even though 332D
eventually 336B
ever 78B, 92D
-ever
– compounds *whoever, whatever, whichever, wherever, whenever, however* 248
every 238
– compounds *everybody, everyone, everything, everywhere* 238
except 302

far
– with the comparative 212C
– *by far* with the superlative 216C
(a) few 242
fewer / the fewest 374
finally 336B
first 336B
firstly 336B
for
– cause and purpose 300A, B
– duration 80, 92B, 94D, 290C
force sb to sth 174A
(be) forced to 148D
fractions 256D
from
– distance 294A
– origin, movement 296C
from… to 290A
furthermore 338A
future
– *going to* 100
– present continuous 110
– present simple 110
– *will* 102, 104, 106
– comparison: *going to,* present continuous and *will* 112
– future continuous 114
– future in the past 318A
– future perfect 114
– future perfect continuous 365

gerund see *–ing* form
get
– in passive sentences 166C
– with means of transport (*into, on, onto, off, out of*) 296D
get sb to do sth 174A
get sth done 174B

369

Index

get used to 232D, + *-ing* form 302
going to
– form and usage 100
– vs present continuous 110
– comparison with *going to*, present continuous and *will* 112
gonna 100A
gotta 146A

had better 154A
hardly ever 286D
have 24
have got 22, 24
have sth done 174B
have (got) to 146, 148
hear sb do / doing sth 176
hear sth being done 176
here is / are 16
how
– interrogative 268
– exclamation 266C
how about 268C
how long 80B, 268C
how many 268B
how much 268B
however 332C, D

If 314A, 320, 322, 324, 338C
if clauses see conditional
if only 326C
imperative 120
in
– after a superlative 216B
– position 292A
– time 288B, 290F
in case 326A, 338C
in front of 294B
in order to 334
in spite of 332D
indefinite article see articles
indefinite adjectives and pronouns 242, 244, 246, 248
indirect questions 314
infinitive
– form and usage 122
– of purpose 334
– after verbs 126, 128
– *ing* clauses 130
– *ing* form
– spelling changes 38B
– form and usage 124
– after verbs 128

– after verbs of perception 176
– after a preposition 130
international phonetic alphabet 359
interrogative adjectives and pronouns 266
into 296B
it's, impersonal usage 18, 122B, 228C

just 76
just in case 326A

lastly 336B
later 336B
(the) least 216D, 220
less 214C, 220
let's 120 C
let sb do sth 174
like (preposition) 302, 338B
linkers 332, 334, 336, 338
little 220,
(a) little 196, 208D, 212C, 242
(a) lot 212C
(a) lot of / lots of 196, 244A

make sb do sth 174
many 196C, 244A
may 140, 371
– present conditional 318C
may have
– past conditional 318C
maybe 140B
might 140, 371
– present conditional 318C
– in type two conditional sentences 322C, 373
– in type three conditional sentences 324C, 373
might have
– past conditional 318C, 373
modals
– *must/have to* 144, 146, 148, 152, 154
– *can/could* 136, 138
– *may/might* 140
– *will/would* 156, 158
– in conditional sentences 318
– related to communicative functions 361
– all tenses 362
– in *if* clauses 363
more
– comparative adjectives 212
– *more and more* 214D
– comparative adverbs 218
– comparative of *much* 220

Index

moreover 338A
most (of) 240D
(the) most 216, 218, 220
much 220
– with uncountable nouns 196C, 244A
– with comparatives 212C
must 144, 371
must have something done 174B
mustn't 146

near 294A
need 148, 371
need to have sth done 174B
neither (of) 240
neither… nor 240E, 332B
neither do I 274
never 78B
next 336B
next to 294A
no 242
– compounds *nobody, no one, nothing, nowhere* 246, 248
nouns
– adjectives used as nouns 200
– collective 200
– compound 194, 210B
– countable 196, 198
– possessive case 202
– nouns used as adjectives 210B
– uncountable 196, 198
– comparatives 222, 374
– plural 192
– irregular plurals 194
none 242D
none (of) 240D, 248B
nor do I 274
numbers
– cardinal 254
– ordinal 256

object pronouns see pronouns
(be) obliged to 148D
of
– preposition 302
– after the superlative 216B
off 296C
on
– place 292C
– time 288C
one / ones 186C, 234B, 236
one another 238

only if 286D
onto 296B
opposite 294B
or 332B
ought to 154B, 361
out of 296C
over
– place 292D
own 230D
on my own 232F

passive
– form 164
– with *get* 166C
– infinitive, modals, conditional 170
– verbs with double object 172A
– perfect tenses, future 168
– present, past tenses 166
– all tenses 365
past
– movement 298C
– time 298C
past conditional 318
past continuous
– form 64
– usage 66
– vs past simple 66
past participle 72
past simple
– form 54, 56
– usage 58
– vs past continuous 66
– vs present perfect simple 82
– irregular verbs 366-367
past perfect continuous 94
past perfect simple
– form 90
– usage 92
– with superlatives 216B
perhaps 140B
(be) permitted to 138G
phrasal verbs 350, 352, 354
plenty (of) 244A
plural nouns see nouns
possessive *'s* 202
possessive adjectives and pronouns 230
prefixes 340
prepositional verbs 346
prepositions
– of movement 296, 298

371

Index

– of place and position 292, 294
– of time 288, 290
– after adjectives 348
– after verbs 346
– position in relative clauses 258C
– followed by the -ing form 130
present conditional 318
present continuous
– form 38, 40
– usage 42
– for the future 110
– vs present simple 44
– comparison: *going to*, present continuous and *will* 112
present participle see *–ing* form
present perfect continuous
– form and usage 86
– vs present perfect simple 88
present perfect simple
– form 74
– with *already, just, ever, yet, not… yet, still… not* 76
– with *ever, never, recently, today…* 78
– with *how long, for, since* 80
– vs past simple 82
– vs present perfect continuous 88
present simple
– form 28, 30
– usage 32, 34
– vs present continuous 44
– with adverbs of frequency 32
– for the future 110
– in conditional sentences 320, 326
pronouns
– personal 228D
– subject 228A
– reciprocal 238E
– reflexive 232
provided / providing (that) 326A, 338C
punctuation marks 360

qualifying adjectives see adjectives
question tags 272
questions
– *Yes/No* questions 270A
– *Wh-* questions 270B
quite 208D, 284B

rather 208D
recently 78C
(to) recommend 314E
reflexive pronouns see pronouns

relative adverbs 262
relative clauses
– pronouns in defining clauses 258
– pronouns in non-defining clauses 260
reported speech
– statements 310, 312
– questions 314
– orders and requests 310

say 308
secondly 336B
see sb do / doing sth 176
see sth being done 176
sequencers 336
shall 152
short answers
– with *be* 12, 40, 52, 64
– with *do, does, did* 30, 56
– with *had* 90, 94
– with *have* 22, 74, 86
- with *can / could* 136
- with *will / would* 102, 156
should 152
–present conditional 318
– in type two conditional sentences 322C, D
should have
– past conditional 318
– in type three conditional sentences 324C
since 80, 92B, 94D, 290C, 334
slightly 212C
so 284F, 334
so as to 334
so do I 274
so far 78C
so that 334
some 196, 198, 242
– compounds *someone, somebody, something, somewhere* 246
some of 248B
spelling rules 28, 38, 54, 212
still, still… not 76E
subject pronouns see pronouns
such a 284F, 334
suffixes 342
suggest with reported speech 314E
superlative of adjectives 216, 220
superlative of adverbs 218

tell 308
time, expressions of

Index

– future 42E, 104E, 110A, 114D
– past 58A
– present 42A
than 212B, 214C, 218B, 338B
that
– conjunction 172B, 338D
– demonstrative 234
– relative pronoun 258
that is (to say) 338D
that's impersonal usage 18
the 184, 186, 188
then 336B,
there is / are 16
there was / were 52G
therefore 334
these 234
this 234
those 234
though 332C, D
through 298A
throughout 290B
till, until 92C, 290E
to 300A, B, D
– purpose 334
– movement 296A
– time 298C
too
– with adjectives and adverbs 122B, 208D, 284A
– with *much/many* 244B
towards 298B

uncountable nouns see nouns
under 292D
underneath 292D
unless 326A, 338C
until 92C, 290E, 336A
up 298D
up to 298B
used to 62, 156D
– vs *be used to* 130C, 302B

verbs
– with double object 300C
– action 46, 88A, 88B, 94D
– of opinion 172B
– of perception 176
– stative 46, 80C, 88A
– irregular 366-367
– modals, general characteristics 136A
– related to communicative functions 361

– tenses 362
– use in *if* clauses 363
– comparatives with verbs 222
– phrasal verbs 350, 352, 354
– prepositional verbs 346
– followed by the *–ing* form 128
– followed by the infinitive 126, 128
– followed by a preposition 346
– conjugation of a regular verb 365
very 208D, 216E, 218D, 284A

wanna 158B
want sb to do sth 158C
want to 158
want to have sth done 174B
what
– exclamation 266C
– interrogative 266
– relative 262D
when
– conjunction 66B, 92C, 110D, 336A
– interrogative 82B, 268
– in conditional clauses 326A
– relative 262B
whenever 248, 336A
where
– interrogative 268
– relative 262A
whether 314C
which
– interrogative 266
– relative 258, 260, 262D
while 66B, 130E, 336A
who
– interrogative 266
– relative 258, 260
(the) whole 244D
whom 258, 260
whose
– interrogative 266
– relative 258, 260
why
– interrogative 268
– relative (*the reason why*) 262
will
– form 102
– for the future 104
– modal 156
wish
– with past perfect 326B

Index

– with past simple 326B
– with *could / would* 326B, 371
with 302
within 290F
without 302
word formation
– prefixes 340
– suffixes 342
word order 286
would
– present conditional 318A
– modal 156
– past habit 62D, 156D
– in type two conditional sentences 322C, D
would have
– past conditional 318B
– in type three conditional sentences 324 B
would like to 158, 371
would prefer to 158D, 371
would rather 158D, 371

yet, not… yet 76D, E

TOP GRAMMAR CD-ROM System Requirements:
Operating systems: all Windows and MAC OS.
CPU: min. Pentium 1 GHz
Memory: min. 256 MB RAM
CD-ROM drive: required
No installation needed.
Requires a browser and Flash Player 9 or higher.